WINNING THE BIG ONES
HOW TEAMS CAPTURE LARGE CONTRACTS

MICHAEL O'GUIN AND KIM KELLY

Contents

Introduction

"Knowledge is experience. Everything else is information"

– Albert Einstein

Ralph Waldo Emerson is credited with saying "If a man can write a better book, preach a better sermon, or make a better mouse trap than his neighbor... the world would beat a path to his door." While scholars consider Emerson to be a great essayist, philosopher, poet, and orator, he was not much of a businessman. Our experience is that the world will not beat a path to one's door. If a man has created a better product, no one will know it unless he goes out and sells it. This book explains how to do just that – in the labyrinthine world of large complex contracts.

This book describes a proven process for teams to win these contracts. Approaching a multi-million dollar or multi-billion dollar procurement effort is complicated, and there are many questions to answer before you even begin: Who exactly is the customer? Which activities merit your precious time and energy? How do you coordinate the actions of multiple team members? What messages do you focus on giving to the customer? Whose needs matter most among the many customer representatives you might speak with? What is most important to the customer in choosing a solution? How do you price your bid? How do you figure out what the competition is offering? This book will answer all these questions and more.

The practices outlined in this book apply to contracts big and small, government and commercial, high tech and no tech, products and services. They are a culmination of our experience chasing a hundred large, complex pursuits, and helping our clients win contracts worth over $286 billion.

Who are we? We're the strategists who conducted the Price-to-Win (PTW) analysis for the Lockheed Martin team that won the Joint Strike Fighter competition -- the world's largest procurement. In 2008, we played a key role in creating the strategy that allowed Northrop Grumman and their European partner EADS to defeat Boeing and win a contract for 179 refueling tankers – the world's second largest procurement. The New York Times called this victory a "stunning upset" and noted military analyst Loren Thompson stated that it was "One of biggest marketing coups in defense-industry history." (Unfortunately, this win was overturned by Boeing's intense political pressure and lobbying campaign).

We have helped our clients sell across such diverse industries as information systems outsourcing, transportation, aerospace, defense, construction, systems integration and electrical power distribution. Our client's customers have ranged from Union Pacific Railroad to the United States Navy, from Reno Nevada casinos to the Republic of Korea, from Intelsat to the Kuwaiti National Guard.

Our names are Michael O'Guin and Kim Kelly. You may not have heard these names before, but our experiences could help you win more business if you bid on large complex contracts.

O'Guin uncovered the processes, tactics and strategies used by top performing companies to consistently win large contracts while leading a landmark strategic benchmarking study at Price Waterhouse in the early 1990s. This study uncovered how top performers consistently won 60 percent of the bids they proposed on, while the industry averaged only 18 percent. O'Guin saw how 24 companies pursued new business and how three did it really well, and their secrets to success became obvious. In 1994, he used these insights to form Knowledge Link, a company that assists companies in winning large contract awards and implementing best business development practices.

While working at IBM in 1991, Kim Kelly invented the revolutionary and now widely used process called Price-to-Win or PTW. This process uses competitive intelligence to determine the optimum price at which to bid and win. It was found decisive in winning contracts worth billions of dollars for their business unit. After Lockheed Martin purchased IBM Federal Systems, executives at Lockheed Martin's corporate headquarters identified Kelly's unique capability to win new business and assigned him to perform PTW for key pursuits across the company. He helped sell ships, aircraft, rockets, commissary services and complex systems for surveillance, training, signal processing, sensing, software and information processing. These products were bid to federal, state and foreign governments, as well as commercial, retail and transportation customers. In 1998, he founded the Lockheed Martin Competitive Intelligence Working Group. Over the next five years this network grew into the largest competitive intelligence network at any company in the world. It elevated awareness of competitive intelligence and facilitated a significant increase in the sharing of competitor intelligence across a company of 140,000 employees. This organization changed the company's culture as the collection and use of competitive intelligence became a common practice throughout the corporation. In short, he transformed Lockheed's contract pursuit culture.

In 2000, Kelly transferred to Lockheed Martin's International Launch Services (ILS) where he implemented a PTW process in the launch vehicle business selling rockets to commercial customers around the world. Over the next 18 months, the PTW process raised Lockheed's launch vehicle market share from 40 percent to 60 percent, making it the market share leader for first time.

After working together on multiple projects including the Joint Strike Fighter, Kim Kelly joined Michael O'Guin at Knowledge Link in 2003. From that point forward, the authors have worked together on 40 campaigns, achieving an 86 percent win rate.

We have helped our clients win billions, and in that process have studied hundreds of campaigns and learned our hardest lessons through our losses.

The intent of this book is to communicate what everyone working on a large campaign should know about the capture process. The intent is not to describe how to architect and write a complex proposal; that would require another book altogether. This book offers the key lessons required to win, and also highlights the common missteps that cause companies to lose the big ones.

One of the things that we do at Knowledge Link is offer capture-training workshops. After these events, the attendees always comment on the vignettes and stories we tell, excited about how these examples bring the theory to life. Throughout this book, we use real-world examples to illustrate the key points we make, just as we do in the workshops. Each story is real, but frequently we have changed the company and pursuit names to avoid disclosing sensitive information or embarrassing any of the companies we have worked with. In most cases, we have also changed some facts to obscure the company's identity without interfering with the point of the story. Sometimes, we will give the players obvious fictional names so that the story is easier to follow. Other stories name the companies involved, as the majority of the story is already in the public domain and nothing proprietary is being disclosed. Look for these real-world examples throughout the upcoming chapters in the sections titled, "Strategy in Action."

Capturing large, complex, multiyear contracts is a high stakes challenge – companies, business lines, plants and careers are at stake. To win, a company must figure out what's important to the customer and then differentiate itself from the competition. It sounds simple. But when a customer has dozens, or even hundreds, of people involved in picking the winner, it is tough to figure out what is important. How can you ensure that your offering is better than what the competition promises? What if your sales team consists of seven or eight, or even a hundred, people? How do you coordinate all of their activities? Often, the winner is decided before the customer even solicits the bid. The company that has best positioned itself up front to influence the customer usually wins. This book describes how to become that company – the one that wins the big contracts. Consistently.

Winning a large complex contract is not a simple one-step sale. It is a detailed sequence of events, referred to as the "capture process." This process evolved during the 1970s in the aerospace industry. Aerospace engineers routinely developed and managed very complex systems and proposals, so some aerospace engineers and marketers applied those systems engineering skills to conceiving a systematic process for winning the complex sale. The result was the capture process.

This book describes how the capture process organizes all the elements of the complex sale into a repeatable process – one that varies significantly from the traditional sale, which focused on one customer and one product. This process applies to multi-million and multi-billion dollar pursuits, but can work for smaller pursuits as well, with the scope and time frames compressed.

Why the Traditional Sales Process Falls Short

Most sales literature and training products focus on the traditional sales process – selling a product to a single buyer; for example, a car or a box of detergent. This singular focus stems from the legacy of American business history. The textile salesman was America's first true salesman, toting samples to distant shops and taking orders for future delivery. With the advent of the railroads, traveling salesmen became a familiar sight, lugging their bulky sample cases along through any town the railroads passed through. During the second half of the nineteenth century, John H. Patterson invented sales innovations including the national sales force, sales training programs and sales quotas. But it was not until 1959 that anyone worked to distill the art of successful selling into a list of specific tactics and techniques. Prior to this, traditional salesmen used intuition, memory and a few notes to develop their strategy, coordinate meetings and send messages. Once the sales process was defined, it became apparent that most traditional sales calls were broken down into the following steps: opening the call, investigating customer needs, highlighting product benefits, handling objections and closing the sale. In this traditional sale – where one product is being sold to one customer – the product is simple, the win strategy is straightforward, the cost of the sale is low, and few customer decision makers are involved. This simple process is geared toward small sales and cannot adequately address the complexities of the large, high-value, complex team sale.

Selling large complex systems differs from the traditional sale in many important ways. Prior to soliciting bids for a large contract, the customer must establish a budget, define requirements and solicit proposals. Once bidders submit proposals, the customer must evaluate the proposals and select the winner. Each of these customer events typically involves a different set of individuals, meaning that there are many customers to influence. The technical staff develops requirements, while a strategic planner or market analyst develops the budget. The contracts administrator writes the request for proposal (RFP). An evaluation teams grades the proposals and executives pick the winner. Because of the duration and complexity of these large sales, potential sellers have ample opportunity to influence the customer's purchasing strategy, requirements, funding and evaluation. Influencing each of these customer events is one of the most important factors in deciding who wins, yet the traditional sales process fails to provide a systematic process for shaping the thoughts of all these different customers.

Buyers of multimillion or billion dollar systems expect to have it "their way." Suppliers engineer large projects to a customer's unique situation and desires. For example, while one oil field floating production system may look like another, they are significantly different in reachable depth, drilling capacity, accommodations and vessel mooring. All of these features affect the solution's cost, project feasibility, operability, and availability – all things that the customer needs to balance when choosing a provider. Unlike the traditional sales process, one must approach the capture of a large contract with a concept, not a product. On a large complex project, the customer often decides on their requirements or budget only after entering discussions with potential sellers. This pre-sale interaction allows the customer to analyze the capabilities of the seller's industry and define their needs, both of which help the customer determine the optimum balance of requirements and budget. The seller must identify and prioritize the customer's requirements to customize their solution. This interaction can last weeks, months or even years. The traditional sales process overlooks this critical pre-sell period and has no feedback loop to integrate the knowledge gained during this process to customize the offering. It also lacks tools to coordinate the actions and messages of the potentially dozens of people on the team trying to sell the customer.

While many companies understand their customers and their own products, they lack any understanding of the competition. If you do not know what the competition is going to offer, how can you send clear messages to the customer contrasting your offerings? Competitive intelligence plays a vital role in winning. Large sales are always fiercely competitive. To win, as this book will describe, top performers can deduce not only what their competitors will offer, but also what prices they will bid. The traditional sales process has no mechanism for collecting competitive intelligence or integrating it into the sales process.

Winning with the Capture Process

As the following examples show, the company with the best fit and most experience does not necessarily win the big contracts – the company that successfully implements the capture process does.

— Strategy In Action —

In 1999, one missile guidance division (MGD) of a large aerospace and defense company faced a declining marketplace. Anxious to find new business, their general manager convened a weekly lunch for their top scientists to brainstorm new business ideas. One of these scientists spotted an opportunity he thought would leverage the division's core competencies in navigation, software development and large system integration. The Kansas Department of Transportation (KDOT) was going to request proposals in six months to develop and install a Positive Train Control (PTC) system. A PTC system supplements the traditional red light, green light signals along the railroad tracks with a system that monitors individual train locations and maintains spacing between trains. This system improves safety and enables high-speed rail service. The company investigated the opportunity and found the railroads were unhappy with their existing suppliers. Current suppliers had a history of late deliveries and blown budgets and also lacked the large-scale system integration experience that a complex project like PTC required. In addition, the existing equipment sales forces were focused on a larger, more lucrative opportunity in New York and not on Kansas. The market was ripe for a new entrant.

However, MGD faced a daunting challenge. Their chief competitor had a railroad heritage going back a hundred years and had teamed with a key equipment supplier. The competitor already had a well-established relationship with the customer. They were already a system integrator for another Union Pacific project – the railroad on which the PTC would be installed. In addition, the KDOT had hired the competitor to conduct their feasibility study. MGD, on the other hand, had no product and no experience in this marketplace. In addition, the track record of defense contractors diversifying into the commercial market was unblemished by success. However, the defense marketplace was so bleak, the MGD decided to pursue this opportunity.

MGD formed a dedicated capture team with the responsibility to win this opportunity. This team visited the customer to identify and understand their needs. The customer was actually a committee of representatives from Kansas Department of Transportation, Federal Railroad Administration and Union Pacific. The capture team learned that these representatives cared most about safety and price. The capture team established a war room to track and manage the team's progress. They assessed their situation, and immediately went to work to create a solution, sell themselves to the customer and overcome their weaknesses.

MGD's competitive analysis found that railroads were frustrated by the current equipment suppliers' proprietary architectures. All of the current prime systems suppliers configured their equipment so that it was not interchangeable with another supplier's. This forced the railroads to buy all spare parts and upgrades from the prime without competition. As a result, the customers felt they were always getting price gouged. MGD's strategy was to provide an open architecture solution that would allow the components to be interchangeable between suppliers. MGD showed the customer how a solution could be designed using an open architecture with commercial off-the-shelf (COTS) components. This approach would allow the customer to compete spare parts and future upgrades for the life of the system, dramatically cutting life cycle costs. After months filled with sales calls providing white papers, presentations and demonstrations, MGD convinced the customer of the benefits of using an open architecture. The customer made proposing an open architecture solution their most important selection criteria.

MGD conducted an extensive competitive analysis, which found that their chief competitor relied on installing track markers along the rail bed to locate trains. MGD's approach was to use sensors on the train to track its motion. The capture team built a prototype using seismic sensor technology from another MGD company. They installed their prototype in a car and drove it around a parking lot to create mapping data. Then, they conducted a demonstration for the customer on a locomotive proving their accuracy to the customer.

To neutralize their weakness in lack of rail experience, MGD teamed with some well respected locomotive equipment suppliers. The capture team had teammate personnel brief the customer at meetings and presented them as prominent members of their team. In addition, MGD needed someone the customer would trust to be program manager. Unfortunately, this division of MGD had no one with railroad experience. The capture team searched, found and transferred in from another division a respected program manager who had led an intelligent transportation project for the Federal Highway Administration. While lacking railroad experience, he had transportation system integration experience and had worked closely, and successfully, with one of the key customer decision makers on this job.

The capture team also brought in software safety expertise from their air traffic control and NASA business units. They created a PTC test integration lab in their facility to collect and analyze the system's data. The customer was so impressed by the lab that the capture team was invited to help the customer write the system's test criteria for the RFP.

MGD's competitive analyst estimated the costs of the competitor's solution and compared it to their competitor's bidding history to calculate their likely bid price. The capture team deployed cost targets to their design team, so that they could under price their competitor. They implemented a formal proposal process to create, in the words of the customer, "the best proposal we had ever seen." As a result of the capture process, MGD won a $34M contract and opened up a new line of business.

MGD won because they followed many of the lessons this book will share. They formed a dedicated that worked hard to understand both the customer and the competitors. They carefully studied the customer to identify key needs, and developed a solution to meet them. MGD effectively teamed with railroad equipment suppliers to bolster their weaknesses along with conducting extensive demonstrations for the customer. They developed an excellent understanding of the competitors, which allowed them to outmaneuver them through every step of the competition.

In another pursuit, Lockheed and Boeing were battling for a contract to develop and produce a new maritime patrol aircraft.

— *Strategy In Action* —

Lockheed had developed and maintained the Navy's very successful P-3 maritime patrol aircraft for 40 years. They knew the customer and mission better than anyone. Lockheed dominated both anti-submarine warfare and long-range surveillance systems. In addition, only Lockheed, by reusing their P-3 airframe, had an aircraft with low enough cruising speed, plus sufficient range and payload to effectively perform the job.

However, in 2000, Boeing formed a dedicated capture team to pursue the United States Navy's Multi-Mission Maritime Aircraft (MMA) contract. This program was intended to replace the aging P-3 patrol aircraft fleet with new aircraft. The first step in Boeing's campaign was to convince the U.S. Navy that Boeing had a valid solution to the maritime patrol mission. Boeing's capture team assessed the customer's needs, desires and concerns. During that year, Boeing provided the Navy with analysis after analysis showing that a 737 was an aircraft that could successfully perform the maritime patrol mission, despite its higher cruising speed and more limited range compared with the P-3. The primary mission of the MMA is hunting submarines — a high tech game of hide-and-seek. A good submarine hunter has long legs so it can loiter over the area where a submarine is suspected to be lurking. Slow speed is helpful, because an aircraft is so much faster than a submarine, and one wants to minimize the time spent flying back and forth.

As a result of Boeing's campaign, the US Navy created a competition that pitted Boeing against Lockheed, the original P-3 supplier. Boeing would propose a new extended range variant of the commercially successful 737. Lockheed would propose reopening their proven P-3 production line with an improved aircraft called Orion 21.

Lockheed was having a tough time. They had trouble staffing up their capture team and the effort was disorganized with different Lockheed companies running the pursuit at different times. The company never built a prototype or even created a detailed artist's rendition of their Orion 21 concept. Lockheed let dust continue to collect on the P-3's production tooling and they did nothing to mitigate the Navy's concerns about the condition of the tooling.

During the fourth quarter of 2002, Boeing sought to familiarize and win over the Navy's P-3 community by taking a 737-700 Boeing Business Jet on a nine-stop, 17-day tour of P-3 bases around the world. At each of the stops, Boeing had Navy P-3 pilots fly the 737, exposing these crews to the plane, and demonstrating its maneuverability and suitability for the MMA mission. Boeing provided the Navy Program Office with simulation results to influence the customer to relax the speed and endurance requirements.

Also during 2002, Boeing worked to mitigate the concerns of Navy officials who worried that cutting into the 737's pressurized airframe to install an internal weapons bay would produce structural fatigue. Boeing formed a team to work with the Navy engineers to stiffen the airframe and dispel the Navy's worries. In 2003, Boeing's team developed and demonstrated key features of the aircraft's mission system, including their open systems architecture, which would integrate well into the Navy's future information infrastructure. Boeing presented the Navy with an extensive analysis showing how they would leverage training and spare parts from the worldwide commercial base of 6,000 737s. This approach would save $3,000 per flight hour over the existing P-3.

Additionally, early schedule delivery was a customer value. Originally, Boeing and their competitor, Lockheed Martin, had similar delivery schedules. Boeing's standard military modification process was to buy a green commercial 737 (a standard, empty aircraft with no unique customer equipment) from Boeing Commercial Aircraft Company in Renton, Washington, and fly it to their Wichita, Kansas facility for disassembly and military modification. Instead, Boeing offered to assemble the aircraft on a dedicated military line in Renton with all the modifications built into the aircraft. This approach cut a year off their initial aircraft delivery, allowing the Navy to start retiring the expensive-to-maintain P-3s earlier.

While Navy credited Lockheed with having "superior aircraft performance," Boeing developed a highly substantiated proposal with a 16 percent lower development cost, and in June of 2004 Boeing edged out Lockheed to win the contract, valued at $20 billion.

Boeing found three issues most important to the Navy's key decision makers: their ability to perform the mission; low life cycle cost; and earliest production delivery. Boeing had to show that their aircraft could perform the mission despite limited range and the limited ability to fly slowly. They also had to differentiate the 737's extensive commercial base, which improved supportability and lowered their life cycle cost from Lockheed's Orion 21. Most importantly, they were able to develop a schedule that provided for production deliveries a year earlier than the competition. Boeing's strategy was to prove that they could offer a lower cost solution, deliver earlier and be as capable as Lockheed in performance.

Boeing's strategy also demonstrated that simple strategies are usually the best. The human mind is attracted to simplicity. The more complex the decision, the harder it is to build consensus, and the more powerful a simple answer becomes. While Boeing's strategy was simple, their implementation was complex. Boeing had to prove to the Navy that they could modify their airframe for an internal weapons bay and still take a year out of their schedule. And Boeing had to create a detailed and persuasive 30 year life cycle cost estimate for a fleet of aircraft and get the customer to agree to it.

As these examples demonstrate, winning a large sale is not a single event, but the culmination of a series of sales contacts and customer decisions leading to the award decision. This book describes a proven systematic process for winning large complex contracts. Before a customer awards a large contract, they develop a procurement plan, define requirements, and write the RFP. Sellers significantly improve their chances of winning by influencing the outcome of each of these customer events and pre-selling their solution. Top performers use the capture process to identify, organize and manage these activities to position themselves to win.

Complex Sales to Complex Customers

The traditional sales process is built on the concept of a single buyer. However, groups of individuals with their own roles, agendas and biases make large sales decisions. For example, when selecting the company that would develop a tax modernization system, the IRS involved their Chief Information Officer, Program Manager and his staff, the office of the Commissioner of Procurement, the Contracting Office, the Privacy Board, various consultants and the Treasury Department. Literally hundreds of people participated in the selection process. In a sale like this, with so many people involved, it becomes difficult for a potential supplier to develop a consensus about what is most important to the customer. Without this consensus, it is impossible to know what optimum solution the supplier should propose. The supplier needs a way to determine what is most important to the customer, an approach that is repeatable and verifiable that will give executives confidence in the results. Then, based on what is determined to be important to the customer, a supplier can decide how to distinguish their solution from anything offered by the competition. Articles and books covering the traditional sales process fail to discuss how suppliers can deduce what their competition is offering, something that is absolutely essential to winning a large complex contract.

A small buy can be considered a discreet transaction. The customer may never see the seller again. Large buys are different. When a company awards a contract to construct a power plant, outsource its IT department, or buy a fleet of earthmoving machines, it is buying a long-term relationship. Success or failure becomes a shared destiny for the supplier and the customer alike. If the customer cannot pay for the project or the supplier cannot deliver, both are in big trouble. Large contracts work a lot like marriages. The time before the award is the romance, where each tries to put their best foot forward and compromise with the other. Then, once they are married, the two parties have to work together, be honest and trust each other. The customer must consider how well the chosen supplier will fit into their long-term business strategy and vice versa.

Also, selling a complex solution requires coordinating the supplier's engineering, operations, marketing, business development, finance, logistics, program management, contracts personnel and executive management. Optimally, all of these diverse people would be sending the same sales messages to potential customers. Every person involved on the supplier side will learn about their customer and the marketplace with each interaction. The sale is helped if all this information is fed back to one source on the sales team, allowing all available intelligence to be used in crafting a final proposal. Information sharing allows the team to improve their offering and position themselves to exceed the competitors' offers. The traditional sales process lacks the structure and has no formal mechanism to systematically identify and evaluate – let alone coordinate – all of these interactions across a large sales team.

There is a Better Way

Start by thinking of your sales campaign the way an author goes about writing a compelling novel. You devise a strategy that brings together the plot, setting, characters and dialogue into a coherent story. The secret to writing the book is not simply having all the right elements, but knowing how to make those elements work together. The same is true for a large sales campaign. The capture process starts with envisioning a strategy based on what's important to the customer decision makers and to the organization's buying behavior. The capture process then converts that strategy into a set of actions designed to influence the customer and contract acquisition, while developing an offering to best suit the customer's needs. Strategy development guides and enables up-front planning, allowing suppliers to take advantage of scarce and costly resources to develop the right solution, influence the customer and pre-sell a solution. The capture process coordinates and communicates activity across the company to support the win.

I. Learn from Winners

Before we discuss the capture process, we must understand the customer's procurement process for a large complex contract award. While the decision-making process differs across customers, Exhibit 1 shows that the customer starts by setting an acquisition strategy. This customer decides what is being bought and how it will be bought (one contract, multiple contracts, fixed priced, etc.). Next, the customer sets the budget for the contract. Then the customer defines the requirements and then creates an RFP and the evaluation criteria. Potential suppliers respond to the RFP and the customer usually separately evaluates the technical proposals and assesses the price. Then, a small group of key decision makers caucus and choose a winner.

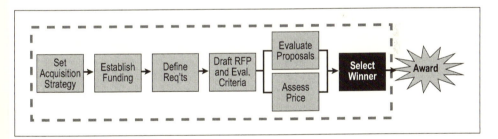

Exhibit 1: The Generic Customer Procurement Process

The capture process acts as a roadmap to a very complex undertaking. The capture process seeks to influence the customer's procurement process. It identifies and schedules a set of messages that the company should transmit to the customer in order to influence the presale and the way that the customer sets out to award their business. As shown in Exhibit 2, the process includes managing the technical evolution of the solution into one that best meets the customer's needs. In addition, it coordinates the tasking of intelligence collection so that the capture team can monitor and understand the customer and deduce the competitor's strategy and offering. The process also integrates collected intelligence, so that strategies and plans evolve across the pursuit using the best information available. The process encompasses how to staff and organize a team to implement the capture plan. The capture process achieves a win, and this book is organized to help your company create and implement a winning capture process.

As Chapter 1 will discuss, companies that consistently win large contracts have a formal and disciplined business acquisition process. The key to winning is creating and then executing a good capture plan. While many companies have a capture process, we have found that only a few consistently implement it. *A company can only fully implement the capture process if it is part of a mandatory, formal business acquisition process and receives executive commitment.* Only by having a well-structured business acquisition process can companies execute their capture process reliably, time and time again. Executives must provide leadership to oversee and enforce the process across individual pursuits to ensure that the company applies the necessary resources. This chapter will describe characteristics demonstrated by top performers in winning large contracts and show how these characteristics allow them to be the most profitable in their industries.

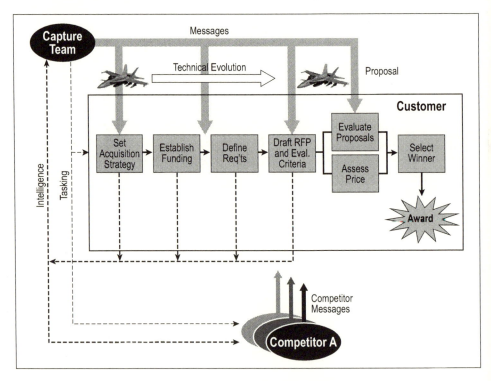

Exhibit 2: The Capture Process

II. Decide What to Pursue

Having a formal business acquisition process is critical, but equally important is the ability of a company to be selective in what it chooses to pursue. In Chapter 2, we will describe the subtle but critical factors necessary in becoming selective. This is the most important factor when working to achieve a high win rate. Few things create more waste than chasing an opportunity and losing. Top performers are very selective about what they pursue. They carefully allocate their scarce resources to a few promising opportunities. However obvious this point may seem, experience shows that it is extremely difficult to implement. Companies who are not selective spread their staff across many opportunities and lose contracts that they could have won with a more concentrated focus. This chapter will illustrate that victory starts with selecting the right battles and putting the right resources toward the job.

III. Start With a Win Strategy

Companies that consistently win do so because they develop and implement effective strategies. Chapters 3, 4 & 5 describe a proven formal process for developing a win strategy. This strategy organizes the critical pursuit of information in a logical fashion from which a company can develop a robust strategy to distinguish its offering from the competition, specifically when it comes to those attributes most important to the key customer decision makers.

As Exhibit 3 shows, when a company implements an effective win strategy, it changes the customer's perception of each player in the competition. Because the customer has the final say in picking the winner, their perception is the only reality that matters. In this diagram, the capture team sells the customer on the value of their features, and that causes the customer's perception of their needs to move closer to the capture team's offering. At the same time, the successful capture team improves their offering by ridding it of expensive features that the customer does not value. This moves the offering closer to the customer's position. By presenting data to the customer that shows that Competitor B is more costly and less desirable, the capture team influences the customer's perception of the competition, too. As the capture team implements their plan, they strive for competitive convergence between their offering and the customer's desires. The desired outcome is to become the closest match to the customer's needs, and the most obvious selection for the customer. A company's strategy is the plan of action that directs its moves across this spectrum and shapes the competition.

The key to the capture process is to start with the end in mind – begin with the envisioned victory and then work backwards, identifying all of the decisions which will predetermine that outcome. The essence of a good strategy is making the choices that will take you from where you are now to the point where victory will be yours. While this concept is straightforward, implementing it is not.

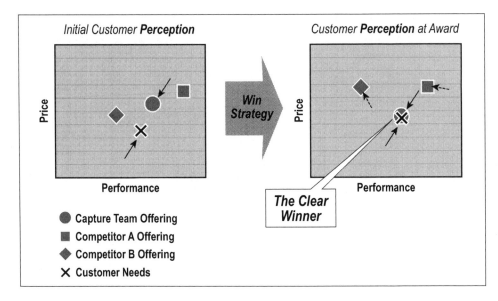

Exhibit 3: Customer Perception

To maximize influence on the customer, the strategy development process should begin as soon as you identify an opportunity – well before the customer sets the requirements and evaluation criteria. This way you can allow your win strategy to guide you in influencing each customer event. We have yet to meet a capture team leader who complained, "We started developing our win strategy too early." Generally speaking, the earlier you begin pursuing a program in earnest – which means developing and executing a win strategy – the greater your chances of winning. An early start provides more time to iterate your win strategy and your solution design. The more times you iterate the strategy development process, the better your win strategy becomes. For example, the earlier you start, the sooner you can identify and work the enabling technology that is required for the pursuit. If there is an enabling technology, this will become a customer's key concern as the pursuit evolves. By starting early, your team can invest in developing the technology and proving it through demonstrations.

IV. Set the Right Price

Price is always important in a source selection, and understanding how the customer weighs price is the key to identifying the correct balance. Exhibit 4 shows that before the key decision makers select a winner, they evaluate the proposals and assess the bid prices. These tasks are a key part of every customer's formal decision-making process. While the key decision makers select a winner, they must use the results of the proposal evaluation and the price to justify their decision. If the offering the decision makers want most is too high in price or scored poorly on the technical evaluation, they may be forced to go with another offering. To win, the capture team must provide an offering with a high enough technical evaluation and a low enough price to allow them to be selected.

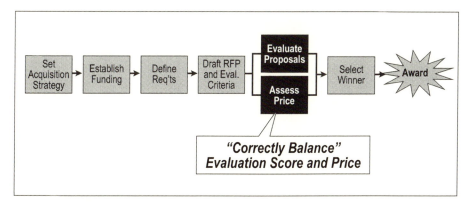

Exhibit 4: Setting the Right Price and Developing the Optimal Evaluation Scoring

In most cases, you cannot have both the lowest price and the highest technical evaluation, so you must analyze the buyer and determine the appropriate balance between the technical evaluation and the price. The key to identifying the right price to bid lies in deducing what the competitors are bidding. It takes a formal competitive analysis to identify your competitors' technical solutions, understand their strengths and weaknesses and deduce their bid price. Determining the optimal technical solution and price so that your team ensures a win is the result of the previously mentioned process called Price-to-Win (PTW). This process will be described in Chapter 6.

V. Prepare a Capture Team and Plan

Chapter 7 describes how to staff and prepare a winning capture team. Crafting the win strategy, shaping the competition, designing the offering, cultivating customer champions, selling your benefits to the customer and preparing for the proposal is a complex and challenging job. To perform these tasks, the top performers assign staff to formal capture teams and hold these teams accountable for winning the contracts. The capture team consists of program managers, engineers, marketers, business development managers, contract administrators and all the other key people required to win. Having a disciplined capture process makes the best use of this cross-functional team. By carefully defining everyone's roles and responsibilities, all the team members know what is expected of them at all times. A disciplined process motivates the team by reducing uncertainty and stress. Top companies try to stand up capture teams before their competitors and well before the customer writes the RFP.

Chapter 8 will describe how to build the capture plan. Developing and executing a good capture plan is key to winning, because it's execution positions your offering. The team that shapes the game better usually wins. The capture plan identifies all the data you need to create, contacts to make, and messages to send to shape the competitive landscape. The plan identifies the responsible party for every action and tracks each action's completion. The capture plan coordinates all of these actions to influence the customer's milestones in an event-driven schedule. As Exhibit 5 shows, the win strategy guides how the capture team attempts to influence all the steps in the customer's acquisition process.

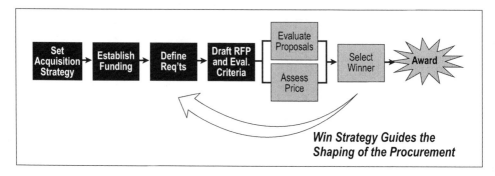

Exhibit 5: Win Strategy Guides the Process

VI. Develop the Contact and Capture Plans

No matter how big or complex the pursuit, a sale eventually comes down to persuading individual customers that your solution's features will solve their problems and provide important benefits that no other competitor can offer. Your greatest strategies will fail if you cannot clearly communicate to the customer why your solution is superior to the competition's. The key planning mechanism enabling this process is the Contact Plan that will be described in detail, along with all the ingredients of a capture plan and how to create one.

VII. Collect Intelligence

Crafting a persuasive win strategy and plan hinges on a thorough understanding of the customer and their needs, as well as the competition and their strategies. The effectiveness of all capture plan activities directly depend on accurate intelligence – about both the customer and competitors. To develop the most desired offering, you must know what is most important to the customer. It is difficult to provide a solution that is better than the competition's if you don't know what the competitors are offering. Chapter 9 discusses how the capture team collects and uses intelligence for a decisive advantage in the capture process. For example, if the capture team discovers that the risk of a particular technology concerns the customer, the team can overcome this fear with a well-executed technology demonstration. However, if this technology is not a concern, performing an expensive demonstration squanders precious resources. Good competitive intelligence allows companies to make the best use of their resources, along with many other benefits.

VIII. Avoid the Common Pitfalls

To win, you must not lose. We have seen even multi-billion bids tripped up by some elementary mistakes. Chapter 10 discusses the common pitfalls we see companies make and how to avoid them. These mistakes include bidding solutions the customer does not want, executives losing the commitment to win when it counts, and teaming with the company your customer hates. We have seen these types of mistakes allow competitors to stumble across the goal line and win, even when their offering was only mediocre.

This chapter will describe how to avoid catering to the wrong customer and how to ensure you bid a winning solution. We will discuss common obstacles to developing a cost effective solution and how to overcome them, and we will describe the undisciplined proposal process. A sales campaign culminates in writing the proposal, and the key to writing an effective proposal is to follow the proposal instructions, making it easy to evaluate. Top performers carefully plan and orchestrate the proposal process to focus their writers on the important issues such as addressing all RFP requirements, dispelling technical concerns and communicating their win strategy. Using a formal proposal methodology allows these companies to increase their reuse of previous proposals and avoid needless reworking of the proposal format. These techniques allow the team to concentrate on the higher leverage tasks.

IX. Close the Deal

After enduring a long campaign and submitting the proposal, many capture teams rest, letting the customer evaluate and decide the winners. But the battle is not over. Chapter 11 will discuss how to successfully manage this crucial post-proposal submittal process. The question and answer period is very important. It is your last chance to explain or adjust your approach before the customer makes a decision. Often, a customer will demand negotiations after proposals have been submitted, giving your company another opportunity to lower the price or otherwise sweeten the offering. Companies lose jobs by being outmaneuvered by the competition or bungling the post-proposal negotiations. Therefore, one needs to have a negotiation strategy before the proposal submittal. Otherwise, you can end up losing your margins on the sale after the proposal goes in. A negotiation strategy is part of the overall pricing strategy. This is also the time when one must carefully monitor the senior levels of the customer's decision-making team. We have seen, in more than one huge pursuit, situations where the customer switched the winner in the last few days before the award announcement. Companies can sometimes make a high-level political play to the final economic decision maker and reverse an award recommendation at the last minute. And even once the contract has been awarded, it might not be over, because many government customers allow post-award protests, which we will also discuss.

Chapter 1: Learning from the Best

"While it is wise to learn from experience, it is wiser to learn from the experience of others."

— Rick Warren, pastor and author

Some companies consistently win the contracts they bid for. Most do not. Obviously, few winning companies are eager to share the secrets to their success with those companies who hold less impressive win records. That's where the experience of the authors will prove invaluable to any company looking to improve their odds of winning future contracts.

As mentioned in the introduction, Michael O'Guin worked on a two-year strategic benchmarking survey of 24 aerospace and defense companies. As the consulting team analyzed the data from these companies, they were startled to find that the average company only won 18 percent of the competitive dollars they bid on. However, three companies won over 60 percent, and one of those companies consistently won 80 percent. How? The study team found that these companies differed significantly in process as well as in performance. This study found that only by applying a formal, disciplined business development process could companies consistently win large complex pursuits. The benchmarking results also revealed that formal processes enabled better performance across the business enterprise, from engineering the product to post-delivery support. Finally, the study showed that superior process performance translates directly into higher profits.

The objective of the study was to compare process performance across the aerospace and defense industry, so companies could implement process improvements. The simple fact is that most companies, regardless of their industry, have no idea how their process performance compares with their industry peers. This study was intended to provide that unique perspective. The study was extensive, taking place over two years and involving 24 different businesses. The benchmarking study collected over one hundred performance metrics at each site and assessed the business practices for all major business processes: acquire business, design product, manage program, provide material, build product, develop software, and support product. The metrics collected included: program budget performance, percent of shop orders released on time, supplier payments released on time, changes per purchasing order and percent on-time deliveries.

The survey process included detailed definitions for each metric and on-site validation of the metrics by a consulting team. To assess the business practices of each company, the consultants interviewed key process owners and scored the company's practices on 850 structured questions. The questionnaires covered topics ranging from design-to-cost practices and program management empowerment, to the level of competitive intelligence collected. Although the participants designed and produced products ranging from rocket motors to computers, the study team found surprisingly few measures skewed by the different technologies used or markets served. The business processes and the characteristics that satisfied internal or external customers varied little from one company to the next. For example, the owners of the manufacturing process at all companies wanted to have their production material on time; it didn't matter if they were assembling a display console or a satellite.

The consultants analyzed the database to identify the characteristics that differentiated top performers and found the companies with more formal processes had consistently better process performance. A company with a rigorous software development and review process delivered more of their code on time than other companies, for example. The analysis also found striking consistency between the processes of the most profitable companies. The most profitable companies in this industry outperformed their peers in five distinct ways:

- Superior new business acquisition – they won more business as measured by competitive win rates.
- Superior customer delivery – more profitable companies had an average on time delivery of 95 percent versus 85 percent for the rest of industry.
- Superior major subcontract delivery – these companies received their major subcontracts on time from their suppliers 95 percent of the time versus 65 percent for the others. Not surprisingly, on time subcontract delivery was highly correlated with on time customer delivery.
- Less change activity – the more profitable companies had almost half as many changes per purchase order and two thirds fewer engineering changes per drawing than the less profitable companies.
- Superior manufacturing quality – the top companies had almost half the repair and rework hours per 1000 direct labor hours and a one-third lower scrap rate.

Surprisingly, better budget performance and material acquisition did not differentiate the more profitable companies. In fact, the more profitable companies consistently performed worse on such material acquisition metrics as "line items received on time," "incoming acceptance rates," and "dollars spent per supplier." This data does not suggest that companies should allow their suppliers to deliver more material late to increase profits. The results merely show that procuring material is not a key leverage point in the aerospace and defense industry. It also reveals that the more profitable companies do not excel at every process. They do, however, excel in the five characteristics noted.

The most startling finding was that the average aerospace and defense company won only 18 percent of the dollars they bid on. The study team's debriefing shocked the participant's executive teams. Win rates are a closely guarded secret, so few executives had any perspective of how they compared. In addition, the study team found that most companies either did not track win rates or they conveniently adjusted the definition of a "win" or "loss" to improve their numbers. For example, a company would classify a follow-on contract award as competitive, because they argued the original award was competitive. After making all of the numbers consistent from company to company, the study team found three companies that won on average over 60 percent of the competitive dollars, one of which consistently won 80 percent over a three-year period.

By conducting this study, O'Guin was given a bird's eye view into the means by which 24 companies pursued new business, and how three did it particularly well. When one interviews the staff at the best-in-class companies, it quickly becomes obvious how they differ from the rest of industry. The data verified those observations and more.

Six years later, the author was able to validate his conclusions while conducting a similar benchmarking study for one of the world's largest aerospace companies. In that study, O'Guin analyzed the eight divisions of the corporation that performed best at winning new business. Performance metrics were collected and business practices were assessed to identify and document best practices in business development so that these practices could be disseminated across the company. This study not only validated the earlier study's findings, but it gave the author more insight into the specific practices that enable superior performance, because this time the author knew what to look for.

While the simple concepts uncovered are easy to grasp and, frankly, pretty obvious; most companies do a poor job of implementing them. This book will reveal the subtle practices that enable superior performance. In addition to the author's experience detailed above, both authors have had the privilege of working over the past fifteen years with eight facilities that are truly best-in-class at winning new business. This chapter distills what the authors have learned from those experiences. For the rest of this chapter these consistently winning companies will be referred to as "best-in-class."

Attributes of Best-in-Class Companies

Best-in-class companies are significantly more profitable than the rest of industry. Companies with win rates over 60 percent achieved a return on sales of 12 percent, while the rest of industry averaged just 8 percent. Their net profit/total investment was 50 percent higher. One of the key factors contributing to this higher profitability was the greater return on discretionary sales, marketing and proposal spending than companies with lower win rates. Lower performing companies – those that win less than half of the dollars they bid on – are wasting most of their marketing and sales resources by chasing opportunities they lose. While one might expect to see a direct relationship between win rate and the productivity (award dollars/discretionary dollars) of business development spending – as your win rate doubles so does your Bid & Proposal (B&P) productivity – this is not the case. Exhibit 1-1 shows that B&P productivity increases faster than expected. A lower performing company winning just 20 percent of their proposed dollars must spend over eight times as much to win contracts with the same value as a company winning 80 percent. The loss of a single large contract forces a company to bid many smaller jobs to win the same backlog of award dollars. However, smaller jobs take proportionally more discretionary resources than larger ones. One particular company's spending can be considered typical: they spent on average $1.5 million chasing a $100 million opportunity (a ratio of 1.5 percent of spending to award value), but spent $800 thousand on a $20 million opportunity (a ratio of 4.0 percent of spending to award value). Therefore, if a company loses one large opportunity they must spend substantially more money chasing an equivalent value in smaller contracts. This results in companies with lower win rates having to spend much more money for each award dollar that they win, which slashes their profit margins.

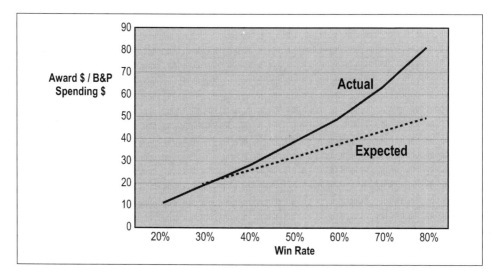

Exhibit 1-1: Improving Your Win Rate Dramatically Raises Your B&P Productivity

Best-in-class companies reap significant benefits beyond higher business development productivity from a high win rate. By winning most of the opportunities they choose to pursue, the best-in-class end up with a backlog consisting of their highest priority pursuits. This mix of contracts should be those best suited to their capabilities. They are then able to tailor all aspects of their business from procurement to sales force training to this select mix of contracts which streamlines overhead, creating a more efficient cost structure and higher profits. As a result of this fit, the best-in-class leverage their research and development (R&D), facilities and knowledge base more effectively. Finally, because their wins match their capabilities, they tend to perform to commitments more often with fewer penalties and less rework, again boosting profitability and creating a positive past performance record that in turn supports more sales. This data proved a hypothesis that the authors had been considering for years ... that winning a lot is good.

Best-in-Class Companies Differ in Process as Well as Performance

One key finding of these studies was that best-in-class companies did not achieve their superior performance by chance, but by developing, institutionalizing and enforcing a formal disciplined business development process. While all of the surveyed companies had a pursuit process, the implementation differed widely between the best-in-class and the rest. Best-in-class do not pursue opportunities haphazardly. When their executives decide to pursue a sale, these companies use a repeatable process to leverage all of the company's marketing, sales, technical and management resources to win. The best-in-class view business acquisition as a structured set of interrelated activities to win new business. Since they view it as process, they work to continuously improve it. The less successful companies treat every opportunity as a discreet and unique event. They do not have dedicated personnel or proposal facilities to help win. It is always an ad hoc effort. These companies spend little time examining and improving their approach or processes. Instead they rely on the experience and capability of individual program managers to win awards. In other words, they work hard and hope for the best.

To Win Consistently, One Needs a Strategy

Superior business development starts with a clear, well-defined business strategy. Best-in-class companies focus their scarce resources on a few markets and opportunities where they will have a decisive advantage. They know what they are good at and what opportunities they can win. Their strategy clearly identifies what they will go after. Conversely, their business strategy also excludes specific potential customers and opportunities because they do not fit the company's strategic objectives or core competencies. Trying to be all things to all people will defuse resources and inhibit their effectiveness.

Best-in-class companies focus on pursuits that are within their core market areas. They bid on contracts to their existing customers and markets with products with which they have experience. Chasing new customers is expensive, and usually vastly underestimated. Data has found that companies are much more successful developing new products for existing customers than trying to take existing products to new customers. In addition, sales outside a core business tend to be less successful since customer understanding and relationships tend to be weaker. However, if the best-in-class decide to chase a new market outside of their traditional business, they do it very judiciously.

— Strategy In Action —

In the early 1990s, IBM Federal Systems Owego forecasted a decline in their traditional defense market. They spotted an emerging market in complex mail sorting systems. This market would leverage their core capabilities in systems integration, implementation of COTS products, complex manufacturing and target recognition. Unfamiliar with this market, they carefully targeted a United States Postal Service opportunity that none of the existing market players had the skills for. IBM may not have known the Postal Service, but they knew how to sell to a government agency. IBM formed a world-class team of experienced postal suppliers early and proceeded to meet with the customer and sell them on their team's capabilities. IBM produced demonstrations of their integration and target recognition skills. They provided white papers to the Postal Service with suggestions on how to improve their Request for Proposal. As a result of their effort, IBM beat out six rivals for a $155 million Postal Service contract to build and install 3,144 sorters that use bar codes to organize letters based on postal carrier delivery routes. Over the next ten years, they grew this market entry into a billion dollar business. They carefully entered this new market.

Best-in-class companies develop realistic market strategies by objectively assessing technological trends and potential customer funding three, five or ten years into the future. These companies diligently work toward a thorough and realistic understanding of a market's future. They conduct market area studies analyzing their markets from different perspectives. First, they analyze their customer base's forecasts and plans in order to understand the market size, trends and dynamics. Next, they examine their customer's customers to understand downstream changes and the underlying foundations of their markets. These companies focus attention on determining where their customers will be spending their money. They estimate the total market size as well as their addressable market (the size of the market their products will compete for). This helps the best-in-class companies determine which products they should develop and push. They study market trends including emerging technologies, changing demographics and evolving customer needs to develop a robust view of how the market is likely to change.

The most significant difference between best-in-class companies and others is that the best-in-class conduct an extensive analysis of their competitors' current and future offerings, investments and strategies. They focus on understanding the competitors' strengths and weaknesses. They work to specifically identify each competitor's weaknesses – holes in their product offering, dissatisfied customers and capacity constraints – because these are good opportunities for expanding their own market share. Into that picture they project their desired position – who will be their customers and what will be their market share, their key differentiators, and lastly their sales and profits.

Once they have those projections, they are able to assess what is achievable. Do they have the necessary resources to do all the things needed to reach their goals? By comparing the company's growth and financial objectives against the resources it will take to be successful, they assess the viability of their strategies. This analysis acts as a check and balance; are they forecasting an unreasonable growth in either their market or their market share? Good strategies are based on facts and analyses, which make them realistic. Only by understanding their competitors' strategies and their customers' future needs and budgets can they develop realistic market forecasts and strategies.

The following example illustrates the importance of accurate market forecasting.

— *Strategy In Action* —

In the mid-1990s a satellite supplier examined the market demand for satellites by forecasting the available market size. They examined the growth of worldwide telecommunications sales, which would provide the revenue for the purchasers of satellites. Companies like Teledesic, Globalstar, Starband, Skynet, ICO and Iridium were planning to meet growing telecommunications demand with satellite-based systems. The satellite company's strategic planners estimated the total expected dollar value of future telecommunication services such as telephone, Internet access and interactive services over the next 20 years. Then they analyzed and compared these revenue projections to the availability of capital for space-based telecommunications investments. They converted this demand into high, nominal and low satellite equivalents. They also assessed the supply of rocket launches to put these satellites into orbit, to determine if there were enough rockets to meet the demand. The planners compared and validated all of these different perspectives against each other to understand how realistic their market sizing was. Their extensive analysis concluded with a forecast that came in significantly below the wildly optimistic projections made by many industry pundits. Phone and cable companies were investing billions in ground-based fiber optic networks that would compete with satellite-based systems for potential users. Their forecast projected that fierce competition from ground-based systems was going to force down telecommunications prices. This meant that the revenue projections all of these financiers were banking on for their satellite systems would most likely never materialize. As a result, the satellite supplier focused their discretionary resources on the slower growing but stable government satellite market. Then, in 2000 when the dot.com bubble burst and caused the telecom industry to implode, they avoided losing tens of millions of dollars.

The approach illustrated above stands in sharp contrast to the approach of less successful companies. The poorer performers concentrate their strategic planning processes on financial analysis in lieu of an in-depth study of evolving customer needs, technologies and demographics. They give mostly cursory attention to their competitors and how they will position themselves in the future. Their strategic planners conduct iteration after iteration of complicated analysis of detailed financial models. However, their results are relatively useless because the underlying market data and competitor understanding is poor. As a result, these companies consistently fall short of their five-year forecasts, while best-in-class companies exceed theirs.

Winners are Selective

The single most significant difference between best-in-class companies and the rest of industry is that the best-in-class have the processes and discipline to be selective in what they pursue.

The common failing of most companies is that they haphazardly chase too many pursuits. Poor performers squander precious staff time and discretionary dollars chasing opportunities that they are destined to lose or that will never materialize. Consequently, because they waste significant resources, poorer performers form their capture teams late in the game, and assign fewer full-time people to chase opportunities than the best-in-class do. Staffing shortfalls curtail everything from customer contacts to performing product demonstrations. As a company spreads its pursuit staff across more and more opportunities, they lose contracts they could have otherwise won.

As Exhibit 1-2 shows, if you are peddling simple products – "small sales" – the more sales opportunities you create, the more sales you make. Think of a sixth grader selling Girl Scout cookies from door to door. Her business is a numbers game – the more doors she knocks on, the more cookies she sells. However, if you are making large complex and competitive sales that require significant customer cultivation, this is not the case. With the large competitive sale, the more time you spend working with the customer, educating them and customizing your solution versus the competition, the greater your chances of winning. The more resources you apply, the higher your win probability. So as a company pursues more large opportunities, it begins to spread its scarce resources thinner and thinner. As a result, at a certain point, the company begins to lose more and more. As the company pursues more, staff spends less time per opportunity, allowing the competition to monopolize the customer cultivation. Exhibit 1-2 shows that you can chase 20 opportunities and win 16 or you can chase 40 and win 8. Best-in-class companies do not try

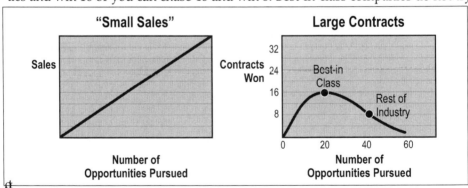

Exhibit 1-2: Best-in-Class Understand the Difference Between Small Sales and Winning Large Contracts

maximize the number of opportunities chased; rather they maximize their chances of winning a select few. As a result, they maximize the number of contracts won, while the rest of industry dissipates their resources and wins significantly less

Best-in-class companies concentrate their resources. These companies typically outspend their opponents by 15-20 percent on the opportunities they commit to winning. However, by chasing fewer opportunities, the best-in-class spend less overall.

Money is important, but it is not the key to winning contracts. The constraining resource is not money; it is people, or more specifically, good people. Within every company there is an "A team" – the company's most innovative engineers, persuasive marketers, and capable program managers. Where one assigns these key individuals largely determines the success or failure of most pursuits. Victory depends on blending the right talent, experience, dedication and aggressiveness into an effective team. While a company can always find more money, people with the right talent cannot be cloned – yet! Where a company's executives decide to assign these people is the most important resource allocation decision they will make.

Starting Early is Key

Just as important as who is assigned, is when these key individuals are assigned. *The earlier a company commits to pursuing an opportunity in earnest – which means developing and executing a win strategy – the greater its chances of winning.* One company's experience is telling: this company has found that they win only 22 percent of dollars they chase if they form a formal capture team less than one year before the RFP receipt. However, their win rate is 79 percent when they form capture teams more than one year before the RFP. Same company, with same processes and people, yet their win rate jumps by almost four times with an early start!

Exhibit 1-3 shows the cumulative new business spending of the best-in-class companies versus the typical supplier. The best-in-class company spends 15-20 percent more overall per pursuit, but if you examine the spending curves carefully, you will notice that after the Draft Request for Proposal (DRFP) receipt, (or after RFQ receipt for commercial bids), both curves become parallel. This means that after that point, both companies spend the same amount. By that point, the best-in-class has already outspent the competitors by a factor of three. This is very important because on the left side of the exhibit is plotted the "Ability to Influence the Customer." During the early phases of the pursuit, potential suppliers have the greatest opportunity to influence the customer. It is during the early phases that the customer is allocating budgets, formulating the acquisition strategy and defining their requirements. They welcome and appreciate a potential supplier's input. Suppliers can provide the customer with trade studies, cost estimates and perform technology demonstrations to influence the program's scope, timing, preferred technical approach, expectations and requirements. This is the best time to foster a close working relationship with the customer, because the customer wants and needs a supplier's help. As the opportunity matures, the customer becomes deluged with supplier visits. The customer becomes wary of suppliers, because late in the process the customers feel the suppliers are just trying to sell them something, not solve their problems. Also, an early start allows the supplier the maximum amount of time to innovate and improve their offering. Time allows the supplier to determine the best solution through trade studies and to develop substantiation of their claims with proof – tests, analyses, and surveys. A supplier's ability to influence drops off precipitously after DRFP receipt. By that time, the buyer has finalized most of their key decisions – set the requirements, funding, contract structure and key evaluation criteria. Once these decisions are made, they become nearly irreversible.

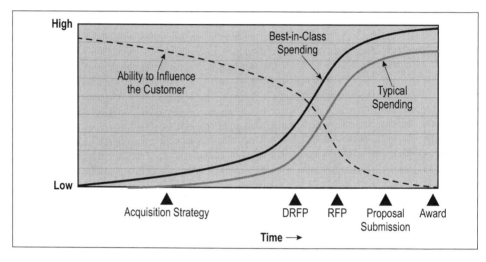

Exhibit 1-3: Influence Versus Cumulative Spending

While the best-in-class companies only outspend the typical company by 15-20 percent overall, they are outspending them by three times when they have the greatest ability to influence the customer. This allows them to shape the procurement to their strengths. ***Therefore, it is not just that best-in-class outspend their competitors, it is when they choose to do so.***

By standing up a capture team late in the process, the typical company has minimal influence on the customer and lacks the time to develop and pre-sell the customer on potentially innovative solutions. As a result, they are trapped with their traditional approaches, may take large risks by bidding a solution that the customer is unfamiliar with and are reactive to the competitive moves of the best-in-class.

— *Strategy in Action* —

A training company was pursuing a job to design and build a family of flight simulators. One of their sister divisions was the Original Equipment Manufacturer (OEM) for the aircraft, but did not make simulators. For two years, the training division tried to interest the OEM division in joining their team. Due to the corporate staffs' inattention to business development, the two divisions agreed to work together just two months before the RFP was received. By that time, the companies had squandered the opportunity to be innovative. If they had teamed earlier, the OEM could have written their flight control software for easy use in the simulator, which would have reduced their costs by millions of dollars. This savings would have created an insurmountable cost advantage over all of the competitors. But with their late teaming, they were stuck competing with low cost competitors bidding into a cost-conscious customer. They lost this bid because they had squandered their inherent advantage.

While most managers understand that opportunities are usually won or lost well before the proposal is delivered, many do not manage that way. The complexity of the solutions, proposal requirements and solution dollar value largely determine how much it will cost to develop a proposal. Only the crucial pre-DRFP monies are truly discretionary. Unfortunately, many executives fail to recognize this fact, much to their company's detriment. We have seen many executives set arbitrarily low capture budgets when compared to historical spending for similar pursuits. The low budget significantly hurts their chances of winning. By underfunding pursuit budgets, management unwittingly puts their capture teams on the typical company's lower spending curve (the gray line on Exhibit 1-3). They under invest when the potential returns are greatest. For example, one capture team leader pursuing an air traffic control system estimated her capture budget at $5 million. The budget included conducting system demonstrations for the customer, trying to assist them in writing the system and test requirements, and creating the proposal. Her executives felt she was padding the demonstration budget and overestimating the proposal costs, despite historical records, which validated her estimates. The executives cut her budget to $3 million. She had to economize on the demonstrations and customer trips, which significantly reduced their effectiveness. In the end, her capture team still overran their budget by $1 million. The competitor successfully used their demonstration and customer visits to persuade the customer to add requirements. These new requirements were expensive for the capture team leader's solution to meet, driving up her company's price and resulting in a loss. As this company discovered, when management underfunds a capture budget, the money they unwittingly cut is the crucial up-front expenditure.

As obvious as these conclusions are, in practice they are very difficult to implement. It has been our experience that the discipline to adhere to a process to select judiciously the best few opportunities early on is the single most important factor in achieving a high win rate. In fact, we have helped five companies to become more selective and within one year, all of these companies had more than doubled their win rate to over 50 percent. In Chapter 2, we will describe the subtle but critical behaviors that enable companies to be selective.

Positioning to Win

Once the pursuit decision is made, the best-in-class companies form formal capture teams to position themselves to win. They hold these capture teams accountable for winning. This multifunctional team includes representatives from all of the disciplines critical to winning the program – program management, business development, finance, pricing, engineering, contracts, operations and logistics. As soon as the team is formed, the best-in-class companies train members in the critical skills needed, including win strategy development, how to influence the customer, and intelligence collection. The team develops the win strategy that guides all of the capture activities. The win strategy identifies how the company will differentiate their offering from the competition in terms of those attributes most important to the customer.

The positioning phase includes developing substantiating data, creating the technical solution, influencing and pre-selling the customer. To plan, budget and schedule all of these activities, the capture team creates a capture plan. The capture plan is the roadmap to victory. A key part of the capture plan is the communications plan, which identifies what messages to send, to whom and when. The capture team attempts to shape the game by influencing the customer's acquisition strategy, funding, requirements and evaluation criteria. To deliver persuasive messages, the capture team must develop supporting facts and data. The capture plan includes an action plan to ensure that all the trade studies, tests, simulations, demonstrations and analyses are available to substantiate the delivery of all messages. If done right, top performing companies shape the procurement toward their strengths. In addition, they convince the customer that their solution best solves their problem, making it the preferred solution. In parallel, the capture team improves their position by acquiring capabilities, selecting the best teammates and suppliers, customizing the solution for the customer's needs and developing proof of benefits for the customer. All of these activities are guided by the win strategy.

But a strategy is only as good as the information on which it is based. How can a company successfully differentiate itself from the competition if it does not know what the competition is going to offer? It cannot. Without facts, one is relying on ignorance, which rarely leads to victory. A capture team builds an effective win strategy only with a thorough understanding of both the customer and the competitor. Best-in-class companies invest resources in establishing a formal business intelligence capability to decipher the competition's strategies and approaches. The benchmarking survey mentioned at the beginning of this chapter found a direct relationship between a company's knowledge of their competitor's technical strengths and weaknesses and their competitive win rate as shown in Exhibit 1-4.

One of the best-in-class' most impressive characteristics is the focus of their intelligence process. They do not try to learn everything about every competitor. Rather, they identify and collect specific information on particular, high-value questions and use this intelligence at key points in the sales cycle to allow more effective executive decision-making. For example, the top performer had their competitive analysts create a mock executive summary of the competitor's proposal. This executive summary highlighted the competitor's key strategies, win themes and likely ghosts of their own proposal. The analysts posted this executive summary in the proposal room where the proposal authors could refer to it throughout their writing process. In this way, they could counter their competitor's likely assertions.

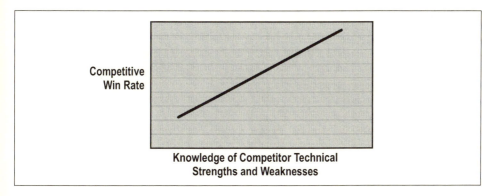

Exhibit 1-4: More Competitive Intelligence Leads to a Higher Win Rate

In addition, best-in-class companies conduct Price-to-Win (PTW) analysis. The objective of the PTW analysis is to identify the highest price a company can bid and still win. A capture team identifies this price by conducting a formal analysis of the purchase, which assesses the customer's buying behavior and the competition's likely solution. The PTW analyst seeks to identify whether the customer awards contracts with price premiums or not, and under what circumstances. A company should bid differently in each of those situations. In addition, the analyst deciphers the competitor's technical approach, and then uses that information to estimate the cost of the competitor's solution. Based on the customer's buying behavior and the competitor's likely bid price, as well as how attractive the competitor's offering is to the customer versus the capture team's, the analyst identifies the winning price for his company.

Writing Effective Proposals

Best-in-class companies consistently create high quality proposals. Despite good positioning, a company can still lose with a poorly written proposal. Best-in-class companies build their proposal teams around a dedicated core staff of proposal developers. This core staff of proposal managers, proposal specialists, and technical writers own a formal proposal methodology. *Our studies found that companies that used dedicated core proposal staff and dedicated facilities significantly outperformed other companies at winning new business.* This dedicated group helps architect the proposal, provides the writing expertise and ensures that lessons learned are passed from one proposal to the next. Their proposal facility includes a centralized proposal library that has training materials, previous proposals, reuse modules, and master resumes. These centers are large enough to allow the company to co-locate their entire proposal team. Using a formal proposal methodology ensures that best practices are consistently applied to each proposal. This avoids the need to reinvent the process and ensures that all steps are followed in the correct sequence. This allows these companies to increase their reuse of previous proposals and avoid needless reworking of the format.

The top three performers also spend the most time on proposal training. For example, before any work begins on the proposal, the core specialists first train the rest of the proposal team in the proposal development methodology. This training includes focus on writing the proposal so it is easy to evaluate as well as how to create good win themes that clearly communicate discriminators and benefits. As owners of the proposal process, the core team always conducts post-proposal and post-award debriefings to gather performance metrics and lessons learned. This data is then used to improve the selection, capture planning, proposal and training processes.

Prior to receiving the RFP, you must develop and implement your strategy. As Exhibit 1-5 shows, once the RFP is received, it is time to document what you have already created. Just like a civil engineer, you cannot build a bridge as you are designing it. Trying to develop and document the story simultaneously leads to disaster.

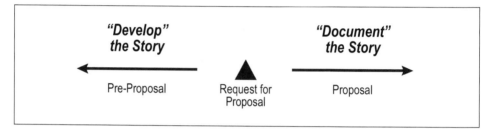

Exhibit 1-5: The Proposal Development Process

One key to creating a well-written proposal is upfront planning and reviews. A proposal process guides the proposal team to carefully plan and orchestrate their efforts. This process ensures that before writing, the authors receive descriptive author packages with clear ground rules, win themes, issues to be addressed and allocated customer requirements. All of this information helps the writers know what to write about in each section. In addition, the proposal methodology ensures that the capture team creates persuasive data and facts for the authors to use to populate each section. The process includes early management reviews of the proposal strategy, pricing and writing. This ensures executive "buy in" to the strategy and themes early in the proposal process. Therefore, the best-in-class avoid management redirection and rewriting at the eleventh hour, when the team should be doing nothing more than polishing up the text. These techniques allow the writers to focus on telling a clear and persuasive story.

None of the poorer performers performed an adequate opportunity selection, causing them to frequently squander resources on poor opportunities while starving otherwise viable prospects. For these poorer performers, capture planning does not begin in earnest until the RFP is imminent or has arrived, precluding any significant customer influencing. Because they start late and do not know the customer very well, their messages are generic and unpersuasive. They tend to ramble on in meetings with the customer and in proposals, listing all of their features, because they do not know what is important to the customer. Proposal planning is often incomplete or cursory. When the RFP arrives at these companies, they typically throw a group of available bodies together in a room. Similarly, they frequently under budget and under staff the effort. Lacking upfront planning, chaos ensues as everyone feverishly reworks the proposal right up until the proposal submission. As a result, these companies submit proposals that are not their best efforts and are filled with errors. The proposal budget is overrun, and the team is exhausted and demoralized. And then they lose. Lacking a core staff that owns the process, poor performers disband the teams and all of their hard-learned lessons are forgotten, destined to be learned again by the next proposal team.

Committing to Winning

One of the most important characteristics of the best-in-class is that they commit to winning. Many executives are simply not committed to winning. While no executive will admit that winning is not important, many clearly communicate it through their actions. Winning is hard. ***Winners make difficult decisions when losers do not think they need to.*** This is a lesson we have seen repeated over and over again. Winners do everything possible to win. For example, on one pursuit the lead division needed work, but it was a high cost facility. Another division had the skills and cost structure that would be a better match for many of the job's tasks. We convinced the lead division that they were not cost competitive and that they should transfer a substantial amount of their work scope to their sister division. This company won, but it was a painful decision for the lead division to give up that work after spending so much money chasing the pursuit. In another case, a company decided to bring their reviled competitor onto their team and give them a prime piece of the work because their products were essential to winning. They won, but probably would have lost without making this difficult choice.

— *Strategy in Action* —

Frequently, the most painful decisions are about people. While pursuing the Joint Strike Fighter (JSF) program, the largest procurement in history, Lockheed Martin realized that the services (JSF was a tri-service program where the customer was the Air Force, Navy and Marine Corps) had lost significant trust and confidence in Lockheed's JSF management team due to cost overruns on their demonstrator development. Lockheed knew it was imperative to correct this problem. When Lockheed's senior executives looked across their company, there was only one person they believed had sufficient stature, management ability and customer confidence to successfully manage the JSF program. That person was Tom Burbage. Unfortunately, Tom Burbage was focused on fixing the problematic F-22 program, the Air Force's largest and most important Air Force development program. Removing Burbage from the F-22 program would anger the Air Force. Lockheed chose to upset their largest customer and move him to the JSF pursuit as their program manager, but it was a necessary step to win the enormous JSF program. Tom Burbage was so well respected, as one high ranking customer told me, their attitude to Lockheed "changed 180 degrees overnight." Without Burbage leading the Lockheed Martin's JSF team, they were unlikely to win. It was a difficult decision. Lockheed made it and won a program worth $200 billion.

At the same time Lockheed Martin was struggling with their JSF competition, they were locked in a heated battle to win a contract to modernize the cockpit of the existing C-130 cargo plane fleet, called C-130AMP. As the OEM on the C-130, this program was critical to Lockheed Martin. Lockheed had invested over a billion dollars of their own money developing the C-130J, a new derivative of the C-130, and the C-130AMP could cannibalize the C-130J's market. If one of their competitors won the modernization program, they would become a potent competitor against their C-130J with a low cost modernization alternative. During the proposal evaluation process and before submitting their last proposal updates, the Air Force informed Lockheed Martin that they had scored poorly on the heavily weighted Past Performance section of the proposal, which was a risk assessment of the contractor's ability to perform based on their previous contract performance history. Ironically, Boeing, one of Lockheed's competitors, also had a past performance problem, but they chose to solve it before the final proposal update. When the government conducts a past performance evaluation, the vast majority of the focus and scoring of the assessment is on the prime or lead division of the team. To address their past performance issue, Boeing made the difficult decision to change the program lead from Anaheim, California to their Long Beach facility 30 miles away. The Long Beach facility had won the prestigious Malcolm Baldrige National Quality Award for their C-17 program a few years earlier, and accordingly had an outstanding past performance record. Changing the program lead is a painful decision because it has a significant impact on executive roles, ego and compensation. While Lockheed had another facility on their team with an outstanding past performance record, they never considered changing the program lead. Instead, Lockheed elected to do what most companies do when they have a past performance problem, they wrote a response to the customer trying to explain away their past performance issues. Boeing's improved past performance rating gave Darleen Druyun, the source selection authority, sufficient justification to award Boeing the contract. Boeing was willing to do something really hard and Lockheed was not. Winners are willing to do hard things when losers don't think they need to.

Executives communicate what is important through the ways they spend their time and by who they reward. At one company, the general manager told us that winning more business was his number one goal for the year. The next day, his proposal manager told us that he had just held a "Red Team" review of a proposal and no one showed up. If winning was really important to that general manager, why did his employees believe that participating in a red team was a low priority? Because the general manager did not spend his time on winning. While he never missed a program or technology review, he did not regularly attend capture strategy reviews or red team debriefings. He led by example, and his example showed that winning was not important.

— *Strategy in Action* —

The best-in-class hire, promote, recognize and reward winners. For example, one company uses many different approaches to reward the people that help them win. They regularly identify eight to ten people on winning proposals for the company-wide employee recognition awards, which include $500 to $1,000 in cash. They provide all proposal team members with plaques, which have a copy of the proposal cover and a list of all of the proposal team participants. The plaques are adorned with red ribbons that read "winner." Management sponsors picnics for the families of capture and proposal team members. These typically occur during the later phases of the proposal when the employees are putting in long hours. They provide key winning capture team members with bonuses. The business development management also throws win parties, and recognizes capture and proposal personnel through articles in a company newsletter, certificates, letters of appreciation, letters to spouses and memos for performance reviews. This ongoing recognition campaign for employees who contribute to winning buttresses morale and helps cultivate support for future competitions. This company clearly recognizes the sacrifice that proposal team members make and provides many small "thank yous" for jobs well done. Most importantly, in this company, leading a winning capture effort is vital to moving up into the executive ranks. This company's capture teams attract their best people. Incidentally, when I remarked to the Vice President of Business Development at this company what a good job they were doing at recognizing and rewarding winners, he responded, "Thank you, but we do not do enough."

Executives at the best-in-class companies devote significant attention to marketing. They spend time on strategic planning; selecting opportunities, capture plan reviews, high level customer contacts, resolving disputes between different organizations and reviewing win strategies. Most importantly, executives who are committed to winning spend the resources necessary to win. But remember, the most important resource is not money; it is people – or more specifically – good people. **Where a company assigns its best people communicates what is really important.** At a company where winning is important, you will find many of the best people staffing capture teams.

Treating Business Development as a Discipline

At another company, the President does not believe that business development is a discipline. He will assign senior level people from program management or engineering into the top spots in business development, either because he trusts them or wants to groom them for the senior executive ranks. Unfortunately, all too frequently these individuals have little idea how marketing operates or how to sell. In addition, some by personality and inclination have no place in sales or marketing.

Since he does not believe in business development as a discipline, the President doesn't believe in training inexperienced personnel when they are hired or join capture teams. The company does little to reward winning capture team leaders, so every capture team leader is anxious to get out of the capture and back to program or line management as soon as possible. If a capture manager does win, he or she is promoted out of business development and capture, so the organization loses their capabilities and the experience that could be shared with other up and coming capture managers. It is always a painful struggle at this company to find someone remotely interested or qualified to run capture efforts.

Unfortunately, we often see capture team leaders with only one or two pursuits under their belt. Even though the customer and competitors are different, the inexperienced tend to latch onto their few lessons learned and view every capture from the limited perspective of their last pursuit. People with more experience know that every pursuit is unique and that there are few cookie cutter answers.

When we have visited the best-in-class companies, we have been struck by how good their business development managers are. They tend to be smart and personable with significant stature. Their people have lots of pursuit experience. While training and education are indispensable, there is no substitute for experience. Capture efforts are incredibly complex and every one is unique. No one should expect that anyone is capable of running such a complex assignment well the first, second or even third time. On each pursuit, there are hundreds of potential tasks, too many to complete. So which ones are the most important? When the customer sends you a signal what does it mean? If the competitor bid very aggressively on their last proposal, will they do it again? Only experience can give someone the judgment to know what is important in each unique situation. As a result of experience, these companies intentionally cultivate capture experience in their staff. They assign young bright staff to work on small proposals and then graduate them up to leading small pursuits. Experienced capture team leaders mentor these young leaders. Through this method, the best-in-class develop a cadre of experienced hunters.

The best-in-class also spend more time on training personnel in the capture process than does the rest of industry. For example, one company has a one-week course for those people who are likely to be on a capture or proposal team. This course is structured around three teams competing for a simulated contract. They run the course offsite two or three times a year using experienced capture team leaders as instructors. The course includes a balance of lectures, workshops and role-play scenarios. The role-playing covers phases from opportunity identification through contract award. The course simulates sales calls, data gathering calls, proposal reviews and internal executive reviews. Each team develops a small mock proposal that the executives evaluate before selecting group and individual winners, who are announced by executives at a luncheon on the last day. At this company, attending this training course is an important career move if an employee aspires to rise into management. By investing in business development, this company is telling everyone that winning is important.

Measuring Performance and Conducting Lessons Learned is Key to Continuous Improvement

It is a management truism that as soon as you start measuring something, it improves. The best-in-class measure their processes and continuously work to improve their performance. They keep their measures simple. Measuring a few things well is more important than measuring a lot of things poorly. Since winning is key, first and foremost, companies that want to win more should track their win rate. Win rate is competitive dollars won versus dollars bid, as well as competitive proposals won versus proposals bid – the win rate is measured both ways to ensure that a company is winning a high percentage of both the big and little pursuits. In addition, they track the size and quality of their sales pipeline including how many opportunities they are pursuing and their value in the different pursuit phases. Top performers have a formal opportunity and lessons learned database which tracks metrics for all their pursuits. All of these things allow them to assess the health of their pursuit process.

When a competition ends, a company's knowledge of the customer and the competitors is highest. It is critical to figure out what the competition did. Not only do you want to know what they bid, but what tactics they employed. This information must be captured and documented. The best-in-class are highly disciplined in collecting lessons learned on all opportunities they pursue. The best way to spot patterns is to compare different situations on dimensions that are similar. Whether a company wins or loses, they must learn from every pursuit. Best-in-class companies always press the customer for a debriefing. Customer feedback is critical to improving their competitive edge.

Too often people focus on the obvious blunders. To effectively adjust processes, a company must compare and contrast different experiences and identify the systemic issues. While each pursuit is different, they all have common elements. Rather than focus on the uniqueness of the campaign, best-in-class companies dissect the experience into common elements. To help identify the recurring issues, they use a common and comprehensive assessment guide to cover all of the critical issues. After a loss, it is critical to focus on the systemic problems that led the customer to select the competitor. Conversely, it is critical to understand why the customer chose whom they did and how the winner positioned itself. Then a company must assess how the capture processes helped or hindered that competition. For example, when they lose, best-in-class companies try to trace key issues back to their opportunity qualification or capture process. Did they identify the reasons that they eventually lost during their gate reviews? If so, why did they discount them? If not, did their capture process fail? The capture leader and the lessons learned leader share the responsibility for improving capture activities, and identifying changes in the opportunity qualification and review processes. The best-in-class continuously analyze their performance and feed those results back into their process to make it more and more effective.

Do Not Succumb to Victory Disease

In 1983, the New York Yacht Club lost the America's Cup. They had successfully defended the Cup for 132 years – the longest winning streak in the sport's history. After their loss, not only were they never able to regain the Cup, they were never able to even sponsor a competitive boat. Just like the New York Yacht Club, we have seen best-in-class companies succumb to victory disease. Everyone learns from experience. When you have a history of winning, the most ego-gratifying conclusion is that you are invulnerable. This belief leads you to insufficiently assess or correct your own decisions. Winners tend to not scrutinize themselves with much vigor. This is further complicated by everyone claiming a larger share of the victory than a dispassionate observer would conclude they deserved. This embellishment often blinds people to what really happened. Complacency leads companies to lose their desire to do the hard things necessary to win. With success, executives are tempted to believe that their processes worked so well last time that they can do it again, but spend less. As a result, they stop looking for innovations, and start searching for economies. In victory, defects are less obvious and it is tempting to focus on embellishing ones' strengths. Losers want to be winners again and are quick to dump old habits. While losers seek to improve themselves and are driven to identify and avoid their mistakes, winners have nowhere to go but down. Over time, the key people with the hard earned lessons get promoted or move on, and the company loses its tribal knowledge of what it takes to win. Also, companies can do a poor job of rewarding those who brought them success. Working proposals is arguably one of the most demanding jobs at most companies. Who else works 14 hours a day during the Thanksgiving or Christmas week? If a company fails to recognize and reward winners, they move on to less demanding assignments.

The inoculation for victory disease seems to be the relentless pursuit of perfection. Complacency leads to decline. As author O'Guin went around debriefing sites on the benchmarking results, he described how the top performers won. Frequently, someone would mention a pursuit where they did everything right – started early, formed a capture team with their top people, influenced the customer and had excellent competitive intelligence. What O'Guin came to understand was that many companies do it right every few years when they have to. In those situations, if they lost that bid, their site would be out of business. The difference was that the top performers selected only the best few opportunities and that forced them to do it right on every one. Since they were going after only a few pursuits, they had to win all of them or they would never achieve their business targets. This kept the top performers driving hard on every pursuit.

Summary

The lessons are clear. It is important to understand how the best consistently win, so that you can emulate their behavior. While it is possible to run an effective capture effort without this structure, it is much harder. The formal business acquisition process of the best-in-class facilitates well-run capture efforts, just as a lack of process impedes them.

Implementing a formal business development process leads to a higher win rate and greater profits. However, developing and maintaining the discipline to carry out these conclusions is hard. Saying "no" to opportunities is hard.

Do your executives know when they have enough intelligence to decide whether to pursue or not? Does your company have a clear strategy, which is widely understood? Have your executives assigned the "right" people to a capture team? How much spending is enough to win? These are some of the difficult questions that the best-in-class companies successfully answer. The fact is that excellence is tough to achieve in any field. As a reward for their wisdom, they spend less and win more.

Companies that consistently win establish formal capture teams early and hold them accountable for victory. These teams develop a win strategy based on meeting the customer's key needs better than the competition. To successfully coordinate and implement this strategy, they require an effective capture plan. However, the strategy is only as good as the information on which it is based. Therefore, the best-in-class invest in conducting competitive analysis to understand their opponents and developing a PTW that is adhered to by the capture team. Companies that win work hard to influence the customer and shape the acquisition. Most importantly, these winners play to win.

Chapter 2: Winning Starts with Selecting the Best Opportunities...and ONLY the Best

"It is easy to become an ace, just pick your targets."

— Brigadier General Chuck Yeager (Retired)

Being selective about which opportunities to pursue is the crucial factor that distinguishes companies with impressive win rates from the rest of industry. Concentrating resources on a select few opportunities is the key to achieving a high win rate. However obvious this conclusion may seem, few companies are good at implementing it. Everybody finds it hard to say no.

The paradox that every executive faces is that in ignorance, all opportunities look great. When an opportunity is in its infancy, little is known about it. It seems promising – no competitor is on the horizon and the customer is open to new ideas and approaches. The customer funding commitment seems assured. The engineers are confident they can solve the customer's problems. As a result, the sales force is optimistic. Enthusiasm is contagious.

Confidence breeds decisiveness. Conversely, lack of information breeds indecision. It seems risky for a manager to halt work on a seemingly good distant opportunity when a company knows little about it. Most managers want to hedge their bets by committing the minimum resources to keep many pursuits in the pipeline until they know more. Unfortunately, the longer one waits to make a decision, the more money is spent and the more momentum a pursuit gains – sales calls made, white papers written and customer commitments promised. Executives fall into the trap of justifying money already spent. This makes stopping the pursuit more and more difficult.

Competitive intelligence gives executives the confidence to be decisive. Intelligence can reveal that a competitor has already been working with the customer and has a new product in development targeted for this customer's application. Customer intelligence can uncover competing customer needs, each of which is fighting for your opportunity's budget. It is only this type of knowledge that gives executives sufficient information about whether an opportunity is one of the best few to pursue.

The top performers have a formal process with go/no-go gates tied to resource allocation. Most importantly, these top performers have the discipline to follow this process. The opportunity champion must complete a detailed opportunity assessment to pass through the gates, which requires focused intelligence collection. And having the right intelligence available at the right time comes only from careful planning and a robust competitive intelligence capability.

A Formal Decision-Making Process

The choice of whether or not to engage in battle is an ancient one. The famous Chinese strategist Sun-Tzu stressed the necessity of formally assessing all engagements before battle. He drew up a list of forty essential elements of intelligence covering such topics as readiness, weaponry, quality of leadership, terrain and deposition of opposing forces to assess the likelihood of victory. Whenever the net assessment showed that the enemy held a decided advantage, his advice was to change the battlefield. His doctrine was to avoid the enemy, assume a defensive posture, or develop tactics that would convert their superiority into weakness, such as harassing them until they became exhausted. This formal decision-making process practiced along the banks of the Luo River over two thousand years ago provides us with a valuable lesson today. We too should employ a formal opportunity assessment process.

Using a formal system facilitates the continual improvement of business development. A formal system allows a business review board to measure the process. This information allows the organization to see clearly what actions and techniques produce wins and which squander resources. The result is an increasing win rate.

Business Review Board

It is management's responsibility to ensure that pursuit teams receive the resources they need to win. To oversee this formal process and make timely decisions, the best-in-class companies have an oversight committee, which we will call the Business Review Board (BRB). The BRB is responsible for allocating new business resources, monitoring capture efforts, and overseeing and refining the process. This group typically includes the General Manager, Chief Financial Officer, legal counsel and the business area executives, business development executives and head of engineering. These executives control the key personnel who staff the capture team. This BRB:

- Coordinates the investigation and qualification of new opportunities
- Assesses all opportunities using a formal and thorough decision-making criteria
- Prioritizes all opportunities
- Tracks the status of capture efforts and opportunities
- Allocates the capture team leaders and other key capture personnel
- Manages the new business resources
- Ensures that capture team leaders and process managers document lessons learned and track the process with metrics

A common mistake that companies make is to organize their BRB at the business unit level or product line level. Instead, companies should strive to optimize resource allocation at the business enterprise level and not the product line. They should work to put resources against the best opportunities across the company. If opportunity assessments occur at the product line level, it is difficult to avoid overspending on some product lines and under spending on others. And decision-making is more objective at the enterprise level – since business unit managers compete for the same scarce pursuit personnel and discretionary budgets, they have significant incentive to be skeptical of their counterparts' assessments of opportunities. The business area managers tend to be aggressive, experienced and knowledgeable of their markets. They usually challenge their counterparts to make good arguments. For example, in one BRB meeting we attended, while the opportunity champion painted a glowing picture of the solution versus the competition's existing product, another business area manager pointed out that the competitor had developed a comparable capability in another product area. Not only was this capability transferable to this opportunity, but he also noted that this competitor had a long-term strategic relationship with the customer as well. This information significantly dampened everyone's enthusiasm for the pursuit.

The BRB should have regularly scheduled reviews so they can evaluate opportunities in a timely manner. Management's responsibility is to decide promptly which opportunities to chase, to allocate resources, and to approve win strategies. A company may have different levels of boards so executives can focus on large opportunities while a lower management level in the organization evaluates smaller opportunities.

The BRB is responsible for allocating and tracking new business resources – selling, bid and proposal dollars. As part of that process, the BRB conducts the formal opportunity assessment at a series of "go/no-go" gates through which all opportunities must pass. The formal process requires approval through these go/no-go decisions whenever a capture effort needs significant resources. Tying resources to go/no-go decisions is crucial for an effective process, because it forces a formal review of pursuits. Unless reviews are compulsory, experience has shown that capture teams put off reviews until they have amassed more information and the opportunity firms up. Without a thorough investigation up front, negative information about the company's prospects may emerge only after prolonged customer contact or some public disclosure by the competition. Unfortunately, by the time the capture team reports this information to the executive team, the pursuit has gained momentum. As a result, poorly positioned pursuits roll on. The BRB is also responsible for tracking the status of all pursuits, to ensure that teams are spending their funds and maintaining progress.

While a formal process helps keep companies from overspending on dead-end pursuits, it also helps companies allocate resources to viable pursuits early enough for them to be put to the best use. At some companies, opportunity champions are unaware how or when to call for a resource commitment. It is difficult to arrange an executive quorum. A haphazard selection process inconsistently assigns resources and often belatedly assigns capture team members. A late or inadequate start cripples a pursuit. The formal process with defined go/no-go points ensures that the BRB makes all opportunity decisions at the right time – not too early or too late. Exhibit 2-1 shows the key phases of the capture effort with the typical go/no-go gates – interest/no interest, pursue/no pursue and bid/no bid. In addition, during the capture phase there may be capture reviews that also provide additional go/no-gates and resource allocation.

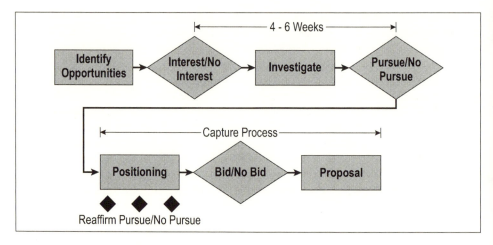

Exhibit 2-1: Go/No-Go Decision Points

Exhibit 2-2 gives a perspective on the typical spending across these phases. As one can see, the investigation phase is limited in time and money while the majority of time and investment is spent in the critical positioning phase. During this phase the capture team is staffed up, and they pre-sell and influence the customer as well as prepare their solution for the proposal. This is typically when a pursuit is won or lost. After receipt of the Draft RFP, the capture team enters the proposal phase when they craft the proposal. Once a team enters the proposal and negotiation phase (post-proposal submittal), they are no longer able to win; they are only able to not lose.

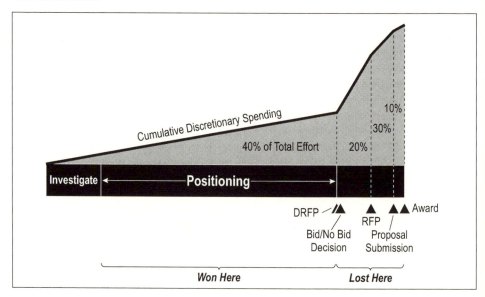

Exhibit 2-2 Early Starts Demand Up Front Investment

The best-in-class companies require the opportunity champion to answer a comprehensive standard set of questions at each review. This opportunity assessment looks at all the critical dimensions of the opportunity – competition, customer's decision-making process, key decision makers, buying tendencies, funding availability, and more. Assessing all of the opportunities with the same criteria makes it easier for the board to compare and prioritize all potential opportunities and allocate resources. These reviews should be interactive with the executive team. This is the chance for the executives to learn about the opportunity and apply their judgment and experience. Executives typically know what works and what doesn't, and they can give valuable advice to the opportunity champion as well as identify potential blind spots that the capture teams are missing. A rigorous analysis and detailed questioning leads to more effective opportunity selection.

Formal Opportunity Assessment Criteria

To effectively prioritize opportunities, the best-in-class companies have a formal, comprehensive and balanced set of assessment criteria. The criteria are a guide to prioritize all potential opportunities and, most importantly, to select the best few to chase. We will call these the Formal Opportunity Assessment Criteria (FOAC). As part of the evaluation process, the capture champion provides the BRB with his or her assessment of the opportunity at the interest/no interest and pursue/no pursue meetings. This assessment is organized into four principle questions which look at the opportunity from different perspectives:

- Does the opportunity support our business strategy?
- Is the opportunity real?
- Will we win?
- Is it worth it?

Unless a company has formal and comprehensive criteria, an opportunity champion may overlook a critical question. Having conducted post mortems on losses, we usually find the key reasons for the loss were known or could have been known early on in the pursuit. However, the capture team and the BRB gave these issues little or no consideration in the opportunity assessment process.

— Strategy in Action —

One company was pursuing the sale of an armored vehicle fleet to an Arab country, and they failed to conduct a thorough investigation. Only after spending over $2 million on extensive field marketing and an in-country product demonstration did their executives request a competitive analysis. A cursory investigation found that a member of the country's royal family owned the French competitor's ammunition supplier. As a result, this royal family member had a substantial financial interest in the French company winning. Given his family position, he would ensure that the French company won. This company's executives should have "no pursued" this capture and saved themselves $2 million for a better opportunity.

— *Strategy in Action* —

Enron's business case for building the $2.8 billion Dabhol power plant in India suffered from a fatal flaw, which their executives should have caught early on. Despite guarantees from the state and the central government, the Maharashtra State Electricity Board (MSEB) lacked the ability to pay for the electricity produced by the plant. Research should have uncovered the fact that the proposed plant's electricity prices were unaffordable. Maharashtra was incredibly poor – the plant's projected power sales would amount to more than state's entire budget for primary and secondary education. If that was not enough, the MSEB suffered from acute cash flow problems due to chronic theft of electricity from their grid. Enron's executives should have assessed these fundamental questions at a pursue/no pursue meeting and realized that this project was not financial viable. While the authors suspect some Enron executives got big bonuses for this contract, Enron lost over a billion dollars. If a customer cannot pay, don't bid.

The BRB discusses, assesses and votes on each of the four questions before moving on to the next question. First they discuss if the opportunity is on strategy and make their determination before going on to assess if the opportunity is real. Addressing the four questions sequentially simplifies the thought processes of the decision makers, bringing greater focus to the debate, greatly increasing the quality of the discussion and improving the chances for consensus.

Below, we describe the intent of each one of these four questions. As you'll see, each question gets broken down into more specific questions. As questions get more specific, they get easier to answer. More detailed questions and answers are easier to assess than broad vague ones. The discussion that follows will show exhibits of sample decompositions of each question, but you must tailor these questions to your specific marketplace.

Formal Opportunity Assessment Criteria:
1. Does the opportunity support our business strategy?

One of the common traps companies fall into is chasing opportunities that do not further their business strategy. If an opportunity is not within a company's strategy, its pursuit dissipates resources and the odds of winning are low. In the unlikely case that a company wins an opportunity outside their strategy, they find that these opportunities frequently cost more than their estimates and usually lose money because of their limited knowledge of the customer, marketplace or technology.

There are always plenty of good reasons why an opportunity is "special" and worth pursuing. However, having focus is the one idea that classic management gurus from Warren Buffet to Peter Drucker and Michael Porter can all agree on. The top performers stick to their business strategy and only bid opportunities within their targeted market. Top performers understand what they are good at, who their customers are and what opportunities they should pursue.

In order to assess whether an opportunity falls within a company's core business strategy, that strategy must be well defined. Unfortunately, many companies lack this fundamental guide. For example, one information technology company proclaimed themselves developers of "world-class" data processing. What was apparent to outsiders was that their true core competencies were high transaction rate processing and managing mega-databases with high security requirements for such clients as credit card companies and stock trading firms. Because their stated strategy was so broad and ill-defined, it did little to screen out opportunities such as bidding on an opportunity to build a desktop networking system, which was not a good fit.

A good strategy provides guidance to business development and acts as a screen, clearly excluding some potential customers and opportunities. Having a poorly defined strategy only encourages chasing far out opportunities. Exhibit 2-3 shows questions to be considered when determining if an opportunity is within a company's strategy. If the opportunity falls clearly within the wording of the company's stated strategy, then there is little question that it is "on strategy."

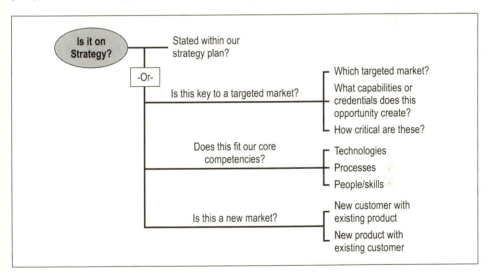

Exhibit 2-3: Strategy Determination – Is the Opportunity on Strategy?

If an opportunity is not within the "stated" strategy, then the executives must ask whether this opportunity fits within their overall strategy in some way. Is this opportunity key to positioning the company in a targeted market? Many times small, low margin jobs are key stepping-stones to larger jobs. The small job may provide a key customer entrée, or prove out a key technology that is critical to a larger, strategic job downstream. The opportunity may be a good fit with a company's existing competencies and a logical business extension into a new market. In this case, how far of a stretch is it? Does the company have the core competencies, facilities, processes and manpower to win and successfully execute the contract? If this opportunity can open a new market, have the strategic planners evaluated that market? If not, they should. Our experience has shown that it is almost always more expensive to enter a new market than an opportunity champion initially claims. Cultivating new customers is expensive and frequently underestimated. You must hire marketers and engineers who understand the market and its technologies. In addition, the company must modify products, create new advertising and open new channels of distribution. In addition to these typical new market costs, remember that every pursuit has an opportunity cost and that spending resources to chase one job is usually robbing resources from another. Choices must be evaluated.

After a thorough discussion of the customer and marketplace, the BRB votes. The board's decision should be unanimous. If there is not consensus about whether an opportunity is on strategy, then one of two problems exists. Either there is not a common understanding of the opportunity and how it fits into the strategy; or there is disagreement about what the company's strategy is. In either case, the result is bad. If there is no consensus, the BRB should put the opportunity on hold until the strategic planner can complete a market analysis and the board reaches agreement. If, however, the BRB agrees that the opportunity is on strategy, they move on to the next question: "Is it real?"

Formal Opportunity Assessment Criteria:
2. Is the Opportunity Real?

The next question in the formal assessment process is, "Is it real?" or "How do we know whether the customer is actually going to spend money on this project?" Every year companies squander tens of millions of dollars chasing opportunities that never materialize. Exhibit 2-4 shows some of the typical questions asked to assess if an opportunity is real. The board must analyze the key reasons for the customer to go forward with the project – things such as the legitimacy of their need and the importance of the project to the organization compared to alternative investments. Many of these questions are points of discussion as well as indicators of how much the opportunity champion understands about the situation. The executives are likely to gain or lose considerable confidence in the opportunity champion's assessment of the customer's funding based on how well he or she understands the customer's budgeting process. If the opportunity champion clearly understands the customer's formal and informal budgeting processes, the executives can conclude that they have a good understanding of whether the customer will approve the project or not.

The opportunity champion describes the evidence that has been collected to indicate whether there is a true need for the project. Does the project solve some pressing customer problem that inhibits their growth or chance of survival? Those are issues that drive real needs. Or, is this a pet project of the CEO? Can the customer afford to solve their problem with a solution like yours? Are there competing solutions? Could the customer consider different approaches to solving their problem? In one applicable example, a country was struggling to improve freight service to their mountainous interior. One project under consideration was a new highway, while there was another plan to build a rail line. The country's freight volumes would not support both, so there was a strong competing solution. The rail construction company had to assess the probability that the country would pursue the road-building project versus the rail line.

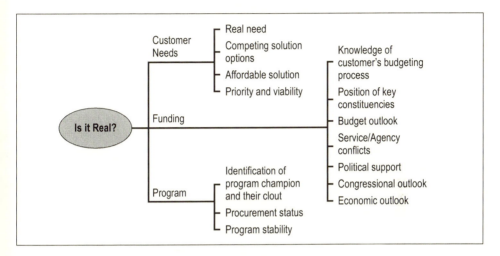

Exhibit 2-4: Determination Strategy: Is the Opportunity Real?

— *Strategy in Action* —

During the 1990s, many companies tried to sell satellites, laser communication links, launch services and ground installations to a customer called Teledesic. Teledesic was a broadband space-based network intended to provide Internet services. It had an estimated cost of over $9 billion to put into orbit a constellation of 840 low orbiting satellites. Its supporters called it "extremely ambitious." However, there were early indicators that this project was "not real." The most telling clues came from a personality analysis of its founder, Craig McCaw. Competitive analysts know that a key predictor of human behavior is that individuals repeat their successes and avoid their failures. Craig McCaw built most of his fortune buying undervalued cellular phone licenses in metropolitan areas around the country for their microwave spectrum allocation. He then leveraged this spectrum as it increased in value to buy telecommunications companies. A competitive analyst would conclude that by making himself a billionaire, Craig McCaw would call that strategy a success.

When he proposed the Teledesic satellite network, the FCC gave him a massive swath of radio spectrum free of charge. One could argue that by investing tens of millions of dollars in "pretending" to develop Teledesic, he was in effect buying an option on some radio spectrum. This strategy would be essentially copying the one that had made him a billionaire – repeating his success. Other signals suggested that the Teledesic deal wasn't "real" as well. Satellite engineers complained that Teledesic wanted components that "violated the laws of physics," indicating their frustration over the fact that the project did not seem technically feasible. Industry observers noticed significant employee turnover in Teledesic's top management and engineering positions, another signal indicating that the success of the project was in doubt. Teledesic suspended work in 2002. Despite the signals that indicated Teledesic wasn't real, companies like Boeing wasted tens of millions of dollars pursuing the project, which never materialized. That was money they could have better spent elsewhere.

Every organization has many potential projects. The question is: how important is this particular one to the organization compared with others, and does the organization have the ability and the desire to fund it? Usually, the best indicator as to whether an opportunity will materialize is whether the customer allocates sufficient funding. To assess this question, you must understand the customer's economic conditions. Methods for determining a customer's financial outlook differ from industry to industry. For example, Royal Dutch Shell's funding plans depend on the price of oil, while Accenture's prospects depend on the forecast for information outsourcing. NASA's depend on who wins the next Presidential election and their vision for space exploration.

Once you've determined that the funding is there, you must determine what other opportunities your pursuit is competing with for that funding. It is critical to understand the customer's budgeting process to determine the key budget players and their influence in the process. It is also a good idea to understand where the customer has spent money in the past and why. Once you've identified the competing constituencies for the budget and each constituency's relative influence, you can try to estimate the likelihood that the customer will fund your opportunity.

Although a customer may have a pressing need and available money, a project may still not materialize without a strong champion or constituency pushing for it. One needs to assess whether there is enough political commitment within the customer's organization to move the project forward. To uncover this, you need to identify the customer's program champion and determine what level of influence they have. You also need to identify where the program is in the internal procurement process and how many more hurdles it must cross. An important indicator of customer commitment is program stability. If the program's requirements, scope and budgets are constantly changing, this indicates that the customer lacks a consensus about how to proceed. Unstable programs lacking consensus have less chance of being approved and more chance of schedule delays than stable programs.

It is also critical to understand whether you have an affordable solution compared with the customer's likely available funding. You'll need to understand how much of the budget the customer will hold back for their own costs, and estimate the full program costs – your product, its support, installation, program management, training, and start-up. Since bidding is always a competition, the award will be made below the available funding. When all these items are subtracted from the customer's likely funding, does the customer have enough money for your solution? If the answer is no, the opportunity is not "real" and you should not pursue it.

The questions asked to assess whether a project is real vary widely by market. So it is critical that every company customize this assessment criteria for their business, technology and customer set. For example, if one is selling hydroelectric projects to third world nations, important questions will include: "What will be their future electricity demand?"; "What is the prospect for alternative power sources?"; "Is there likely to be funding available from the World Bank?" If you are bidding on a new highway through the Brazilian rainforests, you'll need to assess whether environmentalists will block the contract. You'll also need to assess whether the project can pass the regulatory hurdles and obtain rights-of-way, which can derail such a project.

Once the opportunity champion presents their assessment of "is it real," the BRB discusses the issues and votes or scores the opportunity. Then the BRB moves on to the next question.

Formal Opportunity Assessment Criteria:
3. Will we win?

Determining whether you can win is probably the most difficult question to answer objectively. This is where arrogance fills the void created by ignorance. The customer will always tell you that you have a great chance of winning. They want you to bid. In fact, usually the customer's number one priority is to create a competition. If they only have one bidder, they have failed. The customer doesn't give a thought to the millions you may spend chasing his opportunity because they have nothing to lose by encouraging a company to bid. Never be lulled into believing anything the customer says about your chances of winning. You need to be objective. Exhibit 2-5 shows some of the critical questions to assess whether one can win.

People buy from those that they trust. Therefore, one of the most important issues which greatly affects a company's chance of winning is the customer relationship. The first question to answer is how well you know the customer relative to the competition. You are at a significant disadvantage if the competition knows the customer better than you do. Look at how much prior work you have done with the customer versus the competitor. Also, has the competitor hired people from the customer who might be able to give them greater insight than your team has?

The BRB must also assess to what extent the team understands the customer's formal and informal procurement process. This includes how requirements are created, who writes the RFP, how bids are evaluated, who picks the winners and who approves the decision. If a team isn't certain of the customer's selection process, they cannot identify the right decision makers to target within the customer. Win strategies are built on the priorities of these key people, so the quality of a company's information determines the quality of their strategy. Similarly, without an understanding of a customer's process, it is almost impossible to influence it. Lastly, an understanding of the customer's past buying behavior is crucial for knowing how to bid to them – do they like to award low price or high performance? Knowledge is key to winning.

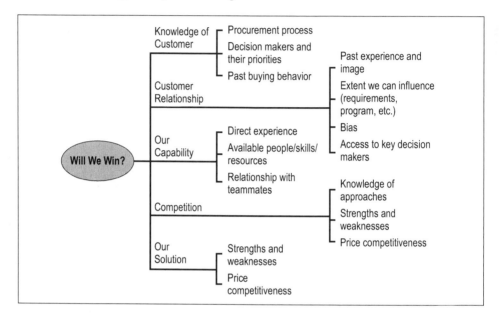

Exhibit 2-5: Determination Strategy: Will We Win?

You must consider past experience with the customer. Do they have a positive image of your company or do you need to prove yourself? This is another area that is tricky to assess objectively. Companies often lull themselves into believing that they have better relationships with the customer than subsequent results show. While customers may not harp on past problems, past problems are rarely forgotten, much less forgiven. Your customer is also unlikely to reveal how they actually feel about your company versus the competition, but marketing departments often take signs of friendship and politeness as indicators of a close relationship. The best sources for objectively assessing relative competitor relationships with customers are former customer employees or employees of other companies, such as teammates or suppliers who have significant contact with the customer. Interviewing these people can be richly informative as long as interviewers are aware of personal biases held by the people interviewed. The capture team should also evaluate their competitors' customer relationships, and past performance records. In the train control pursuit described in the introduction, the competitors' troubled customer relationships were a key reason why the defense company felt they could win in this tangent market.

As you assess the situation, an important question to ask is: to what extent do you know the key decision makers and how much access do you have to them? If your competitor has access and you do not, you are at an immense disadvantage. One company could not get an audience with the Royal family in Kuwait because they did not have the right agent. In another situation, a company was not able to access the decision makers because there were many bidders and the customer had too tight a schedule. Since the customer's executives did not have the time to meet with all the bidders, they forbade any contact except with purchasing. Unfortunately, a competitor had current work with the customer, and despite the blackout they were able to meet with the customer's executives under the guise of talking about their current program. In both cases, the companies who could not meet the key decision makers lost.

The company that most successfully shapes the customer's acquisition strategy and requirements usually wins. So a key question is whether your team has more or less ability to shape the procurement process than the competition does. This can depend on not only customer knowledge and relationships, but also on company aggressiveness, capture team experience and even the availability of talent to work with the customer. Does intelligence indicate that any competitor is already working the customer? Has your team already seen evidence of your competitor's influence on the customer's stated requirements? Some companies start late and never attempt to shape the acquisition, while it is a standard tactic with others.

This all boils down to assessing your company's chances of winning. Is there a match between your capabilities, resources, people and skills to execute the job? Do you have direct experience with this job and market? Are you selling a solution that you have sold before? If you are lacking key experience, it might require you to "reinvent the wheel," which is expensive, risky and unattractive to a customer. Do you have experience in every aspect of the scope of work required by this customer? If you don't have all the necessary experience, you may find that you are not competitive unless you are committed to finding a teammate with the missing experience.

If you lack people or the manufacturing capacity to execute the job, the customer is likely to realize this and hold it against you in their evaluation. You'll be rated as high risk. On the other side of that coin, winning a job you cannot perform is bad business. It leads to cost overruns, missed schedule commitments and customer dissatisfaction, all of which damage a company's reputation and long-term market position.

To win, a company must devise a solution that differentiates itself from the competition in those attributes most important to the customer. If companies know little about their competitors, they usually discount their competitors' capabilities and relationships with the customer. Only by conducting a competitive analysis and accumulating facts can companies develop an unbiased perspective about the competition. It is important to note that when conducting this analysis you need to consider the strengths and weaknesses of your competitor's team and not just the competitor's, because you are competing against the team. But before you seek to assess your relative competitive position, you need to first determine to what extent your capture champion understands the competitors' likely approaches and strategies. The BRB needs to understand the quality and depth of the competitive intelligence. Is the assessment based on current intelligence or suppositions? The BRB should ask, "Who did the analysis and what sources did they use?"

An analysis short on facts, but long on speculation can underestimate or overestimate the competition. Both are bad. Underestimating can lead a company to lose a winnable opportunity; overestimating the competition can lead a company to not bid on a winnable job, taking on unnecessary risks, squandering precious resources or bidding too low on price. Studies have shown that people will knowingly make decisions using flawed, inaccurate or inappropriate information if they have no other information. A bad analysis is worse than none because it distorts the competition and executives will make important decisions based on it. At least with no analysis, executives are aware that they do not know what the competition is doing. The BRB executives should always require a competitive analysis and set rigorous standards for its quality. They should also probe the opportunity champion to understand where the champion collected their knowledge and how reliable it is.

Top performers at winning develop a good understanding of their competitors' strengths and weaknesses. They know how cost competitive their offerings are likely to be. Does your competition have insurmountable discriminators such as a key agent, a low cost supplier or some unique product that perfectly fits this application and will make them the de facto winner? You'll want to ask yourself, if your competition is formidable, is this really one of your best few opportunities?

One of the important factors when assessing your competition is understanding their past relationship with the customer. What is the competitor's track record with this customer? Is the customer favorably disposed to the competitor or not?

When competing against an incumbent, assessing their position is always tricky. In the services industry this is one of the most important factors in the competition. If the customer is happy with the incumbent, they are often very difficult to dislodge. However, some customers, such as the U.S. Department of Energy, consistently award to a new player, regardless of their satisfaction with the incumbent. Other customers are very loyal. If a services customer is satisfied with the incumbent and has a history of loyalty to the incumbents, you best choice is to "no pursue." So, before jumping in, you'll need to analyze the customer's buying history and uncover their history. You need to answer the two key questions: To what extent does this customer tend to switch suppliers?; and, is the customer happy with the incumbent?

Incumbents tend to be loaded with advantages, but experience has taught us that incumbents frequently squander advantage. Incumbents usually behave cautiously and their thinking is stuck in the past. They rarely propose an innovative solution, because the incumbent's attitude is wed to their current approach and its success. It is hard for them to claim any improvements, because they have been already doing the work. They tend not to assign their best people to the pursuit or listen to the customer, because they are complacent. This complacency makes it possible to defeat incumbents.

One critical issue that sometimes comes into play is that of winning too much of one customer's business. Some customers will not award the majority of their business to just one supplier. This is mostly the case with government contracting. We have seen cases where a government agency will not award to a supplier simply because earlier that same year they awarded another big contract to the same supplier. No matter how compelling the proposal, the customer does not want to look like they are directing all of their business to one company, so they won't.

Formal Opportunity Assessment Criteria:
4. Is It Worth It?

An opportunity may be real and winnable, but is it worth it to dedicate the resources necessary to win? To answer this final question see Exhibit 2-6, a company must address three critical issues: 1) does the opportunity represent a prudent financial investment; 2) what are the strategic implications of winning or losing the opportunity; and 3) what is the opportunity cost?

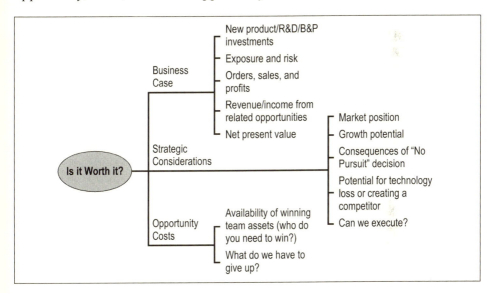

Exhibit 2-6: Determination Strategy: Is it Worth It?

Looking at the financial aspect is straightforward. The preliminary financial analysis looks at a cost/sales forecast profile, estimate of profit, new business acquisition costs, and investments required. The business case is the mechanism for accumulating and analyzing the financial aspects of the opportunity. What are the project's cash flow, risk, and ROI? We have seen cases where companies pass up bids to the UK Ministry of Defense (MOD) because the MOD wants highly customized products (with high development costs) at fixed "off-the-shelf" prices. The projects rarely look profitable. Likewise, we have seen companies pursue these opportunities and find out later that they cannot make money.

When assessing exposure and risk, market experience is important. If the project is outside a company's traditional market, they simply may not know what they don't know.

— *Strategy in Action* —

One company was bidding for a large technically complex project into a Middle Eastern country where they had no experience. This country, which employed world-class negotiators, rigidly held contractors to the strictest interpretation of each performance requirement, had onerous penalty clauses and held up payments with the slightest excuse as negotiating leverage. This company brought on a consultant with significant local experience. The consultant advised the company on the dangers of the contract and persuaded them to restart negotiations. In doing so, the company narrowly avoided signing a contract that likely would have cost them hundreds of millions in losses. Their own lack of experience almost made their opportunity a financial abyss.

It is important to look at the entire business case for an opportunity and not consider it as an isolated program.

— *Strategy in Action* —

When Boeing bid on the Australian Airborne Early Warning (AEW) Aircraft program in 1999, called Project Wedgetail, they did not bid it as an isolated seven aircraft buy. Wedgetail was a strategic bid for Boeing, who dominated the large AEW market with their Airborne Warning and Control System (AWACS) (on a 707 airframe) and the Japanese 767 version. However, these aircraft were too large and expensive for most countries. Wedgetail was the first sale of a midsized AEW aircraft. Therefore, Wedgetail offered the opportunity to pay for developing a smaller export-focused product and to rack up a prestigious win. Boeing believed that the winner would be the only company with a developed product for the midsized market. If a competitor such as Lockheed or Raytheon won Wedgetail, they could in the future threaten Boeing's large AWACS market franchise. Boeing amortized a significant portion of their nonrecurring expense (NRE) for developing Wedgetail, not across seven aircraft, but across a conservative market size estimate of over forty aircraft. This resulted in Boeing submitting a significantly lower price than their competitors (who amortized their NRE across only seven aircraft) and helped them win the Wedgetail contract.

Unfortunately, this story does not have a happy ending for Boeing, despite winning subsequent contracts for eight more aircraft in Turkey and South Korea. Boeing encountered significant aircraft and radar integration problems on Wedgetail. This resulted in aircraft deliveries four years late and a billion dollar overrun.

The strategic considerations involved with pursuing an opportunity can be numerous. How does this opportunity fit into the company's long-term strategy? Is this opportunity a stepping-stone to a much bigger opportunity? In a previous example we discussed Lockheed Martin's bid to enter the postal business. In order to do this, they targeted a contract to build a sorting machine for the Postal Service. While this contract was not big, profitable or prestigious, it was strategic for them because it provided valuable marketplace credentials and customer relationships.

One must also consider the consequences of a "no pursue" decision. For example, will a decision not to pursue allow a competitor to gain a strategic foothold in your market? Or, are there other consequences of a decision not to bid that must be considered as the following example illustrates:

— *Strategy in Action* —

The U.S. Special Forces operate a small fleet of AC-130 gunships. These aircraft carry a variety of weapons including cannons to provide air support to troops on the ground. The supplier of gun control systems for the Special Forces AC-130 gunship was a small division of one of the largest U.S. defense contractors. This division manufactured a wide variety of stabilized gimbaled systems, including the AC-130 gun control system, which was a complex, low volume and troublesome product. Despite being sole source, the division made little money on this product and it consumed an inordinate amount of engineering and management attention. When the Special Operations Command requested a quote from the division for a system modification, the division, tired of a problematic product, opted to "no bid" the request. Within 24 hours, the CEO of the corporation called the division general manager. The CEO explained that he had just fielded an angry call from the Secretary of the Air Force asking him why his company did not believe in supporting the Special Forces. The CEO assured the Secretary that his company supported the Special Forces and there must be some mistake. Then, the CEO called the general manager of the facility and directed him to bid the Special Forces Command's job. A no pursue decision on this work had a significant negative consequence.

Another difficult question to answer is: what is the opportunity cost of pursuit? For every pursuit you choose to bid, you give up the chance to chase something else or potentially erode the chances of winning everything you are pursuing by spreading your resources too thin. When deciding whether to chase an opportunity, executives tend to focus on how many dollars the opportunity will cost. They weigh the capture budget against their discretionary budget and frequently try to negotiate the spending plan down with the capture leader. They usually discuss squeezing other pursuit spending plans and spend much angst sorting out the money. While this is important and necessary, it distracts the executives from an even more important constraint – good people.

In reality, good people are the constraining resource in a pursuit. Good people win. Within any company, there is usually a small cadre of top hunters – the experienced capture team leader who knows how to win, the great engineer who can develop and sell the customer on innovative solutions, and the talented marketer who can decipher the customer's true needs and sell them on your solution. While a company can almost always find more money for chasing a good opportunity, they cannot clone good people. For that reason, one key to making the go/no-go decision effective is having the last slide of the presentation to the BRB be a list of the key staff required for the capture team. Invariably, this list includes the top people, who are always very busy. This final slide should show their current assignments and responsibilities, so that the executives understand the sacrifices required to assign those people. When a company runs out of "A team" players, it can no longer pursue new opportunities unless the BRB drops something else. This is not say that your entire capture team must consist only of A team players, but a successful capture team requires a significant number of them. You will not be successful pursuing opportunities with only B and C players, so don't bid. The proposed staffing list makes the pursue decision difficult for executives. If the executives are committed to winning, they will assign those key individuals or make only a few substitutions. No opportunity champion can expect to get everyone they want, but if they get no one, the executives are sending a clear message that they do not believe this opportunity is one of the best few – it is not worth it. If the executives cheat, and try to double or triple-book individuals on multiple full-time assignments, that also shows a lack of commitment.

Putting the Results Together

If the BRB determines that an opportunity is not within their strategy, they should drop the opportunity. If the BRB agrees an opportunity is on strategy, then they decide if the opportunity is one of their best few by assessing whether it is real, can be won, and is worth it. What is important in completing this assessment is to identify all the facts, speculations and unknowns about these pursuits, so the BRB can make a fully informed decision. The BRB must weigh all of these factors to determine how good the opportunity is. The BRB must then decide whether to allocate the necessary staff and resources to this opportunity.

We recommend that when the board addresses each "real," "winnable," and "worth" question, that they score the opportunity. This facilitates ranking the opportunities on how confident they are. Ranking opportunities on a numerical scale can be a useful tool, helping weigh alternatives and facilitate process improvement; however it will never replace management judgment. Picking the best few opportunities to pursue is a complex decision; it requires judgment and discipline.

Another benefit to performing a comprehensive analysis is that it forces the capture team to identify and address unknowns and weaknesses. Through preparation for review and through questioning by the executives, weaknesses are identified. The capture team can then develop new actions to address these issues. And because executives have broad purviews, they frequently suggest ways that other elements of the company can help, or mention some distant employee who has relevant experience that is unknown to the capture team. Overall, the reviews enroll the executives in helping the team win the pursuit.

The capture team documents the outcome of each review, as well as the issues raised. This gives the company a chance to analyze the effectiveness of their process qualification over time. For example, if the BRB approves an opportunity at the pursue/no pursue point, but then the customer cancels the opportunity, the BRB can look back at the pursue/no pursue minutes and see if the process identified the issues which eventually led to the cancellation.

It must be mentioned that some companies pursue opportunities with no intention of winning. They bid strictly to hurt a competitor – to drag the procurement out, force the competitor to spend more money pursuing it, and bid lower margins. In one example, there were a group of customers who would always award contracts to a particular company because they had common geopolitical relationships. The competing company knew they would never win these bids, so they always put in lowball bids that they knew the customers would use to negotiate down the competitor's bid. If hurting a competitor is the objective of your capture team, you manage it differently. The capture team leader should not be held accountable for winning, but for how much he or she can hurt the competitor. Instead of trying to win, you work to minimize your expenditures, and disrupt the competition to stall the customer's decision-making.

Go/No-Go Decision Points and Phases of the Pursuit

Exhibit 2-1 shows a formal selection process. These gates ensure management input and readiness to proceed, and also provide a disciplined approach to chasing new business, improving a company's win probability. This process brings together enough intelligence to allow the executives the confidence to decide whether or not to proceed, so each of these gates is tied to resource allocation and requires specific intelligence. Each pursuit process has, at a minimum, three go/no-go decision points or gates – the interest/no interest, the pursue/no pursue and the bid/no-bid. Each gate has a different role in the process and is discussed in detail below. As Exhibit 2-7 shows, many opportunities pass the interest/no-interest gate and join the interest list. Then there is a big reduction in their numbers as the pursue/no-pursue meeting cuts the list significantly, resulting in a much shorter pursuit list. A few more opportunities fall out during the pursuit process and later, at the bid/no bid.

These gates are scheduled around two key milestones. The first is the need to stand up a capture team and the second is the need to start the proposal process. When an opportunity has developed to the point where it is necessary to stand up a capture team, the interest/no-interest and pursue/no pursue gates are triggered. The capture team schedules the interest/no-interest meeting about four to six weeks before the pursue/no-pursue meeting, because the purpose of the interest/no interest gate is to prepare for the pursue/no pursue gate. The team schedules the bid/no bid before ramping up for the proposal development phase.

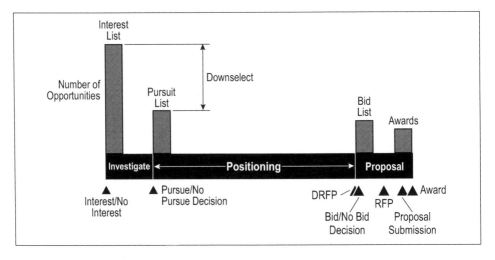

Exhibit 2-7: The Best-in-Class Significantly Reduce the Number of Opportunities Chased

The Interest/No Interest Decision

During a sales campaign, the need arises for the company to form a capture team. This is a critical event in the pursuit selection process. But before the BRB decides to form a capture team, make any large resource outlay, or make a public commitment to a new opportunity, they must approve a pursue decision. However, even before they can make a pursue decision, the opportunity must pass an interest decision. The role of the interest/no interest (I/NI) is two-fold: It will provide a cursory screening to eliminate poor opportunities, and it will ensure that the capture team develops the information needed to make an effective pursue/no pursue decision downstream, see Exhibit 2-8.

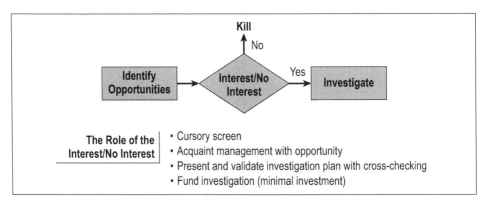

Exhibit 2-8: Interest/No Interest Decision Prepares One for the Pursue/No Pursue

Business development professionals prospect, identify and develop new opportunities. The business development professional is the point person for listening to and communicating with the customer in order to obtain information about their opportunity, including needs, funding, program objectives, costs, preferred approach and potential competitors. The business development manager learns about the customer's problems and begins helping the customer to resolve them. As the manager sees that the opportunity is sufficiently mature for the company to consider standing up a capture team within two months, they schedule an interest/no interest review with the BRB. The business development professional presents the opportunity at the interest/no interest review.

The interest/no interest review plays an important role in acquainting the entire executive team with the opportunity and starts building consensus about whether or not to pursue the opportunity. It is difficult for executives to have confidence in committing significant funds to pursuing or killing an opportunity in a first discussion. By acquainting the executives with the opportunity at the interest/no interest meeting, it mentally prepares the executives for the upcoming pursue/no pursue decision.

The key components of the interest/no interest are:
- Formal Opportunity Assessment Criteria – these were the four questions described in detail earlier in the chapter.
- Investigation Plan – the proposed intelligence plan to answer the questions of the Formal Opportunity Assessment Criteria in preparation for the pursue/no pursue.

At the interest/no interest review, the opportunity champion presents the opportunity against the FOAC. Though the opportunity champion answers questions at the most detailed level possible, the answers will be much more detailed at subsequent reviews. At the interest/no interest, there will be unknowns and incomplete answers. This is a critical part of the process because it highlights the need for thorough intelligence collection prior to the pursue/no pursue review.

The opportunity champion presents an investigation plan to the board that seeks to provide answers to all of the FOAC questions at the pursue/no pursue. Because one of the critical outputs of the interest/no interest is the BRB's approval of the investigation plan, the BRB carefully examines the plan to ensure that the capture team conducts a comprehensive assessment. The plan identifies the information to be collected, and the sources and the parties responsible for collecting it. The board members add questions that they want answered before they commit to the opportunity. This enrolls the executives in the evaluation process. As part of the interest/no interest, the BRB approves the investigation plan, committing the team to collecting the necessary intelligence to answer any outstanding questions prior to the pursue/no pursue.

Typically the BRB must approve some modest funding for customer visits, competitive analysis or market studies to complete the investigation plan. This is a wise investment, because spending a few thousand dollars significantly improves the down selection decision and averts wasting millions of dollars on opportunities that a company is destined to lose.

— *Strategy in Action* —

Due to some well-publicized problems with their computer systems, the IRS was in a hurry to modernize their computer systems. An information technology (IT) company hired an external consultant to conduct a customer assessment of the IRS to feed into their pursue/no pursue decision. The IT company was considering spending millions bidding on the IRS modernization program and wanted to objectively assess their chances of winning. By interviewing key decision makers and influencers at the IRS, the consulting firm determined that the IT company had some unique capabilities that the IRS desired. However, the IRS did not know the IT company well enough, and due to the IRS's urgency, the IT company lacked the time to build a trusting relationship. The customer analysis also identified the leading competitor to win the IRS contract. As a result of this $70,000 study, the IT company's executives decided not to pursue the opportunity as a prime contractor. They avoided spending over $2 million in earmarked new business funds to chase this opportunity – money they certainly would have wasted. In addition, the IT company approached the favored competitor and used the customer analysis to substantiate their contention that the IRS valued their discriminators. This information allowed the IT company to obtain some meaningful work share on the competitor's team. Performing this investigation was money well spent.

If the board agrees that the opportunity is within the company's strategy, is real, can be won and is worth investigating, they approve the investigation spending plan. The BRB then funds the investigation and schedules the pursue/no pursue decision.

Investigation

After the interest/no interest, the opportunity champion collects all the necessary intelligence identified in the investigation plan. To keep the investigation process from dragging on, and to prevent resources from being squandered without a commitment, the capture team should schedule the pursue/no pursue no more than eight weeks after the interest/no interest.

The investigation should include intelligence assignments to a broad set of people with customer, competitor or market contacts. In this way, employees from across the company contact various sources in the marketplace – budgeters, engineers, users and suppliers. We call this process "cross-checking." Pulsing contacts across the customer ensures that the company gets a broad perspective of the opportunity. Cross-checking helps avoid optimistic marketing bias where the company's opportunity champion only talks to the customer's opportunity champion, whose interactions usually focus on how good the opportunity is and how well positioned the company's team is. While the rest of the team reports all intelligence back to the champion, the opportunity champion does not have a monopoly on the information. This is another important check and balance on the selection process. By enrolling people across the organization in the opportunity qualification process, not only are more diverse sources of information tapped, but more people in the company develop independent views of the opportunity. This dissemination of information also helps encourage the creation of a culture that seeks multiple opinions, and ultimately, the truth.

The Pursue/No Pursue

The pursue/no pursue is the critical decision making gate. This is when the executives commit to invest in standing up an expensive capture team. Conversely, this is also when companies should drop most potential opportunities. The company conducts a pursue/no pursue before any significant spending on a pursuit. Also, a company should hold a pursue/no pursue review before making a marketplace commitment such as signing a teaming agreement, formally announcing a product or hiring a representative (i.e. agent or consultant) in a foreign country. However, the most common trigger for a pursue/no pursue is the need to form a capture team.

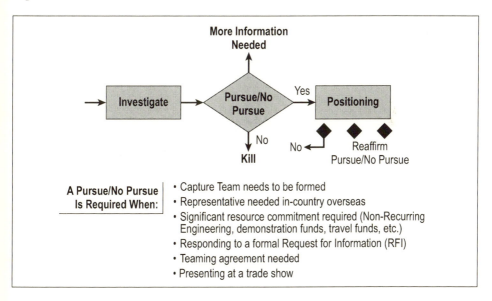

Exhibit 2-9: Is This One of Our Best Opportunities?

After a thorough investigation, the opportunity champion consolidates all of the intelligence gathered from across the organization as tasked by the intelligence plan. The pursue/no pursue focuses on answering the same four questions as the interest/no interest, except in significantly greater detail, along with any additional questions that the BRB requested answers to at the interest/no interest. At the end of the meeting, the executives decide if this opportunity is one of their best few.

This is the gate when executives make the tough decisions. Do they want to assign the right people or not? The industry top performers understand that they must be selective, and say "no" to opportunities. The worst-in-class companies say "maybe." Worst-in-class executives will tell the capture team that they are "allowed to bid." This means the executives are half-heartedly supporting the pursuit – they are unwilling say no, but not committed enough to assign the necessary resources to win. As a result, the company continues to squander resources on an opportunity while its competitors are beginning to improve their own positions.

Large pursuits are extremely complex. To help focus the executives and the capture team on the critical issues, the BRB identifies "Red Flags." While red flags connote danger at the beach, they do not mean that it is closed entirely to the public. Red flags are warnings. They identify the issues to watch – either dangers or uncertainties. These flags will be the key issues that will have a significant impact on a company's ability to win, or will signal key missing information. Red flags can include:

- Missing critical information
- Key customer constituency not contacted
- Onerous requirement or terms and conditions
- Unrealistic customer expectations
- Potential overwhelming discriminator of a competitor
- Substantial internal problem
- Customer reorganization

For example, in one situation the competitor was developing a new product that would significantly outperform our client's. This competitor was having significant development problems, so the capture team had to monitor closely the competitor's progress to determine how much of a threat this new product was going to be. This is the type of issue that gets documented as a red flag, so management will monitor its development. These issues get documented during the interest/no interest and items are added or dropped as the campaign progresses. The red flag list ensures that the executives concentrate and query the capture team on these critical issues. It also ensures that the capture team monitors these issues and attempts to influence them if possible.

It is critical to manage resources and cut losses if the chances of winning worsen. Within the red flags, the BRB identifies "Exit Criteria." Exit criteria are occurrences that will lead the company to discontinue their pursuit. Companies sometimes embark on the pursuit based on one or more assumptions, such as:

- The ability to team with a certain company with a critical discriminator
- The ability to convince the customer to include a requirement which gives their team a critical advantage
- The likelihood that two formidable competitors with complimentary skills will not team up

- The customer securing a sufficient level of funding to afford the solution

Sometimes these assumptions prove wrong. After the BRB commitment to proceed, the pursuit gathers momentum that can be difficult to stop. If, at a later date, these assumptions prove wrong, it is easy for managers to rationalize these concerns away. The existence of predetermined exit criteria allows the company the opportunity to discontinue a pursuit if signs indicate that: the customer will cancel the program, your company will lose, or the win will be unprofitable. Documenting exit criteria up front and requiring a new pursue/no pursue forces the BRB and the capture team to rethink the pursuit if any of these events occurs.

Positioning Phase

The positioning phase begins with the commitment to pursue and continues until the proposal process starts. During the positioning phase, the team works to influence the customer, collect intelligence, develop the solution and conduct other activities to improve their position. This phase includes regular formal capture reviews to assess progress, ensures the company applies satisfactory resources, refines the win strategy and continually revalidates the pursue/no pursue decision. At the formal capture reviews, the executives do not need to review the whole pursue/no pursue briefing, only significant changes. Each of these reviews is an opportunity to stop a pursuit if the competitive environment deteriorates or if the customer's commitment to the project collapses. However, if the capture team needs an infusion of more funds or if circumstances trigger any of the exit criteria, the capture team leader must schedule a new pursue/no pursue where the capture team updates the briefing and then the BRB reassesses the opportunity.

Bid/No Bid

In commercial pursuits, the bid/no bid review is another chance to decide whether to pursue or not. However, since proposal preparation costs for commercial pursuits are relatively small, the big decisions are all on the win strategy, pricing and the negotiation strategy. During this review it is imperative that the capture team gains the executive's concurrence on the capture team's win strategy. Failure by the executives to agree on the win strategy before starting the proposal results in significant proposal rework and usually produces a low quality proposal.

Other key considerations are what price to bid and how to bid it. What price will it take to win and what message will the price send to the marketplace? For example, if you give a customer a low bid and this customer is likely to leak it to other customers, you must consider the impact that this price will have on future sales. You must also decide how much to bid and how much to hold back as a price concession for subsequent rounds of negotiation.

For jobs with large complex RFPs, the proposals can cost millions to create. With these proposals, the bid/no bid considerations are different. The bid/no bid is time to decide whether to approve the proposal expenditures. The top performers have few no bids because they are usually successful at stopping opportunities before they get this far. The BRB should eliminate poor opportunities at earlier gates. However, the top performers do demonstrate the discipline to no bid when their competitive position has deteriorated. Since the proposal cost may be as high as 60 percent of the total cost of the pursuit, by no bidding, a company can still avoid squandering a significant portion of their discretionary funds. In addition, companies pay a huge opportunity cost when they waste their staff on opportunities they lose. That same staff could have been working a more promising opportunity and their absence hurts that pursuit.

A few words about pop-ups. The bid/no bid meetings are sometimes confronted with "pop-ups." Pop-ups are surprise RFPs which are not in the sales forecast and that no one in the company has been working on. These opportunities have not gone through the interest/no interest or pursuit/no pursuit gates. Even so, some pop-ups are great – those where the customer has an urgent need and no competitor has a distinct advantage.

— *Strategy in Action* —

On October 23, 1986, Mikhail Gorbachev retaliated for the expulsion of Soviet spies in the U.S. by banning all local Russian staff from the U.S. Embassy in Moscow and Leningrad. Since American embassies depend on foreign nationals for secretaries, receptionists, maids, mechanics, cooks and cleaners, this action profoundly upset life for the diplomats and their families. The State Department rushed out an RFP for a contractor to quickly secure new American staff willing to relocate to the Soviet Union. This was a surprise to everyone in the industry and no competitor had an edge. Pacific Architects and Engineers (PAE) quickly mobilized a team to respond to the RFP. PAE scoured Russian Literature departments at universities across the country looking for Russian majors who had the necessary trade skills. They searched for students who were working themselves through college as janitors, typists, chefs, plumbers and truck drivers and would love to spend a couple of years exploring Moscow or Leningrad. The Department of State was impressed by PAE's proactive and innovative approach. PAE secured the lucrative contract, proving that being responsive is an enormous discriminator on a pop-up opportunity like this.

Because these pop-ups usually are meeting some important, emergent need; winning them can lead a company, like PAE, into an entire new business area. These pop-ups are good. Pop-ups that a competitor knew about and has been working on for a while are bad. Rarely does any customer define all of their requirements without talking to any suppliers. If the customer wasn't talking with your company, they were talking to your competition. Occasionally, the competitor who worked on the requirements has dropped out of the competition, which leaves the remaining competitors on an equal footing, but this is a rare occurrence. One of the top priorities of any customer is to have a valid competition, which typically means having multiple bidders to choose from. The customers want multiple companies to bid, and to get them to bid, they tell suppliers how good their chances of winning are. But if you are late to the pursuit, these opportunities epitomize the warning: "In ignorance, all opportunities look good." With these pop-ups, you usually know little about the competition, lack the time to develop a trusting relationship with the customer or even discover what's really important to them. In addition, you have missed the opportunity to pre-sell the customer or influence the RFP. As a result, you usually lose these pop-ups. One needs to understand each opportunity's history. It is possible to win a pop-up, but the BRB must assess them with skepticism. Unplanned efforts are especially disruptive to other pursuits because they suddenly pull key people off those teams. The key question about a pop-up is whether the opportunity is a surprise to the whole industry or just to your company. If it's a surprise to everyone, can you be responsive? If it is a surprise to just your company, it is probably not one of your best few.

Optimally, the bid/no bid should take place just after receiving and analyzing the Draft RFP. With this schedule, the capture team can gain approval to proceed with the best industry practice of beginning to write the proposal against the draft RFP. If there is no draft, the bid/no bid should take place just before a company intends to start creating the proposal. The board should review an update of the formal assessment with changes from the previous presentations highlighted in color.

The primary role of the bid/no bid decision gate is not to screen out opportunities, it is to ensure the company is ready for the proposal process and that the executives agree with the capture team's proposal strategy and approach. The capture team should present the win strategy, technical approach, pricing strategy, proposal schedule, proposal team assignments and resource requirements. It is critical to get agreement on the pricing and win strategy before writing the proposal, so the team can freeze the technical baseline and complete the estimating process. Failure to gain concurrence on the strategies until late in the process always results in substantial rework, proposal budget overruns and poor proposal quality.

In some cases it may become necessary to hold a second bid/no bid. An opportunity may pass through the bid/no bid based on the draft RFP looking good, only to find that the final RFP contains significant changes such as onerous new terms and conditions. If there is a significant change, you need to find out what caused it. If the customer surprises you, your chances of winning drop. If you don't know why a change occurred, you don't know the customer as well as you thought. If the competitor drove these sudden customer changes, it demonstrates that they have influence. This second bid/no bid is a company's last opportunity to avoid squandering resources on something they cannot win or would prefer not to attempt.

Summary

The road to victory starts with selecting the right opportunities. We have seen companies start out with a weak initial position; but with a lot of talent, effort, time, money and a great strategy, convert it into a win. However, this is not the way to win consistently. The best-in-class pick their best opportunities and then concentrate their best resources on those. The weaker the initial position, the more resources a company must apply to be competitive. The best-in-class select opportunities early and outspend the competitors, especially in the critical early phases of the customer's acquisition process. The best-in-class recognize that success depends on judicious management of their limited new business resources. The only effective way to manage these resources is with a formal process that brings together enough intelligence at the moment that they have to commit their precious resources to an opportunity. It is critically important that these executives clearly understand the opportunity cost of a pursuit. Without picking only the best few, executives cannot hope to win consistently the opportunities they chase. Picking the best few is good for morale, too. Everyone would rather do a few things well than many things poorly.

While it is easy to understand this philosophy, it is hard to implement. It is scary for executives to forgo distant opportunities and commit to a critical few. But this is exactly what works. Being the best is only for the brave.

Chapter 3: Strategy Starts with Identifying Customer Values

"I don't know the key to success, but the key to failure is trying to please everybody."

— Bill Cosby

In 216 B.C. at Cannae, Hannibal led a ragged outnumbered band against the largest Roman army ever assembled. The Roman legions consisted of the world's most formidable soldiers with the best weapons, training, and squad-level leadership bolstered by their infamous Roman discipline. Hannibal lured the Roman infantry into a headlong attack into his lines. Hannibal's center retreated, bringing the Romans forward. Unfortunately for the Romans, as they advanced, Hannibal's powerful wings gave up less ground than their center, creating a crescent shaped line. So as the Romans in the center surged forward they became more and more compressed, losing their ability to maneuver and fight. Hannibal's cavalry struck the Roman cavalry guarding the Roman infantry's flanks and drove them from the field. Next, Hannibal's elite African mercenaries swung around and attacked the undefended Roman flanks. The Roman formations could not easily pivot and effectively defend themselves against a flanking attack. Hannibal's cavalry completed the encirclement and an epic slaughter ensued. Hannibal's strategy was so superior that the Roman advantages proved inconsequential; Hannibal's Carthaginians soundly defeated the Romans. The lesson is clear; a superior strategy can overcome many disadvantages.

— Strategy in Action —

When Don Rice, the Secretary of the Air Force, announced the award of the Advanced Tactical Fighter competition to Lockheed, he said that the award "went to the lowest risk contractor." That was not a coincidence. Lockheed worked for five years to build a win strategy that would culminate in this final statement. Lockheed correctly identified that the most important consideration for Rice, and for the other key customer decision makers, was a low risk program. As a result of this insight and the strategy they employed to be the "low risk contractor," Lockheed flew a "state-of-the-art" prototype cockpit in its demonstrator aircraft. The company used this cockpit to demonstrate a reduced pilot workload. Overloading the pilot with too much information was a key risk area and a personal hot button of Joe Ralston, another key decision maker. Lockheed's competitor, Northrop, on the other hand, used a modified F-15C cockpit in their demonstrator aircraft and did little to address the pilot workload issue. During their prototype's flight test program, Lockheed worked hard to ensure a higher flight rate than Northrop, demonstrating the robustness of their design and implicitly its lower risk. Both companies' aircraft would need to carry an internal missile, and the Air Force's technical team considered launching this to be the program's highest risk item. Lockheed stunned the Air Force and Northrop by firing an internally carried missile during their demonstrator's flight tests, proving that they could meet this objective. These are just a few of the many examples showing how Lockheed systematically worked to reduce their solution's risk and win over the key decision makers. Arguably, Northrop had the better aircraft, as it was significantly faster in "super-cruise" performance, could do sustained supersonic turns and had better all-aspect stealth performance than the Lockheed plane. Yet, Lockheed's better strategy outmaneuvered them.

Strategy comes from the Greek work strategos, which means "general," and refers to the art of the generalship, or setting up of the forces before the battle. And as Sun-Tzu said, "Most battles are decided before the first shot is fired." The winner for a major sales campaign is usually determined the same way, well before a company submits its proposal. The key to victory is developing a win strategy that successfully differentiates your offering from your competitor's in those areas most important to the customer.

Beginning with the end in mind is the basis of strategy. Envision how victory will happen, and then take all the steps necessary to create that vision. Winning would be easy if you could always offer the best performance at the lowest price, but these two characteristics rarely go together. Life is not that simple; you must make choices that balance competing customer desires. The win strategy relates your starting position to your destination, guiding your choices at each step. The strategy process is designed to construct an approach that differentiates your offering from the competition's in those matters most important to the customer. This is reflected across the capture process: Who's on our team? What should we offer? What messages do we send? What's our price and what's our guarantee? The win strategy guides your choices, and your choices become the implementation of that strategy.

To envision the end, our strategy development process starts by looking at the customer's decision-making process, since this is the process we intend to influence. Exhibit 3-1 shows the generic customer program development and source selection process all customers go through when choosing a supplier for a large complex contract. While the decision-making process differs across customers, all customers start by setting acquisition strategy where what is being bought is decided, as is the way it will be bought (one contract, multiple contracts, fixed priced, etc.). Next, the customer sets the budget for the contract. Then the customer defines the requirements and creates a Request for Proposal (RFP) and the evaluation criteria. Potential suppliers respond to the RFP and the customer usually separately evaluates the proposal content and the price. Then, a small group of key decision makers caucus and choose a winner.

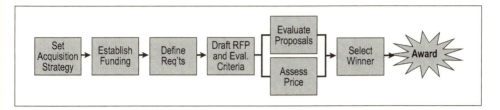

Exhibit 3-1: Generic Customer Program Development and Source Selection Process

We have worked on bids where our team had the lowest price offering and the highest evaluation score and still lost. Our team lost because the key decision makers wanted the other team more. Key decision makers can pick whomever they want. However, this is not enough to ensure victory. The key decision makers must use the proposal and price evaluation to justify their decision. In addition, they must be willing to accept any resulting political ramifications of their decision. We have seen companies lose for having a poor proposal evaluation or too high a price, despite being desired by the key decision makers. Their poor proposal evaluation made it too painful for the decision makers to justify awarding to them. The way to assure victory is to be the offering the key decision makers want most <u>and</u> to "correctly" balance the proposal evaluation and price. By correctly balancing the proposal evaluation and price, you make it very easy for the decision makers to justify selecting you. We will discuss how to "correctly" balance the proposal evaluation and price in Chapter 6.

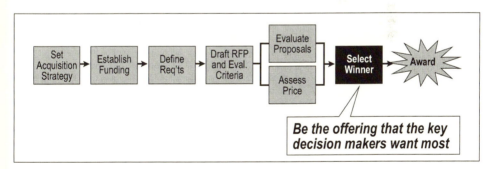

Exhibit 3-2: The Road to Victory, Being Selected as the Winner

Exhibit 3-2 shows the vision of the end; what you want to do is provide the offering the key decision makers want most – the offering they select. You build your strategy to create that offering. The strategy must consider the initial position of the customer, your team, and the competition. Exhibit 3-3 shows the steps that lay out a strategy process to create a winning offer – the offering the key decision makers want most. Throughout the next three chapters, we will explore each of these specific steps, which organize the critical pursuit information in a logical fashion and develop a robust strategy. The results will differentiate your offering from the competition's by giving key customer decision makers precisely what it is they want most. Focusing the strategy on the key decision makers unites and focuses your capture team. This win strategy creates clarity and purpose out of complexity. Even though you may begin developing your strategy before the opportunity itself has crystallized, your win strategy must be fact-based and realistic.

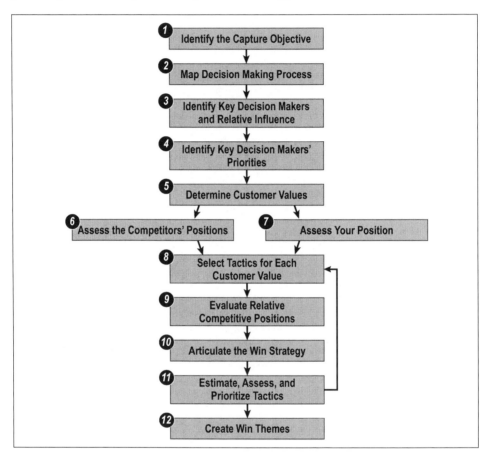

Exhibit 3-3: Win Strategy Development Process

The strategy development process should be focused on a single objective, such as winning the pursuit. Keep it as simple as possible, especially for initial campaigns, or you run the risk of confusing yourself, your team and your executives. Keeping the process simple creates straightforward strategies. The most powerful and successful strategies are clear, direct and simple.

However, for a campaign, you'll also want to develop a strategy to keep the program funded. If this is the case, you must develop a separate strategy. To do this, you'll use the same process described here, but the decision makers will be the budgeters who allocate program funds, and the competitors are the alternative projects that the customer could invest in.

This chapter, and the two that follow, lays out a formal process for developing a win strategy. In describing the process, we discuss exceptions to almost every principle. It is important to note that every procurement is unique. We describe scenarios in which exceptions should be considered and we point out common pitfalls that capture teams face when implementing this process. T.S. Elliot summed it up when he said, "It's not wise to violate the rules until you know how to observe them." The same holds true here. Picasso mastered the classical human form before he dared to paint both eyes on the same side of the face. Read and re-read this section if you consider deviating from our guidance. This process requires judgment.

Step 1: Identify the Capture Objective

The first step in the strategy development process is to document the goal of the capture process. The essence of strategy is to envision the end and build a path to that conclusion. Therefore, it is critical that everyone on your team understands exactly what you want to accomplish. This may seem obvious, but while the usual goal is to win a particular challenge, this may not always be the case. A company may wish to obtain a particular work scope, so the most successful strategy might be to position themselves as a subcontractor on the winning team. The actual objective might not be the near term opportunity, but a follow-on award.

For example, if the customer is having a "two-step down select" – picking two winners from three competitors, and then choosing one winner from those two – a company can easily fall into the wrong strategy. On a three to two down select, the mostly likely win strategy is to be innovative, to offer the customer something that is unique from the offerings of the other two competitors. Because the customer typically wants a choice, they tend to like to select two different offerings at a three to two down select. The problem is that in the final selection customers tend to select the least risky, most robust offering, which typically is not the most innovative. As a result, creating a strategy for winning the three to two can poorly position one to win the final selection.

Alternately, you may have little chance of winning, so your goal might be to hurt the competition. In that case, your capture team's strategy might be to force down the competitor's price as much as possible. To accomplish this, you work to appear a valid competitor in order to force the competition to bid more aggressively at lower margins. This was one billionaire's plan when his company was bidding for the PCS frequencies in a government auction. His bidding objective was not to win, but to make sure that his large competitors bid so much that it would leave them with little money to compete against his existing services.

When documenting the capture objective, be specific. State the specific customer event and outcome that you want. For example: win Citibank's Data Center Operations contract; win a sole source award for the Navy's XV-15 Maintenance contract; or achieve the Canadian Parliament's approval for $350 million for an Air Traffic Center upgrade.

Step 2: Map the Decision Making Process

After you document your objective, you need to map the customer's decision-making process that leads to that outcome. You must also identify the evaluation and approval process that the decision makers go through. In our example case, we will focus on the objective of winning a sale.

No matter how large or complex a procurement might be, one does not sell to organizations: one sells to a set of individuals. Organizations are groups of individuals within which hundreds of people can be called customers. Many people may influence the source selection decision. However, in any organization only a small set of people make the actual source selection decision. Therefore, identifying these key decision-makers is one of the most important elements in the competition. There may be many different people who write the requirements and set the funding, but you build your strategy on those key decision makers who will fulfill your objective – selecting you as the winner. This is the premise of our approach. You build your solution to satisfy the key decision makers more completely than the competition.

Identifying the key decision makers is one of the most important elements in the competition. Despite its importance, most companies do a poor job of it. Many team members jump to erroneous assumptions about what is important to the customer. These assumptions are frequently based on their own opinions of what is most important. Many competitors focus strictly on the written evaluation criteria, which may, but usually will not, reflect what's really important. Companies misread the customer and make incorrect assumptions about which customer community is making the source selection. Companies frequently focus on the technical evaluators or the users since they are usually the most vocal in customer meetings. As a result, these companies develop their win strategy around the wrong set of customer needs.

— *Strategy in Action* —

Working on a Foreign Military Sale (FMS) to Taiwan, the capture team initially focused on how to satisfy the Taiwanese Air Force. However, when they mapped the source selection process, it became clear that the U.S. Air Force conducted FMS acquisitions and made the source selection decision with only limited input from the Taiwanese. As a result, the capture team changed their strategy. The capture team constructed their strategy around those issues most important to the U.S. Air Force program office – a low risk solution and jobs for the U.S. Air Force technical staff. They adjusted their solution to threshold compliance with existing technologies to minimize development and integration risk. The capture team committed to establishing a new facility near the Air Force base, and contracted with the Air Force laboratories to perform specific technically challenging tasks on the FMS sale. The competitor focused on the Taiwan Air Force leadership's desire for a superior logistics system, and lost.

Selecting winners is a complex multi-participant process; every organization and procurement is different. Most government procurements have a well-defined acquisition process complete with published procedures and evaluation criteria. Large corporations tend to have well-structured formal processes, but these may not be disclosed to outsiders. Some other customers lack any structured process at all, and many large procurements are shrouded in mystery. But whatever level of disclosure exists, you must uncover your customer's process to develop an effective strategy.

Customers generally don't use the same decision makers when deciding to buy $100 million dollar information systems versus million dollar machine tools. As a result, you must look for "precedent programs"— similar purchases in comparable size and complexity. Looking at the customer's past buying behavior is critical to projecting how the current competition might proceed. Like individuals, customers have personalities and norms of behavior. Even though personnel and circumstances change over time, customer behaviors tend to be consistent for years.

Start by analyzing the customer's procurement rules and procedures. Who conducts the evaluation? Are different commitment teams looking at different aspects of the proposal? Are separate committees conducting the technical evaluation and the industrial participation package? Different sized jobs require different levels of approval. Who approves this size procurement?

To answer these questions, you should look at how the customer has made similar decisions in the past. For example, the U.S. government publishes procurement policies and regulations, award announcements and competitive results, and they debrief all participants. This information is readily available. Even for a closed government like Kuwait there is a wealth of information – press releases, magazine articles, local bankers, Ministry of Industry officials, former customer personnel, former vendors, local company executives and embassy personnel. These people all have excellent insight into past procurements. Selling to a large corporation is no different; you can interview the customer's personnel, people who have sold to this customer before and former customer employees.

Using this information, you'll build a process chart of all the required steps in the customer's source selection process. Map the process from proposal submittal through award announcement, identifying each committee, board or individual who reviews and approves the proposal, resulting evaluation and award recommendation. Once you have analyzed the past programs, you can identify from what organizations your customer is likely to draw the key decision makers for your pursuit. Then you try to identify each decision maker by name. Next, take those names and define their positions and functions at the time of the procurement.

As you work to identify the process and everyone's role in it, you need to understand how the process really works, and then add any informal excursions to the process. For example, one capture team discovered that the divisional president's staff, while not included in the formal decision making process, was actually conducting the evaluation. Through interviews with former employees, we learned that before evaluative results ever went to corporate for the final decision, his subordinates briefed him. This divisional president was also well known for his strong preferences for certain solutions, and he was quite willing to exert influence on the analysis before it was sent up the chain of command. In this case, we added a step in the flow diagram for the divisional president as shown in Exhibit 3-4.

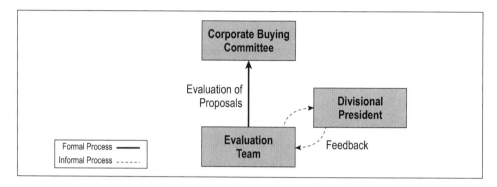

Exhibit 3-4: Commercial Source Selection Process

Discovering the who, how and when of a specific source selection can be a formidable task. Sometimes you will have to contend with misinformation. Each individual on the customer's team will naively assume that they have more power than they really do. They will tell you, "I'll be the one who is going to make the final decision on this source selection." As the acquisition progresses, these individuals will find, often to their own surprise, that lots of senior people want to be involved in the major decisions. They'll discover that they are not the final decision maker, but just one of many who have a voice in the selection.

Sometimes the official decision-making process is merely for show and only the informal process matters. For example, when selling to the Kingdom of Saudi Arabia, the official process includes the Supreme Economic Council and The Ministry of Planning. When you ask a Saudi official when they will make a decision, their reply is usually no more revealing than, "Insha'allah" (when God wills it). In reality, the purchasing decision is not made by these committees at all, but by the inner circle of the Royal Family. They typically make their decisions as they sit around the campfire after a day of hunting with falcons in the desert. To sell to this group, you must decipher how all of these individuals will interact to select the winner. One of the most common sales blunders occurs in not identifying the true source selection process.

Your strategy should be built around the customer's decision-making process. It may not be published, announced or even decided, but you have to figure out what it will be. You may need to do this years before the customer has even figured it out. Experience has shown that projecting what a customer will do is not as difficult as it sounds. Customers, like you and I, are creatures of habit.

— *Strategy in Action* —

The competition was for a large aerospace procurement called the Advanced Attack Fighter (AAF). The AAF program called for the design and production of 1,000 multi-role fighters for the U.S. Air Force. This aircraft was going to be an aircraft that could vertical lift to a take-off in order to allow it to be deployed close to the troops. We'll call the two competitors "Goliath" and "Huge Aircraft Corporation." We will show the strategy development from Goliath's perspective on this procurement.

To develop the win strategy well before the source selection, the Goliath team needed to know what process the customer would use and who the final decision maker would be. The U.S. armed services each have well formulated, well-defined and documented source selection processes. Exhibit 3-5 shows the Air Force's process. The Source Selection Evaluation Board's (SSEB) technical team evaluates the proposals independently for proposal merit and risk against the RFP requirements. They do not compare the competitors' proposals. The cost team evaluates each competitor's bid price. The cost team then adjusts for risk by adding additional cost to the bid price for unrealistic estimates, and missing components and activities. They create an estimate called the "most probable cost (MPC)" – what the Air Force believes it will realistically cost for the contractor to do the job they propose. The past performance team assesses each company's performance on previous contracts and rates them on past performance risk. These evaluations are passed on to the Source Selection Advisory Council (SSAC), which is composed of senior executive personnel from interested organizations. The SSAC compiles the results and compares the competitor's scores, and then recommends a winner to the Source Selection Authority (SSA). The SSA is responsible for making the final award decision. This process is not completely sequential and there are many feedback loops. As the SSEB evaluates the proposals, the SSAC and SSA are briefed, issues are raised, and questions are fed back to the SSEB. Substantial time occurs between the initial proposal submittal and the award decision; eight months passed in the case of AAF, allowing many reviews and much interaction that allowed the competitor's time to influence the evaluation process and the resulting ratings.

Step 3: Identify Key Decision Makers and their Relative Influence

One does not sell to an organization; one sells to people. Identifying the people who will select the winner is critical in developing an effective win strategy. In fact, we base our strategy on what's important to the key customer decision makers, so do a good job of it!

Often, when members of a capture team are asked what is important to the customer, a great argument ensues. Everyone has an opinion and those opinions are frequently in conflict.

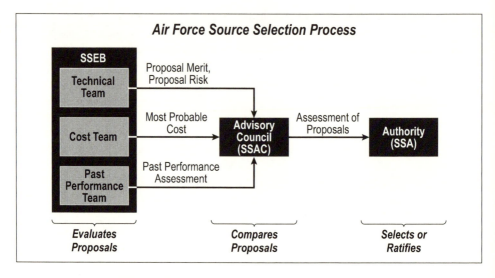

Exhibit 3-5: Air Force Source Selection Process

— *Strategy in Action* —

We once began a win strategy development session by asking the capture team's key leads what would win a competition for building an armored vehicle for the Canadian Army. The chief engineer replied, "A better fire control system." He thought that the ability to put more rounds on target was most important to the customer. The capture team's program manager chimed in that since the Canadian Army was bogged down in Bosnia and insurgents were shooting up their vehicles, he thought that better armor protection was most important. However, when we analyzed the key decision makers to uncover what was important to each individual, we found a surprising answer: jobs, or more specifically—jobs in Quebec. The key decision makers wanted to award to a contractor who would provide the most local work and jobs in Quebec. This competition took place while Quebec's separatist sentiment was running high and the biggest concern of the key decision makers was keeping Quebec happy and their country together. As a result of this strategy development process, the chief engineer realized that his most important mission would not be to design a better fire control computer, but to source all the circuit cards in the existing computer to companies in Quebec. The most important person on the capture team became the procurement director. She developed an entire sales campaign around "Jobs in Canada." She sourced many of the armored vehicle components to Canadian industry, and then used those same suppliers for production going into the company's other products being sold to Taiwan, Thailand, Saudi Arabia and the United States Marine Corps. As a result, this client beat out a French competitor with a manufacturing plant in Quebec for the $650 million contract. The number of jobs in Quebec was not mentioned in the proposal evaluation criteria, but it was the key to winning.

The key decision makers are those people who, through their role in the acquisition process and their authority and initiative, dominate the customer's source selection process. In spite of complex procurement processes and elaborate evaluations, experience has taught us that approximately seven people dominate most source selection decisions.

It is critically important to always keep in mind that the strategic focus should be on those people who will decide which supplier wins the award, and not on those who will formulate the requirements or make funding decisions. We see lots of people get confused and think that Congress matters in the source selection process for U.S. government contracts. They do not. They play no role in the source selection decision. However, they play a crucial role in keeping projects funded, but that is a different decision and one that takes place after the source selection is decided.

While we focus on these key decision makers, there are many who influence the decision makers by providing technical, management, and economic advice. We refer to these people as the influencers. Many people confuse influencers with decision makers. Decision makers have the power to vote and make the choice. Influencers, on the other hand, only give advice. Occasionally, an influencer may have such high informal authority that their advice makes them a de-facto decision maker. In these cases an influencer can have so much power and expertise that he or she can be considered a decision maker, but this is rare. A frequent mistake that capture teams make is labeling influencers as decision makers. This happens because influencers are often outspoken technical experts and capture teams are frequently kept busy responding to their questions and direction. But in the end, they merely provide advice on the source selection and do not select the winners.

Focus your win strategy on key decision makers, not influencers, because these decision makers have the final word. And when you focus on the decision makers, take into account how the influencers will likely affect their priorities. ***Remember, contacting influencers, listening to them, communicating with them, pre-selling and managing them is critical to winning; but don't build your strategy around an influencer's priorities!***

To identify the key decision makers, analyze the steps in your map of the customer's decision-making process for selecting the winner. Sometimes a step is performed by a single individual and sometimes by a committee. Either way, those who make the critical decisions along the way are the most influential people in selecting the winner. You must look at each decision-making body and determine how much relative influence it has. Then determine which steps in the process have the most significant impact on the resulting award decision and which steps have the least impact. You must understand the influence of each step in the process and who controls that step. Then identify by name the individuals who will be the key decision makers.

Some advisory groups oversee selections in certain companies, but provide only a cursory evaluation with little impact on the final decision. Some evaluation groups have only veto power. If an evaluation group has only "pass/fail" power, we almost always exclude that body from our list of decision makers, because rarely does just one company "pass" the evaluation process. For example, in many countries there are "industrial participation" requirements, or laws requiring quotas of local work content. Councils conduct an assessment of the competing companies and basically approve or disapprove of the bidder's proposed industrial package. If the councils deem that the work content meets the target, they usually have no further influence in deciding which contractor will win the award, so these industrial participation council members would not be considered key decision makers.

Virtually every large source selection decision uses committees as part of the evaluation process. You will need to determine who the important players will be on each committee, and who the leaders of each committee are. You do not need to know every single person on each committee because even though a step may be a committee decision, certain individuals will dominate that committee. You need to identify the few people who will dominate the committee's decision-making and recommendations.

Customer procedures may establish firm evaluation and selection committee membership, or the procedures may be very flexible. If the procurement rules do not define the membership, you must look at the customer's prior buying behavior to understand which functions or organizations are likely to be represented on the committees. Typically you will find executives on the selection committee who represent those organizations to be most impacted by the procurement – operators, implementers and representatives of finance and contracts. In addition, you should discern the rank or level (manager, director, vice president, etc.) of each person assigned. Examine the customer's organizational charts, identify who is prominent at supplier briefings, and note those names mentioned frequently during meetings with the customer. These people or their organizations are going to be involved in the decision-making. The best way to discover who is likely to be on a board or committee is to cultivate and interview customer insiders. It is critical to develop personal relationships with knowledgeable people inside the customer organization. These friends can then coach you on deciphering the customer's true decision-making processes. We find that the more structured the decision-making process, the more predictable the outcome usually is.

You should also strive to identify the key individuals on the board. A chairperson usually has significantly more influence than any other member. Develop a list of those candidates whom you think are likely to be the most influential in the source selection decision and chart these key decision makers and their positions as shown in Exhibit 3-6.

Unless there is an evaluation board that makes the ultimate choice, proposal evaluators are not considered key decision makers. Technical evaluators typically work within narrow bounds and can only influence a limited portion of the evaluation. The evaluators are forced to assess each offeror against predetermined criteria and these criteria constrain their influence. They usually have limited ability to drive the selection toward one contractor or another. However, the technical evaluation board chairman has significant latitude to influence many areas of the evaluation. He or she can apply their judgment to their evaluation findings. Similarly, he can ask questions of the evaluators and send them back to incorporate new analysis. The chairman packages the findings using his experience and judgment, and this typically influences how the board presents each competitor's strengths and weaknesses. As a result, the evaluation board chair has significant influence on the selection of the winner and should be considered a key customer decision maker. However, if the customer has only a final decision maker and a technical evaluation board, then a few of the evaluators will be key decision makers. In this situation, the evaluation board usually makes a recommendation greatly influenced by these key evaluators.

It is also very important to note that while technical evaluators may not be able to select you or influence the selection toward your offering, they can effectively veto your selection. If you propose a solution that an influential technical evaluator really hates, he or she can evaluate you as "high risk," destroying your chances of winning. For this reason, it is very important not to propose a solution that will get a veto from someone in the technical community. The capture team must test and pre-sell their technical solution with the customer's technical evaluators to ensure that their solution will not be thrown out. Since these technical evaluators can only fail your solution, you do not build your strategy around their desires; you must only pass muster with them, and then win with the key decision makers, who will select from those solutions that were not technically vetoed.

Typically, buyers, legal counsel, and contracts administrators are not key decision makers. They design and monitor the process but do not usually weigh in on who wins. Capture teams are often misled into thinking that the buyer is very important because he dominates their formal communication with the customer. In fact, he oversees the bureaucratic process, but does not usually choose or influence the selection of the winner.

Because **all decision makers are not equal**, the next step after identifying a candidate list is to assess each key decision maker's relative influence on the source selection decision. Some decision makers have more power than others; this is tempered by the fact that some decision makers are more willing to exert their power than others. Therefore, each decision maker's influence must be assessed based on these two considerations.

As part of our process, we will quantify the relative *influence* of each decision maker. *Influence* reflects how much relative power the individual will use to affect the decision in question. We measure *influence* as a percentage. The sum of all of the decision makers' influence equals one (see Exhibit 3-6). Their relative level of *influence* depends on two factors:

- Power – Formal authority of the position and the role in the decision-making process. To what extent can this individual make decisions on issues and to what extent can they make those decisions independently of other individuals? The more unilaterally

they can act on important issues, the greater their power.
* Salience – The willingness to exert political capital on this decision. Salience reflects how important the outcome is to this individual, and correspondingly, how willing they are to expend their political capital. Salience ranges from a decision maker's disinterest in the outcome to their willingness to invest all of their prestige to affect the outcome.

Decision Makers and Position	Relative Influence	Likely Source Selection Role
Walter Peyton, Secretary of Air Force	35	Likely final decision maker (SSA)
Debbie Davies, Deputy Assistant SECAF(AQ)	25	Likely SSAC Chair
Gen. Marshall Reese, AF Chief of Staff	10	Likely SSAC member
Gen. Robert Conway, Dir. of Tactical Progs.	5	Likely SSAC member
Gen. Frank Martin, Com of Air Combat	5	Likely SSAC member
Gen. Mark Howard, AAF Program Mgr.	20	Likely SSEB Chair

Exhibit 3-6: Key Decision Makers, Roles and Relative Level of Influence For AAF

The final decision maker will frequently have the authority to make a unilateral decision, but their salience is such that they do not want to. Salience is affected by how important the issue is to them. Does the result impact their job? A customer program manager who will have to live with the results of the source selection for years will likely expend every ounce of their power to avoid a selection they do not like. Another decision maker may view the principle of the decision as important, because it communicates a statement to the rest of the organization, such as, "things are different now." Other factors can affect a decision maker's salience too, such as their need for dominance over an archrival, or their support of a political alliance.

Your assessment of each individual's power and salience allows you to estimate each player's relative influence. To determine the level of influence, first rank the decision makers from most to least influential. Then estimate how much relative influence each player has versus another player, where the total of all the key decision makers' influence equals 100 percent. Examine each individual and compare his or her influence to the other decision makers on your list. This process of dividing up influence helps cull the list of decision makers. People with a small relative level of influence (less than three percent) can be dropped from the list. While this distribution of influence may seem inexact, it is more rational than assuming each decision maker has equal relative influence. Remember, the number of true key decision makers is usually seven to eight individuals. If you identify more than twelve, you don't understand the customer well enough, and will need to do more research.

— *Strategy in Action* —

In the decision-making process for AAF, the SSEB focused on three aspects of each contractor's proposal: cost, technical aspects and past performance. The SSEB evaluated the proposals independently for over-all merit and risk against the RFP requirements. They did not compare the competitor's proposals to one another. None of the evaluators on the SSEB were key decision makers except the chairperson of the SSEB, which was the program manager for AAF, General Mark Howard.

The program manager is responsible for preparing the source selection documents, writing the RFP, and developing the detailed evaluation criteria. Even if the program manager is supplied with detailed guidelines, such as performance requirements and top-level evaluation criteria, he or she still has tremendous influence on how the source selection process is run, and therefore is usually considered a key decision maker. In this case he was also the SSEB chairperson. The SSEB chairperson runs the evaluation, and as such, exerts significant influence over the evaluation scoring. The SSEB chair will direct the team in how to undertake the evaluation and focus the team on particular issues. As the evaluation team is scoring the proposal, it is not unusual for the chairperson to question the team's assessment and send the team back for more analysis. As a result, they have tremendous influence on the final evaluation scoring. If the team rates a product poorly, it is very difficult for the other key decision makers to overrule that decision without impinging on the integrity of the procurement process.

The SSEB's assessments are passed on to the SSAC. To protect the integrity of the procurement process, it is a violation of federal regulations to disclose or learn the identity of members of the SSAC. However, bidding contractors are free to guess who might be on this council, and they should. To identify "likely" SSAC members, bidders research prior similar procurements by this customer to learn from where the customer traditionally draws its SSAC members. Prior customer debriefings can be examined and former customers should be interviewed. In the case of the Air Force, the SSAC is made up of senior executive personnel from the user, in this case, Air Combat Command, and requirements organizations represented by Tactical Programs. From each of these organizations, bidding contractors select a person who appears to have sufficient stature and the appropriate background (aviation or acquisition experience) for the committee.

The SSAC compiles the results and compares the contractor's scores; they then recommend a winner to the SSA. As the recommenders, the SSAC exerts significant influence. They also receive briefings as the evaluation is being conducted, during which they may raise questions and send recommendations back to the SSEB. Key members of the SSAC are going to carry a significant amount of weight in the source selection, with the chairperson typically having the most influence. Just as with the SSEB, the chairperson typically dominates the group. They usually have significant discretion in how they run their counsel and what they focus on. As a result, the chairperson usually has the most influence of all key decision makers.

When the SSA receives the recommendation, they can accept or overrule it. The SSA is the single person responsible for making the final award decision. While they have total authority over the final decision, in reality the SSAs usually have many issues to contend with, so they often delegate the source selection process to a large degree to the SSAC and SSEB. Because the process is usually for them to ratify or veto the SSAC's recommendation, they must expend a lot of political capital to overturn a recommendation. So while the SSA has all of the authority to choose whichever contractor they want, rarely do they exercise that prerogative.

In the case of AAF, we analyzed the previous five major fighter procurements and found that in each case the Secretary of the Air Force was the ultimate decision maker. Based on this selection process, we identified the key decision makers in the AAF procurement as shown in Exhibit 3-6.

It is not unusual for us to conduct this analysis two years before the actual source selection and in the end to find that our initial assessment closely matches the actual source selection composition.

Step 4: Identify the Key Decision Makers' Priorities

The key to victory lies in knowing the customer's values. The customer's values are derived from the priorities of the individual key decision makers. Priorities are the customer's perception of their most important needs. The meeting of these needs is the primary factor upon which the key decision makers will base their decision. Customer values are identified by analyzing what is most important to the individual key decision maker. Using your list of key decision makers, you identify and rank each individual's personal priorities for the procurement. These priorities are the most important aspects of the competitors' solutions, the items that each decision maker will use in choosing one offer over another. These priorities reflect what the decision maker believes is most important to the organization.

Most source selection decisions require the decision makers to make trade-offs between the attributes of one competitor versus another. To be very important to a key decision maker, an attribute must be relatively difficult to satisfy. If it is easy to satisfy it will not be a point of differentiation between the competitors. Keep in mind, there is never a perfect offering; there are always trade-offs between buying desires. The different priorities must compete with one another for the optimum solution. For example, a key decision maker may want a longer-range aircraft, but this would require larger fuel tanks and less payload capacity. Obviously, range and payload capacity are both relatively difficult to satisfy simultaneously.

An attribute cannot be a priority unless it serves to differentiate the competitors. If there is little or no differentiation between the competitors for a given attribute, the attribute will play no role in the source selection decision. For example, a minimum performance requirement cannot be a priority. If a company did not meet the threshold, the customer would disqualify them and the attribute would not be used by evaluators to choose a winner. Also, pass/fail criteria are unlikely to be a customer value, because unless all of the competitors fail to pass the criteria there will be no differentiation between them. Avoiding a protest is not a priority for selecting one contractor over another. While many government customers absolutely do not want their award decisions protested, that concern rarely influences which contractor they select. To avoid a protest, they must adhere to the procurement rules and not demonstrate any undue favoritism toward any competitor.

Also, a key decision maker may have an overwhelming priority that overshadows all of the other considerations. For it to be on the list however, it must be relevant to this procurement. For example, while chasing a sale to the Greek government, the only priority of the Prime Minister was getting reelected. However, neither our client nor the competitor would be voting in the upcoming election. The question became: how do this procurement's attributes affect the Prime Minister's perception of his chances for reelection? The two issues that the competitors could influence were job creation in Greece, and the potential political influence of the competitors' governments on Cyprus's entry into the European Monetary Union (EMU). Based on this knowledge, we translated the PM's priorities to "Jobs in Greece" and "EMU support."

Customer values are usually benefits and not features. As salesmen have found for thousands of years, while people may infer benefits from features, it is benefits that motivate people to buy. Many people confuse benefits with features. Features are the characteristics of a product, and benefits are what someone gains from the features – lower cost, lower risk, more reliability, faster delivery, or improved performance. Benefits motivate people to buy, but features prove that the benefits are true. Therefore, to make a strategy as precise and persuasive as possible, you will usually define decision makers' true priorities as the benefits they seek.

To determine customer values, analyze the desires of each key source selection decision maker. The key is to understand what each decision maker perceives as most important. Identify and rank, in descending order, the personal priorities for the procurement for each individual (see Exhibit 3-7). Identify what is most important to that person in choosing one contractor over another, making these priorities as specific as possible. The greater your understanding of their desires, the more specifically you can articulate their needs. For example, instead of settling on a customer's assertion that aircraft performance is the most important attribute, you should try to find out what characteristics the decision maker most closely associates with performance, such as speed, range, or cargo capacity. The more specific your understanding, the more focused and more powerful your strategies and sales messages will become.

Where people stand depends on where they sit. You'll find that you can predict – with a surprising degree of accuracy – how people will make decisions is based on their position and responsibilities. You can also often make a good guess about someone's individual priorities by carefully studying their past decisions and personalities. For example, a CEO wants value for money as he or she is trying to balance a project against other expenditures. This tends to make acquisition price an important priority to the CEO. In addition, the CEO is usually very concerned about any political issues associated with the project that might be raised by the board of directors. It is helpful to understand how the key decision makers are compensated and rewarded by the organization. Line managers are usually most concerned with operational issues and to some degree overall economics, while the program manager is inherently interested in performance capabilities and low risk, since he will be held accountable for successful implementation as well as problems and schedule slips. Price is not typically a high priority for a program manager. Frequently they are given a budget, and as long as it is not exceeded, they have no incentive to give money back.

Key Decision Maker	Relative Influence	Priorities			
		#1	#2	#3	#4
Walter Peyton, Secretary of AF	35	Unit Cost (AUPC) **1**	Life Cycle Cost **1**	Risk **1**	Growth Capability **2**
Debbie Davies, Dep. Asst. SECAF(AQ)	25	Management Team **1**	Unit Cost (AUPC) **1**	Risk **2**	Life Cycle Cost **3**
Gen. Marshall Reese, AF Chief of Staff	10	Unit Cost (AUPC) **1**	Risk **1**	Interoperability **3**	Survivability **4**
Gen. Robert Conway, Dir. of Tactical Progs.	5	Pilot Load **2**	Survivability **3**	Ground Attack **3**	Risk **4**
Gen. Frank Martin, Com of Air Combat	5	Ground Attack **2**	Survivability **3**	Risk **3**	Life Cycle Cost **3**
Gen. Mark Howard, Program Mgr.	20	Past Perf. **1**	Ground Attack **2**	Risk **2**	Life Cycle Cost **3**

Confidence:	**1** Very High	**2** High	**3** Some	**4** Low

Exhibit 3-7: Key Decision Maker Priority Matrix for AAF Competition

All decision makers have opinions and biases that factor into the source selection. It is important to assess each key decision maker individually to try to get inside his or her head as much as possible. Everyone is a product of their past experiences. You may find important clues to each person's priorities and perspective by examining their career history, past successes, and failures. What training and previous positions lined the decision maker's career path? A person's background can cause them to interpret requirements and their order of importance differently. For example, when selecting an Information Technology outsourcing vendor, the Chief Financial Officer (CFO) and the Chief Operating Officer (COO) could have very different priorities based on their backgrounds. The CFO may have just watched an electronic commerce system go $10 million over budget, while the COO, in a previous position as an operations vice president, might have successfully implemented a new material requirements planning system.

Assuming that executives and their subordinates have the same priorities is a common mistake. While there might be substantial overlap because they represent the same organization, key decision makers are individuals. It is very important to analyze and listen to each person as an individual.

Filling out this matrix accurately is difficult. It is challenging to identify the correct decision makers. But once you have their names, you can determine their priorities with some modest effort through careful listening. While the decision makers want to communicate their priorities, most people have trouble listening. We tend to allow our own biases to distort the customer's assertions. To determine an individual's priorities, it is important to listen carefully to what they say. Key decision makers will tell you their priorities in many ways throughout the competition; you must listen for the issues that they return to and continually articulate. You must examine what they write about the program and how they describe it. What are their perceptions of the needs of the organization? They broadcast their key concerns and issues through their questions, assertions, speeches, source selection documents and so on. In addition, listen to the questions they ask; what terms and language do they use, what are the topics that create an emotional response, to whom do they listen, and from whom do they solicit advice? What truths do they believe and hold dear? It is more difficult to identify someone's third and fourth priority desires. Their top concerns usually dominate their decision-making and their discussions, but you must seek out their lower priorities as well. Not surprisingly, the best way to learn a decision maker's priorities is to ask them. They want to tell you what's important to them. And seek to understand not only their first and second priority, but their third and fourth.

A common mistake people make is to assume that a decision maker's priority is a process, like ISO 9000, Open Systems, and Just-in-Time. People buy benefits, not processes. Decision makers may ask lots of questions about processes because they are trying to infer benefits. Decision makers want Just-in-Time because they desire the benefits of high quality and on-time delivery. Focus on benefits, not processes.

Typically, you will first attempt to fill out this matrix in a brainstorming session. People who know the key decision makers will describe their personalities, background, current positions and responsibilities. They will identify what they believe are the priorities of each individual. Experience has shown that when a group of people attempts to identify the most important attributes of the customer, significant arguments and disagreements result. However, when the matrix approach is used, and people focus on what is important to individual decision makers, you will find that a surprisingly rapid consensus forms about what's important to each individual.

A systematic approach is required to seek out, verify and record the decision maker's priorities. Establish a contact plan to meet and query them, and use meetings, briefings, demonstrations, plant tours, and golf outings to discuss their values and priorities with them. Every one of your employees who is in contact with these decision makers should engage in this listening process. Test your list of priorities by asking the decision makers questions that reveal their priorities. For example, you can ask, "Are you willing to pay more money upfront for a reliability guarantee?" Continually compare their remarks with what you have recorded as their priorities. Each team member should listen for the points stressed and quotes should be recorded verbatim because it is very easy to misinterpret remarks. It is helpful for the capture team members to review all background material on the key decision makers, including the current assessment of their priorities, before making contact. The more information your interviewer starts with, the more information he or she can obtain.

Some high-level decision makers, such as the CEO of IBM or the King of Kuwait, may be difficult to access in person. In such cases, you must attempt to infer their priorities from discussions with people who know the target. Analyze their background; review their speeches, carefully read press articles where they are quoted and interview people who know them.

Completing this matrix is a big step toward winning. If you are able to accurately complete this matrix, you will usually win. Completing this matrix encourages the whole team to listen and understand the customer and focuses a capture team on providing a solution that matches the customer's key needs. It is extremely important that the capture team does its homework, refines, retests and refines again.

— *Strategy in Action* —

In the AAF example, the Secretary of the Air Force's principle concerns revolved around having low cost aircraft so that the Air Force could afford to buy and support large numbers of them. This is why his first priority was low unit cost, and his second priority was low life cycle cost. General Robert Conway, on the other hand, was concerned that his pilots were being overwhelmed with information. His number one concern was whether the aircraft would overload the pilots and render them ineffective, so his key priority was pilot workload. He also wanted a highly survivable aircraft that could attack heavily defended targets. Debbie Davies, Deputy Assistant for Air Force Acquisition, believed that having a good management team was the most important factor in having a successful program, so that was her number one priority.

Priority Definitions:
Past Performance: How well the contractor performed on schedule and budget on similar prior programs.
Risk: The relative perceived risk of one contractor's program offer over the competitor in terms of ability to stay within budget and on schedule.
Life Cycle Cost: The total program cost of each competitor including acquisition, operations and support over 30 years.
Ground Attack: How well each competitor's aircraft would attack ground targets.
Survivability: How well the aircraft could likely meet and survive future air-to-air and ground-to-air threats.
Pilot Workload: How well the aircraft managed the presentation of information to the pilot.
Average Unit Production Cost: The average costs of the variants when they reached production, weighed by the number of each type to be produced.

Interoperability: How well the competitor's aircraft could fit into the existing and future force structure and perform missions with all of the services.

Management Team: The perceived competence of the contractor's management team to deliver the program on budget and schedule.

Early in the pursuit, you may lack confidence in your Decision Maker Priority matrix. Until you work to validate the positions of each of the decision makers and their priorities, the matrix may be incorrect. And since the entire strategy is driven by this matrix, it is critical to validate this information. By coding both the key decision makers and their priorities as shown in Exhibit 3-7 (because this book is black & white, the coding is shown as a 1-4 scale, but it should be colored coded blue, green yellow or red for easy identification, see definitions in Exhibit 3-8), management can assess and track your confidence in the information on which your strategy is based. Color-coding ensures that the capture team makes a determined effort to validate the decision makers and their priorities in order to improve their color scores. When the team first completes the matrix, it may have a large number of yellows and reds; but by the time of proposal submittal, if the team has worked concertedly, it should be mostly blues and greens.

Confidence Level	Key Decision Maker	Priority
Very High	Understand customer decision making process and have very high confidence that you know this person's role in the source selection process	Excellent understanding of this person's priorities for this project, learned by hearing them articulate this priority relative to other priorities
High	Understand customer source selection process well and you believe this person will likely fill a key decision making position	Have had discussions with this person about their issues for this procurement
Some	Understand customer source selection process, this person or equivalent will probably be a key decision maker	Know this person and what is generally important to them, but have not discussed their specific issues for this procurement
Low	Speculation – not sure of how customer will structure source slection decision making	Speculation based on this person's position

Exhibit 3-8: Guidelines for Identifying Matrix Confidence

Step 5: Determine the Customer Values

One premise of our strategy development process is that some customer needs are more important than others. While all requirements must be satisfied (except in some international campaigns which will be discussed in Chapter 4), you build your strategy around the customer values. This concentrates your efforts on the highest leverage areas – the attributes that the decision makers want most from the program. Since most bidders meet all requirements, the final decision will usually be based upon the relative ranking of the proposals against a subset of customer needs.

We consolidate these critical needs in a list of the customer values. Typically these include:

- Low acquisition cost
- Low risk
- Rapid payback

- Lowest operating cost
- High operational availability
- On-time schedule completion

To create the customer values list, you cull the key decision makers' priorities. The first step is combining similar or directly related priorities. You combine priorities such as technical risk and schedule risk into simply "risk," and reliability and sustainability into "supportability."

A decision maker's first priority is significantly more important than their second or third. So, you need to weigh each priority on the list accordingly. The sum of the priority weights for each decision maker equals one.

By weighting each decision maker's influence multiplied by their relative priorities, you can calculate a score for the priorities. You'll rank the weighted priorities by score, and arbitrarily truncate the list to focus on the top few priorities. In Exhibit 3-9, we took the top five, which were 75 percent of the total weighted scores (the sum of the relative scores of the customer values does not add up to 100). This weighted scoring list comprises the customer values. Typically, a capture team will have four to eight customer values. Fewer customer values are better because they drive the capture team to a more focused win strategy.

Key Decision Maker	Relative Influence	Priorities			
		#1	#2	#3	#4
Walter Peyton, Secretary of AF	35	Unit Cost (AUPC) [1]	Life Cycle Cost [1]	Risk [1]	Growth Capability [2]
Debbie Davies, Dep. Asst. SECAF(AQ)	25	Management Team [1]	Unit Cost (AUPC) [1]	Risk [2]	Life Cycle Cost [3]
Gen. Marshall Reese, AF Chief of Staff	10	Unit Cost (AUPC) [1]	Risk [1]	Interoperability [3]	Survivability [4]
Gen. Robert Conway, Dir. of Tactical Progs.	5	Pilot Load [2]	Survivability [3]	Ground Attack [3]	Risk [4]
Gen. Frank Martin, Com of Air Combat	5	Ground Attack [2]	Survivability [3]	Risk [3]	Life Cycle Cost [3]
Gen. Mark Howard, Program Mgr.	20	Past Perf. [1]	Ground Attack [2]	Risk [2]	Life Cycle Cost [3]
Confidence:	[1] Very High	[2] High	[3] Some	[4] Low	

Customer Values	Relative Score
AUPC	24
Risk	21
Management Team	11
LCC	11
Ground Attack	8

Exhibit 3-9: Weighted Customer Values

Always include price as a customer value, even if price does not bubble up to the top of the customer priority matrix. Price is always important to a customer, but frequently people understate its importance when identifying priorities for individuals. Decision-makers always trade off desirability with its cost, so price is always a customer value because developing cost and price strategies is always important to winning. Price can be expressed as a customer value in many ways. In the AAF example, price is represented as Average Unit Production Unit Cost (AUPC) and Life Cycle Cost. It also can be represented as acquisition cost, most probable cost or a whole variety of other ways.

The key to victory lies in knowing the customer values. These are the factors most important to the customer, and we build our strategy around Customer Values.

— *Strategy in Action* —

It is very insightful for the team to see what is not on the list of customer values. Engineers realize that the features they have been pushing are not that important to the customer. For example, on AAF, "air-to-air combat capability" was not a customer value, while unit cost and risk were the most highly rated values. As a result, if an engineer was pushing to replace the off-the-shelf air combat radar with a new expensive and technically risky radar, the AAF capture team would be smart to propose keeping the existing system.

The list of customer values will usually differ from the evaluation criteria, sometimes significantly. The customer values are derived from the wants of the key decision makers. The evaluation criteria, on the other hand, are developed by the procurement organization or program office. The evaluation criteria are designed to be a comprehensive evaluation of the solution's ability to satisfy all of the requirements. But the definition of a customer value is a need that is most important to key decision makers – the customer values are a significant subset of all the characteristics to be evaluated as shown in Exhibit 3-10. Because the program office must allocate the evaluation weighting across so many factors, customer values end up with little of the total weighting. As a result, the technical evaluation process will bury the few critical customer values beneath the more numerous, but less important, evaluation factors. In most cases, the evaluation criteria and customer values overlap. The amount of overlap depends on the complexity of the project and the responsiveness of the procurement organization or program office to the needs of the key decision makers. Typically, the larger and more complex procurement organization is less responsive, and we see less overlap. In other cases, key decision maker desires may not even be factored into the evaluation, such as the "Jobs in Canada" example earlier in the chapter.

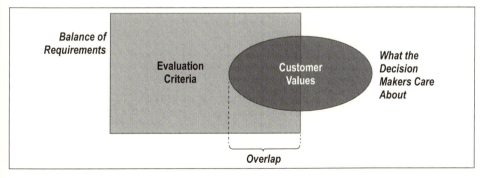

Exhibit 3-10: The Evaluation Criteria and Customer Values Overlap

— *Strategy in Action* —

In another similar example, a company was trying to sell a set of ships, planes and communications systems for rescue operations and drug interdiction to the Coast Guard. The most important customer value for the Coast Guard admirals was not drug intercepts, but "Big Ships." All of the customer's key decision makers were former ship commanders and longed for their days at sea. While one contractor had an innovative, low cost solution using small boats, remote sensors and unmanned aircraft, which simulations showed to be highly effective, they found little enthusiasm from the customer for their approach. What the admirals really wanted was their own Navy. The admirals selected the contractor who built a proposal strategy around "Big Ships." In each of these cases, no one in the customer community ever publically admitted their priorities, but the suppliers with the strategies built on "Jobs in Quebec" in our previous example and "Big Ships" in this one both won.

The key decision makers may influence the weighting of the evaluation factors, but the most powerful decision makers usually delegate the development of the evaluation process and are divorced from it. They frequently have low salience about pressing their priorities until differentiation between the competitors becomes pronounced. However, the most powerful decision makers will force change in the evaluation process if they see a significant divergence between their desires and the RFP and evaluation criteria. As a result, if the decision makers force changes in the evaluation criteria, they are usually significant.

For each customer value, you must write a detailed definition for your team; every member of the capture team must understand what the term means. The definition must clearly articulate your understanding of each customer value and what it means to the key decision makers. With customer values, phrasing and terminology are critical. You should always articulate the priority in the language the customer would use in describing their desire. A common language indicates to the decision makers that you are listening to them and understand their needs. It is important that your language resonates with the customer. You are going to attempt to build rapport with your customers around these concepts during your sales process and using the same language creates feelings of connection. It demonstrates your understanding of their issues.

A strategy is only as good is the information on which it is based. Customer values are essential because they form the basis for evaluating all of your alternatives; they drive your strategy development. Identifying the customer values is one of the keys to winning, so it is critical to confirm your key decision maker and priority list as soon as possible. The capture team should make a concerted effort to meet with people who know the decision makers well, and then with the decision makers themselves.

Fortunately, decision makers want to share their concerns, needs, desires and issues; simply ask and listen. Discussing priorities with the key decision makers helps them formulate those priorities that they may not have yet articulated. Also, this confirmation process demonstrates that you are listening and attempting to understand their needs, allowing you to build rapport. Experience shows that even a single meeting with the decision makers, or an interview with someone who knows the key decision makers well, will significantly improve the accuracy of the list.

Once the list has been confirmed to be extremely accurate, it should be reconfirmed. And reconfirmed again. This process of validating key decision makers and their priorities continues throughout the pursuit. Experience has shown that the initial brainstorming of key decision makers is usually wrong by one or two names. Errors in priorities are common as well. But, figuring out what you do not have confidence in or do not know is a critical step toward victory. Priorities change over the course of the pursuit and the organization's needs may evolve as available funding falls or new competitive threats emerge. Key decision makers may be replaced or are successfully influenced by you or the competition. Developing the strategy is an iterative process that continues until the contract is inked.

Summary

The essence of a winning strategy lies in differentiating your solution from that of your competitors in the specific attributes deemed to be most important to the key decision makers. These attributes, or customer values, once identified, will guide the strategy formulation. Creating a solution with strengths linked directly to these specific attributes – and knowing how the competition is positioned in relation to these areas – is crucial to creating a strategy that will help you to out-maneuver the competition and ultimately win the contract. The key to winning is figuring out what is most important to the customer's key decision makers. While there are a lot of customers, the key decision makers are the ones you build your strategy around.

Chapter 4: Crafting the Win Strategy Starts With Assessing Your Relative Position

> "One day Alice came to a fork in the road and saw a Cheshire cat in a tree. 'Which road do I take?' she asked.
>
> His response was a question: 'Where do you want to go?'
>
> 'I don't know,' Alice answered.
>
> 'Then,' said the cat, 'It doesn't matter.'"

— Lewis Carroll, Alice's Adventures in Wonderland

A battle fought without a strategy is almost always lost. This is equally true when battling the enemy in the jungles of Vietnam, prosecuting a murder in the Orange County courthouse, playing football in the Coliseum, or treating a cancer patient at John Hopkins. Rarely does anyone succeed who seeks success blindly.

This idea is fundamental, yet many companies begin pursuits with win strategies that are weak at best. Every contractor plans to win by meeting the customer needs better than the competition, but this objective is not a strategy in itself. Over the last twenty-one years, our experience has found that most capture team personnel do not know what a win strategy is. As a result, many capture teams rely on hope and luck to win, both of which are poor substitutes for a strategy.

This chapter will lead the reader through a proven process to assess their current position. This chapter will take the us through steps six through eight of Exhibit 4-1, continuing to build on the five areas outlined in Chapter 3, guiding us through the formal process needed to develop a successful win strategy.

Step 6: Assess the Competitors' Positions

The selection of a strategy should be based on how your offering compares to the competitors' for each of the customer values. Once the customer values have been identified, as directed in Chapter 3, you must assess the strengths and weaknesses of all the serious competitors against those specific values. Crafting a win strategy requires an understanding of specifically how you differ from your competitors in the areas most crucial to the customer.

Discriminators are unique differences between two or more competitors as perceived by the customer. These differences can exist in the offering or in a company's capabilities, and they are what sell a solution. People buy things that are different – they buy things that are bigger, smaller, cheaper, faster, louder, quieter or tougher. If you and your competitor are great shipbuilders, that is not a discriminator, even if shipbuilding is the number one evaluation category.

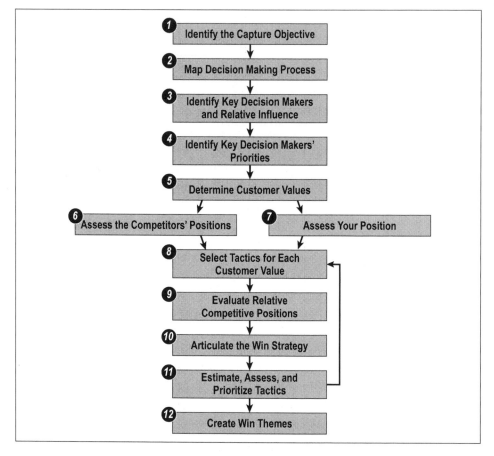

Exhibit 4-1: Formulating the Win Strategy

Discriminators are the differences between the way you build your ship and the way they build theirs. Each competitor's team will have a diverse set of differentiators that help or hurt their position. Competitors always have many things in common, and unless exploited or perceived differently, similarities do not matter. Selecting winners is always based on discriminators.

Creating discriminators is very important and can be difficult. As the famous marketing professor, Theodore Levitt once said, "Differentiation is one of the most important strategic and tactical activities in which companies must constantly engage. It is not discretionary. And everything can be differentiated, even so-called commodities."

You can differentiate anything. A few examples:

- Evian differentiates water and even charges more for it than is charged for a Coke.
- When Frank Perdue learned that customers preferred their chickens plump and yellow, he developed a new breeding and feeding

program to invent a superior chicken.
- While working with a utility, one of our capture teams learned to create discriminators for supplying electricity to ski resorts and casinos.

All competitions are based on discrimination. Creating discrimination between you and your competition is the key to winning.

The next step in the strategy development process is to document the strengths and weaknesses of each competitor for each customer value, as shown in Exhibit 4-2. Strengths are discriminators that make a company or offering more attractive to the customer relative to a particular customer value, while a weakness makes the company less desirable. The battle to win takes place solely in the customer's mind; so discriminators do not need to be real. However, if the customer thinks they are real, then they must be addressed.

In a brainstorming process, the team should identify those strengths and weaknesses that have a possibility of making a difference to the customer for each customer value. A team's typical strengths might include:
- Unique features of their offering
- Process capabilities
- Previous experience making this or similar products
- Proprietary technologies
- Low manufacturing labor rates
- Existing customer relationships or knowledge
- Established logistics networks

It is important to focus this process on those discriminators that are important. After you go through each customer value from the brainstorming, eliminate those discriminators with little importance. The key is to focus this process on the critical few and not the trivial many. Next, go through the lists of competitor strengths and weaknesses and highlight in bold or in red those that are very significant. That way when you start to develop your tactics, you can be sure to focus in on the most important discriminators.

A common mistake made by capture teams just beginning their competitive analysis is to assume that a competitor is more formidable than they actually are. Overestimating the competition is almost as bad as underestimating them. If you overestimate the competition, you will underbid, take risky and unnecessary actions and potentially ruin your proposal.

As part of this step, the capture team must also identify the actions that the competitor is likely to take to improve their position on each customer value. A competitor is likely to try to neutralize any weaknesses and leverage their strengths. Examine the competitor's past capture efforts to look for patterns that reveal how they compete. Some companies consistently try to be the low price offer, others compete on early schedule delivery, and others attempt to always have the best technical performance. The capture team should also review their competitor's marketing materials for the procurement; these materials tend to broadcast the competitor's intentions and strategies.

— *Strategy in Action* —

In the AAF example, as shown in Exhibit 4-2 (shows only excerpts from two customer values and not all five), Huge Aircraft had discriminators that would lower their program risk. Huge Aircraft did not have a complex lift fan like Goliath, and therefore had a simpler aircraft. Huge Aircraft also had flying test bed aircraft and the best fighter simulation capabilities in the world, which could be used to mitigate risk. Huge Aircraft's risk weaknesses included an immature aircraft design (their prototype had a different tail than their proposed aircraft), and a limited design margin. Huge Aircraft's projected aircraft performance allowed little additional weight, and new aircraft programs consistently experience weight growth as they enter production. Their design also had poor handling qualities at slow speed, making slow bomb runs difficult, resulting in poor ground attack capabilities.

In many previous competitions, Huge Aircraft had established relatively easy to achieve schedules and budgets during pre-proposal program phases. They then trumpeted about beating schedules and under-running budgets. Huge Aircraft's bidding behavior also signaled that they often tried to be the low price option. In addition, in their AAF ads they broadcast their strategy to be the lowest unit priced contractor.

To address their design maturity weakness, one element of Huge Aircraft's likely strategy was to establish a development process to rapidly respond to new requirements, while still meeting their schedule and under-running their budgets. This approach leveraged their simulation and rapid prototyping strengths, while allowing them to argue that the AAF program was changing, and would continue to undergo many changes, so that both contractors would be forced to continually adjust their design. This strategy tried to convert Huge Aircraft's weakness – their immature design – into a strength.

Customer Value	Competitor Strengths	Competitor Weaknesses	Most Likely Strategy
Unit Cost (AUPC)	• **Lighter Aircraft** • Designed for Producibility • Manufacturing Simulation • Use of Adv. Manuf. Techniques	• Failed to Meet Past Cost Targets • Use of Some Unproven Processes	• Digital Design for Manufacture (including SPF, unitized structure, high speed machining, flexible tooling) • Use of COTS
Risk	• **Simpler Aircraft** • Weapons Testing and Simulation • **Open System Architecture** • Sensor Fusion Experience • Flying Testbed • Rapid Prototyping Capability	• **Limited Design Margin** • **Design Maturity**	• Sell Evolutionary Concept Not Point Design • Mitigate Risk Through Simulation and Rapid Prototyping • Demonstrate Effective PM and Under Run Budgets • Prove Manuf. Processes on Risk Reduction Program

Exhibit 4-2: Competitive Assessment – Huge Aircraft AAF

Exhibit 4-2 demonstrates the matrix that was constructed in the AAF example to help pinpoint the competitor's likely strategy relative to specific customer values. In order to identify the key discriminators for each customer value, the entire scope of the customer's desired work must be considered, and the most significant factors for each value must be identified. For example, if the customer value is "risk," you need to focus on the elements of each competitive solution that will have the most impact on risk. The Exhibit also shows a few of the discriminators in bold to reflect those that are most important. This helps focus the capture team when identifying tactics.

In the AAF example, one of the key program risks was whether the aircraft could make range with the required bomb payload. Huge Aircraft's strategy was to be low cost; so they designed a very lightweight fighter with little design margin, meaning their aircraft's weight could not afford to grow much heavier and still meet the bomb payload requirements. This made Huge Aircraft's limited design margin an important weakness.

It is important to be as realistic and honest as possible when developing this matrix. It is human nature to dismiss our competitors until we discover just how good they really are. An opinion of the competition frequently changes once we learn of the technologies that the competitor is developing, their positive past performance history, or the unique features of their current product offerings. A clear understanding of the competition's approach and benefits encourages capture teams to develop the best possible solution for the customer.

Trying to complete this matrix highlights the critical pieces of information that a company lacks. The information voids become the team's intelligence requirements – the information that still needs to be collected. Typically, the first time a team goes through this process, they are surprised to realize how much they do not know about the pursuit and their competition, even if they have been working on the pursuit for months or years. Recognizing the gaps in critical information is the first and most important step in filling them in.

The quality of a strategy depends on the quality of the information on which it is based. If a company has a competitive analyst, having them participate in the win strategy development process is priceless. Having good competitive intelligence is critical to positioning the offering. Developing competitive intelligence is something a company should invest in to help teams develop effective capture strategies. In Chapter 9 we will discuss how to collect and analyze competitive intelligence in support of a capture effort.

Step 7: Assessing Your Position

The same process used to identify the competition's strengths and weaknesses should be applied to your own team for each customer value. However, do not attempt to develop "likely strategies" for each value at this step. Exhibit 4-3 provides an example.

— Strategy in Action —

The following matrix highlights some of the strengths and weaknesses of Goliath for each customer value. In production unit cost, Goliath designed their aircraft using a set of standard part families – this allows them to produce fewer unique parts at higher volumes. However, as a weakness, Goliath has a larger and more complex aircraft, something that drives up production costs. In Ground Attack, they have a larger weapons bay, allowing them more mission flexibility. In addition, they also planned to propose an advanced ground attack radar, and a bubble canopy that would allow the pilot to have an excellent view of the ground when flying.

Customer Value	Our Strengths	Our Weaknesses
Unit Cost (AUPC)	• Use of Part Families • Flexible Tooling • Lean Manufacturing	• **Complex Design** • **Larger Aircraft**
Risk	• Significant Design Margin • Extensive Simulation and Modeling • Conventional Structure • Risk Management Processes	• **Lift Fan Unproven** • **Clutch Unproven** • Weak System Integration Process
Management Team	• F-27 Experience • F-12 Experience	• C-122 Experience • Complex Management Structure
Life Cycle Cost	• Open Business Model • Stealth Maintenance Experience • Extensive Prognostics	• Use of Some Unproven Processes
Ground Attack	• Larger Weapons Bay • Ground Attack Radar • Bubble Canopy with Good View • Advanced Cockpit Attack Modes	• Mission Radius

Exhibit 4-3: Goliath's Self-Assessment Matrix

The capture team should list all relevant capabilities of their company and identify any teammates that could be of value, even if these resources are not currently scheduled to be employed on the pursuit. The team can even include capabilities at other sites within the corporation if there is a possibility that they could be leveraged. Identify as many strengths as possible during this brainstorming process. This information gives your team more tools to work with to create the winning offering. The customer will use each competitor's discriminators to select the winner, so you need discriminators. In addition, you need to make sure that the evaluator clearly recognizes the positive differences between your solution and the competition.

Next, identify your weaknesses. How solid is your past performance? Is your team missing any capability or experience needed to provide a complete customer solution? Include any potential weaknesses perceived by the customer as well. Review your pursue/no pursue briefing for issues. It is critical to be as objective as possible in this analysis because the first step in overcoming a weakness is to acknowledge it.

Sometimes, you will have a discriminator that can be considered both a strength and weakness, so list it on both sides of the chart. For example, when bidding on a train control system, if the company had a very similar system in development for another customer, this experience and capability would be a strength.

However, if the system was also a year behind schedule, its schedule performance would be a weakness.

It is not enough to simply identify strengths and weaknesses; the team has to do something with these discriminators to position themselves to win. In the next sections, we'll discuss how to leverage this information to formulate the win strategy.

Step 8: Select Tactics for Each Customer Value

Tactics are actions that build discriminators. While you will use tactics to fulfill your strategy, you must brainstorm these tactics before initially defining that strategy. You do this because everyone has a certain set of discriminators entering the competition – their strengths and weaknesses, as discussed above. In addition, one creates discriminators as they progress through the pursuit process. Once these have been identified, it is much easier to identify specific actions to be taken to maximize the strengths and minimize weaknesses than it is to conceptualize full-blown strategies. Before you decide on your win strategy, you hypothesize potential discriminators. This will help you to select the best possible strategy.

Tactics are not the "spin" or the stories you are going to write about in the proposal; tactics are actions that, when properly executed, improve your customer value position relative to the competition. Tactics create discriminators that you will write about in the proposal. You must document your tactics using an action verb such as: develop, demonstrate, establish, or complete. Typical tactics include:

- Sign up a teammate who brings critical strengths
- Conduct a demonstration
- Prototype a high risk subsystem
- Persuade the customer to change the requirements
- Develop a risk mitigation plan
- Conduct research and development
- Develop a computer simulation
- Create independent substantiation
- Develop and apply lessons learned prior to the proposal
- Influence the customer to heavily weight responsiveness in the proposal evaluation
- Conduct joint customer study
- Patent a solution

It is important to note that for most customers, you must satisfy all of their requirements. If you fail to meet any requirements, they will disqualify you. However, some customers, like the Indian government, don't insist that you meet all of their requirements. Some international customers routinely ask for the Cadillac, when they only have a Chevy budget. These customers like to ask for everything and then use that as the starting point for negotiations. With these customers, part of one's strategy is to be strategically compliant. You are compliant on the key requirements and choose not to be compliant on the expensive ones that the customer does not really care about. Intentionally not meeting a requirement can be a tactic to lower risk or cost. But it is critical to employ it only if you have a customer that can award to non-compliant offerings.

Using the templates created above, review your strengths and weaknesses relative to each competitor for each specific customer value. Compare and contrast all of the competitor strengths, weaknesses and likely tactics to your own. Based on this analysis you'll identify tactics for each customer value which:

- Heighten or create new strengths
- Counter the competitor's strengths
- Magnify the competitor's weaknesses
- Neutralize your weaknesses

You do not need to address every single strength and weakness of every competitor, but it is important to address all of the critical strengths and weaknesses – those that will have a large impact on the customer's perceptions. The capture team must examine all of the strengths and weaknesses of both the competition and their own company, selecting those deemed most significant. Pay special attention to those discriminators that your team bolded or colored red in the matrix, because those are the most important. Then the team should identify tactics to address those key strengths and weaknesses. Typically, capture teams do this through a brainstorming process. We tell the capture teams we work with that quality is more important than quantity. A few good tactics tend to be substantially more effective than many trivial ones. Exhibit 4-4 shows how a team identified three critical strengths or weaknesses with circles, and then brainstormed to counter a competitor's strength, heighten one of their own strengths and neutralize a weakness. As this sample campaign progresses, the team will add more effective tactics.

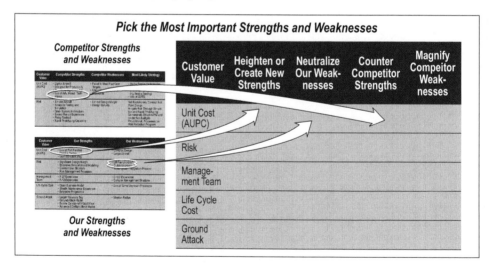

Exhibit 4-4: Example Matrix Development

Heighten or Create New Strengths

To create a new strength, the capture team must examine the customer values to identify a feature or capability that could be added to their offer to heighten a capability or solve a customer problem better than the competition.

— *Strategy in Action* —

Lockheed created a host of strengths in their pursuit of NASA's Reusable Launch Vehicle program. The objective of this program was for industry to develop and operate a space transport system that would replace the space shuttle. Some of NASA's customer values were low risk, low cost, and commercial viability. To make their business case feasible, Lockheed removed the flight crew from their spacecraft and with it, the need to "man rate" the vehicle. If a vehicle carries people it must be proven safe, requiring an exhaustive and extremely expensive test program, as well as substantial system redundancy, which significantly drives up development, acquisition and operating costs. Lockheed developed a rapid recovery and launch turnaround concept that slashed operating costs. They created an investor-based business case, which relied on a realistic number of flights and did not require the traditional government progress payments or loan guarantees. These are just some of the changes in approach that Lockheed used to create new strengths. These changes helped Lockheed make the case that their solution was commercially feasible and they beat out rivals Boeing and McDonnell Douglas. Unfortunately for Lockheed, test failures of the composite fuel tank in the X-33 technical demonstrator doomed the project, leading NASA to cancel the program.

Entirely new discriminators can be created by leveraging capabilities from other areas of the company, including new products or innovative approaches.

— *Strategy in Action* —

Two companies were bidding on a new aircraft to collect intelligence from the battlefield for the U.S. Navy. Since this was an urgent need, the program requirements were somewhat unclear about what the customer wanted. During a pre-proposal one-on-one customer exchange, the customer asked Contractor A's capture leader if they were going to be providing analyzed intelligence as part of the contract or just raw collected data. To provide analyzed intelligence the contractor would have to provide analysts to correlate the raw intelligence into specific targeting as well as assessments of the enemy's capabilities and intentions. The capture leader immediately deduced that the customer did not want to recruit and train dozens of new analysts and so he said, "Absolutely, we will provide analyzed intelligence." This was a gutsy call, as they had no intelligence analyst capability nor any plans to include it in their solution concept. The capture leader then returned to his facility and built this into his offering – providing intelligence analysts. He contacted and teamed up with a sister division with extensive intelligence capability. The competitor merely provided a simple ground station that would deluge the Navy with a mountain of data. Contractor A created a new strength and won the program at a significantly higher price than the competitor.

Another way to create a new discriminator is to develop evidence to prove to the customer that you understand their problems, or that you can solve their problems in innovative ways.

— *Strategy in Action* —

On one pursuit, our customer was receiving significant pressure from one of their most important customers to complete a new national communications system. The customer wanted to roll out the entire system in two years, but because of budget constraints, the program was going to take over three years. The capture team decided to create a new strength by proposing a two-year implementation schedule with a three-year payment scheme. The company's executives agreed to finance part of the project to implement the strategy and win the business. As the capture team was estimating the costs of this accelerated schedule they were pleased to discover the accelerated schedule would also save them money. This new discriminator made the capture team's offering very attractive, as it achieved the goal of their customer's customer.

An existing strength can also be heightened by expanding its benefits – showcasing it so that it seems more beneficial. For example, one of T-Mobile's strengths is their claim to provide the "fewest dropped calls." Their billboard shows an older woman hanging from the top of the billboard, with the text, "Don't Drop Grandma." This message evokes a strong image and emotional response. Many elderly people are uncomfortable with new technology like cell phones. The billboard creates the fear that if we go with another carrier, that service will lose Grandma's connection and we'll experience the pain of a confused grandparent.

— *Strategy in Action* —

In another case, a construction equipment manufacturer was trying to sell a fleet of excavators, dozers, backhoes and assorted other equipment to a mining company operating in a remote part of South America. The mining company's executives were very concerned about spare parts availability, which would be needed to keep their equipment running in this harsh environment. Parts and service were a key strength of the manufacturer, as well as a weakness of the competition. At the start of a meeting at the customer's headquarters, the manufacturer gave the mining company president a long spare parts list and asked him to pick a part. Five hours later, a manufacturer's service representative walked in and gave the president a box. In the box was the spare part he had chosen. The deliveryman showed the president the stock picking ticket, and the aircraft flight plan that was used to get that part to him. This stunt highlighted the manufacturer's strength by giving the customer a vivid demonstration of their spares response time. It also led to the customer asking the competitor how long it would take to get a spare part from their warehouses. Their answer? Days. Through this practical example, the manufacturer heightened the value of their strength by contrasting it with the competition.

You can create a strength by adding a feature that solves or reduces an important customer problem. To successfully sell a new feature, you must ensure that the customer understands the value of your solution. You must take them mentally through three steps. First, identify the customer's problem and its root cause. Next, help the customer understand the value of solving the root cause to their problem. Lastly, show them how your solution solves the root cause of their problem. Only after convincing the customer that your feature solves the root cause of their problem will they understand the benefit of your feature.

— *Strategy in Action* —

A commercial aircraft manufacturer was trying to sell a fleet of aircraft to an airline. They followed the three steps outlined above. The aircraft featured an on-board maintenance diagnostic system that communicated with the ground. This diagnostic system would improve an airline's on-time departure performance. First, the manufacturer showed the airline that they understood their problem (late departures) well enough to identify the root cause. In this case, the analysis showed that a certain number of the late takeoffs were caused by maintenance problems, and specifically showed how many maintenance fixes that could be accomplished between flights if repair crews and materials were available. Next, the manufacturer helped the airline quantify the value of solving their problem. They worked with the airline's maintenance planners to calculate the value of improving repair crew and materials availability when an aircraft lands on a stopover. Lastly, the manufacturer showed how their capability addressed the root cause of the customer's problem. The manufacturer provided the airline with data from other customers showing how real-time maintenance status cut flight delays. If a plane landing at Dulles Airport had a stopped up toilet and was equipped with the manufacturer's maintenance diagnostic communications system, a repair crew could be waiting when they landed. The airline could avoid a costly delay or even a canceled flight. The airline manufacturer was able to show the airline how this system increased aircraft availability and on-time performance, information that the airline was able to convert into increased revenues and lowered costs.

Many people make the mistake of taking for granted that the customer will be able to intuitively understand a feature's worth. This is a dangerous assumption. To sell your strengths you must take the customer through the sales process.

Some of the most important tactics to identify are those that can shape the procurement. These tactics heighten your strengths or magnify a competitor's weaknesses by influencing how the customer designs the procurement. You can capitalize on a strength by convincing the customer to grade your strength as an evaluation criteria. For example, one company had excellent processes to engineer their products for quick and efficient repair and field support. To shape the RFP, they provided the customer with white papers showing how maintaining products in the field was eating into the customer's meager operating budget. They also showed that great strides could be made in reducing these costs if the customer induced their suppliers to design their products for ease of repair. To do this, the company suggested that the customer include supportability as an evaluation factor in the RFP. The customer accepted this suggestion, which improved the company's competitive position because they knew they would score very well on supportability. Shaping the procurement to bolster your competitive position is one of the most important aspects of the capture process and we will discuss at length how to plan and execute shaping in Chapter 8.

Sometimes companies create false strengths. For example, Ivory Soap claims it is 99 and 44/100ths percent pure. Though a chemist verified that Ivory only contained 56/100 percent impurities, this feature provides no real benefit to the customer. Nonetheless, this claim gave the soap an image of quality and innovation, and catapulted it to becoming the best selling soap in the United States. In another example, during the late '70s actor Ricardo Montalbán touted the luxurious feel of rich "Corinthian leather" in ads for the Chrysler Cordoba. Interestingly, Chrysler's marketing department invented the phrase "Corinthian leather." We recommend against inventing fallacious strengths, as the competitors can easily expose them, undermining your credibility.

Counter the Competitors' Strengths

Featuring your strengths is one of the most important aspects in positioning to win. However, this is only half the battle. You must take the fight to the enemy and attack your competitors' strengths. A capture team can counter a competitor's strength by minimizing, neutralizing or discrediting it. You can minimize a strength by showing that it is not as valuable or as beneficial as it first seems. If the strength is valuable, you need to show that it has a significant downside as well. Better yet, turn a competitor's strength into a weakness.

— Strategy in Action —

Lockheed Martin was pursuing a contract to be the system integrator of combat systems for a new aircraft carrier. The capture team's competitive analysis of Raytheon revealed what appeared to be an insurmountable strength: Raytheon supplied almost all of the major subsystems that went into the combat suite. This gave Raytheon a huge advantage in knowing the capabilities, limitations, interfaces and nuances of the systems by substantially reducing their risk as the system integrator. The Lockheed Martin competitive assessment was bleak; and we told the capture team leaders that they either had to develop a brilliant strategy or choose to no bid. The Lockheed capture leaders rose to the challenge and developed a brilliant strategy. They invented an approach they called the "Open Business Model^{TM}" (OBM). Traditionally, suppliers would sign agreements prior to the proposal to support the integrator's proposal effort with cost and technical information in return for a work share commitment if the team won. Using the OBM approach, Lockheed would not make any work share commitments until after they won. Lockheed's team argued that their negotiating position would be significantly improved with the potential suppliers *after* they won the contract. Lockheed could use their winning position as negotiating leverage with suppliers and avoid long-term uncompetitive commitments. This would allow Lockheed to maintain continuous competition between component suppliers across the thirty-year life cycle of the program, which they argued would reduce risk and cost. In addition, since Lockheed did not produce any of the components, they would focus solely on selecting the best hardware for the Navy. Lockheed would be an honest broker.

This assertion directly attacked Raytheon's position, since the Navy perceived Raytheon as being biased toward their own products. Lockheed argued that their Open Business Model, by leveraging their negotiating position after award and maintaining competition across the entire cycle, would cut costs and reduce risk. This was a brilliant strategy because it converted Raytheon's key strength – that they had all of the components – into a weakness. Because of this strategy, Lockheed won a contract worth $500 million.

You can neutralize a competitor's strength by adopting it. For example, the Apaches terrorized settlers in the Arizona Territory during the late nineteenth century using guerrilla-style hit and run tactics. The U.S. Army seemed powerless to stop this elusive foe. Then General George Crook hired disaffected Apaches to serve as scouts and teach his troops the Apache style of tracking and fighting. He replaced his road-bound supply wagon trains with pack mules, which significantly increased the range and speed of his troops. Adapting their fast moving techniques, Crook's troops were finally able to chase down and defeat the Apaches. The army had neutralized the Apache's key strength of mobility by adopting it. This is precisely what Raytheon's naval systems division did after losing the above example. For years after this loss, Raytheon would propose their own version of the open business model when competing against their archrival Lockheed Martin.

You can discredit a strength by demonstrating that it is not real, or at least by creating that perception.

— *Strategy in Action* —

During the 2004 Presidential campaign, John Kerry's military career was a strength that conveyed his apparent heroism and leadership. Then the Swift Boat Veterans for Truth initiated a series of advertisements questioning the legitimacy of his war record and criticizing his antiwar activities following his military service. The news coverage of these ads turned his military service into a weakness by questioning his honesty and his fitness to serve as commander in chief. Initially, John Kerry tried to ignore the Swift Boat controversy and watched his poll numbers slip. The Swift Boat campaign destroyed John Kerry's strength: his military career. His campaign staff learned an expensive lesson – the longer it takes you to counter an argument, the more ingrained the argument becomes in the consciousness of your competition and customers, making it more difficult to counter. The sooner you counter a competitor's strength or an argument, the better.

It is naïve to assume that the customer will realize that a competitor's strength is overstated or untrue. It is your job to tell them. Unless addressed or countered, a customer will assume the competitor's claim to be true. For example, Karl Malden's "Don't leave home without 'em" commercials made American Express' Travelers Checks famous. These television spots embedded American Express in the collective American consciousness. Ironically, all travelers check companies provide replacements for lost or stolen checks. Amex's expounded differentiator was in fact not a differentiator at all, but their competition left this strength unaddressed, and suffered market share loss to American Express. Companies must strike back. Frequently, the counter punch can be more powerful than the initial assertion.

— *Strategy in Action* —

In 2005, when Frito-Lay launched Stax, a potato crisp product, they took out ads in USA Today and other newspapers boasting, "America Prefers the Taste of Lay's Stax Over Pringles." Stax directly assailed Pringles strength, their taste. Procter and Gamble, the maker of Pringles, being the aggressive competitor they are, immediately countered with a commercial featuring a researcher interviewing a typical middle-aged American man at a taste test booth in a supermarket. The viewers saw him crunching a Pringles in front of a can of Pringles and a Stax-colored can. The market researcher asked, "So, sir, which tastes better?" "Oh, the Pringles taste better," the man said. "Is that because they're less greasy?" the researcher asked. "No, just taste better," the man said, eating another Pringles chip and smiling. "You know, a lot of people love these cans," the researcher said, "maybe it's the can you like?" The man looked down at the Pringles can, picked it up and took a bite out of it. "No. It's not the can," he said, "It's the Pringles." When their product's strength was attacked as not as tasty, P&G immediately responded. By quickly countering the attack, P&G sapped the energy of the competitor's assault.

The surest way to win is to identify your competitor's strengths and then discredit them. On the other hand, if you attempt to discredit a competitor's strength and are unsuccessful, you've discovered the surest way to lose.

— *Strategy in Action* —

On another pursuit, two companies were teamed and heavily favored to win a contract to provide a comprehensive safety and maintenance monitoring system to a large chemical manufacturing complex. In fact, it looked like no other company would even bid against them. The key component in the entire system was a set of chemical detection sensors that were able to report real time chemical mixes. The first company was principally a hardware manufacturing company and had just developed a more accurate sensor that promised significantly improved plant operating efficiency. The second company was a systems company that would provide the operating software and communications links. The hardware company believed that their sensor virtually guaranteed victory and attempted to renegotiate their teaming agreement to gain greater work share and revenue. The systems company refused, and the teaming agreement dissolved in acrimony all around. The hardware company had limited software and integration capabilities, but their chief strength was their sensor – the sensor's capabilities alone were likely to win the contract. The systems company recognized that they needed to counter their competitor's sensor, so they found a small engineering house that produced some prototype sensors. The systems company contracted with the leading experts in sensor technology to help the engineering house improve their processes and combined the sensors into a single package. The resulting sensor package provided comparable performance to the hardware company's single sensor. The systems company also found a microchip production house that could bring the engineering house's sensors into production. In the end, these three companies working together developed a sensor package whose performance consistently exceeded that of the hardware company's and they went on to win the contract. They identified their competitor's key strength and successfully countered it.

One can also counter a competitor's strength by showing that its benefits are offset by other weaknesses. For example, in 2005 while both Gillette and Schick were pushing multi-blade shavers, Norelco aired a humorous commercial announcing a new product with fifteen blades – the "Quintippio Multi-Shave." In the commercial, a puzzled man looks at it wondering how he is going to shave his face with it. A voiceover says, "Everyone's talking more blades - we're talking less irritation." The spot then describes Norelco's electric shaver, which dispenses Nivea skin cream as a shaving lubricant and moisturizer. The spot ends with the claim "As close as a blade with less irritation." This ad directly attacked Gillette and Schick's, more is better multi-blade obsession, by arguing that Norelco's electric shearer matched them on a close shave, but also reduced chafing.

"Ghosting" is another technique that can be used to attack a competitor's strength. Bringing up ghosts involves igniting discussion of issues that your team does not face, but that the competitor does. It is important when ghosting that you do not mention your competitor by name. You should only attack their approach and characteristics, not the competitor. Criticizing a competitor to a customer diminishes you in their eyes and adds a sense of unpleasantness to the relationship. Ghosts raise doubts about the competitor's approach or capability by seeding fear, doubts and uncertainty in the customer's mind about the competitor's approach. The objective of ghosting is to plant the idea there is a clear difference between you and the competition and that their approach has significant drawbacks. Ghosting allows you to not just sell yourself, but to unsell your competition. Remember, you are doing your customer evaluator a service by identifying the shortcomings of the competitor's approach. You are helping the customer with their due diligence. Then, the evaluator will look for those differences when they review the competitor's proposal. For example, as the incumbent bidding on a contract renewal, you could describe to the customer the value of all your experience. Then, you could ghost all of the competitors by describing what inefficiencies and problems your company has learned to avoid and how lacking your unique experience they would most likely suffer severe delivery problems.

— *Strategy in Action* —

When trying to win a ship development contract, one competitor was proposing a trimaran (ship with three hulls) while the capture team for Company X was proposing a monohull (a single hulled ship). In seeking to win the business, the X's capture team did not attack the competitor directly; they attacked the competitor's approach. In the proposal, they showed an extensive analysis that credited the trimaran with such highly prized customer desires as speed and a large deck area. In this way, the capture team built credibility by acknowledging the competitor's strengths. However, the analysis also showed that Company X's capture team had rejected the trimaran themselves, because the trimaran sized to meet the customer's payload requirements would not fit into any of the customer's existing dock space. The capture team showed a diagram of the customer's port facilities with an overlay of a trimaran trying to fit into the space. The picture clearly showed that a trimaran would not fit. The analysis estimated the costs to modify or acquire new wharfs (even though it was unlikely they could actually do either of these) and they were prohibitive. The analysis demonstrated that the capture team had honestly and logically evaluated an alternate approach and concluded that the competitor's choice would not work.

Most engineers are reluctant to perform this type of analysis because they do not have exact competitor information, and engineers despise inaccuracy. But you do not need to be precise to sell the customer. Customers don't expect you to have perfect information. Trade study results are usually so overwhelmingly convincing that one can afford to make engineering estimates and still produce an accurate conclusion. In the example above, the capture team did not have exact information on the competitor's performance, but they were able to calculate it based on the competitor's published artist drawings and marketing literature. They also gave the competitor's approach the benefit of the doubt when necessary. In that way, when the customer examined the competitor's data they would find it less compelling than the approach the capture team had logically eliminated.

Sometimes, attacking a competitor's strength can backfire, such as when American West charged in ads that Southwest Airlines passengers should be embarrassed to fly on such a no-frills airline. Southwest Chairman Herb Kelleher promptly responded by appearing in a TV spot with a paper bag over his head. He offered the bag to anyone ashamed of flying on Southwest, suggesting they could use it to hold, "all of the money you'll save flying us." Herb Kelleher countered the competitor's assertion and he did it quickly.

One last important point is that your counters must be valid. If you overstate a counter to the competitor's strength you will have a problem. You might not have had all of the information on the competitor's approach, and as a result your claims may be somewhat inaccurate. The customer is likely to forgive you if the customer believes you are acting in good faith. However, if the customer comes to believe that you are raising invalid arguments without good basis, it hurts your credibility with the customer. The customer, then, will wonder what else you are embellishing.

Magnify the Competitor's Weaknesses

— Strategy in Action —

Apple does an entertaining job of highlighting their competitors' weaknesses in their commercials. A cool young guy in jeans and a t-shirt introduces himself, "Hello, I'm a Mac." Another slightly nerdy guy in a suit, says, "Hello, I'm a PC." The Mac guy starts to explain that, "We've got a lot in common these days," and then both say, "We both run Microsoft Office." The PC guy continues, "We share files, it's great - we just get along," and then abruptly stops in mid-sentence. Looking concerned the Mac guy asks, "PC?!?" and pats him on the back. The PC guy starts up again saying, "Hi, I'm a PC," and the Mac guy interrupts him saying that they've already covered that. "Yeah, I had to restart there - you know how that is," says the PC guy. "No - actually I don't," replies the Mac guy. "Oh, what? Macs don't have to ..." and poor PC freezes again. The Mac guy scratches his head, "we had him and we lost him." This ad reminds viewers of the frustration caused by the common system interruptions of a Microsoft-based system.

A capture team should expose, exploit, and magnify the weaknesses of every important competitor. You should never assume that the customer is aware of your competitor's weaknesses. Sometimes, customers don't do all of their homework. A customer might be buying your product for the first time and may not understand all the potential pitfalls inherent in your industry. You perform a service for your customer by exposing the shortcomings of the competition.

— *Strategy in Action* —

A telecommunications company was buying a set of rocket launches for the first time. An American rocket supplier provided the customer with an analysis of the European rocket supplier's launch manifest. The analysis graphically showed the European company's publicly committed launch schedule versus the lead-time and capacity to produce, assemble and service these rockets. Drawings showed that the competitor could not be assembling five rockets at the same time because their assembly building only had four assembly bays. The competitor could not meet all of their promises without canceling current commitments. This information was based on publicly available information, and undermined the competitor's credibility. The information was also greatly appreciated by the customer, who learned a great deal about this new market in the process.

While identifying a competitor's weaknesses can be seen as doing a great service for the customer, you must be careful how you approach the customer with this information. Some customers will readily accept data showing a competitor's flaws or inaccuracies. Others find this "bad-mouthing" offensive. A capture team must understand the customer's culture to know what is considered acceptable competitive behavior and what is not, to avoid offending them. Once this is understood, the capture team can present the comparisons in the most effective way.

For example, if an engine supplier were trying to sell a gasoline engine to a warehousing vehicle manufacturer, they would explain why they rejected a diesel engine. "While the diesel engine provides better fuel economy and longer engine life, we rejected it because diesel operation in warehouses is prohibited in 16 states under current air quality laws." The engine supplier gives the diesel credit for its benefits, but argues that those benefits are outweighed by its faults. No specific competitor was named, and no mud was slung – the engine supplier simply produced facts that would lead the customer to their own conclusion – and to select the supplier's product.

— *Strategy in Action* —

In a competition to design and build a large airport, the selection was down to two design and construction companies: a local company, and a foreign company with extensive airport construction experience. To heighten their competitor's weakness, the foreign company built an "Airport Design Center" just blocks from their customer, the local airport authority. The Airport Design Center included both design staff and a large display center showing the company's airport design heritage. The exhibit included models and pictures of previous projects, as well as airport traffic and structural simulations. The displays highlighted their design build process, which integrated architectural design, engineering design and construction services. The display served to illustrate how their streamlined process with its single point of accountability, and design for construction approach could shorten a schedule, cut costs and most importantly, ensure a high quality of design and construction. The company invited the airport authority, politicians and civic groups to take tours. The intent of this public relations campaign was to impress on all of these people the technical complexity involved in building an airport, and to demonstrate that only their company had the necessary experience to tackle the job. The company also produced a video about their quality control system, which showed how they prevented common construction problems like poor workmanship, management and use of substandard materials. The video also described the resulting budget overruns, late completions, recriminations and political fallout resulting from these problems in other cities. The video was a ghost, pointing to the competitor's lack of experience. The company heightened the competitor's lack of experience by educating the customer about the value that experience brought to this type of project. The entire center acted as a giant ghost, creating fear and doubt in the customer about the competitor's lack of experience.

You can magnify a competitor's weaknesses by getting that item written into the customer's requirements. You want to convince the customer of the importance of requirements that will be impossible or difficult for the competitor to meet. If successful, this can cause the competitors to drop out of the competition altogether or expend a lot of time and money in meeting a requirement.

— *Strategy in Action* —

Two helicopter companies were competing for a VIP fleet sale to a foreign government. The customer had an aggressive desired delivery schedule as well as unique requirements that would result in some development for both competitors. Company A had an older proven aircraft in high volume production that was well-suited for the mission. Company B was proposing a newer, somewhat larger and more costly aircraft. Company B, realizing that they were at a disadvantage, decided to shape the procurement to their favor. Since safety of their VIP's was paramount to the customer, Company B convinced the customer that having their aircraft certified FAA DO-178B would result in a safer aircraft and should be a requirement. DO-178B is a rigorous software development process for assuring the safety of airborne systems. Company B knew that Company A had written their flight management software before the advent of DO-178B. To go back and certify their existing software to DO-178B was going to cost Company A time and money. While the money would not be onerous, the time to certify would make achieving customer's delivery schedule impossible. By getting this requirement inserted into the customer's Request for Tender, Company B became to be the only company which could meet the customer's delivery schedule. With this advantage, Company B went on to win the competition, in spite of having a more expensive offering.

A great way to highlight a competitor's weaknesses is to compare it your strengths. When providing a direct comparison between your offering and the competition's, you must show that it is fair, objective, and perceived to be unbiased.

— *Strategy in Action* —

Working on one assignment, our client claimed that their aircraft had substantially lower maintenance costs than the competitor. Since the client's aircraft was smaller and designed with the latest condition-based maintenance technology, this assertion made sense. However, the competitor's aircraft advertised nearly the same operating maintenance cost per flight hour as our client's. What was strange about the competitor's claim was that their aircraft had three engines to our client's two. Engines are by far the biggest maintenance items on the aircraft. Just to make it more obvious that something funny was going, the competitor's engines were not only the same horsepower as our client's, they were the exact same engine! So, the competitor must have been incurring at least a 50 percent greater engine maintenance costs. There was something seriously wrong with somebody's numbers.

Fortunately for us, a few years earlier the competitor had bid on a contract to a foreign Navy, who published every bidder's proposal after the competition. Because the competitor's proposal was in the public domain, we were able to obtain, translate and analyze a copy of it, which included a detailed breakdown of their maintenance cost per flight hour. By analyzing this data, we found that the competitor was consistently understating their scheduled and unscheduled maintenance hours, repair and spares costs by 33-60 percent. This fallacious data explained why the competitor claimed such low costs.

To counter this, in our proposal we highlighted our lower maintenance costs per hour and how they were achieved. We also discussed that different companies calculated maintenance costs differently and pointed out that to ensure a fair and accurate evaluation one needed to compare the detailed maintenance numbers by component between different proposals and industry benchmarks. Our proposal showed our scheduled and unscheduled maintenance hours, repair and spares costs by component compared with industry benchmarks. We also showed the customer where they could access the industry benchmarks. We made maintenance costs so prominent that the customer could not miss that something was wrong in somebody's numbers. Within the tables we provided with our proposal, we made it very easy for the customer to compare these factors, so they could easily discover that the competitor was intentionally understating their maintenance costs. After reading and analyzing the proposals, the customer adjusted the competitor's proposed costs accordingly and could not help but wonder what else the competitor was not forthcoming about.

The key to the success of this approach was that the capture team provided data that the customer could substantiate. The analysis was completely objective. If a customer perceives a bias in such a situation, they will ignore the study and begin to question other assertions.

Done well, ghosting can be decisive. But it can be a distraction and a big waste of time if it focuses on an issue of little important to the customer.

— *Strategy in Action* —

In one competition to build and service a head of state aircraft for the U.S. government, there was a domestic aircraft manufacturer and a domestic system integrator teamed with a foreign aircraft manufacturer. The system integrator's team was going to propose a variant of a foreign-designed and built aircraft. While the system integrator promised to assemble the aircraft inside the country, many of its parts would be made outside the United States. The domestic company believed that this high foreign content was the competitor's key weakness and decided to base their win strategy around this weakness.

Under United States regulations, every worker who builds or repairs a presidential transport, from limousines to helicopters to aircraft, must have a special clearance. The domestic company argued that a company could not build a product with foreign parts and preserve security, so the domestic manufacturer took on the risk, dumped their global suppliers and pressed the government to eliminate the system integrator from the competition. Meanwhile, the system integrator worked with the government to develop security procedures that allowed them to compete. The domestic manufacturer should have realized that their chances of having the competitor eliminated were small.

The first job of any customer's acquisition personnel is to foster a valid competition. Customers will go to great lengths to qualify suppliers so they can have more than one bidder. If they have only one bidder, they have failed. Nonetheless, the domestic company in the example above persisted with their strategy, including running ads touting their "All-Locally Manufactured" aircraft. Unfortunately for this domestic manufacturer, domestic content was not important to any of the key decision makers. Under the law, a contractor must have 50 percent domestic content and both companies met this threshold. The domestic company spent their resources switching out their suppliers instead of improving the aircraft's communications suite, which was very important to the customer. The domestic company wasted opportunities to send messages to the customer by discussing domestic content rather than focusing on their exceptional safety record and their competitor's high crash rate. The government's key decision makers did not value more domestic content and as a result, the domestic company lost. Strategies do not work if they focus on the wrong things.

Neutralize Your Weaknesses

Everybody has weaknesses. You should always assume that your customer and competitor are competent at finding yours and that your customers will be looking for mitigation of these items, while your competitors will seek to exploit them. To foil the possibility of capitalization by your competitors, your capture team must objectively identify every weakness and bolster it effectively. A charge made against you is a charge believed unless and until you refute it, so you should never ignore or bury weaknesses.

When Apple and its CEO, Steve Jobs, were besieged by criticism that their iPhone 4's antenna caused reception problems, they minimized the problem. In an e-mail, Jobs called users' reception gripes a "non-issue." Apple claimed that the problem was rooted in a software problem that could be easily fixed. It finally took Consumer Reports to bring the problem to a crescendo. The magazine's analysis found that the phone lost reception when held a certain way, running counter to Apple's claims and saying it could not recommend buying the phone. Eventually, Apple admitted their problems and offered a free "bumper" case to iPhone 4 customers, but not until after doing their image some serious damage.

If weaknesses remain unaddressed, the customer will assume the worst. If customers have concerns about you or your solution, these concerns are bound to influence their judgments, and until you remove them, they will remain factors in the competition. Even if the issues are only subconscious concerns, they still hurt your chances of winning. The longer a weakness endures, the more difficult it will be to change your customer's mind about it. The sooner a team acknowledges a weakness and neutralizes it, the better.

The capture team must admit weaknesses to themselves first and then to their customer. Everyone has faults; a key differentiator is how a team deals with them. Defensiveness and contentiousness never sell well, while being open and honest can build trust. To neutralize weaknesses, a capture team must take corrective action and prove to the customer that the team is stronger for it. Once the situation has been corrected, the team will need to provide the customer with substantiation to resolve the issue entirely. Another way to turn a weakness to a strength is to very publicly admit the problem and solve it in an equally visible way.

— *Strategy in Action* —

Performing on a maintenance service contract, one company experienced terrible start-up problems as they tried to stand up a new facility in a war zone. The company, in a rush to get the contract staff, allowed the hiring of unqualified mechanics, and failed to implement effective processes. In addition, the customer was unable to deliver the spare parts required and agree on a consistent acceptance criteria. Without an agreed on acceptance criteria, repaired items would sit accumulating "late" time while the customer and the contractor squabbled about whether the unit was fixed. These problems led to poor documented turnaround times for equipment, late deliveries and missed production targets. The press lambasted the contractor and there were Congressional hearings on the contractor's performance. The contractor worked hard to correct the problems and implemented some very successful six sigma and "lean" production techniques in their repair departments that dramatically improved performance. However, as the company was up to recomplete for the contract, they faced the stigma of their early problems. To overcome this weakness, the company applied for and won a national quality award for their lean production implementation. This quality award turned everyone, including the customer, into heroes and helped the company convert their weakness into a strength.

If you are the first to tell the customer of your weakness, you take control of the story. Admitting that you have a problem establishes credibility that you can then use to define the problem in a way that keeps the damage to a minimum. It allows you to put the problem in context. If you do not take control of the story, the competition will. When New York Mayor Ed Koch suffered a minor stroke and was recovering in the hospital, city council president and longtime political rival Andrew Stein visited the mayor. After the meeting, Stein told reporters that Koch was speaking very slowly. Mayor Koch's communications advisor David Garth knew that this political jab could erode the public's confidence in the mayor's competency. He took control of the story by telling the media, "What people don't understand is that when Ed talks to Andy, he always speaks slowly." This response deflected the issue of Mayor Koch's condition.

As Garth's retort shows, humor is a great way of deflating an attack. In 1984, Ronald Reagan was the oldest President to ever run for reelection. Many Americans were concerned about his ability to withstand the rigors of office for four more years. During the second debate, when asked by the moderator if he saw his age affecting his ability to perform his duties, Reagan replied that "… I will not make age an issue in this campaign. I'm not going to exploit for political purposes my opponent's youth and inexperience." Even Mondale laughed and the issue of Reagan's age disappeared from the campaign.

In another case, a company was trying to sell a large complex system to a customer. Rumors flew about a similar system installation by the company that had gone awry. The company knew that the customer would think the worst about this problem program, so they took the problem program's manager to brief the customer. He explained the current status of the program and went into detail explaining the problems. The company took responsibility for their mistakes and identified how customer changes in requirements and funding had exacerbated all of their problems. They showed that the program was not the nightmare that rumors suggested, but that the company made mistakes and learned from them. They took control of the story and put it into perspective. Customers don't like bad news, but the fact that the company did not try to cover it up did inspire confidence in their integrity.

A team can bring on a teammate or invest funds to overcome weaknesses. For example, on one bid, a bidder's stretched logistics organization concerned the customer and they doubted that the bidder could provide the global support required. To mitigate this weakness, the company brought in a well-regarded teammate to provide the logistics system and budgeted 20 percent more than usual in logistics to ensure that they proposed a well-staffed and stocked product support solution.

Weaknesses can be purely imaginary. Even if a weakness is unreal, a capture team must refute it. Great advertising frequently attacks these imaginary weaknesses. For example, in the early 1960's, Honda found selling motorcycles in the United States to be surprisingly difficult. They conducted an extensive market survey and discovered that few Americans wanted to be associated with motorcycles. The study found that when the public thought of motorcycles, they pictured Marlon Brando and his gang taking over the small town of Wrightsville in the film "The Wild One." Honda decided to directly challenge this image with their cute advertising campaign, "You meet the nicest people on a Honda." This long-running and extensive advertising campaign depicted housewives, a parent and child, young couples, and other respectable members of society riding Hondas for various purposes. This campaign drove a significant sales increase in all demographic groups and an overall 500 percent increase in motorcycles registrations over the next ten years.

— *Strategy in Action* —

For the AAF program, risk was one of the most important customer values. Huge Aircraft Corporation was proposing an open systems architecture that allowed the use of commercial off-the-shelf components. Integrating a group of commercial off-the-shelf products had significantly less risk than developing a completely proprietary system. In order to neutralize this discriminator, Goliath decided to develop their own open system architecture. But the greatest risk issue for Goliath's team was their lift fan system. The lift fan was located in the center of the aircraft and pushed their aircraft up into the sky. The lift fan was connected to the engine by a drive shaft rotating at thousands of revolutions per second. Engaging the clutch to the rotating shaft was a tough technical problem, unlike anything attempted before. To mitigate its risks, some of Goliath's tactics included (Exhibit 4-5):

- Establishing a world-class transmission team of the top suppliers from around the world to design the clutch
- Testing the propulsion system's clutch to more than double the operating time and 10,000 engagements
- Flying their prototype from a vertical take off and then taking the

aircraft supersonic showed the maturity of their solution

Implementing these tactics helped Goliath retire significant risk on their pursuit. By reducing the solution's risk, they convinced the customer that the lift fan system would work and provide an aircraft with superior performance.

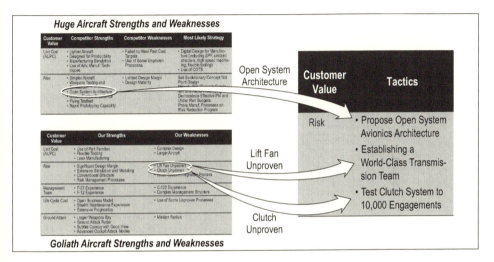

Exhibit 4-5: Tactics to Counter Weaknesses

Summary

Winning is about positioning. To position yourself, you need to know where you stand. By assessing your strengths and weaknesses versus the competition, you gain an understanding of how you stack up on what's important to the customer. Then you can start to identify actions to improve your position. Shaping the procurement is one of the most powerful techniques in winning. After identifying your strengths and weaknesses vis-a-vis the competition, you should work to convince the customer to value your strengths and require your unique capabilities. If you shape well, you usually win.

As you brainstorm tactics to enhance your strengths and mitigate your weaknesses, it is critical that you focus on the most important issues. Which issues are going to decide the competition? *It is important to be bold early.* Early is when you have the time and resources to be innovative and to substantially change your position. Time can allow you to develop a decisive edge. Take advantage of it.

Next, you have to assess your competitive position and started to enhance it. The next chapter will describe how to turn your position into a winning one by developing an effective win strategy.

Chapter 5: Crafting the Win Strategy

"Nothing is more difficult than the art of maneuvering for advantageous positions."

— Sun Tzu, Renowned Chinese General and Military Strategist

Our process sifts through all of the customer needs and builds a strategy around the most important ones – the customer values. In Chapter 3 we described how to determine those customer values. In the past chapter, we showed how to synthesize key information about the customer, competitors and your own company to create an objective assessment of the pursuit. Then, we began to identify the actions needed to build a win strategy. In this chapter, we'll consider steps nine through twelve of the win strategy formulation process. This chapter will describe how to test the effectiveness of a strategy – how to know if it is going to be a winner. Then, we will articulate the win strategy – creating the simple statement that answers the question, "Why should the customer choose us?" This win strategy should, in total, be more attractive to the customer than that of the competitors. In addition, this chapter will explain how to detail and substantiate your strategy to make it more persuasive.

Continuing with the win strategy formulation process:

Step 9: Evaluate Relative Competitor Positions

One fundamental challenge facing every capture team lies in knowing whether or not their strategy is any good. To address this challenge, we will quantify the relative positions of the competitors on the customer values. This analysis allows us to quantitatively assess whether our tactics will improve our competitive position sufficiently to defeat the competition.

After you have identified tactics to improve your position for each customer value, you can determine your overall relative competitive position. Whether or not you are going to win depends on how your offering stacks up to the competition on the customer values. You must assess your relative position for each customer value. For the competition, you must only focus on where they will be at the end – the final proposal evaluation. However, for your position, there are two relevant times – where you are now and where you can be. The first point of interest is this: how does your offering stack up right now, to where the competitor will be in the end game? The second point is: where will your team will be at the final customer evaluation, if you implement your proposal strategies and plans? These two views allow you to weigh the impact of implementing your tactics as well as the impact of choosing not to implement them. Therefore, for each customer value, you will assess your competitor's position at the final proposal evaluation and your own position at two points – now, and at final proposal evaluation.

For each customer value, we recommend that you have a competitive analyst rate the various offerings. If you lack a competitive analyst, assign someone who is knowledgeable and independent of the capture team. It is important to weigh evidence when making this assessment. The analyst examines each competitor's strengths, weakness and their most likely tactics for each customer value. They then rate each offering on a scale of one to ten. This rating reflects the customer's likely satisfaction with an offering. A "one" would be considered unsatisfactory, "three" is marginal, "five" is satisfactory, and so on. This assessment (see Exhibit 5-1) attempts to foresee how attractive each competitive offer will be to the customer at final proposal evaluation.

The next step is to rate the capture team's offering relative to the competitor for the same customer value. The analyst should assess their team's current position relative to the competitor's expected position at proposal evaluation, as if the capture team chose to implement none of the tactics proposed during the strategy development process. This assessment baselines the company's current position and gives the team and their executives a reference point for comparing your position if no further actions are taken to improve your position. You score your offering relative to the competition. Will your offering be viewed more or less favorably versus the competition on each value from the customer's perspective? If there is a difference, the competitive analyst should estimate the magnitude of the difference based on how much more or less satisfied the customer will be with your offering versus the competition.

Next, the competitive analyst assesses your team's likely position at proposal evaluation relative to the competitor's if they implement all of the current plans and tactics identified in Step 8. This allows the team to compare their final likely position if they implement their proposed tactics versus their position if they don't. This allows your team to quantify the impact of implementing your tactics on each customer value. This analysis can justify the cost of implementing those tactics. Also, if the company chooses not to improve their position, the executives can see what the resulting impact will likely be on their customer values.

— *Strategy in Action* —

Two years before the proposal submission, Huge Aircraft still had many outstanding risk issues, including proving their ability to make range. But the capture team of Goliath projected that Huge would resolve most of these issues with their flight test program. Regardless of improvements that they might make, their offering was inherently riskier than Goliath's, since their aircraft had a small design margin. If the aircraft came in over its projected weight, as almost all aircraft do when they transition from design to production, it could potentially fail to meet the critical range requirement. As a result, the analyst projected Huge's score with this one risk item to be a six, or slightly better than satisfactory. In the meantime, Goliath was still carrying a lot of risk in their solution, but was planning a large number of actions, including demonstrations, ground tests and extensive flight tests to lower their risk. The competitive analyst thought that with all of these actions, Goliath could move their risk rating from a satisfactory (5) to a very good (8).

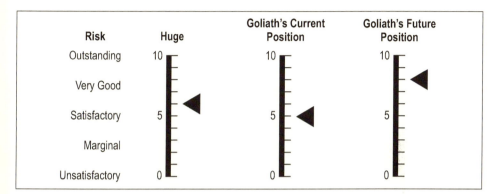

Exhibit 5-1: Evaluate Relative Competitive Positions for Each Customer Value

This process measures the relative gaps for each competitor for each customer value, and communicates to management how well you are currently positioned relative to the competition if you do nothing and also how well you'll be positioned if you implement your current plans. This allows the team to assess whether it is worth it to undertake the tactics you brainstormed in the strategy session. If management is reluctant to invest more in the pursuit, this information can overcome their complacency. This process clearly illustrates the value of making investments to improve your position.

If there is a large gap for one customer value, hopefully this process will spur the team into dreaming up innovative approaches to close it. Even though you have made trade-offs and identified the customer values for which you will be superior to the competitor, it is essential to work to close all relative gaps on all of the customer values where you are behind. Leaving a wide gap between your team and the competitor puts you in peril. With some effort, you can usually close the gap. This was Microsoft's strategy in the 1980s when the Macintosh operating environment was significantly more user-friendly than Microsoft's DOS. When Microsoft released Windows, it attempted to mimic many of the features of the Macintosh's graphical user interface. While Windows' features did not close the user friendliness gap, they did significantly reduce it, thus eroding one of Mac's key discriminators.

— Strategy in Action —

A good strategy works all the angles as demonstrated on the 2008 KC-135 Tanker Replacement program. The KC-135 Tanker Replacement program looked like an easy win for Boeing, who had produced every aerial refueling tanker for the U.S. Air Force in the last 50 years. Boeing had a prototype KC-767 built for the Air Force and had already made sales to Italy and Japan. The company enjoyed very close relationships with the refueling and the airlift communities in the Air Force, as well with their buying command. Most importantly, the Air Force designed the procurement – the funding, schedule and requirements, based on Boeing's KC-767 offering. Northrop Grumman had no tanker experience. Their teammate was EADS, a European aerospace company that was very unpopular with the "Buy American" crowd. While EADS had built a few tankers before, they had never developed and flown the critical refueling boom – the fuel pipe with wings that sticks out of the back of the plane.

Northrop knew that defeating this incumbent would be difficult, so they worked to neutralized Boeing's advantages. Northrop proposed a 23 percent larger tanker than their Boeing competitor, which allowed them to carry significantly more fuel and cargo. Unfortunately, since the acquisition was designed around the capabilities of Boeing's 767, Northrop's greater capability would receive little credit in the evaluation. Since it was larger, their tanker was inherently more expensive. Northrop's capture team quantified their advantages and showed the Air Force that their larger A330 aircraft could retire dozens more aircraft than the same number of KC-767s. Earlier retirement of the KC-135s would save the Air Force billions of dollars. Northrop suggested to the Air Force that they should include an assessment of the number of equivalent tankers it took to perform a set of missions. They argued that it could be easily and accurately modeled. The Air Force concluded that this made good sense and included just such a factor in the RFP.

Northrop leveraged EADS's Australian tanker design to the greatest extent possible to minimize their aircraft development and create a low risk schedule. Both Northrop and EADS worked with their customers to ensure an exemplary past performance record. They established an early Price-to-Win target and drove down their costs to ensure that they had an affordable offering, which was close in cost to Boeing's.

In the end, public documents showed that the Northrop Grumman – EADS team outscored Boeing on four of the five evaluation factors: Mission Capability, Past Performance, Aerial Refueling Factor and Cost/Price while tying with them in Proposal Risk. When Northrop won, Loren B. Thompson, a well-known defense industry analyst said, "This isn't an upset, it's an earthquake." Boeing was defeated by a superior strategy, which outscored them across the board

Step 10: Articulate the Win Strategy

You may have different options about how to solve a customer's problem, such as modifying an existing product or proposing one that is under development. In competitions, companies are required to make trade-offs between customer values. Achieving outstanding performance in one customer value usually creates conflict with another. For example, when buying a car, fast acceleration requires lots of horsepower, which results in lower fuel economy. Few companies can ever be both high performance and low cost. You evaluate your options against the customer value scoring to choose the best approach. Rate the best tactics for each option and compare them to the competition to see how much each will close the gap between you. Document your assessment of your selected options – then look for the opportunity to share your analysis with your customer. The more options you identify, the more flexibility you will have to trade one approach for another. This helps to ensure that you are selecting the optimum solution and demonstrates to the customer that you have done your homework to select the best solutions for them. If you discover that your options won't guarantee victory, then it's time to go back to the prior step and look for new approaches that will provide a unique way to meet the customer's real need. Undertaking and collecting all of this analysis not only ensures you are providing the best solution, but provides the database to present to the customer that will justify your offering and in some cases, ghost the competition.

The mind is the ultimate marketing battleground. The human mind has evolved over millions of years, and it did not survive through conceptual and abstract thought alone. It evolved making simple decisions. "See lion, climb tree." The mind likes clarity and abhors confusion. That is why a capture team needs to clearly articulate to the customer the values on which they intend to exceed their competition. If you cannot reduce your arguments into a few crisp words and phrases, there's something wrong with the argument. The more complex the decision, the harder it is to build consensus, and the more powerful a simple answer becomes. A win strategy is a clear answer to the question, "why us?" A win strategy is not a win theme. It states on what basis your team intends to win the job. This strategy describes around which customer values your team intends to provide greater benefits to the customer than your competition. This strategy then guides the team in how to design their offering to influence the customer. A win theme, as we will discuss further in the chapter, is a declarative statement describing how our features provide benefits to the customer.

You're constantly communicating to the customer how you intend to win their business. Just as important as that communication is the communication with your own team. Capture teams are typically working hundreds of action items and it is difficult to align them without a clear strategy. Developing and communicating a persuasive win strategy is the key to ensuring that your team understands how you intend to differentiate yourself so they can clearly communicate that message to the customer. To develop this simple statement, the capture team quantifies their position relative to that of the competitors' for each customer value.

The key to developing an effective win strategy is to decide which customer's needs to focus on. Where can you outperform the competition? There are many customer needs, but only a few are decisive. Our win strategy process helps you identify the critical few – the customer values as shown in Exhibit 5-2. Then, to develop your strategy, you need to determine for which of these customer values your offering will outperform competition's. We call those the winning customer values. ***The choice of which customer values to select is the essence of strategy, and what you choose makes or breaks your pursuit. From these "winning customer values," one crafts a win strategy.***

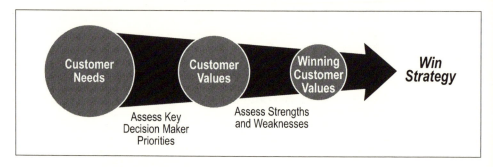

Exhibit 5-2: Which Customer Values Will We Win On?

To assess the validity of your strategy, you must quantify its relative worth to the key decision makers. To do this, multiply the customer value weight times the ratings given to each competitor, the capture team's current position, and the capture team's future position. Then, add up and average these numbers to create a "total score," as shown in Exhibit 5-3. This total score quantifies the relative overall desirability of each competitor's offering to the key decision makers. If your future total score is higher than the competition's, you have a winner. If not, you have more work to do. This analysis validates whether or not your company can achieve a winning position.

Customer Value	Weight	Huge Final	Current Goliath	Future Goliath
Unit Cost (AUPC)	24%	8	5	8
Risk	21%	6	5	8
Management Team	11%	9	5	8
Life Cycle Cost	11%	6	4	5
Ground Attack	8%	6	7	8
Total Score		7.1	5.1	7.6

Exhibit 5-3: Evaluate Relative Positions on Customer Values

— *Strategy in Action* —

In this case, the analysis shows that Goliath will lose if they do not improve their position. However, the analysis also shows that Goliath could overtake Huge if they successfully implement their identified tactics. Quantitatively, Goliath would have a 7 percent advantage over Huge (7.6/7.1). While not large, it is significant and indicates a winning position.

As shown in Exhibit 5-4, you can then identify those customer values on which your team plans to outscore the competition. These are your "winning values."

In the case below, Goliath's winning customer values are "Risk" and "Ground Attack" performance. Once you have selected the values on which you will win, craft a simple statement using your "winning values" to articulate a "why us" statement. It is important to note that integral to Goliath's strategy was to be equal to Huge on cost; since this is the customer's most important value and the thrust of Huge's strategy. That said, the simple win strategy for Goliath became, "provide the lowest risk solution with the best ground attack at the same cost." This is a simple statement that clearly describes how the team intends to win. This statement articulates your win strategy.

Customer Value	Weight	Huge Final	Current Goliath	Future Goliath
Unit Cost (AUPC)	24%	8	5	8
Risk	21%	6	5	8
Management Team	11%	9	5	8
Life Cycle Cost	11%	6	4	5
Ground Attack	8%	6	7	8
Total Score		7.1	5.1	7.6

Winning Customer Values

Exhibit 5-4: Determine on Which Customer Values You Will Win

After developing your win strategy statement, you'll still need to ask yourself two simple questions: Is this statement compelling? And, if your capture team makes this statement true, will you win? If the answer is "yes," the company's executives will have to decide if this opportunity is worth the cost to implement all the tactics needed to make the win strategy true. If the answer is no, then your team should reconsider the strategy and look to adding new tactics to significantly change your relative position. For example, we were working a job where the scoring gave the capture team a small advantage with their strategy, but when we asked the team if they felt they would win if they made the win strategy true, they said "no." The team intuitively believed their strategy was not compelling enough to win. In this case, the competitor was likely to bid a lower price. The team believed that even with their advantages, the customer would not pay a price premium for their solution. As a result, the team adjusted their strategy to become the lowest priced offering in addition to maintaining their other advantages. This change gave the capture team the confidence that they would win. This process does not replace judgment; it supplements it.

Strategy assessment is crucial. While this process may seem subjective, it should not be if you stay focused on facts, conclusions and judgments rather than opinions or feelings. This process provides traceability from facts, conclusions, and assumptions that lead to a score for your strategy. This score focuses your team on identifying the critical assumptions and conclusions which help you assess your confidence in your work. Identifying those critical assumptions can then guide further competitive intelligence collection, which improves your knowledge base. You will never have perfect information, but this process goes a long way to improve what you do have. It helps select and validate a winning approach. Without this process, capture teams lack a way to assess the effectiveness of their win strategy until the award announcement, and then it is too late.

A company needs to assess how well their strategy is being implemented or they may get an unpleasant surprise as demonstrated by the following example:

Customer Value	Weight	Huge Final	Current Goliath	Future Goliath
Unit Cost (AUPC)	24%	8	5	8
Risk	21%	6	5	8
Management Team	11%	9	5	8
Life Cycle Cost	11%	6	4	5
Ground Attack	8%	6	7	8
Total Score		7.1	5.1	7.6

Winning Customer Values
(Why Us!)

> *"Goliath's Fighter is the lowest risk solution with the best ground attack at the same cost."*

Exhibit 5-5: Articulate Your Win Strategy Based the Winning Customer Values

— *Strategy in Action* —

Boeing's victory on the 2008 KC-135 Tanker Replacement program was considered so certain in this competition that prior to the award announcement many Wall Street analysts did something they rarely do, they factored the contract into their economic forecasts for the company.

Boeing's strategy was to be the low risk and low cost solution. They failed miserably to follow their strategy. Boeing had a prototype aircraft, but it was based on a 767-200, which could not carry as much gas as the KC-135 and therefore would be marginally compliant at best. A larger 767-400 could carry much more gas but at a significantly higher price. They decided to cobble together a new configuration, nicknamed the "Frankentanker," with a 767-200 airframe, -300F wings, and -400ER tail, which the Air Force believed added time to their schedule and considerable risk to the program. Their competitive analysis was flawed. Boeing thought the A330 had a much higher fuel burn and higher maintenance costs than the KC-767, which lulled them into thinking that they had a substantial cost advantage in total life cycle costs, where none existed. As a result, they did not bid as aggressively as Northrop. Boeing lost because they undercut their own win strategy. Their Frankentanker was not low risk or low cost. Boeing failed to accurately assess how their strategy implementation was going to be evaluated.

However, the 2008 tanker saga took another turn after Northrop won. Boeing then began the most contentious and relentless protest in American history. They instituted a massive and unprecedented legal, public relations and lobbying campaign to overturn the decision. Boeing's pressure worked and the Government Accountability Office (GAO) sustained Boeing's protest. Boeing put so much political pressure on the Department of Defense that their leadership mandated a new source selection be conducted which was "protest proof." The Air Force did this by removing any evaluation criteria Boeing had protested or any opportunity for the Air Force to apply judgment in the source selection decision. As a result, the factors where Northrop Grumman outperformed Boeing were slashed – past performance, program risk, program schedule, cargo capacity, and extra fuel carry. The award criteria were based almost exclusively on cost. And since Boeing's aircraft was 23 percent smaller, and inherently less costly, the outcome was not in doubt. Northrop Grumman believed they could not win this new competition and elected not to bid.

Step 11: Estimate, Assess and Prioritize Tactics

A campaign is a balance of ends and means. The capture team might have the best strategy, but unless they have the means to implement it, it is worthless, so after selecting a strategy, you will need to re-evaluate your current plans and the tactics that resulted from the brainstorming session. Your action plans must be evaluated based on the cost, time and resources to implement them, as part of creating the capture budget. Some tactics may not be worth the cost, or you may not have sufficient time to implement them. Once the costs are totaled and tactics are prioritized, the team should drop tactics that are too expensive to implement for the value they provide. When this analysis is done, update your customer value scoring. Then take this plan to your executives for approval. The executives can then assess their confidence in your strategy and your relative competitive position. Finally, they can apply their judgment about whether the company should allocate the resources demanded to implement your proposed strategy with its accompanying tactics.

Once the strategy is selected, a capture team must stick with it, even when it gets hard. Not staying consistent with the chosen win strategy undermines your "why us" statement and is a quick way to ensure a loss.

— *Strategy in Action* —

When working on a pursuit to sell a radar system to the U.S. Air Force, Company X had an existing system successfully operating in Australia. Their competitor was a small lean company who provided the Air Force's existing system. The Air Force required a new solution with much more sophisticated processing than the existing program, which would be a technical challenge for the smaller company. The customer was also struggling with a rash of problem-plagued development programs including the incumbent's program. As a result, the Air Force was looking for a low risk solution. Company X's strategy was simple – leverage their proven Australian solution to provide the lowest risk offering. However, their chief engineer had other ideas, much better ideas in his mind. Just after the pursue decision, he convinced the capture team leader to swap out the Australian antenna design for a smaller one using newer technology. A few months later it became clear that Company X had a problem with their tuners, which were the core of the system. The Australian solution's tuners would not quite meet the Air Force's requirements. So, instead of trying to convince the Air Force to relax the requirements or just upgrade the tuners, the chief engineer convinced the team to replace the tuners with a new architecture. Months later, when Company X stood up its proposal team, the recently assigned proposal manager expressed surprise. "What happened to the Australian solution? The Air Force loved it!" The capture team had forgotten their strategy and they went on to lose the pursuit, and lose it badly at that. The lesson is clear: get everybody on board with your strategy and stick with it.

You need to identify any cases where your tactics for one customer value conflict with your win strategy. Capture teams face many trade-offs and the win strategy should guide the selection of which tactics to employ. A capture team can make a few small compromises, but they must be made sparingly so that the company continues to "win" the customer values they have chosen. For example, in the above case, the prime probably would probably have been successful if they just swapped out the antenna, because it was not that much of a leap in technology, and it did not add much risk. But changing the tuner architecture negated the assertion that they were reusing the Australian solution, and the new architecture was unproven and not low risk. As a result of their actions, the prime's new de facto strategy was now to offer the most capable system at a higher price. This was a bad strategy for this customer. As this example shows, changing your strategy mid pursuit is rarely a good idea.

After completing this step, the goal is to have a win strategy that you believe will be compelling to the customer. You have confidence that your win strategy will succeed. You have identified the tactics you need to implement the strategy and successfully resourced them. If not, then you need to consider changing the rules of the game.

Changing the Rules of the Game

More than once after leading a capture team through this assessment, the situation looked bleak – the competitor was just too formidable. In these cases, we recommend the team either drop the pursuit or change the game.

Changing the game means influencing the customer to reshape the acquisition in your favor. A capture team can seek to change the customer's acquisition strategy, requirements, funding, decision-making process, or key decision makers. To change the game, you need three things. First, you need good intelligence, especially about the customer's decision-making process and their needs and priorities. Second, you need a compelling customer benefit for changing the acquisition. Third, you need time. It takes time to influence the customer and it takes time for the customer to change the acquisition.

— *Strategy in Action* —

In a satellite competition, one company (Competitor A) had developed an advanced sensor, and the customer wanted the performance that it offered. No one else had a comparable sensor and this was so important to the satellite's mission that this company was surely going to win. One competitor – we'll refer to them as Competitor B – went to the customer and convinced them that with their current acquisition plan, only Competitor A could win. As a result, they suggested, Competitor A would price gouge the customer. Competitor B suggested that the customer buy the sensor sole source, run the competition for the satellite minus the sensor, and then provide the satellite manufacturer with the sensor for them to integrate. The customer agreed. A disappointed Competitor A received a sole source contract for the sensor, but ended up losing the satellite since they were complacent and their sensor was just about their only significant discriminator. Competitor B could not win initially, so they changed the rules of the game and won. Competitor B understood the competition and most importantly, they understood that their customer wanted to ensure a good deal for the taxpayers.

In the above example, shaping the acquisition was decisive in determining the winner. The key to changing the game is to clearly identify all of your strengths and all of the problems facing the customer. Then, envision how you can help solve their problems with your strengths. Remember that the best way to obtain the contract may be to avoid a competition altogether and to have the customer award you a sole source award.

Changing the rules of the game can be a difficult endeavor. It usually takes a well-orchestrated and implemented capture plan to be successful. However, changing the rules can be one of the most satisfying ways to win, and removing competitive pressures is usually good for a company's profit margins, as the following example illustrates:

— *Strategy in Action* —

A competition was formed to remove and replace the wings of a fleet of U.S. Air Force training aircraft. A recent change in the training program had significantly increased operating stress on the planes and the fleet was rapidly running out of useable safe flying hours in their wings. Wings, like other structural components, are designed with a certain amount of flying hours after which they must be replaced or the aircraft grounded. New wings would extend the trainer's operational life for another 15 years. If any aircraft reached their flight safety limit prior to rewinging, the Air Force would be forced to ground that aircraft.

Three companies were vying for this rewinging contract. One of the competitors was the trainer's OEM. It was their analysis of the trainers' operating tempo that originally alerted the Air Force to the accelerated loss of safe flying hours. As it became apparent that there was going to be a competition, the OEM analyzed the customer's past buying behavior and determined that the Air Force would select the lowest priced provider to rewing the aircraft. Unfortunately, their competitive analysis also found that one of their competitors was a small lean aerostructures modifier that lacked the large engineering staff of the OEM and its accompanying overhead cost. In addition, this company had inexpensive facilities and a non-unionized workforce that resulted in their manufacturing cost per hour being 45 percent lower than the OEM's. Another competitor was an airframe manufacturer with extensive engineering capabilities and sophisticated automated manufacturing facilities. For one of their ongoing aircraft production programs, they had invested in automated drilling machines, which eliminated significant labor for hand drilling and countersinking operations. This technology could be applied to the rewing program and significantly reduce assembly costs. In addition, this manufacturer had an extensive manufacturing and design engineering staff that could handle any of the Air Force's technical needs. The OEM's capture team realized that if this competition were a "price shootout," both of these competitors would handily defeat them.

During a strategy session, we realized that we could not win a price competition, so we decided to shape the acquisition. The OEM had a few unique strengths – they knew the aircraft's design, use and manufacturing processes better than anyone, including the Air Force. The capture team leader had their operations analyst review the trainer's flight data. He found that the Air Force had underestimated the operational tempo and that their need for the wings was more urgent than they thought. The Air Force's current acquisition schedule would not keep their pilots from exhausting the fleet's safe flying hours before the rewinging program could supply new wings. The Air Force didn't know it yet, but they had to accelerate their schedule.

While the Air Force owned the trainer's tooling, the OEM physically possessed it and knew all of its shortcomings. In addition, the OEM possessed the trainer's wing assembly sequence. The assembly sequence defined the order in which the wing fasteners were installed to apply the optimum stress in the wing. Developing the proper assembly sequence was a costly and time consuming process requiring extensive stress analysis as well as "trial and error" on the shop floor. The OEM's capture team decided that the only way they could win was to forgo a competition and have the Air Force award them a sole source contract. To achieve this, the capture team had to convince the customer of the true schedule urgency while simultaneously making the case that only the OEM could meet that accelerated schedule. Importantly, a unique ability to meet a schedule is one of the seven reasons the U.S. Government can use to justify a sole source award.

The OEM's engineering staff worked with the Air Force operations analysts to assess the current and projected fleet flying schedule. This analysis concluded that the Air Force must accelerate their schedule. Also, the OEM's team began to present white papers to the Air Force program office showing the time and money required to relocate and "debug" the tooling plus develop the assembly sequence plans. The OEM convinced the Air Force that only they could meet the accelerated schedule because all of the other competitors had to reinvent the assembly sequence. As a result of these actions, the Air Force gave the OEM a sole source award for an interim production lot of wings worth $35 million. However, the Air Force would still compete the full rate production contract, so the OEM used this interim production lot to position themselves to win the follow-on production lots. They invested in and proved out automated drilling machines for the wings that would dramatically cut their bid price. As a result of their actions, the OEM won the subsequent $620 million contract.

The example above illustrates that for the OEM to "change the game," they had to leverage their discriminators. They used their unique manufacturing process to create a schedule advantage. In addition, they used their operations analyst group and their unique knowledge of the trainer's operating tempo to turn this discriminator into a decisive advantage. The OEM took a losing situation and implemented an effective capture effort to win an enormous contract.

There is one more important point to make on this topic, however: if you are not competitive and are unable to change the game, you should no bid.

Step 12: Create Win Themes

To successfully sell a solution, you have to communicate its benefits. But as sales and solutions get bigger and more complex, it becomes more difficult to clearly communicate "why us" to the customer. As we discussed earlier, even the most intelligent mind struggles with complexity, so sales messages should be simple in order to maximize their effectiveness. The mind is attracted to simplicity – simple is beautiful; simple is easy to remember. The last step in the strategy development process is to create these simple messages – your win themes. You must develop and repeat simple win themes throughout the campaign to sell your strategy. Win themes are the statements that sell your strategy and prove the value of your benefits. A win theme should be so simple and clear that anyone can understand it quickly without having to think about what it means.

Win themes can be defined as the conclusive reasons why the customer should select your company over the competition. The goal of a win theme is to create a compelling message that resonates with the customer – a message that says your solution satisfies a crucial need. If you joined your key decision maker in the first floor elevator and were going to the twentieth, you should be able to communicate to him or her one of your win themes in that brief amount of time. Incidentally, if you did have this opportunity, you should pick your best win theme – the one that addresses his or her highest priority customer value.

Win themes help organize customer messages and simplify the proposal by providing a few central benefits. *Permeate your sales campaign with win themes, including them in your presentations, white papers, briefings, advertising and, ultimately, your proposal.* You want the customer to hear these themes enough times that they associate your win themes with your solution. As a result, the customer will remember the simple reasons to select your solution. One note of caution, it is also important to protect some discriminators from disclosure to the competition, and this issue will be discussed in Chapter 8.

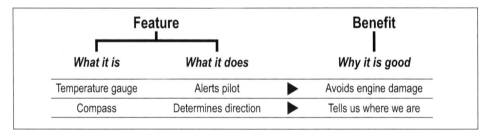

Exhibit 5-6: Win Themes Have Features, Proof and Benefits

The win theme should be focused on a customer value or one of its elements, thereby reinforcing its importance. *A good win theme has a feature, proof and a benefit.* As touched upon in the previous chapter, a common mistake is to confuse features and benefits. A feature is *what the product is or what it does* as shown in Exhibit 5-6. A feature is an attribute or characteristic of the product that provides a benefit. People don't buy what something is; they buy what it does for them. Benefits are why people buy a product. Benefits are what the buyer gains from the features. Benefits are things like lower cost, lower risk, better reliability, faster delivery, or improved performance. Benefits motivate people to buy, but features prove that the benefits are true. For example, the Porsche 996 Turbo's twin turbocharged 3.6-liter engine is the feature that produces a benefit to the customer of a zero to sixty sprint time in just 4.2 seconds. Customers desire fast acceleration – that is the benefit. The finely crafted 3.6-liter engine is merely the feature which helps achieve the benefit. Another example: look at how Siemens sells MRI machines, by not selling MRI machines. They sell *"a faster and more accurate diagnosis of serious health problems."* Siemens sells benefits, and so must you.

Too often, engineers or proposal writers assume that a benefit is self-evident to their customer. Never make that assumption. You must identify benefits for customers and show them how they solve a particular concern.

— Strategy in Action —

For example, when Boeing was chasing NASA's Consolidated Space Operations Contract, one of their press releases was indicative of their poor sales messaging. A Boeing Vice President stated: "Boeing has combined its traditional strengths – detailed customer knowledge, space operations expertise, large-scale systems integration and lean, efficient production systems – with the commercial savvy of these world-class, strategically aligned companies renowned for their leadership, innovation and commercial focus." This run-on sentence listed lots of features. However, nowhere in this sales message did Boeing state any benefits of these features to the customer. This was a prevalent problem for Boeing on this campaign. After Boeing lost this $2 billion opportunity, a well informed industry analyst told us that one of the key reasons Boeing had lost was that they never tied their "best commercial practices" to any tangible benefits, such as cost savings to the customer.

Developing Proof of Benefits

Every win theme should have a proof to show that what you are saying is true. Proposed concepts without supporting details and data will lack credibility, despite any technical merits. People have to believe it to buy it. Proposal evaluators need quantifiable proofs that verify claims and differentiate a solution from the competitors. They need data to justify their selection.

We often see proofs missing from ads, white papers and proposals. Without proof, a win theme is just an unsubstantiated claim. Providing some form of proof for each benefit is critical to selling. For example, "The Blue Fish Café offers the best food in Long Beach," is an unsubstantiated claim, while "The Blue Fish Café has won the Long Beach Herald's Critics Choice for Best Seafood two years running," has proof and is persuasive. The proof you include in your proposal gives the decision makers the rationale they can use to convince their stakeholders that they made the right decision in selecting you.

For example, some meaningful win themes follow. Each has a feature, a proof and a benefit to the customer:

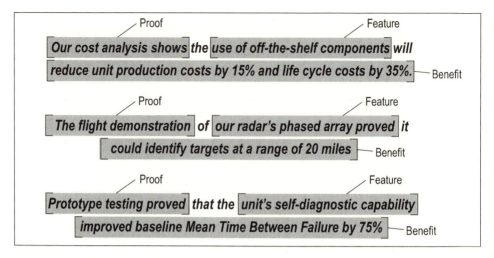

Exhibit 5-7: A Good Win Theme Has a Feature, Proof and Benefit

The ultimate test of a win theme is this: after you read it, ask yourself if the customer will say "so what?" Is your win theme meaningful to the customer? If not, try again! The most powerful win themes are those that describe your discriminators and have been vetted with the customer in advance. These selling points must be true for you and not be true for at least one of your competitors. Once again, competitive intelligence is important. When you claim to have a unique approach and but do not, you lose credibility.

To make win themes more powerful and persuasive, you add specifics. The surest way to arouse and hold the attention of the reader is to be specific, definite and concrete. Be exact and precise whenever possible. Precision makes what is said more believable. Be specific, and it's likely that you'll find that your products or services will appear more interesting and desirable. Customers look for details to confirm that an approach is proven and that you are prepared to do the job. For example, Crest did not say, "many dentists recommend Crest," they said, "four out of five dentists recommend Crest."

As we add more details, our statements become more persuasive:

> "Our past construction projects had dependable schedules," Or,

> "Our past 15 construction projects had dependable schedules and were all completed on-time, ensuring an on-time completion for your job." Or,

> "Our past 15 construction projects met 98 percent of the schedule milestones and were all completed on-time, ensuring an on-time completion for your job."

Start developing win themes for each customer value. Identify the features for each customer value, describe its benefits and the way you will prove that the benefits are true, as shown in the construction project on Exhibit 5-8. In this example, the capture team documented a set of features that will help the company ensure an on-time project completion. Next, they identified each feature's benefit to the customer. Finally, they brainstormed how to prove that each claim was true.

As we have discussed, in some cases the customer values do not align with the evaluation criteria. After developing win themes for each customer value, develop win themes for each likely proposal evaluation criteria. This process will help your team refine other important sales messages and drive the capture team to develop proof of benefits for the proposal evaluation. These win themes will help sell the benefits of features to maximize your proposal evaluation score. Since the customer values are the most important concerns to the customer, you will organize your proposal's executive summary around the customer values and then provide the win themes from the proposal evaluation.

The construction company in our example has three discriminators for each customer value. As shown below, once the feature, proof and benefit are identified, it is easy to put together a powerful win theme.

Customer Value	Feature	Benefit	Proof	Win Theme
On-Time Completion	Modular Construction	Eliminated low volume parts with poor delivery performance, improving our ability to meet schedule	Computer Aided Design (CAD) system reports 1,500 fewer unique parts	Our CAD system showed that our modular construction approach slashed 1,500 low volume parts with poor delivery performance from your project, enhancing our ability to make your schedule
	Design-Build Process	28% reduction in unscheduled rework, improving our ability to meet schedule	Based on Burnwell project results	Using our new Design-Build Process on the Burnwell project cut unscheduled rework by 28%, improving our ability to meet your schedule
	Integrated Schedule Planning System	93% of materials received on-time, improving our ability to meet schedule	Data from two most recent projects	Data from two projects showed that using our integrated schedule planning system resulted in 93% of our materials being received on-time, helping to ensure on-time completion
Construction Quality	Craftsman Training and Apprentice Program	Reduced workmanship defects by 65%, improving construction quality	Workmanship audits over last three years	Workmanship audits over the last three years showed that our Craftsman Training and Apprentice Program reduced workmanship defects by 65%, improving overall project quality
	Design-Build Process	28% reduction in unscheduled rework, improving construction quality	Based on Burnwell project results	Using our new Design-Build Process on the Burnwell project cut unscheduled rework by 28%, improving our construction quality
	Vendor Quality Rating System	Reduced material defects by 43%, improving construction quality	Receiving inspection reports	We have improved construction quality by reducing incoming material defects by 43% using our Vendor Quality Rating System, as shown by our inspection reports

Exhibit 5-8: Features and Benefits Matched to Customer Values

The key to selling resides in making the customer believe that the features of your offering translate into meaningful benefits for them. A capture team must substantiate or validate their benefits. Providing proof is the key to building credibility. Most sophisticated customers – those that typically buy large complex systems – use disciplined reasoning to question anything that is not substantiated with facts. Specific details can be generated only by doing your engineering homework and planning. Developing win themes forces a capture team to develop a comprehensive set of proofs, which in turn make the proposal very compelling. So after creating win themes, the next step is to develop a plan for creating these proofs.

To develop proofs, start by identifying how the customer measures their values or how they will measure the benefit you are trying to prove. Copy that measurement. If you can measure something, you can manage it. Once you have a mechanism or approach for measuring something, you can quantify changes and differences based on different inputs and this becomes the basis of proof.

— *Strategy in Action* —

L'Oreal wanted to claim that its Fructis Fortifying shampoo would make hair shinier. The shampoo smooths the hair cuticle by targeting damaged and rough areas of the hair fiber. When hair fibers are better aligned, with a smoother cuticle layer, there is better light reflection from the hair surface, resulting in increased shine. L'Oreal developed lab tests that ran a probe along the surface of the hair fiber to measure its roughness. By comparing the results before and after washing, they were able to develop their proof that their shampoo will make hair, "twice as strong and more than three times as shiny."

If you want to prove that your solution will have the lowest life cycle cost, you must develop a comprehensive life cycle cost (LCC) model for the customer's costs. Once you develop the model, you can analyze how various alternate solutions affect the model's inputs and change the customer's life cycle costs. The results provide proof of your benefits. You can enhance your credibility further if you can get the customer to validate your model.

Remember that the purpose of the proof is to show how your features deliver benefits. To create quantitative proof, consider:

- Performing tests
- Conducting operational analyses
- Modeling
- Developing simulations
- Conducting surveys
- Performing demonstrations
- Highlighting awards
- Publicizing endorsements by respected individuals

Some examples of imaginative proofs:

- One company learned that supplier responsiveness was important to their customer. Fortunately, the company prided itself on responsiveness. To prove that they were responsive to their customers, they hired a Big Six accounting firm to conduct a customer satisfaction survey of their marketplace. In their proposal, the company could legitimately claim to be "the most responsive in the market as found by a recent survey conducted by…" Hiring an outside organization to conduct an independent study or analysis for you enhances the proof's credibility.

- A company showed their vehicle was "combat proven" by reprinting a U.S. Marine Corps General's quote extolling their vehicle's wartime performance in Operation Iraqi Freedom.
- Reliability was very important to the customer. One company had designed a high degree of reliability into their product. Their competitor's design was older and not designed with reliability in mind, but the competitor claimed matching reliability levels. Concerned that the customer would not believe them or might simply discount both companies' claims, the company decided to guarantee their reliability performance. They committed to pay penalties if their product failed to meet a conservative level of reliability. With their reliability investment, they calculated this guarantee had a very limited financial liability. But they knew that it would be financially onerous for the competitor to match. This tactic proved to the customer that the company's reliability claims were true.

We have all seen creative proofs in advertising:

- To demonstrate his confidence in the identity theft protection that his firm LifeLock provides, CEO Todd Davis posts his social security number on their billboards and advertisements, daring thieves to try to beat their security. What makes this proof so startling and memorable is that it violates everyone's instinct to carefully guard his or her personal identification numbers.
- For 20 years, Timex took a tongue-in-cheek approach with a poker-faced John Cameron Swayze standing by and commenting upon an outrageous stunt, like Acapulco cliff diving, or being dragged by a racecar across the desert floor. Each of these situations might have been fatal to the participant and was certainly bad for a timepiece, proving the durability of Timex watches. This "takes a licking and keeps on ticking" advertising campaign helped to propel Timex to number one in the American market, allowing them to boast that more than half of all watches worn are Timexes.
- In a direct response to critics who allege that Coca-Cola and Pepsi-Cola were identical drinks, Pepsi Cola conducted the "Pepsi Challenge." These televised blind taste tests always showed the participants choosing Pepsi over Coca-Cola.

Once the proofs are identified, the capture team leader assigns a responsible party to take action (see Exhibit 5-9). It is important to visualize how the proof's data will be presented when designing the proof. It is said that a picture is worth a thousand words, so save a few words when possible and show a picture or graph when you can. If you plan to use the results in a graph, then your action plan should generate data that will produce a persuasive picture. If you are conducting a test or developing a prototype, invest a little more money and make the item look like the final product. These subtle details have a powerful influence on the customer's perception. They give the impression that you are farther down the technology curve than you may actually be. You might video a test to make its results more exciting and compelling. Due dates need to be set early enough to allow you to incorporate your results into the strategy process and have an opportunity to pre-sell the results to the customer. Experimental and analytical work often takes a long time, so your dates need to be realistic and monitored by the capture team leader as part of the action plan (which will be discussed in Chapter 7).

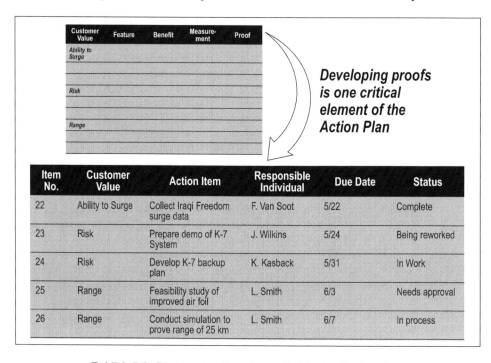

Exhibit 5-9: Developing Proofs are Put in the Action Plan

It is critical to develop proofs for all of the customer values, and going through this process early in the pursuit is important. It gives the capture team time to develop substantiation of their claims. By providing substantiation of each claim, you give the evaluator no choice but to believe your proposal. Proofs are the gist of one's proposal – the evidence that your solution is the best.

Iterating the Win Strategy

Hopefully, you and your team have started developing your win strategy well before the writing your proposal. If that is the case, then you have time to iterate your win strategy as the pursuit evolves. During the pursuit, things change. As you test your ideas on the customer, you gain more information about what works and what does not. As the campaign progresses, your team picks up more clues about what the competition is up to, and by listening to the customer, you get a better idea about what is important to them. You attempt to reach agreement with potential teammates. You conduct analysis to prove your discriminators, which sometimes do not work, and you constantly search for more discriminators to improve your position. Based on all these efforts, you need to continuously refine your strategy with this information.

Since strategy development is iterative, the best way to assure that the iterations happen at the optimum time is to schedule them in advance. Schedule reviews around the key event schedule, either just before a key opportunity or after an event that will reveal more information. Typically, every other month, the leader should conduct a win strategy and capture plan update. During these reviews, the capture team updates their win strategy with the core capture team (capture team leader, program manager, business development (BD) managers, technical director and key technical leads) and selected subject matter experts from outside the organization. The team should refine their strategies and tactics and be continually asking themselves: "is the strategy working and what adjustments need to be made?" These sessions help to manage the campaign and ensure that the team is developing and sending the right messages to the customer, as well as collecting the right intelligence. These reviews will result in the assignment of new actions and planning of new contacts. You iterate your strategy by updating your templates back to Step 3 as shown in Exhibit 5-10.

The strategy can become hard to implement. Your technical solution may not be evolving as you had hoped, or the right program manager might not be available. Maybe the designers cannot get their costs down to their targets or you might find the customer less enamored with your solution than you'd hoped. With this information you iterate your strategy, but don't throw it out when it gets hard – add or change tactics. Implementing your tactics or inventing new ones can be very hard, but hard work is what wins.

Summary

The key to selling resides in making the customer believe that the features of your offering provide more meaningful benefits to them than do your competitors' for those specific attributes most important to them. A win strategy is built around this simple objective.

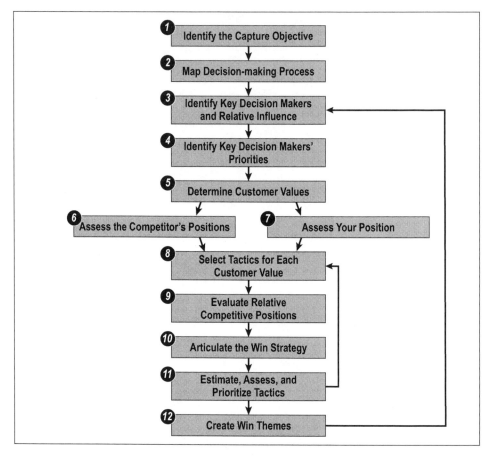

The flowchart steps are:

1. Identify the Capture Objective
2. Map Decision-making Process
3. Identify Key Decision Makers and Relative Influence
4. Identify Key Decision Makers' Priorities
5. Determine Customer Values
6. Assess the Competitor's Positions
7. Assess Your Position
8. Select Tactics for Each Customer Value
9. Evaluate Relative Competitive Positions
10. Articulate the Win Strategy
11. Estimate, Assess, and Prioritize Tactics
12. Create Win Themes

Exhibit 5-10: Iterate the Win Strategy

Identifying and documenting your strengths and weaknesses as well as those of the competition will give you a clear picture of where you stand in the competition. From this perspective, you'll see how to create greater differentiation and improve your relative position. Then you'll be able to select the customer values on which you intend to win, maximizing your strengths and minimizing your weaknesses while potentially highlighting your competition's weaknesses and downplaying their advantages.

Remember, it is not enough for your capture team to understand which customer values are going to differentiate you and make you the winner. The customer must understand this clearly as well, which is why you must be able to clearly articulate your win strategy for the customer – or answer the question, "why us?" And just telling the customer about the features of a solution will rarely win a contract. Every customer value must relate directly to at least one feature, proof of this feature, and the benefit that will be derived from it.

If you find you cannot win, be imaginative and change the game. Shaping the acquisition is a difficult task to accomplish, but if implemented well it can snatch victory from the jaws of defeat. The key to shaping is to understand the needs of the customer and to figure out how your solution could best benefit them. Then, you must influence the customer to change the acquisition rules to your advantage.

As the process moves forward, your team must stick with your win strategy even when it gets hard. This is not to say the win strategy does not evolve as you get more intelligence on the customer and the competitors. But it is important to avoid complacency, keep resources applied and send consistent messages to the customer.

Develop effective win themes to communicate the benefits of your features. That means developing and including persuasive proofs in your messages. The win themes should be easily understood and included throughout your proposal.

This methodology is not foolproof. It is a tool that you can use to organize your information about the pursuit. This method is repeatable and verifiable, but it is still only a tool. It will not replace sound judgment.

Chapter 6: The Secrets to Setting the Price-to-Win

"Pricing is the moment of truth – all marketing comes into focus in the pricing decision."

— Raymond Corey, Harvard Business School

Bid price is paramount to success in competitions for major contracts. Outsourcing, digitalization, corporate consolidation, free trade and even the Internet are leveling technological advantages between competitors across the globe. This is reducing discrimination on technical issues between competitors on major bids. As discrimination between solutions decreases, the importance of price increases (see Exhibit 6-1). However, that does not mean that the lowest price always wins, far from it. While your business may be different, our analysis of 155 recent major contract awards (all over $40 million and within the last six years) found that the offeror with the lowest price won 54 percent of the time. Also, when examining the buying behavior of over 50 international customers, we found that more than 90 percent of customers have picked a higher priced solution at one time or another. Therefore, determining the winning bid price is complicated at best.

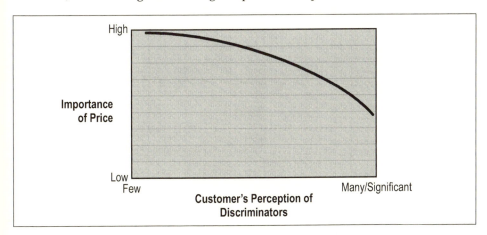

Exhibit 6-1: Decreasing Discriminators versus Importance of Price

Despite the increasing importance of pricing, most capture teams allow their solution design to determine their pricing. They allow its costs, irrespective of competitive forces, to dictate pricing, as opposed to identifying the winning price and then ensuring that the solution design fits the price. Then, as the proposal submittal date nears, management often decides their price is too high and demands that it be slashed. Management usually bases the new price on conjecture rather than facts. To reach management's desired price, the capture team suddenly finds itself desperately scrambling to reduce costs and frequently jettisons the features and discriminators which they spent weeks and months selling to the customer. This late price cut also forces management to make painful choices including cutting profit margins, committing millions in R&D, and risking cost overruns, all of which jeopardize the win and future returns.

Executives from a construction company were delivering a proposal to the California Department of Transportation (Caltrans). This $650 million bid to expand and repair freeways across the state was critical to their business unit. As their car pulled into the Caltrans's parking lot, one of the executive's cell phones rang. The construction company's president was on the line. He knew Caltrans always went to the lowest price contractor and he was concerned that their bid was too high. He told them to cut the bid price by $30 million. They changed the proposal's bid price in the Caltrans parking lot. They won. They had underbid every competitor by $70 million. This meant that the executive had forfeited $30 million in profit in 15 minutes on the phone in the parking lot without any competitive intelligence. Our analysis of 25 recent large pursuits found that winners significantly underbid one quarter of the time. In these cases, companies had significant cost advantages, which would have allowed them to increase their bid price and still win. However, these companies failed to leverage their cost discriminators into a higher price. There is a better way to price bids.

Setting the "Right" Price

Developing a winning price, while upholding margins, is critical to victory and to increasing shareholder value. But determining the "winning" number is one of industry's most difficult challenges. For best-in-class companies, achieving the "winning" price, which is not always the lowest price, is not the result of luck. It is the result of a systematic and repeatable, yet rarely discussed process called "Price-to-Win (PTW)."

PTW is shaped by external factors – namely a customer and the competitors. The PTW has nothing to do with your ability to meet the price determined. A PTW analysis is a market-based analysis of an opportunity, conducted to identify the highest price a company can bid and still win. As Exhibit 6-2 shows, this formal process includes systematically analyzing the customer's buying patterns and evaluation process, to predict the customer's likely source selection behavior. The analysis includes a top-down estimate of the competitor's likely bid price based strictly on their past bidding behavior. In parallel, a rigorous competitive analysis deciphers the competitor's offering from a bottom up estimate of their costs and their likely bid price. An important component of the competitive cost analysis is comparing the competition's costs to a "should cost" analysis on the capture team's offering. A "should cost" is the capture team's current cost baseline minus cost inefficiencies, which will be described in detail later in this chapter. Comparing these cost baselines allows the PTW analyst to identify and quantify differences between the capture team's offering and the competitors. By estimating the competitor's bid and how the customer is likely to make their source selection, the PTW analyst identifies the highest possible winning bid price with the right balance of capabilities. This comprehensive analysis significantly increases a company's win probability by independently validating and refining the capture team's strategy.

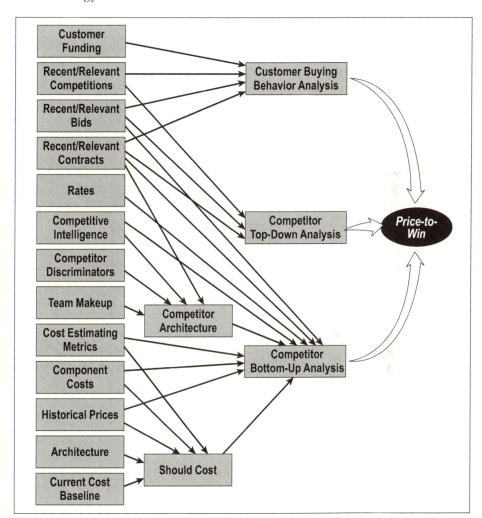

Exhibit 6-2: The PTW Analysis Process – Significant Data Multiple Approaches

Developing the PTW is a mix of art and science. It combines the science of cost engineering with the art of competitive analysis. The analyst must project the competitor's likely approach and bid aggressiveness, and deduce their solution architecture. They must overcome all of the ambiguity of the situation and make judgments about how the competitor will behave. Since large pursuits are complex, developing the diverse skills to accurately predict the competition's bid is challenging.

Some managers mistakenly believe that a PTW is merely a justification for slashing profit margins, but it is not. PTW is a process for managing costs while maximizing win probability. Establishing an early market-based price and subtracting out the desired profit margin allows management to set and deploy cost targets for the offering. These cost targets feed the design-to-cost (DTC) or cost as an independent variable (CAIV) process. The technical team then develops a solution that meets a market-derived price. Starting early allows design teams to achieve challenging cost targets.

— *Strategy in Action* —

For example, in 1996, Air Force General Merrill McPeak decided that the Joint Direct Attack Munitions (JDAM) contract should have an average unit price of under $40,000 per unit. He based this number not on an in-depth engineering analysis of the requirements, but on how much he thought the defense budget could afford. Initially, McDonnell Douglas's JDAM engineering team thought that no one could produce a guided weapon at that cost. Their original estimate was $68,000 each. However, when told by their business development manager that the company was going to "No Pursuit" if the engineers stuck to that position, the engineers reconsidered. McDonnell Douglas was motivated to win. Having recently lost a major competition for the sole source production of the Tomahawk missile, they realized that if they wanted to remain in the precision-guided munitions business, they had to win JDAM. The design team committed to beating this challenging target. Eventually, McDonnell Douglas won the competition with a bid of $14,100 per unit. Their competitor was a mere $300 per unit higher. Setting an aggressive cost target forced the design teams of both companies to break paradigms and use innovative technologies and approaches to achieve their huge cost reductions. That is the power of setting early upfront cost targets.

Results in the space launch business between 2000 and 2002 clearly demonstrated the power of the Price-to-Win process.

— *Strategy in Action* —

In April 2000, one of the authors, Kim Kelly, transferred into Lockheed Martin's International Launch Services (ILS). He began implementing a PTW process for rocket launch sales to commercial satellite companies around the world. By studying his competitor's bids, he was able to decode their pricing formulas. As ILS institutionalized the process over the next year and a half, ILS's pricing became more effective. They raised their win rate from 50 to 80 percent. ILS's market share increased to over 60 percent, becoming the market share leader for the first time in history. Their revenue increased by almost $500 million while profits skyrocketed. ILS's principle competitor, Arianespace, failed to respond and continued to lose sale after sale. Arianespace had no comparable Price-to-Win capability. They did not understand what was happening in their market. In 2002, while ILS's executives were receiving record bonuses, Arianespace's board of directors ousted their entire executive team.

As discussed in Chapter 3 and shown in Exhibit 6-3, the key decision makers must use the proposal and price evaluation to justify their decision. The way to assure victory is to be the offering the key decision makers want most and "correctly" balance the proposal evaluation and price. By correctly balancing the proposal evaluation and price you make it easy for the decision makers to justify selecting you. The PTW process is how one determines the correct balance of evaluation score and price. As part of the PTW process, you assess all of the competitors' likely evaluation scores and then determine what you need to bid to win.

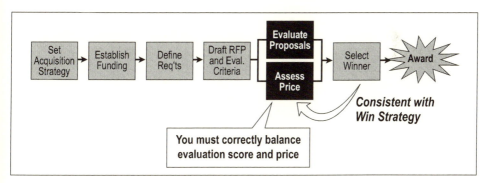

Exhibit 6-3: To Win You Must Correctly Balance Evaluation Score and Price

An important point to remember is that you will have to take actions to achieve your price target and your desired proposal scoring. These actions must be consistent with your win strategy. That means that your win strategy tactics should not conflict with actions you employ when getting your price down to achieve your PTW, nor should they conflict with your approach to improving your evaluation scoring.

Figuring Out How Much the Customer Has to Spend

The first step in conducting a PTW analysis is to determine how much money the customer has to spend on your work scope. The funding frames the entire competitive landscape and bounds all of the solutions. It's no fun wasting time chasing an opportunity with a solution that the customer cannot afford. Many governments publish their project funding, and commercial customers will often tell you how much money they have available. This forthright approach saves everyone time. However, many customers are not so enlightened, and in those cases, bidders have to figure it out. Someone in the customer's company has a specific dollar amount in mind and it's best to find out who it is and what they know. The available funding will determine what requirements the customer can afford. It is also important to understand their funding expectations. The customer expectations can determine how open they are to different solutions, or to bidding lesser requirements, as well as whether the proposed project is realistic.

To identify available funding, a capture team should try to determine what logic and data sources the customer used to estimate the project's budget:

- Is this a repeat buy?
- Did they conduct a market study?
- Did they receive any prior Rough Order of Magnitude (ROM) or unsolicited proposal prices?
- Did they use a comparable project as the basis?
- Did they request pricing in a Request for Information (RFI)?

Once you identify the sources, you need to ask yourself whether these estimates are comparable. More importantly, does the customer think they are comparable, and what adjustments did they make? You'll also need to examine the project's affordability with their overall budget. Can they afford the project as currently scoped? If not, the capture team needs to consider this as they develop their approach. When trying to project future funding, examine the organization's likely revenue growth. Within most bureaucracies, looking at a department's percentage of total funding works as a fair guide. Departments mightily resist any threat to their relative status, such as a reduction in their budget to increase that of another department, so a capture team should be skeptical if the customer is projecting that their department's funding is growing as a percentage of the customer's overall funding.

— *Strategy in Action* —

When strategizing about how to win an electronic archives program for the National Archives, architecting a solution around the available funding was very important. The National Archives was projecting the program budget to be $100 million per year for six years. Our experience told us that the National Archives' program manager would hold on to his belief until proven wrong, so he would stick to his assertions that the project would be fully funded. However, Congress has traditionally underfunded the agency and restrained budget growth. The National Archives would need an overall budget increase of 20 percent to fully fund their archives project. This seemed unlikely given the limited clout of their Congressional oversight committee and the tight budget environment. Therefore, the capture team needed to design a solution which could satisfy a program with a $100 million/year budget, but that could also be scalable to a project with half that amount, a target we estimated was more realistic. This scalable strategy provided a distinct advantage over the competition because the competitors believed the program manager. The competitors were then forced to slash their system's scope when Congress published the National Archives reduced budget.

When customers publish budgets, they don't always break out all of the other distributions that will come out of that budget. The capture team must sift out the management reserves that program managers bury in their budget numbers. Once the team has identified the actual project budget, they must understand how much of the budget is available for the contractor.

Surprisingly, we have seen many multibillion-dollar proposals submitted with bids over the published customer available funding. ***Never bid above the customer's available funding.*** Customers cannot commit to a contract unless it is within their budget. And they can rarely go back and get more money. If a customer is ever presented with one bid over their available funding and another below it, they will pick the competitor who came in within their funding.

If the project is commercially funded, then the availability of funding depends on the project's financing and the company's business case. Bidders will need to forecast the project's revenues and expenses. The business case needs to consider all of the project's risks, from receiving government approvals to avoiding labor problems and currency exchange fluctuations. Then they'll need to assess the eligibility of debt and equity financing to this customer to determine how big a budget the project will have.

Identifying the Customer's Buying Behavior

The next step is for the PTW analyst to examine the customer's buying behavior. Procurement departments and executives usually follow the same formal procedures from one purchase to the next. Executives and contracting staff tend to have longevity and organizations develop norms of behavior. As a result, customers usually have consistent buying behaviors over the years. For the PTW analysis, consistent means predictable. Identifying these behaviors is of strategic importance, yet few companies conduct even an elementary analysis of how their customers actually buy.

Examining a customer's buying patterns allows one to understand a customer's true value in the source selection decision – if, how much, and under what circumstances they are willing to pay a price premium. While the U.S. Coast Guard claims to always buy "best value," a look at their buying history over the last 12 years reveals their true buying behavior. They have selected the lowest price bidder in every case. Once they even chose the lowest bidder despite their technical evaluation team determining that the "winning" shipyard was incapable of building the ship proposed. NASA, on the other hand, which also claims to award on "best value," consistently awards to low risk or higher performing technical solutions. And NASA will pay a premium for their preferred choice. It is crucial to identify your customer's behavior, so that you can best architect your bid and avoid leaving "money on the table."

Even within customers, different organizations buy differently from one another. For example, NAVSEA, the contracting office responsible for buying the U.S. Navy's ships, is very cost conscious and tends to technically level competitors. NAVAIR, the branch of the Navy that buys airplanes, on the other hand, is one of the world's most risk averse customers. They often pay large price premiums for more sophisticated solutions. When bidding a contract, a winning strategy of low cost works well for NAVSEA, but is a terrible strategy for NAVAIR.

The customer analysis focuses on understanding how and why the customer has made source selection decisions. This analysis looks at specific similar sales, at who was selected and why. Did they pick the lowest price or did the winner have a price premium? What reasons did the customer give for picking the winner – greatest capability, lowest risk, or fastest schedule? Who were the key customer decision makers and what roles did they play? Did the customer rigidly adhere to their rules or were the rules flexible? Does the customer request a Best and Final Offer (BAFO) or multiple rounds of price concessions? As you accumulate answers to these questions, you will uncover the patterns that the customer repeats over and over again.

— *Strategy in Action* —

Customer analysis provides excellent insight about how to position your company. For example, a bidder can see an interesting pattern when examining the Australian Ministry of Defense's (MOD) selection behavior. The MOD always likes to have three bidders and uses the three players as leverage against each other in lengthy negotiations before announcing a winner. They often go with someone other than the low price bidder, such as on the Lead-In Fighter, F-18, P-3 Upgrade and Penguin Missile programs. When the MOD intends to select a higher priced offering, they tend to behave in a consistent way. They start defining and interpreting the requirements to disqualify the low cost offerings as noncompliant. Knowing this, a shrewd supplier can discern where a competition is going by watching how the MOD is evolving the requirements. However, most importantly, this knowledge helps guide the team in developing an influencing plan to shape the competition toward your offering.

One critical issue that some proposal teams neglect to fully consider is what price the customer will evaluate. Some customers evaluate development cost, some consider unit production cost and still others look at the entire expected life cycle cost of the program. NAVAIR, at Patuxent River, asks for development costs, low rate production costs and life cycle costs as part of their RFPs. However, when analyzing their behavior, you will find that they focus almost exclusively on development costs. The Air Force at Wright Patterson, on the other hand, has traditionally assessed price as total life cycle cost, while Qantas Airways measures a total rolled up cost per seat mile when deciding what model of aircraft to buy. Analyzing prior purchases can help the capture team answer the question: What will be priced? Failing to answer this question can cost you the competition, as one contractor discovered on a guided bomb bid. The contractor knew that the Air Force would pick the lowest price for this program, so the contractor set an aggressive price target for their bomb and rigorously drove their design team to meet it. Unfortunately, the RFP surprised them. They found that the customer would evaluate the cost as the bomb plus the bomb carriage. The contractor had not optimized the bomb carriage for low cost and its high cost was a key reason they lost.

Like in the commercial rocket launch business, the price you submit isn't the number the customer evaluates. Customers add launch insurance costs to each supplier's bid to create an evaluated price. Launch insurance covers the buyer in case of a launch failure and is based on their track record, so the proven Proton rocket with its nearly perfect record has a proportionally smaller premium than other launch vehicles. Customers like the U.S. Army, Navy, Air Force, NASA and the U.K. Ministry of Defense all adjust one's bid for risk. We have seen these customers add dollars for risk adjustments up to 50 percent on a bidder's price to generate the evaluated price.

In projects where the supplier requires financing, price may be only a part of the evaluation. In these cases, one does not provide a price per se, but a business deal. With a business deal there will be revenue and risk sharing, which offset price. For example, when General Motors decided to outsource its information technology (IT), they struck a deal with EDS. EDS agreed to take over GM's existing IT staff and assets and then sell its data processing and computer services back to GM. In this deal, there are two key prices: the price EDS was willing to pay for GM's IT department, and the service fees EDS was willing to charge GM.

The customer evaluates the overall return of a supplier's offering versus its perceived risk. In these cases, you do not conduct a Price-to-Win. Instead, the analyst conducts a Deal-to-Win. The Deal-to-Win is an analysis that determines the competitor's likely business proposition to the customer and recommends your winning deal. In this case, the analyst must understand the competitor's financing capabilities, willingness to accept risk, and return expectations, as well as their bid aggressiveness.

Exhibit 6-4 shows the award behavior for one customer. Of the five awards examined (we replaced program names with letters), this customer awarded to the higher priced bid in three cases. In those four awards, the customer awarded to the company with the higher technical evaluation score. For example, in XYZ, the winner had a higher evaluation in two of the five evaluation categories. In KRVT, the loser had a higher evaluation score in two areas, but was 20 percent higher in price. The conclusion one can draw from this analysis is that the customer will award to a company with a higher evaluation score (in at least two areas) as long as their price is within 12 percent of the lowest priced offer (as it was in FABC and AAMC), but not to a bidder with a 20 percent higher price. Customer buying behavior can be commodity specific. Customers are much more willing to pay a premium for a higher performing solution that addresses a significant mission shortfall than for one that improves a non-mission critical support service. For example, one construction company always chooses the lowest cost bidder when selecting a concrete supplier. However, they believe that the quality of the architectural and engineering (A&E) firm's design determines the success or failure of their projects. As a result, they are willing to pay a significant price premium for the firm they think is most technically competent.

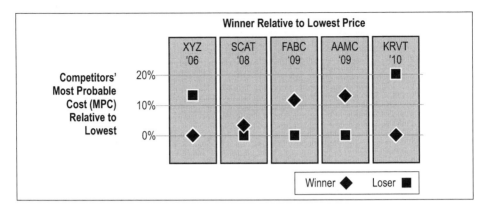

Exhibit 6-4: Tracking Customer Award Behavior

The capture team needs to understand the context of each past procurement – how important was this competition to the organization's mission, and what were the funding constraints and other environmental pressures on the organization when this procurement was decided? For example, in 2002 the Transportation Safety Administration (TSA) paid a large price premium for the Boeing/Siemens Airport Explosive Detection System (EDS) to field a system quickly in the 9/11 aftermath. Boeing got lucky because TSA, in their urgency to get under contract, has never paid a similar price premium since. Therefore, when a PTW analyst assesses TSA's buying behavior they should realize that the EDS buy was a unique situation and did not represent TSA's typical buying behavior.

Including inappropriate purchases in the precedent program analysis is a fairly common mistake that capture teams make. Buying behaviors are a function of an organization's procedures, precedents and individuals. Therefore, when analyzing precedent programs it is important to only examine purchases that were made by the same procurement organization that you are selling to. For example, when you try to sell a ship to the U.S. Navy, DDX, their next generation destroyer, would be a good precedent program. Ships like DDX are purchased by the NAVSEA Command. You would not examine the Presidential Helicopter competition, which was bid into NAVAIR, which buys all the U.S. Navy aviation assets. NAVSEA and NAVAIR have some similar procedures, but their buying behaviors are very different. If you were selling the same ship to the English Navy, it would be insightful to analyze their buying behavior on other complex development jobs such as a command center or aircraft, as well as ships, because the Ministry of Defense (MOD) centralizes all military purchases.

A customer's buying behavior can change. General Motors dramatically changed their buying behavior with the promotion of Jose Ignacio Lopez to the head of Worldwide Procurement. Lopez was aiming to obtain cost savings of 20 to 40 percent out of their suppliers to help GM avert a financial crisis. Lopez destroyed GM's cozy supplier relationships by reopening contracts and ruthlessly competing supplier contracts to drive down prices. Lopez changed GM's buying behavior overnight. Changing an organization's buying behavior brings a significant cultural change as well. These changes are typically well publicized both in and outside the company as leadership tries to implement its desires.

The customer analysis helps to determine where the price needs to be relative to the competition, as shown in Exhibit 6-5 for two different customers, NASA and the U.S. Coast Guard. To win a Coast Guard procurement, one must bid a lower price than any other competitor. However, when selling to NASA, the winning price depends on how desirable your offering is relative to the competitors'. The more desirable your offering over the competition, the greater price premium the customer can justify. Conversely, if the competition's offering is more desirable, you must be much lower in price.

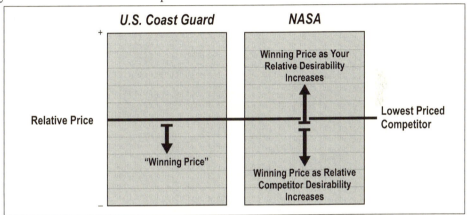

Exhibit 6-5: Using Customer Analysis for the PTW

Building the "Should Cost" Model

One starting point for estimating a competitor's bid price is their past bids. If you have a past bid, you need to do your homework to understand what the number included. You need to discover what the work scope, order size, and delivery schedule of the bid were, in addition to understanding how competitive it was. Once you determine this information, you adjust the bid for inflation, differences in quantities, bid aggressiveness and technical differences to develop a cost baseline. In some cases we have list prices for the competitor's product or at least part of their solution. For example, when estimating the competitor's bid price for a search and rescue helicopter program, we were able start with the competitor's list pricing. After interviewing the sales force to determine the competitor's discounting policies, we estimated their green aircraft price (a green aircraft is the base flyable aircraft with no interiors or customer equipment). Because this competitor had not bid on any search and rescue configurations yet, we then had to use our "should cost" approach to estimate the additional costs of their aircraft modifications and avionics suite.

Another point of departure for developing an estimate for the competitor's bid is your cost baseline. Your current cost baseline incorporates a significant amount of knowledge. The cost baseline incorporates much of the company's knowledge about how much it will cost to satisfy the potential customer's requirements. The PTW analysis is going to use this knowledge together with competitive intelligence to calculate the differences in the two cost baselines. Unfortunately, initial program cost estimates frequently contain errors and cannot always be used. By the time a proposal goes to the customer, its pricing has gone through many reviews and management has wrung out most of the cost inefficiencies. Some competitive intelligence professionals mistakenly use this initial cost baseline for developing a competitor cost buildup. If they do, they embed these inefficiencies into their estimate of the competitor's costs. As a result, the projected competitor's cost is too high and the PTW is inaccurate.

Since the PTW analysis is always trying to predict the "endgame" – the final competitor price; analysts must develop accurate estimates early on, before this wringing out process is complete. A key part of the PTW process is to analyze the company's current cost baseline and develop a "should cost." To create this "should cost," the PTW analyst builds a cost model going down to at least the third level of the work breakdown structure and usually the fourth or fifth level. The "should cost" is an estimate of the company's proposal price with all of their costing and design inefficiencies eliminated. We call it a "should cost," but it might be more appropriate to call it a "should price," because it does include profit margin. Later in the process we use the "should cost" as the basis for estimating the competitor's bid price. We do that by making adjustments to the "should cost" for the differences in approaches between the offerings.

The first step in creating the "should cost" is to analyze your team's current cost baseline, or invent one if they haven't started yet. When a "should cost" is done effectively, it uncovers cost savings ideas from across the capture team and company. The capture team evaluates all of these factors against the customer's requirements to eliminate over-scoping, redundancies, unnecessary features and poor bidding practices. A good PTW analyst is experienced and knows cost estimating relationships. This allows them to spot uncompetitive functions and support ratios that are out of line. For example, the "should cost" may find that management has under budgeted some functional areas. Under budgeted functions can result in overruns and schedule delays once the contract is awarded.

The "should cost" process typically reduces the overall program budget by a double-digit percentage. Some "should cost" findings have included:

- Support ratios for quality assurance, document control, reliability and production control are double what they should be (based on similar programs).
- Logistics padded their budget by 50 percent because they were used to having their budget slashed in the review process.
- A supplier of a key component learned that the prime contractor knew little about their costs and decided to include a large nonrecurring development cost in their bid.

- Another supplier buried first class travel in their bid to support an overseas project.
- Substantial low skill work has been earmarked to an underutilized high cost facility.

Using the current cost baseline you identify the key cost drivers for your company. These cost drivers are likely to be the same for the competition, which helps focus the competitive analysis on the most important questions that need to be addressed. Through interviewing your own engineers, you can determine what cost trade-off alternatives the capture team engineers faced in developing their estimates. Usually, these will be the same trade-offs that the competition faced. The PTW analyst then second-guesses all of the major trades and assumptions driving cost. They look for divergent opinions in the company's own staff as well as competitive intelligence about what the competitors are doing. For example, the analyst can discover that one engineer believes that a requirement interpretation might create discrepancies in the bids between teams. A single assumption can create huge cost differences between competing solutions. We have seen many situations where an engineer has made a very conservative interpretation of a requirement that results in a significant increase in a proposed solution's estimate.

— Strategy in Action —

One engineer working on a train control system concluded that to be "absolutely certain" of never losing a signal between control relay stations, the antennas must never be more than four miles apart. Another engineer found there would be no operational impact due to lost signals if the antennas were six miles apart. Putting the antennas two miles farther apart reduced the bid cost by over 15 percent. In an analysis like this, where a requirements interpretation has a significant cost impact, it is critical that the engineers bring these issues forward to management. Management should decide how much risk they want to take on to win the business.

Competitive intelligence can also help develop the "should cost."

— Strategy in Action —

In one case, a company was designing a new handheld gas detector for an upcoming pursuit. The engineering staff insisted that the design required twelve batteries. However, the company's PTW analyst was concerned about the battery count because the customer would evaluate the life cycle cost of the solutions. In fact, battery costs dwarfed the price of the gas detectors over their life. The competitive analyst went to a trade show and visited the competitor's booth. He found the competitor's unit on display. He picked it up, turned it over and found that it had slots for only eight batteries. When he returned to his company, he informed the executives and the engineers of his finding and the competitor's low estimated evaluated price. Given their previous reluctance to consider a design with fewer batteries, he commented, "we are going to lose, because their engineers are better than ours." That was all the company's engineers needed to hear. The engineers took up the challenge and were able to redesign the unit with improved power management, reducing the battery requirement to eight and achieved the PTW, thus eliminating a key competitive disadvantage. The PTW analyst's "should cost" pointed the engineering staff to an improved solution.

The PTW analyst needs to examine the customer's likely evaluation criteria and compare these to the solution, removing features that are costly and have minimal impact on the evaluation criteria. We have seen features included that the customer didn't require, and that provided only an additional two percent of evaluation credit, but that drove up the solution's cost by more than 20 percent. The capture leader must remove features like this from the proposal baseline, but could offer these features as an option. This makes the customer's job easier, because they won't need to justify the high cost of these features in their source selection decision, but will still have the choice to add them.

The "should cost" should exclude any engineering "pet rocks." Pet rocks are features or exciting technologies your marketing or engineering departments are dying to get into production that are not desired by the customer. Since these features are not required or desired by the customer, they won't be in the competitor's solution and they'll provide little or no evaluation credit. If pet rocks are bid, they create a competitive disadvantage.

The analyst should assess the solution's cost trade-offs versus the customer's likely evaluation scoring. Costly technical features need to be assessed against their likely evaluation credit. For example, on an unmanned air vehicle program, the engineers were pushing to propose a radar under development instead of a commercial off-the-shelf item. The development radar would have added millions to the bid price, six months to the flight test program and a huge amount of risk for a mere three percent improvement in the evaluation score. The analyst put the off-the-shelf radar's price into the "should cost" and not the development radar.

Estimating the Competitor's Bid Price

The "should cost" is critical to modeling the competitor's bid, as shown in Exhibit 6-2. Typically, this cost, without inefficiencies, is the starting point for developing an estimate of the competitor's bid. Once the PTW analyst deduces the competitor's technical approach, they make adjustments to the "should cost" based on differences with the competitor. Developing the PTW requires a thorough understanding of the competitor's likely approach. It is our experience that it's usually better to concentrate on the strongest competitor than to analyze many. You uncover greater insights by going in depth into a single competitor's technical solution, but if you spread your resources across many, you conduct a less thorough analysis and miss critical subtleties that can drive the analysis. One accurate competitive bid number is better than two inaccurate ones. However, sometimes we do analyze more than one competitor. This might be done, for example, if the competitors have very different approaches where each one has some unique discriminators highly valued by the customer. If the competitors have different approaches, one of which may lead to a drastically lower price that we are not able to confirm without conducting a second detailed cost analysis, then more than one competitor may be analyzed.

The analyst begins by conducting an analysis of the field of competitors to identify the top competitor. This is a critically important step. The authors have lost two pursuits by focusing on the wrong competitor. In both of those situations the customer sent mixed messages about what they wanted which made it difficult to select the most formidable competitive solution. The best approach is to assess which competitor will have the best price and evaluation from the customer's perspective. You conduct your competitive analysis and cost analysis on the most formidable competitors and delve into more and more detail until you can deduce with confidence who is the strongest. This is a critically important step, because getting it wrong can cost you the win.

The next step is to deduce the architecture of the competitor's likely solution. For most bids, differences in their architectures, not variations in labor and overhead rates, drive most of the cost differences. The analyst should focus on the messages that this competitor is communicating to the marketplace. Are they trying to be low risk/low cost solution or provide the highest performance? In most procurements, a company's basic strategy is widely broadcast. They announce it in press releases and product brochures, and they communicate their strategy through actions: who they team with, who they hire, what components they buy, and what messages they send. The PTW analyst should systematically seek out these signals, piecing together data to assemble a picture of their offering as will be discussed in Chapter 9.

Once you have identified the competitor's technical solution, you want to estimate its cost. While competitive intelligence alone is a powerful motivator for executives to change their assumptions and ideas, its influence is magnified if you dollarize it. For example, while competing for a maintenance services contract in the Middle East, the two companies bidding both used a mix of Americans and Foreign nationals as mechanics, warehousemen and truck drivers. When the PTW analyst told the executives that their proposed ratio of American nationals to foreign nationals was one-to-one while the competitor was likely to bid a one-to-three ratio they expressed mild interest. However, when they were told that the competitor's staffing mix cut their competitor's cost by $60M, their interest level jumped.

Using knowledge of the competitor's technical architecture, the PTW analyst works with the various internal experts (engineering, procurement, business management, etc.) to create a bill of material for all the significant cost items. *One of the biggest challenges in developing a PTW is converting qualitative competitive intelligence into a cost estimate.* A PTW analyst seeks to quantify the cost impact of all of the qualitative differences in the competitor's architecture. At the lowest level they can identify cost differences between your solution and the competition's, within the constraints of time. For each purchased component in the bill of material, they'll determine whether the competitor's component will be more or less expensive than your components based on the source or its level of complexity. For the competitor's software, they'll assess the product's functionality and consider what new functionality they must build to meet the customer's requirements. For software, assembly, engineering, installation and other labor tasks, the PTW analyst should estimate the labor-months required for the solution and apply to that estimate the competitor's labor rates and burdens to determine their likely final bid. Labor rates can be estimated by comparing and correlating market intelligence with such factors such as geographic location, structure, size and levels of automation. For each major cost, the PTW analyst looks for adjustments to the cost baseline.

Working with your technical staff to estimate cost differences is key. While engineers frequently are precision-oriented and reluctant to make "guesses" on anything less than perfect information, it is imperative that they do. By making rough estimates at a low level in the work breakdown structure, one finds a high level of accuracy at the system level. Underestimating some elements is compensated by overestimating on others, and rolling these costs up with the appropriate burdens and overhead rates leads to a more accurate system estimate than if the engineers did not offer their best estimate.

The following example illustrates how the PTW analyst assessed a vessel tracking system bid to a port authority.

— *Strategy in Action* —

A vessel tracking system consists of a control station connected to a series of radars that locate, identify, track and direct all ships into a port to prevent collisions. In previous competitions, the port authority always went to the lowest price. The analyst started the process by developing a Current Bid Baseline (the first cost column), which priced the sum of all of the functional cost estimates (see Exhibit 6-6). Next, the PTW analyst adjusted this baseline to eliminate expensive and unnecessary software development and hardware that could have been proposed as future upgrades. In addition, the analyst added in missing bill of material items and revised some of the overhead factors to develop the "should cost" (the second cost column).

To develop the competitor bottom up cost, the PTW analyst studied the system's cost drivers. One of the most significant costs of a vessel tracking system is the design and installation of the radar towers. From the competitor's marketing literature, the analyst identified the competitor's radar frequency while a press release announced their radar supplier. Knowing the supplier and frequency allowed the PTW analyst to identify the competitor's radar from its specification in the supplier's catalog. The competitor's radar was larger, more expensive and more capable than the capture team's radar. When the capture team's engineers overlaid the competitor's radar capabilities on the port's geography, they calculated that the competition would need only 20 radar towers to the team's 27. Each tower had to have a foundation sunk into the river and a tower erected, so each tower required a geographic survey, foundation design, foundation placement, power and communications interconnection design, and radar attachment. The competitor's per tower erection cost would be the same as the capture team's, despite the heavier radar. Since the cost of the "Radar & Tower Hardware," "Location & Design" and "Tower Erection" were directly proportional to the number of radar towers the competitor required, with fewer towers they had a $3 million cost advantage (see the third cost column). The company's position looked bleak.

When the PTW analyst presented this information, the capture team brainstormed how to get their costs down to meet the competitor's. One engineer came up with the idea of using existing towers or buildings instead of erecting new towers. The team explored this idea and discovered that their smaller radar could be installed on 12 existing towers or buildings. This approach eliminated the erection costs for 12 towers and slashed the location and design costs resulting in a "revised should cost" (the fourth column in Exhibit 6-6). In addition, because they were able to remove so much cost, the company was able to incorporate some additional features in their software development and increase their profit margin while keeping their price well below the competitor.

	Current Bid Baseline	Should Cost	Compeitor Bid Baseline	Revised Should Cost
Radar and Tower Hardware	$945	$945	$952	$945
Location and Design	$5,535	$5,535	$4,100	$3,495
Tower Erection	$12,150	$12,150	$9,000	$6,750
Control Center Equipment	$210	$120	$165	$120
Communications	$130	$130	$240	$130
Software Development	$4,800	$3,900	$5,100	$4,485
Systems Integration & Test	$1,440	$1,170	$1,530	$1,346
Program Management	$3,373	$3,238	$2,730	$2,210
General & Administrative (G&A)	$6,860	$6,525	$6,431	$4,675
Profit	$5,316	$4,046	$4,537	$4,831
Total	$40,759	$37,758	$34,785	$28,986
Number of New Sites	27	27	20	15

Exhibit 6-6: Using Competitive Analysis to Set the Cost

With competitive insight, the company was able to innovate and win. This is a simple representation of a PTW analysis. The "should cost" analysis was actually conducted at a much greater level of detail, and the customer and the competitive analysis were significantly more complex than what was presented here.

The following three examples show how the PTW analysis uses a variety and combination of techniques to develop the competitor's "should cost" and to accurately deduce their bid price:

— *Strategy in Action* —

An analyst needed to know the bid price of a large quantity of sophisticated multi-spectrum cameras for a pursuit. In this case, the analyst started with a "should cost" analysis of the company's product to identify the key cost drivers for the competitor's solution. From a photograph of the competitor's unit, the analyst concluded that the competitor had one more lens, and from the size and shape of their box, the analyst could tell that the competitor had only one large circuit card versus their smaller two. As a result, the competitor would not require a flex cable like the analyst's company used to connect their two cards. The analyst estimated that as a smaller, more entrepreneurial company, the competitor's labor rates were about nine percent lower. The system's key component was a focal plane array (FPA) – a sensor that converted an image into electronic signals. The competitor had purchased an FPA factory the year before, so the analyst believed they would have designed their product using their newly acquired FPAs. Since the analyst's company had purchased FPAs from that plant prior to the acquisition, their engineers had a good idea what prices the competitor's FPA factory charged. The analyst assessed the competitor's bidding history and found them winning new business and no market signals indicating that the competition would bid any more aggressively than they had in the past, so the analyst concluded that the competitor would bid their standard margins. Working with the capture team's engineering and procurement personnel, the analyst estimated the costs of all these differences and was able to predict the competitor's final price within five percent and win the program.

— *Strategy in Action* —

On another pursuit, our client was bidding on a train navigation system, and the electronic enclosures to protect the equipment from heat and vibration were a significant cost driver. To determine the competitor's enclosures cost per unit we analyzed their design versus ours and found one substantial cost difference. From our engineers we learned that the competitor wired their units differently than we had. They required more electromagnetic interference (EMI) filters and therefore more assembly time. Through interviews with our enclosure supplier, we found that the competition had similar production volumes in their plant, but had greater levels of automation for fabricating sheet metal. We also learned that both suppliers bought the maximum buying unit quantities of material, so neither had an advantage in buying economies. We adjusted the competitor's costs for the automation and their plant's lower labor rates, as their's was located in Mississippi versus our supplier's being in Michigan. Our supplier's Vice President told us that he had been competing with this competitor for the last ten years and he believed his company had a consistent eight to nine percent price advantage. Our client's procurement specialists had experience buying from both companies over the years and confirmed this assessment. We did not understand why our supplier appeared to have a price advantage when the competitor had less costly processes. Which brings up a critical point, **when conducting a Price-to-Win, you need to resolve discrepancies in your findings. Because an erroneous conclusion which results in a few percentage points higher cost can make the difference between winning and losing.** We continued our investigation and discovered that the competitor's factory carried the cost of an R&D Center at their facility in their overhead. When we included an estimate of the R&D Center's cost in the competitor's overhead it explained our cost advantage despite their manufacturing's location and automation cost advantages. Having understood the competitor's cost buildup, we were then able to accurately estimate the competitor's bid and win the program.

— *Strategy in Action* —

This example describes how a PTW analyst developed a Price-to-Win for a field services contract to the Navy. The Navy required all of the bidders to propose staffing and an hourly labor rate for a large set of job categories. Because their principle competitor had won a similar field service contract to the Army in 2007, the PTW analyst used this as a baseline for identifying cost differences between the companies. The analyst's company had lost this bid to the competitor, therefore, the analyst had his company's failed bid as a starting point for the analysis. The analyst knew the competitor's winning price, as well as his company's losing price and their cost proposal. The analyst then collected intelligence on the competitor to identify and explain differences between the competitor' bids. For example, the competitor claimed that their spares forecasting was so sophisticated that it typically reduced warehousing demands by 12-15 percent, so the analyst estimated how many fewer hours of warehousing and inventory control the competitor would have likely bid. To determine the hourly labor rate for each labor category, the analyst started with overall competitors bid and staffing levels to derive an average labor rate. Then the analyst used other labor rate data sources for the type of job categories used in the program, such as published General Services Administration (GSA – which are blanket government buying contracts) rates and labor rates in previous contracts. The analyst adjusted these rates for such issues as inflation, changes in work rules, and different locations. To estimate the cost impacts of these changes, the analyst needed to dissect the competitor's current fringe benefits offering and its costs. The analyst visited the competitor's web site to determine their vacation, health care, and retirement policies. Then the analyst worked with his own human resources manager to estimate the costs impact of these policies and the changes for the new proposal. The analyst estimated how differences in such items as supervision ratios, rent and utilities affected overhead. From this intelligence and analysis, the analyst was able to reconstruct the competitor's 2007 bid price. Once he understood those differences, the analyst was able to project how these differences would apply to the Navy job. Their resulting estimate was within a few percentage points and won the job.

Sometimes a competitor's product may be different enough from yours in design, production processes or culture that extrapolating from your cost baseline is not appropriate. In these cases, you should seek out some top down intelligence on the competitor's pricing to validate or supersede your bottom up cost build. For example, on one bid for an Arctic-based processing facility, one key component was a pumping station. The competitor's pumping system was designed for different applications and would require significant modifications to survive the Arctic weather and meet the required safety standards. The company's engineers estimated their competitor's modified system would cost $23 million. Yet we picked up intelligence from three independent sources that the competitors were quoting prices of $16 million. We believed our engineers' estimates truly reflected what it would take to build this pumping station, but because the competitor lacked prior Arctic experience, we also believed they did not fully understand the true cost of adapting their product to operate in prolonged subzero conditions. As a result, we believed that the competitor would bid $16 million, not knowing their system would quickly break down if they won. It became critical for the capture team to educate the customer on how our solution was designed for the harsh arctic conditions, how our competitor's was not, and how this difference would affect the customer's operations.

In estimating your competitor's price, the analyst must make many judgments about the competitor's approach. He or she will develop a range for various cost elements and must predict what the competitor will choose to do. As we discussed earlier, the analysts use their knowledge of the competitor's culture and outlook to make these predictions. Does the competitor think this cost element is important? How is the competitor going to interpret the customer's requirements? For example, if you are trying to estimate how much the competitor is going to bid to support a customer service help desk, you can estimate approximate staffing based on the service levels that the customer requires. But to estimate what the competitor will precisely bid, you need to understand how that competitor views itself and the customer's needs. If the competitor prides itself on being responsive and having excellent customer satisfaction, they will propose higher staffing levels for lower help desk wait times and call abandon rates. However, if the competitor always tries to be the low cost provider they will staff to the bare minimum.

Amazingly, sometimes the competitors will even tell you what their pricing strategy is. On the Joint Strike Fighter pursuit, the customer had set price targets for each of the aircraft variants. Lockheed's executives believed these cost targets were going to be very difficult to achieve and they were focusing on providing the maximum capability for that cost. However, Boeing broadcast their strategy in their advertisements, "The Air Force is Committed to a Joint Strike Fighter that's *Affordable*. So Are We." Affordable is code for low price. Most importantly, Boeing's capture team leader told the press that his team was going to come in well below the customer's price targets. He gave away his pricing strategy on a $200 billion pursuit! One axiom of competitive intelligence is: **big people tell big secrets.**

The capture team should also analyze the competitor's past bidding behavior. On what basis do they traditionally differentiate their offerings (technical features, low price, minimal risk, support)? This information is used to help focus the analysis of how the competition is likely to behave – where and how they are likely to innovate. The PTW analyst identifies the opportunities on which the competitor has bid aggressively in the past, and those on which they have not. Analysts do not blindly use history as a predictor of the future, however. They look for patterns and discontinuities to understand the competitor's underlying behavior.

— *Strategy in Action* —

For example, Exhibit 6-7 shows one competitor's erratic bidding pattern.

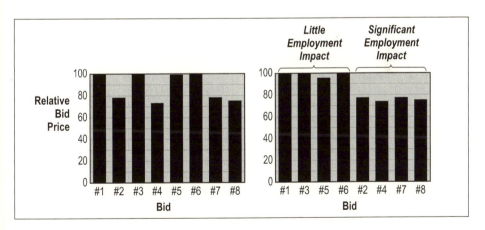

Exhibit 6-7: Example Buying Behavior

It shows the competitor bidding aggressively on some projects compared to our company, but not on others. Further analysis of these bids found that the aggressive bids coincided with those having a potentially large impact on the factory's employment. This conclusion made sense, the company had a large skilled labor force that was difficult to ramp up or down. In addition, the company president was promoted out of human resources and was an extroverted, gregarious, feeling-oriented, "people" person. Due to this background, the company president bid to try to stabilize their staffing. This analysis helped us understand that the competitor would bid aggressively on future opportunities only if that bid would have a significant effect on the company's staffing level.

— *Strategy in Action* —

In another situation, we were analyzing a competitor's past bids. We'll call this competitor "TB" for the purposes of this example. TB's business strategy was to invest in cutting edge products to dominate emerging markets. We found that in two cases TB had significantly dropped their price during campaigns. We wanted to understand this pricing behavior, so we interviewed the marketing managers on those jobs. In the first pursuit, we found that initially, due to the customer's challenging performance requirements, TB thought they were the only viable bidder. However, when it became apparent that another company met the minimum requirements, TB's price dropped 21 percent. In the second competition, the customer was going to award a sole source contract to TB because the customer demanded a very quick delivery schedule. When another company protested the customer's decision to give TB a sole source award, the customer decided to initiate an accelerated procurement. In that case, TB dropped their price 15 percent. These findings were important because in the competition we were working on, TB was trying to create interest in the program and quoting prices in the press. We believed those prices reflected their belief that they had no competition. Our conclusion was that this competitor raised their prices 15-21 percent when they believed they had no competitors and they cut their prices that amount whenever a competitive threat loomed. When we took 20 percent off of their quoted public prices this target aligned with the bottom up estimate we had developed for their solution, so we set a price below this target for the client's engineering team. They designed a more affordable solution that won the competition.

A company's bid aggressiveness also depends on the competition. If a company is competing for a contract and a known low cost company is bidding, it usually causes all of the other bidders to lower their prices. For example, a European telecom equipment provider was competing with their traditional rivals for a multimillion-dollar contract in Africa. When a low cost Asian competitor entered the competition, all of the competitors cut their pricing to historic new levels to compete.

Once the analyst has estimated the competitor's technical approach and understands their bidding behavior, he or she will add in profit and subtract out any likely competitor investment. From the competitor's past bidding history, the analyst should be able to deduce what margins the competitor targets. Do they bid lower or higher margins, and under what circumstances? To assess the competitor's business considerations and bid aggressiveness, you need to "get inside their head." To do that, look for signals including the corporate web site and press announcements. You'll also want to assess the caliber of their capture team. Do they have their A team on the program? If a company assigns a top executive to win an opportunity, it communicates the opportunity's importance. How much are they spending on advertising and demonstrations, and have they hired expensive consultants to help them win? If a competitor is promoting the opportunity to its shareholders, that says a lot. These are signals that indicate how important the pursuit is to the competition, which gives you an idea how much they're willing to invest or cut margins to win.

Conversely, if a company knows that their approach is significantly less costly than the competitors', they can bid with significant margins and still be confident of proposing the lowest price. It is important to note that if a company does not have competitive intelligence and PTW capability, they will not know if they have a cost advantage and may fail to take advantage of cost discriminators. Our experience is that companies bid significantly lower than necessary to win about a quarter of the time. These companies' lack of competitive intelligence and PTW precludes them from leveraging cost advantages, and they squander shareholder value. One must consider how each company views an opportunity in order to project behavior.

We have seen competitions where a company thought they had an insurmountable advantage, so they proposed a monster bid – as much as they thought the market would bear. The PTW analyst should assess how strategically important this opportunity is to the competitor. On the other hand, if a company has experienced a string of losses, they usually start to dive on price. For example, we saw one company bid thin margins and cut budgets despite having many discriminators and a customer who hated their competitor. They wanted to get their price as low as possible because after having lost three big jobs in a row, the executive team thought that if they lost again, they would also lose their jobs.

The more you understand about the competition's thinking, the more precise your pricing can become. For example, a company that sold a line of expensive products implemented the PTW process. Their PTW analyst studied every sale and the executive team tried to price each sale optimally – adjusting their price up or down by millions depending on their relative competitive position. This approach significantly improved their win rate and profit margins. By studying the competition, the PTW analyst knew that the competitor was more bureaucratic and that they used a standard, but complicated, pricing model. By studying the competitor's pricing over time, the analyst was able to reverse engineer their pricing formula. The analyst's company started beating the competitor time after time, even winning with some of their competitor's long favored customers. The analyst's company kept waiting for the competitor to respond by changing their pricing policy. Finally, the competitor lowered their price on a small bid in an obscure market by seven percent. The PTW analyst spotted the price change. Because the competitor lacked any PTW analysis capability, the PTW analyst could imagine the competitor's executive team struggling with loss after loss, not understanding how they were being beaten time and time again. They probably had a long series of executive meetings to change their pricing policy. This small sale was the first sale after the likely policy change and revealed the size of their price cut. The PTW analyst got his executive team to adjust their pricing immediately to this change. His company then continued to ring up a whole new set of sales while the competitor took months to respond again.

In order to obtain a high level of confidence in the prediction of the competitor's bid price, you must try to triangulate your bottom up cost analysis. Optimally, you'll have three independent approaches for estimating the competitor's prices to verify each other. One good method is to look at your competitor's past bidding behavior to understand how aggressively they tend to price. You can also use lateral analysis by asking industry experts for their estimates of competitors' costs, and create a parametric estimate based on similar types of project prices. If these three approaches line up, we have confidence in our estimates as shown on the left in Exhibit 6-8. However, if the bottom up competitor estimate falls outside the other approaches, then you either need to find an explanation for the disconnect or look for errors in the analysis. The most detailed and highly weighted analysis is usually the bottom-up "should cost."

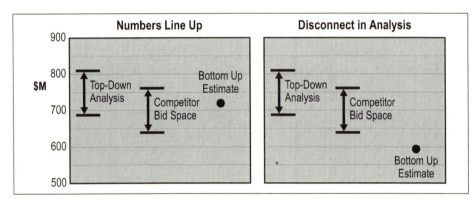

Exhibit 6-8: How Accurate Analysis Affects Pricing

How accurate can this process be? On the KC-135 Tanker Replacement Program, we used six different approaches to estimate the competitor's price. In the end, our estimate was off by $1 billion, which may seem like a lot, but it was out of an evaluated cost of $108 billion, or less than 1 percent.

Developing the Evaluation

After the PTW analyst develops the competitor price estimate, he or she determines where to put the company's price relative to the competition. This does not always mean a lower price than the competition; people are willing to pay more for some attributes. The methodology must identify and justify the differences in value between your solution and the competition's. This value difference allows you to optimize your price and still win. Since commercial customers usually use relatively simple evaluation scoring, while government customers tend to use formal and very detailed evaluations, we will describe two different methodologies for estimating value – one for commercial sales and one for government sales.

For commercial sales, competing solutions differ in terms of characteristics such as capacity, range, quality, reliability, schedule and safety. Every product is different, but any product can be described, and measured, in terms of a list of attributes that characterize its performance from the customer's perspective. It is challenging to calculate directly the monetary value of all of the performance differences among products. However, using the right methodology, you can infer the worth of your comparative advantages and disadvantages. If you know how your product stacks up attribute by attribute, you can evaluate its overall performance and determine an appropriate price premium or discount. To do this, you must assess your desirability to the customer versus the competition to know where to place your bid relative to the competitor's. As you recall, in chapters 3, 4 and 5, we described just how to identify customer values. We will use this analysis as a starting point to quantify price differentials between the competitors once you've determined the relative performance difference between the competitors on these key customer values.

Examine the customer's past buying history to understand to what extent they pay price premiums. How much and what was the value differential? Did they pay a small price premium, even though one product was far superior to the other? Or did they pay a large price premium for a product that was only marginally better? Obviously, if the customer pays large premiums for marginally better products, this would indicate that you could bid a large price premium if you had a similarly important purchase and a better solution. The converse is true also. If you have many examples of suppliers proposing significantly better solutions at higher prices and they always lose, that says bidding anything but low price is a risky strategy.

Next, analyze the customer's business case to understand how much your advantages (or those of your competitor) are worth to their business.

— Strategy in Action —

For example, Acme Construction and Conway Brothers were competing for an industrial construction project. A PTW analyst employed by Acme identified Conway's likely bid price as $100 million and quantified their discriminators. From discussions with people who worked with the customer before, the analyst learned that the customer was a sophisticated buyer of construction services and considered such factors as schedule and construction quality in the evaluation. The most important customer value for this bid was the project's completion date. The sooner the construction was complete, the sooner the customer would be able to begin to lease out the property. Acme was promising a 21-month schedule, while Conway was proposing a 24-month schedule. This earlier schedule would allow the customer to begin leasing the property three months earlier, which translates into $9 million of additional revenue for those three months. The customer had already sold the leases on the property, so if the construction were not finished on time, the customer would have to pay stiff penalties. This meant that schedule confidence was also very important to the customer's key decision makers. The customer had more confidence in Acme's ability to make their completion commitment, based on their industry track record. Since Conway's industry reputation was that they tend to miss completion dates, Acme's PTW analyst estimated that the customer would conservatively add another month to Conway's proposed schedule. As a result, improved schedule confidence was estimated to be worth $3 million. This customer highlighted the high quality of the facility's foundation, plumbing and electrical systems to their potential tenants, so the customer was likely to value high quality. Acme had a good reputation for providing higher quality construction. The analyst estimated that Acme's higher quality would translate into a slighter higher lease price for the space under construction, which was estimated at $5 million. All told, the PTW analyst estimates that Acme's bid was worth $17 million more to the customer than Conway's, as shown in Exhibit 6-9. Since Conway was likely to bid $100 million, Acme could win if they bid less than $117 million.

Customer Values	Acme Construction	Value (in $M)	Conway Brothers	Value (in $M)
Completion Date	21 months	$9	24 months	--
Construction Quality	High	$5	Fair	--
Schedule Confidence	0	--	+1 month	($3)
Total		$14		($3)
Greater Value		$17		

Exhibit 6-9: Determining Bid Value to Customer

While it is difficult to quantify value by tracking and analyzing award behavior, with time, intelligence and experience you can begin to predict outcomes. The rewards for this investment are great – they significantly improve a company's win rate and profit margins. Most companies on large projects consider non-price attributes in their decision making and these non-price attributes can be translated into dollars. The trick is quantifying them. It is important to note that if one calculated a $17 million advantage, as in the above example, that does not mean you have to bid as if you will receive all of that additional value. You discount the $17 million based on your level of confidence; this gives you room for error but still protects your profits.

In the case of government acquisitions, the PTW analyst tries to duplicate the customer's proposal evaluation criteria, and then score both their offering and the competitor's against it. This mock customer evaluation should be completed as soon in the pursuit as possible, usually before the customer has published any guidance. From the customer's past evaluations, as well as any published rules or guidelines on source selections, you should try to identify where the customer's evaluation factors come from and how are they scored. The best sources for this information are past debriefings and RFPs that your company has bid on for this customer. Finding and interviewing former customer employees involved in these source selections is invaluable to understanding how both the formal and informal process works. The analyst should attempt to replicate the customer's likely evaluation criteria and weightings, and should also try to duplicate the form and even the presentation of the evaluation to be as consistent with the customer's evaluation as possible. The more accurate you make the analysis, the more insight you will gain into the customer's thinking. Like the rest of the PTW analysis, this mock customer evaluation should be updated as the customer provides your team with their actual evaluation or more insight.

Once the evaluation criteria are developed, the analyst should identify strengths and weaknesses for the competitors and for themselves against each evaluation factor. When examining the strengths and weaknesses, the analyst will try to put himself or herself in the evaluator's place and objectively assess each competitor's offering against the evaluation criteria, creating a score. The scores are then compiled using the same method that the customer will use. From this analysis, the capture team is able to estimate each competitor's relative score.

— *Strategy in Action* —

Exhibit 6-10 shows an example of how NAVAIR might evaluate the offerings from Elite and Gold Wing for a new reconnaissance aircraft for the U.S. Navy. As the Exhibit shows, NAVAIR has four major evaluation categories: technical, past performance, similar experience and cost.

To estimate a quantitative category like "Effective Range," the PTW analyst would provide competitive intelligence to the company's aero dynamists. They would assess the drag, payload, fuel capacity and burn rate of the competitor's aircraft to estimate its effective range. In the example above, the PTW analyst found that Gold Wing's aircraft could barely meet the customer's minimum range requirements, which would result in a "Marginal" scoring. Elite's aircraft would easily exceed the customer's requirements and provide significant additional benefits to the customer, so the analyst projected they would be scored an "Outstanding."

Technical is further decomposed into technical approach and program schedule. The analyst tries to break the evaluation down to the lowest level evaluation factors possible. As with most competitive cost and technical analyses, the more detailed the assessment, the more accurate it becomes.

Proposal Ratings	Weights	Merit Rating	
		Gold Wing	Elite
A. Technical	60%	Mar	HS
1. Technical Approach	40%	Mar	HS
a. Effective Range	7%	Mar	Out
b. Cruising Altitude	7%	HS	Mar
c. Speed	7%	Mar	Out
d. Sensor Capability	7%	Mar	HS
e. Logistics and Readiness	6%	Sat	HS
f. Ease of Maintenance	6%	HS	Mar
2. Program and Schedule	20%	Mar	Sat
a. Risk Analysis	5%	Sat	HS
b. Ability to Achieve Schedule	5%	HS	HS
c. Test & Eval. Approach	5%	Mar	Sat
d. Software Risk	5%	Mar	Sat
B. Past Performance	10%	Low	Mod
C. Similar Experience	10%	HS	Out
D. Cost	20%		
Total Score		53%	68%

Merit

Out	Outstanding
HS	Highly Satisfactory
Sat	Satisfactory
Mar	Marginal
Unsat	Unsatisfactory

Past Performance Risk

VL	Very Low
Low	Low
Mod	Moderate
High	High
VH	Very High
Unk	Unknown

Exhibit 6-10: Example Proposal Scoring

For qualitative categories, like "Ease of Maintenance," the analyst lists strengths and weaknesses for Elite and then compares them to Gold Wing to create a relative scoring. In this case, Gold Wing's simple design offered easy access to the engines and avionics compartment, while Elite's systems were more difficult to access. As a result, Gold Wing was rated "Highly Satisfactory" and Elite was rated "Marginal." It is important to use the likely evaluation criteria as a guide to collect intelligence on the competitor's capability in those areas. It is frequently difficult to get good specific competitive intelligence on elements of the evaluation, but one needs to collect enough to make good judgments. For example, it is unlikely that an analyst will know many details of a competitor's software development process, but one can get a good sense of whether their software capability is a strength or a weakness compared to their industry peers. By conducting searches of papers written, press releases, association memberships and hiring ads, a competitive intelligence analysis can determine whether a company is leading, following or pacing the industry's software development practices. If the company is publishing several cutting edge papers and has industry renowned personnel, one can assume a state-of-the-art capability. If they never claim software as a core competency and they are hiring managers requiring only basic qualifications, the competitor may be lagging behind the rest of the industry. It is critically important to remain dispassionately objective when conducting this analysis. It is just as important not to overestimate a competitor as it is not to underestimate them. A biased analysis can cost you the competition.

In the above example, Elite had a rather significant evaluation advantage over Gold Wing. If their customer's key decision makers favored Elite's offering and the customer historically paid price premiums, Elite's Price-to-Win target could be set significantly higher than Gold Wing's estimated bid price. How much higher would be based on the size and consistency of the customer's historical price premium.

Setting the Price

We have seen companies with the solution that key decision makers want most lose because their price was too high or their evaluation score too low. And we have seen companies with the highest evaluation score and lowest price lose because the key decision makers desired the competition more. In order to ensure a victory, you must have the solution the key decision makers want most *AND* your solution must balance the price and the evaluation score so that it is easy for the key decision makers to justify selecting your solution. For example, the Kwajalein Reagan Test Site (RTS) is used to track Intercontinental Ballistic Missiles fired from California into the South Pacific. The Army awarded Bechtel the management of the RTS, even with a $600 million higher bid price (29 percent), which is a really big price premium. The Army justified this price premium by saying that the technical and management criteria were of much more importance than the cost because of "the critical importance and extremely high cost of the customer programs supported by the RTS." Individual tests often cost in excess of $100 million each and were critical to national security. Despite the size of the price premium, the Army decision makers could easily justify it.

Key decision makers can choose whoever they want, if they are willing to take the political backlash from their Board of Directors, elected officials or procurement bureaucrats to whom they must justify their actions. Choosing the lowest priced offeror is always easy to explain. The bigger the gap between the lowest offeror's price and the winner's, the more scrutiny the decision is likely to receive. The greater the transparency of the decision and the less autonomy the procurement team has, the more pressure they are susceptible to. NASA has a great deal of transparency and oversight from the GAO and Congress, for example, while no one questions the decisions of Saudi Arabia's royal family. Typically, as potential political pressure increases, more reluctant decision makers begin to award larger price premiums. On the other hand, the more sophisticated the procurement organization, the greater their ability to justify higher prices with analysis. So NASA, despite its transparency and oversight, allows its talented organization to justify choosing significantly higher priced bidders if they can create a persuasive rationale.

The correct balance between the evaluation score and the price comes down to how much higher an evaluation score needs to be in order to justify a higher price. The acceptable balance is based on the norms of behavior of the customer and key decision makers. Some customers seem unable to justify a three percent price premium, while others routinely justify twenty percent. It is not just the magnitude of the price difference, but also the relationship between the evaluation score difference and the price difference. The wider the gap between the two evaluation scores, the greater the customer's ability to justify a price premium.

Using your assessment of the customer's likely evaluation scoring and routine buying behavior, you can determine where your price needs to be, relative to the competitor, and how big the gap can be. If your solution will likely receive a higher score, and customer's buying behavior shows a willingness to pay a price premium, then you can set your price higher than the competitor's. If your score is equal to or less than that of the competitor, then your team should set a PTW target comfortably lower than the competitor.

The PTW target is the final price after all rounds of the post proposal submittals or negotiation. You must shoot for the end game of the competition. After developing your PTW, you must develop your negotiation strategy so that you can set your proposal price. Your negotiating strategy determines what price concessions you are willing to make from the proposal price to the final negotiation so you need to include this pad in your proposal price. Developing the negotiating strategy is discussed in Chapter 11.

Sometimes an important customer will say, "Bid the funding line, we want you to spend all of the budget." If you are bidding on a research and development contract this may be true. Otherwise ignore this direction. The customer program manager is naively saying this because he or she has worked hard to get their budget and has no incentive to give unspent money back. However, they forget that there is a competition and that if one company bids 20 percent below the funding line while your company bids the funding line… it doesn't take a rocket scientist to figure this one out. The other guy wins. The decision makers need to justify awarding a price premium, and while the program manager is only worried about his or her project, the decision makers usually have lots of projects to fund. If they can save some money on one project then they can spend it elsewhere.

Packaging the Price

When the PTW analyst has completed the analysis and is prepared to present their recommendations and target price, it is important that this information be presented to senior management, especially the CFO. Senior management will make the pricing decisions in the end and they need to understand the rationale behind the PTW.

From our experience, approximately three quarters of the time the capture team's current cost baseline is above the PTW target. In those cases, the PTW analyst needs to show a roadmap of low risk cost reductions that take the current cost baseline down to the PTW target. The analyst uses ideas gleaned from the "should cost" and from the competitive analysis to provide a set of cost reductions. Developing this roadmap enhances the "believability" of the analysis by reconciling the PTW target with the current price estimate and "should cost." This process helps the PTW analyst sell the PTW target. If it seems unachievable, the PTW target gets ignored at the company's peril. We have seen a few cases where it was impossible to get a company's "should cost" down to the PTW. In those cases, the company either needed to make an investment or no bid. In cases where our clients have bid significantly below our "should cost," the clients won but their programs went significantly over their budget contract execution. Bidding below the "should cost" is a very bad idea.

— *Strategy in Action* —

We worked on the Price-to-Win for a data collection system where the majority of the cost consisted of hand held data collection devices. We determined that our client needed to lower their bid cost by $60 million or 25 percent to undercut the competitor in price. When we studied the client's solution, we found that one of the most expensive components of the handheld devices was the transmitter. The client's operational concept was for their data collectors to transmit data to headquarters after each reading. We also learned that the data collectors meet with their supervisor each day. Therefore, since all of the handhelds had Bluetooth capability (it could electronically transmit data within a few feet), we recommended that instead of having a transmitter in every handheld, the client install one in only the supervisor's unit. When the supervisor met with the data collector, he (or she) could transfer all of his readings to the supervisor using Bluetooth and then the supervisor could upload all of the data from their data collectors to headquarters in one transaction. By requiring only the supervisor's handheld to have a transmitter, this solution eliminated the need for 90 percent of the transmitters saving $60 million. We also estimated that by having the supervisor consolidate all of the data into a single transaction, it would reduce daily data transmission volume by more than a factor of a hundred. We believed that this reduction would significantly reduce the complexity of receiving and processing telecommunications transactions at headquarters, as well as operator training requirements because they would not have to deal with transmission errors and resends. The client capture team believed that the customer thought of handhelds like smart phones and would think of non-transmitting handhelds as antiquated technology. However, the "should cost" analysis using the non-transmitting handhelds showed to the client that the PTW was achievable – they had previously thought it was impossible. The client's engineering team went to work and developed a new design that included a transmitter in every unit, a very aggressive cost challenge, which hit the PTW target and won the program. However, the program ended up being cancelled due to program management failures, and technical problems achieving the cost target and data transmissions overloading the telecommunications system.

Interestingly, we find that the most resistance to our PTW targets is in the twenty five percent of the cases where we recommend raising the capture team's price. The objective of the PTW is to identify the highest price a company can bid and still win. Frequently, the only advocate for this objective is usually the CFO. The capture team leaders are incentivized to win. They typically behave like typical salesmen and want the price target as low as possible to increase their probably of winning. Whether the company can perform or make a profit holds less importance to them. The analysis is also an independent view of the pursuit and some of the recommendations may go against the positions pushed by the capture team leader. We have seen capture team leaders hide the PTW results from their senior management because they disagreed with those results.

For example, we were working on a large pursuit with four companies competing where the customer was going to award two contracts. Our client was desperate for a win, as they had lost their last two major pursuits and many of their executives believed they would be fired if they lost another one. Before we were brought on to conduct our PTW analysis, the capture team had made all the right decisions – they had selected the right strategy, chosen the right technologies and picked the right teammates. The competitors had revealed enough information in the press about their solutions that we could accurately estimate their costs. We did extensive competitive analysis leveraging the world's most renowned designers to build our cost analysis. We found that all three of the competitors had significant risk and cost problems. In fact, we believed there was a good chance that two of the competitors would be disqualified because their technology was so immature. We told the capture team leader that the company could raise his price by $60 million and still have a 95 percent win probability. In our experience it is significantly more difficult to get executives to raise prices than to drop them, and this situation was no different. The capture team leader wanted a very low price because he wanted to make sure they won. He had no prior pursuit experience and did not want to believe what we were telling him, despite the overwhelming evidence. He hid the PTW results from his executives. After finishing our PTW analysis, he had us update our analysis twice with new intelligence, hoping we would raise our estimates for the competitors. Each time, as we gained more intelligence and improved our understanding, all three of the competitors' relative positions grew worse. Finally, he hired another consulting firm to give him the answer he was looking for – that the competition would be close and that his team needed to bid extremely low. He bid low and won. The ironic result was that this customer published the two winning bidder's prices showing that our client had under bid their competitor by $70 million. When the CEO of the corporation called the capture team leader after the announcement, he did not congratulate him. Instead, the CEO asked, "Why did we bid so low?" It is critical to have the PTW analysts brief the senior executives so they can make informed pricing decisions and maximize shareholder value.

Deploying Cost Targets

The PTW process does not end with providing a price target. It should also produce a host of actionable recommendations for improving one's competitive position. A PTW is a comprehensive analysis, and the process always brings to the surface many critical competitive issues. It can provide executives with an unparalleled and independent assessment of the capture team's win and pricing strategy. For example, the Joint Strike Fighter PTW identified some significant issues that triggered changes in the avionics architecture, the allocation of engineering resources, and the operations and support approach.

Once management has agreed on the PTW target, finance and the PTW analyst need to work together to set cost targets with support from the leaders of the functional organizations. Costs targets should cover all the elements of cost that the customer will evaluate as price. For example, if the customer is including operations and support (O&S) in their price assessment, then cost targets for O&S should be developed. From the PTW process, your finance manager should flow down cost targets, called "bogies," to the functional departments and be consistent with the Work Breakdown Structure (WBS). If business management sets cost targets at too high a level, the cost target will encompass areas outside one manager's area of responsibility and no one will have accountability for hitting the number. The cost targets need to be set at a level at which budget estimates are made and used for design-to-cost (DTC) or CAIV targets. The targets should be broken down so functions such as tool design, production control and software quality control have their own cost targets. By having business management develop this baseline, it ensures that burdens, G&A and fee are also included, items which the technical staff so often forgets. This avoids lots of rework later.

When deploying these cost targets, it is important to explain their rationale to cost area managers so that they understand that the numbers are not arbitrary and have logic behind them. This helps them accept the targets. Once the cost targets are set and deployed, the team's business manager must manage to those targets. They should have a spreadsheet where the cost targets are tracked against the functional estimates and are updated as revisions come in.

While we have frequently heard the comment, "The functions should develop grassroots estimates without targets, otherwise they won't make their best efforts," our experience is that functional organizations rarely estimate too low, and that people almost always over scope their work. By deploying cost targets prior to the estimating process, the capture team sizes the work upfront and brings up scope issues before engineers spend countless hours estimating to the wrong assumptions. Likewise, people have difficulty going down to a target after they have created and justified a higher number. Functions and subcontractors end up thinking that you are trying to squeeze them out of profit, hours or work scope. It is better to set cost targets early on and let them drive the design. If a company has trouble meeting the target, they need to get innovative like McDonnell Douglas did on JDAM.

The PTW must be derived early enough to allow it to drive the solution architecture. Also, the resulting cost targets become critical design parameters. Only by having the market-derived PTW drive product development, can profit margins be maintained while creating a winning approach. The business manager should monitor and record in a database how each group is progressing against their cost target. In this way, the business manager can keep the technical lead and the program manager abreast of progress toward the PTW target. Continuous dialog with the functions and subcontractors is necessary so that neither side is surprised as costs are refined. The technical lead must ensure these cost targets are a key design parameter and monitored across the development process.

When Should a PTW be Conducted?

Effective pricing is critical to winning. A company must know early on if they have an affordable solution for their customer. If not, they should "no pursue" and find other opportunities. The company also needs to ensure that the solution they will be proposing is cost competitive. They must avoid making any decisions that put them in a cost bind. Even early on in the pursuit, the customer may ask questions whose answers may lead to the company being burdened with a costly solution. It is imperative to develop a price target very early in the pursuit.

As Exhibit 6-11 shows, the PTW is iterated throughout the capture process. It also shows the percent of the PTW work during each phase. The analysis becomes more detailed and evolved as the opportunity matures. The analyst adjusts the targets as the customer changes their acquisition strategy, requirements or available funding and as more competitor intelligence is uncovered. In addition, the capture team continually assesses their own progress in meeting the targets.

An initial PTW target is developed prior to the company's "pursue/no pursue" decision, well before the company has made significant investments. At this point, the PTW should consist of a top-level parametric estimate compared to the customer's likely budget as well as rough order analysis of the competitors' likely bid prices. This analysis validates whether you have a solution that will fit within the customer's funding and is affordable compared to the competitors. If there is insufficient funding or a significantly lower priced competitor, you should not bid. Initial PTWs resulting in "no pursues" keep companies from squandering millions in discretionary marketing and sales funds.

Once a capture team is committed, they should have an extensive PTW analysis conducted, which includes the "should cost" and competitive bottom up cost analysis. Even though this may be well before the customer has finalized their requirements, it allows the capture team to develop and deploy cost targets early. The PTW process brings up the key cost issues and focuses the team on designing in affordability at the program outset. The PTW guides teammate selection, avoiding commitments to unaffordable work share agreements or products. The more time the capture team has to work on cost, the more innovative they can be.

Conversely, over time, capture teams become more entrenched in their existing solutions and less able to sell internally and externally innovative approaches. They are forced to fall back on traditional and potentially uncompetitive approaches. Once lost, time is impossible to make up.

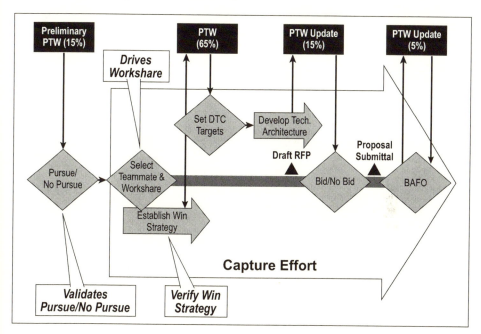

Exhibit 6-11: PTW Iterated throughout the Pursuit

The PTW analysis is updated whenever a significant customer event occurs such as the release of the Draft RFP and the Best and Final Offer (BAFO). With this further definition of the customer requirements, some adjustments are typically required to the overall PTW target. The PTW may also need to be updated if significant new intelligence is uncovered which has a sizable impact on the likely price.

The PTW process continues after the award decision to understand how the customer made their decision and what the competitors proposed. This process helps the companies adjust their future competitiveness by understanding what really happened on a competition. Without a competitive cost analysis, we see executives miss the opportunity to learn from experience. Frequently, they dismiss their losses by assuming that the other company bid below cost just to get the business, stating "the competition bought into the program." Despite this common sentiment, we have rarely seen American companies intentionally bid under cost (Electric Boat's bids on some large cost plus contracts in the '70s and Boeing's 2011 tanker bid are notable exceptions. French, Spanish, and Chinese firms are another story). This observation was ironically demonstrated in the satellite business a few years ago.

— *Strategy in Action* —

After losing a big satellite program, the Vice Chairman of Company X bitterly decried in the press that his company could not bid as low as Company Y because "my shareholders demand an adequate return." However, had the Vice Chairman's company conducted a competitive analysis they would have discovered that Company Y did not win the program at a loss. In fact, Company Y had incorporated new technologies into their satellites and proposed a new information management system that significantly reduced their program management and engineering costs. Just six months later, the Vice Chairman's company won a major satellite program by dramatically undercutting Company Y's price. Ironically, Company Y's president whined in the press the following week about how the Vice Chairman's company was "buying the program." When, in fact, Company X had elected to use some discounted rocket launches on this bid that they had obtained from an unrelated business deal. The rocket launch savings slashed their bid cost.

In neither case were the companies intentionally bidding at a loss (we say intentionally because satellite manufactures are notorious for frequent cost overruns). Because these firms did not conduct a competitive analysis after the award, they remained ignorant of their competitor's successful tactics and failed to learn the correct lessons from their losses.

— *Strategy in Action* —

In another case, a small competitor underbid a large communication system company by 50 percent on three consecutive space-based transmitter bids. Many executives in the larger company jumped to the conclusion that the smaller company was cheaper because of lower labor rates. The PTW analyst assigned to examine these losses was skeptical of this conclusion. The analyst assessed the bids and found that the largest cost driver in the transmitter design was a set of radiation-hardened chips. These chips are required in space applications to enable the hardware to continue working properly when bombarded with interstellar radiation. These chips must go through a long and expensive manufacturing process. The large company made radiation-hardened chips, while the smaller competitor bought them from third parties. As a result, the large company's engineers had significant motivation to use radiation-hardened chips throughout their design. The large company's chief engineer insisted that all of the hardened chips in his design were essential. However, even after accounting for their lower labor and overhead costs, the analyst found that the only way to explain the remaining cost difference was if the smaller company was not using as many radiation-hardened chips. The analyst did further research and found that there was a method of sample testing that allowed companies to certify, significantly less expensive, commercial chips for some radiation-hardened use. The analyst replaced the cost of some of the radiation-hardened chips with the commercial ones in his cost model of the competitor and found the spreadsheet hit the competitor's prices on their last three bids exactly. Initially, the chief engineer was unimpressed with the analysis. He had worked in the industry for over 30 years and had forgotten more about radiation hardened chips than the competitive analyst would ever know. However, when the analyst told the engineer that he was going to brief the divisional President on his findings and the engineer would need to explain why the competition could use commercial chips and his company could not, the engineer decided to rethink his position. When the President held a meeting to discuss the PTW results, the chief engineer concluded that his company could also bid sampled commercial chips. The large company changed their approach to selecting chips and won the next bid against their small competitor for the first time in five years.

Over the last ten years, global consolidation has created a handful of lean and largely technically level companies who battle over a small set of "make or break" programs. Within this fiercely competitive environment, companies spend hundreds of millions of dollars on proposal development each year, but only a few top companies have an effective PTW process. Based on our experience working on over 100 pursuits, we have learned that developing an early and effective PTW, and implementing its recommendations, is the single most important factor in securing a victory.

It is very important to keep in mind that to ensure victory, a company must be certain that they are most desired by the customer's key decision makers AND that they have the correct balance between the price and the proposal evaluations. If a team fails to do both, the competition is a toss up. To ensure victory, the key decision-makers must want your offering the most, and you must make it easy for them to justify selecting you. Fail to accomplish both of these activities at your own peril.

Chapter 7: Staffing and Leading the Capture Team

"Alone we can do so little; together we can do so much."

— Helen Keller, blind author and political activist

You work as a team, you win as a team and you lose as a team. ***Identifying and securing the right people for the capture team is one of the greatest challenges facing executives on every major pursuit.*** Almost always, the most talented people needed for the capture team are also the busiest. The right staffing for the capture is the company's "dream team." Ideally, the company's most dynamic and aggressive vice president will lead the dream team. It will include the company's top engineer, the one who can solve any problem; the business development manager who can charm every customer; and the business manager who always comes up with an innovative solution. A company's probability of winning is directly related to the quality of their capture team.

To staff the capture team with the right personnel demands sacrifice. A company must compromise today's contract execution for tomorrow's future business, just like Lockheed Martin did when they assigned Tom Burbage to the JSF pursuit discussed in Chapter 1. Making this trade-off is a difficult decision for executives. It is also the decision that typically separates winners from losers. ***Winners assign the "right" team; losers make do with who is available. Assigning the right people is always a difficult decision.***

Getting the best people assigned early on is usually the problem. "Early on," as shown in Exhibit 7-1, is when the company has the greatest ability to influence the customer. Ironically, companies are almost always willing to throw money and their best people at an opportunity at the eleventh hour when the situation is desperate. The challenge, and the key to victory, is to assign the best people early on when they can have the most impact on the solution concept and the customer. When the executives finally assign their top talent as the proposal is being patched together, all the company stars can do is try to fix their predecessors most egregious mistakes.

No leader can achieve their vision alone. Once a company conducts the pursue/no pursue, and commits to winning an opportunity, they assign the capture team, the cross-functional team held accountable for winning the opportunity. This team, under the direction of the capture team leader, formulates the win strategy. They then convert that strategy into a capture plan, which details all the tasks the company must complete to position themselves as the winner. The team then carries out that plan, iterating and evolving it throughout the pursuit with new intelligence as needed.

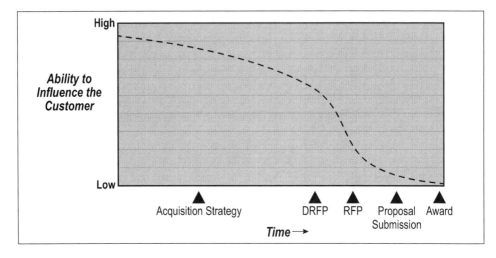

Exhibit 7-1: Assign the Top Team Early

The composition of a capture team will vary from one pursuit to another based on the opportunity's size, importance, customer concerns and technical characteristics. A capture team pursuing a critical multibillion-dollar opportunity can consist of dozens of full-time people for years, while a smaller pursuit may consist of a handful of people for a few weeks.

The capture team brings together all the critical skills needed to develop and sell the solution. A typical moderately sized capture team as shown in Exhibit 7-2 includes a program manager, technical director, business manager, contracts manager, business development/account executive and proposal manager. The teams usually start with a small core team with functional representatives phased in as needed. Then, depending on the customer needs and key contract requirements, the company will add staff from other disciplines. For example, if the opportunity has significant product support needs, the capture should include a logistics specialist. If there is a large production component requiring supply chain integration with the customer, the capture team should include supply chain management or manufacturing representatives.

It is the capture team leader's responsibility to ensure that every member has a clearly defined role and responsibility. Below, we describe the typical responsibilities of the key capture positions.

The Capture Team Leader

A company's choice of capture team leader can make or break the pursuit. The capture team leader develops and implements the overall strategy to win the pursuit and has the final authority in strategy decisions, as well as day-to-day responsibility for positioning the solution with the customer.

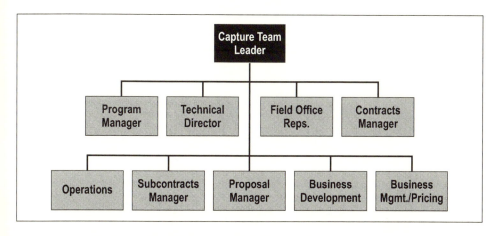

Exhibit 7-2: The Typical Capture Team – Everyone Has a Role

Running a capture effort is an incredibly complex and difficult task. And it becomes increasingly difficult as the number of people involved grows. The key challenge for the capture team leader is to avoid being drawn into the mundane details of the pursuit and losing sight of the strategy implementation. Pursuits are overwhelming, and it is easy to lose focus. The capture team requires discipline to implement all the elements of the capture – keeping up the intelligence collection, getting the logistics system defined and working to influence the customer. As new information is collected and problems arise, the plan and the leader must adapt. Leading a capture effort will test the capture team's program management skills to the utmost.

The capture team leader is responsible for:
- Leading the win strategy development
- Overseeing the creation of the capture plan
- Directing and monitoring implementation of capture plan
- Orchestrating customer shaping
- Managing the pursuit budget
- Managing teammate relationships
- Conducting capture team meetings
- Facilitating executive reviews and selling the pursuit internally – getting the resources to win
- Ensuring an effective Price-to-Win is conducted with cost targets deployed and tracked
- Overseeing the proposal development

A capture team leader can be a vice president or an account manager. He or she must have stature relative to the program value, and must be able to negotiate work scope and contractual commitments with teammates. Stature is important for the leader, in order for him or her to be able to quickly access the company's senior executives to resolve problems. This stature will help to get the right people and resources assigned. The capture team leader must be able to successfully fight for the resources necessary to win. These resources could be facilities, R&D or help from a sister division.

— *Strategy in Action* —

For example, after Frank Cappuccio, the Lockheed Martin JSF capture leader, learned from the competitive analysis that Boeing's open architecture solution was a significant discriminator, he called Bob Coutts. Bob Coutts was one of the top four Vice Presidents at Lockheed who led the Electronics Sector. Frank Cappuccio asked Coutts to form a "world-class" team to assess the JSF team's avionics solution and recommend improvements. The request for help was unprecedented within Lockheed, as the Vice President of the Aeronautics Sector, where JSF was led, and Coutts of the Electronics Sector were rivals. But Cappuccio knew the best avionics capabilities did not reside in his sector. So putting egos aside, he did something hard. He asked for help from outside his sector. Coutts assembled a team of top experts from across his sector, drawing on expertise from ten different Lockheed companies and a key teammate. Many were pulled from critical projects. The team assessed Lockheed's JSF solution and found it wanting. They revamped Lockheed's solution, changing it from a military-focused proprietary solution to a commercial open systems architecture. Frank Cappuccio's stature allowed him to quickly access Coutts and persuade him to help. Cappuccio had the clout to get the resources he needed to win; maybe no one else within Lockheed could have successfully reached out to another sector for such assistance. This also demonstrates another key lesson: winners do hard things. Calling another sector for help on their biggest program was hard.

Capture experience is essential for a capture team leader. They need experience in pursuits of comparable size. We have seen many billion dollar pursuits led by excellent smart leaders who have never been on a pursuit before. No matter how good the person, inexperienced capture team leaders almost always lose large pursuits. People rarely do anything well their first time trying, and this is no different. Managing a large complex sale is one of the most difficult jobs in any company. Experience teaches a person what's important and whose advice they should ignore. Without experience, capture team leaders do not know what is most important, what tasks cost, and how important intelligence is. Rookies make catastrophic errors. One inexperienced capture team leader chasing a multibillion-dollar opportunity told a reporter, "it is going to come down to price ... so we are going to have to bid accordingly." This statement sent a message. It was a message that went directly to the competitive intelligence analyst at his competitor. And the message was: we intend to bid low. This is absolutely one of the worse messages one can send. It drives everyone in the competition to lower their prices. And by driving anyone's price down, you reduce your ability to differentiate yourself on cost. This capture team leader did not even end up driving his team's price very low as he said he would in the article. But the competitor took this comment very seriously and drove their price down by a billion dollars and won by being significantly lower in price.

Unfortunately, the reality is that at many companies there are few people with suitable capture experience, skills, personality, and stature to lead all the critical pursuits. To have a pool of experienced capture team leaders, the best-in-class cultivate a tribe of great hunters by providing significant incentives and rewards to hunters. These companies identify ambitious young marketers, engineers and program managers. They assign them to proposals, train them in capture and start assigning them to capture efforts to develop winning skills. Over time, these people develop competitive experience and are mentored to become seasoned leaders. At these companies, winning a key pursuit is an important step toward advancing into senior management. Top performers demonstrate that winning is important.

At some of the poorer performing companies, we see a different behavior. These companies assigned failed program managers to run capture teams until they win something to redeem themselves. These companies treat their capture leaders like Sisyphus. The Gods sentenced Sisyphus to Hell, pushing a large boulder uphill only to watch it roll back to the bottom where his job awaited him again. At many poor performing companies, running a capture effort is purgatory.

In the case where circumstances force a company to assign a senior executive who lacks pursuit experience as capture team leader, it is vital that the company provide the leader with an experienced capture mentor. We have seen retired executives or consultants fill this role well.

A capture leader on a major pursuit should have not just capture experience, but company experience as well – he or she should not be a new hire. The leader must know the company's strengths and weaknesses, must write proposals well, and know how to estimate costs and plan logistics. This is imperative so they know what capabilities to leverage and what to compensate for. They also have to know whether they are getting the right personnel assigned to their team. The leader does not have the luxury of time in the middle of a pursuit to figure these things out. This person must also have the trust of the company's executives. Executives can become paralyzed by indecision if they do not know whether to believe their capture leader. Running a major pursuit requires the capture team leader to ask the executives to make tough decisions, and the company's executives must have confidence that when the capture team leader asks for something, it is something that he or she really needs. That can only come from trust built over time.

A good capture leader must be comfortable making decisions even when faced with ambiguity. In a capture effort, one cannot wait to have all the information desired to make a decision, you never know exactly what the customer wants, much less what the competitor is really doing. Leaders must make decisions.

To help ensure that the capture team leader has "buy in," best-in-class companies typically assign the capture team leader just prior to or after the pursue/no pursue decision. That way, the leader is able to propose "his or her team" and the resources they believe are required to win. Recruiting their own team increases their personal commitment to winning. The capture team leader continues to lead the pursuit until after victory and can then turn over all of their responsibilities to the program manager. Many companies struggle with whether they should have the program manager, who will ultimately run the program, also lead the capture effort. Companies with the highest win rates have specialized capture team leaders. These companies recognize that capture team leaders and program managers have different personalities. Rarely do we find people that do both jobs well. It is important to note that, as this chapter will explain, the capture team leader and the program manager are two different jobs and should be held by two different people. The exception to this rule is when the pursuit is small and it cannot afford two people.

Good capture team leaders have a "hunter" personality – they are the strong, aggressive entrepreneurs. They must like to compete. They must have lots of persistence in the face of obstacles – there will be many obstacles on all big campaigns. These hunters are visionaries and strategists – people who can take a complex, ill-defined situation and imagine a path to victory. They are good communicators, as they need to articulate their vision to the customer, teammates, executives, and capture team members. They must have a good technical understanding of the solution to allow them to develop an effective strategy.

A capture team leader must have excellent program management skills to plan, organize and lead a team in the complex and unstructured environment of a pursuit. Capture team leaders should be natural organizers who are good at being objective and forceful in carrying out their commitments. They must be excellent at schedule management, because time is such a critical resource on a pursuit. Missing deadlines in a pursuit can be fatal. Cost control is a necessary skill, but capture team leaders must know where and when to spend their budget, and even go over if they must. We have never heard of executives firing a capture team leader for going over-budget and winning. But we have seen capture team leaders fired for losing. If a capture team leader goes over budget, they better be right. With a large complex team, they must be able to delegate as well as be able to accept and learn from criticism.

A good capture leader must be a persistent, disciplined risk-taker. Pursuits that succeed are those where people are willing to take risks. The capture team leader must encourage risk taking, which means supporting a team member's unsuccessful effort when necessary. When a team member tries something innovative and it does not work, the leader gives support by sitting down with that team member and saying, "Let's look at what happened and what we can learn from it." Losing is a big part of winning. Learning from failure is often the key to future success.

The capture lead must be flexible in applying process. As we've emphasized in previous chapters, structured capture processes are a key reason that the best-in-class win more business. Processes are critical, but they must be tailored to the pursuit. For example, government customers require elaborate proposals, while many others suffice with a single page letter. Different things are important on different pursuits and a capture leader must be able to adapt and carefully manage time and resources to identify what is important. In addition, the capture leader must be good at seeing what is illogical, inconsistent, impractical or inefficient.

Beware of the capture team leader who insists on doing things their way, neglecting proven practices. The person who reinvents everything and goes around the functional department heads and process owners loses the big pursuits. These "cowboys" isolate their capture team to keep outsiders from interfering in "their" pursuits. These people tend to have big egos or insecurity. Amazingly enough, on small pursuits, these cowboys usually have a good track record. With small, less competitive pursuits, a focused, hard-charging leader can win. On small pursuits, one can afford to make some mistakes and does not need to leverage the entire company's resources as in a large pursuit where using the best practices is a must. The best capture team leaders are open to outside help and take advantage of the entire company's capabilities.

The Program Manager

The program manager will be responsible for program execution and success after contract award. The program manager's responsibilities include:

- Developing the statement of work
- Managing the solution development
- Defining technical and execution organization baselines
- Developing the Work Breakdown Structure (WBS)
- Developing program plans, schedules and budgets
- Developing risk mitigation plans
- Performing make/buy analysis

Identifying and committing the proposed program manager during the capture phase is vital. It is critical that the capture team "sell" this person and their abilities to the customer. This individual is the most important member of the capture team to the customer. The success or failure of the project usually rides on their shoulders, so this person must inspire confidence in the customer. To inspire this confidence, the program manager should have program management experience on a similar scale and scope to the proposed project. Experience within the customer's marketplace is also important, because it gives the customer confidence that their program manager understands their business. Being a successful program manager is all about meeting the customer's requirements on schedule and within budget. It is their experience and personality which must convince the customer that they are the individual to ensure the project is a success. During the capture phase, the capture team must introduce the program manager to the key customer decision makers and provide him or her with opportunities to demonstrate skill and competency. For example, on a customer visit to your facility, you would have the program manager brief the customer about your company's relevant experience. The program manager would use this opportunity to highlight some of his or her personal experiences, and the lessons learned from those programs.

Waiting until just before the proposal submittal to name the program manager shows a lack of commitment. It means that the pursuit team lacks a guiding force behind configuring the program. And most importantly, the customer never has the opportunity to meet the person that they are being asked to bet on. You cannot expect to win under these conditions.

Assigning an individual with all the necessary qualifications can be challenging.

— *Strategy in Action* —

A company was bidding a complex training system to an airline. The company had hired a very experienced executive from the airline who knew the customer's requirements very well. The customer's decision makers knew and respected this executive, and he had been instrumental in creating the training job at the customer. Originally, he was assigned to the high profile position of program manager. Unfortunately, this individual had never managed the development and implementation of a training system before. Given this lack of development experience, assigning him as the program manager was undermining the company's strategy to be the low risk solution. The company's executives recognized his lack of experience and developed a new plan. The company brought in another individual with the appropriate development program management experience to win. The former airline executive was kept on the program, but they created a position for him to be the customer relationship manager. He was no longer in the critical position as program manager, but became the individual responsible for interfacing with the customer.

Program managers have a different personality than capture team leaders. While capture team leaders are "hunters," program managers are often called "skinners." They are thorough, well organized, and can delegate. They are detail oriented risk mitigators, and they are conservative customer advocates. They like long-term customer relationships, and good program managers are very disciplined process people who manage customer expectations. Program managers are trained and experienced at working to mitigate risk and manage to schedule and budgets. They believe in accountability and focus on meeting the schedules and budgets they are given.

Skinners should manage programs, not lead pursuits. Program managers typically do not like risk nor do they believe in spending what it takes to win. For example, many times a capture team leader will initially receive too little funding or the procurement will stretch out costing more than budgeted. The risk taking and driven capture team leader will go back and fight the executive team for more funding. The program manager will manage his program through adversity, cut back and freeze spending. We have seen program managers bring their capture effort within budget and lose.

Never have the capture team leader manage a program. One company had an accomplished capture leader, a true hunter, who had racked up five consecutive victories. He wanted to do something different. He wanted to manage one of the programs he had won. Being a persuasive individual and one who could call in favors after winning so much business, the company's executives appointed him program manager. His tenure lasted just over three months as the program's scope and budget grew and its scheduled slipped. It is not a good idea to have a risk-taking entrepreneur manage a program.

The program manager plays a key role in developing the successful customer solution. He or she focuses on organizing the execution team and developing the execution plan. As the reader may have noticed in the Capture Team Structure shown in Exhibit 7-2, the program manager is shown reporting to the capture team leader. This is because winning is the primary objective of the capture team. We recommend that program managers report to capture team leaders for the same reasons that one has hunters lead pursuits and not skinners. The capture team will take on the personality of its leader. If a program manager is running the pursuit, the capture team will behave like a cautious risk mitigator. If the capture team is led by a hunter, the team will be innovative and entrepreneurial and won't mind risk taking.

Some worry that having the program managers subordinate to capture leaders will result in unexecutable (programs going over budget and falling behind schedule) contracts. Our experience is that these two individuals frequently act as a counterbalance to each other. While the capture team leader will tend to be a risk taker, the program manager will act as the company advocate. The program manager works closely with the capture leader during all phases of the pursuit. A program manager for a large complex program should not be a shrinking violet who allows the capture leader to propose imprudent solutions or make difficult promises. If your program manager would allow such behavior, you have the wrong person. The program manager needs to be of sufficient stature and capability to run the program. They must be able to stand up to the capture team leader and get a hearing with the executives if the capture team is proposing a solution that the program manager believes cannot be executed, or one that exposes the company to significant financial liability. If they cannot stand up for the company, they have no place in their position.

Unfortunately, based on the size of many opportunities, many companies cannot afford the luxury of having both a capture team leader and a program manager; they must be the same person. In these situations, the company executives need to provide much oversight. If they have a hunter leading the pursuit, they must carefully watch his or her promises. Also, if they have a skinner leading, they must push them to innovate and be aggressive. In those cases, the company must work hard to develop people with necessary skills as both a capture team leader and program manager.

Technical Lead

The technical lead is the individual who directs the engineering effort. This person, like the program manager, must inspire trust in the customer. He or she will be the person responsible for making the solution work after the capture team wins.

Specifically, the technical lead is responsible for:
- Formulating concepts and configuration
- Leading the overall engineering effort

- Establishing the technical approach and baseline
- Overseeing any supporting R&D
- Defining and managing trade studies so the choice for all realistic alternative approaches are explained, especially why a competitor's approach was rejected
- Managing the Design-to-Cost process so the solution meets the PTW target
- Developing the proof plan
- Assisting in analyzing competitor's technical approach
- Selling oneself to the customer
- Assisting customer in writing the requirements and developing the evaluation process

One of the most important elements of leading the engineering effort is for the technical lead to ensure his team conducts all of the appropriate trade studies. Trade studies provide an analytical comparison of cost and performance between two or more system design alternatives. The technical team should conduct trade studies to identify cost sensitivities and ensure that all key technical, design, and management alternatives are assessed and choices documented. The technical lead is responsible for ensuring that trade studies assess all potential alternatives, especially those chosen by the competition. This data allows the team to explain to the customer why they chose the approach they did. The technical lead also develops the proof plan. The proof plan defines all the actions needed to create persuasive data and facts for all of the key sales claims.

The technical lead and his or her staff help in analyzing the competitor's technical approach. To solve the customer's problems, design teams make trade-offs. In most cases, the competitor's design team faces many of the same trade-offs as your team. The technical lead can identify for the competitive analyst the key trade-offs each competitor will face – which processor to use, what type of antenna, or what hull form. Each of these choices has their own pros and cons. The competitive analyst can scour the marketplace for clues that will reveal which fork in the road the competitor took. Then, as the competitive analyst picks up clues, the technical lead can help deduce the competitor's choices and their resulting impact on the competitor's cost or desirability to the customer.

— *Strategy in Action* —

Working on a bid for constructing a telecommunications operations center, displays were a major cost driver. Since the competitor made displays, we were able to work with a company engineer to pick the one that best fit the customer requirements right out of their catalog, along with its price and specifications. When we discussed this display with the engineers from our display supplier, they told us about all the field problems that the competitor's display was having. In fact, our supplier was replacing those displays in the field because the customer was having so many problems. We then used this information to ghost the competition in the proposal. The technical lead's involvement in the competitive analysis was essential to gaining this competitive insight.

The technical lead must ensure that cost targets based on the PTW target are decomposed and distributed to the design team. The cost targets are broken down into meaningful targets so each group and subcontractor estimate has its own cost target and can be held accountable for meeting the target. The technical lead should ensure these cost targets are a key design parameter and monitored across the development process. The technical lead should work with business management to monitor how each group is doing against their cost target. In this way, the technical lead, program manager and business manager can all keep abreast of progress toward the PTW target.

The most successful capture team technical leads thrive on opportunity. They are comfortable with uncertainty. They enjoy working with end users to solve problems while building something new. However, they should not become so enamored with a new technology that they lose sight of what's important to the customer.

The technical lead needs to have the appropriate technical discipline and project experience for the proposed solution. The customer will scrutinize their background to gain confidence that they can lead the technical work to success. The customer must have complete confidence that the technical lead understands their problems and can meet its challenges. A customer will see through a company's proposed use of a software engineer, when a system engineer is really required, as we saw one bidder try to do. If the customer does not see your company assigning the right people during the competition, they conclude that they won't get the right people after the award, when they lose their leverage. Also, the technical lead must organize and control, in most cases, a complex development undertaking, so having program management experience is highly desired.

The technical lead should brief the approach to the customer's technical evaluation team. To whatever extent possible, the technical lead and staff should try to develop a close relationship with the customer's technical staff and work collaboratively with them to solve their problems. The win strategy should define how the capture team would like the customer's requirements shaped to improve their competitive position. This shaping requires the capture team to develop persuasive white papers, simulations and trade studies to be provided to the customer to justify the position you would like them to take. The technical lead ensures these materials are created and delivers them to the customers in briefings and demonstrations. The most effective technical leads become so close to the customer that they are invited by the customer to write the system specification or technical evaluation. This gives the technical lead the opportunity to compose those documents to best present the capture team's solution.

Business Development/Account Manager

Listening to the customer's needs and understanding their buying problems helps us develop the best solution while gaining a competitive advantage. This is the principle job of the business development manager. They are the chief customer interface and advocate. It is their job to get inside the customer's mind and understand how they think. The business development manager is also the team's lead intelligence collector and he or she maintains the overall intelligence focal point on both customer and competition. They should determine the customer's source selection process and key decision makers and their priorities. Plus, they must supply intelligence about what the customer thinks of their company and the competition. They must be able to confidently say, "I don't know, but I will find out."

The business development manager assists in formulating the strategy, managing the customer contacts and "romancing" the customer. They are responsible for developing customer contacts who are knowledgeable and who help guide a team through the sale. A good customer coach can provide key intelligence on the customer as well as help identify and meet the key decision makers. These managers are also the team's chief communicators to the customer. They should be in constant contact with the customer, sending messages to influencers and decision makers.

The characteristics of a great business development manager are: entrepreneurial drive, appropriate stature, sound business judgment, aggressive nature, and being "homework" oriented. They must be good communicators and listeners, and they must have a good personality fit with the customer's culture. As someone who has frequent contact with the customer, appearance, technical competence, and follow-through are noticed by the customer and reflect on your entire company and your solution. The business development manager must possess customer knowledge, marketing capability, and proposal experience.

Specific responsibilities of the business development manager are:

- Identifying the key customer decision makers
- Maintaining the key decision maker priority matrix
- Determining, understanding and influencing the customer values
- Developing and maintaining the capture plan, including:
  - Developing the communications plan, including messages, media, targets and timing
  - Making intelligence assignments
  - Developing and maintaining the contact plan
  - Orchestrating the advertising campaign
- Managing internal interfaces (disseminates information across team, company, corporate headquarters and customer)
- Managing customer, competitive analysis and PTW and acting as the central repository of all intelligence
- Assisting with identifying follow-on opportunities for creating the business case
- Monitoring the customer budgeting process and funding for the project

Business Management

This manager is the fiduciary conscience of the team. The business manager advises the capture team leader and the company's executives about whether they are making wise business decisions. The CFO looks to this person to verify that the cost estimate is realistic and counts on them to assess the risks. This position is largely one of coordination between the capture leader and the finance, contracts and legal organizations.

Business management responsibilities include:

- Assisting in developing, tracking and controlling the capture budget
- Managing the team to meet the PTW targets
- Overseeing cost estimating
- Assessing the impact of the terms and conditions
- Working with teammates and key subcontractors to establish their work scope
- Preparing price estimate briefings to management for review and approval
- Working with Business Development to create revenue projections
- Developing the business case

One of business management's critical tasks is to begin working cost early to ensure that the team can meet the PTW target. They lead the cost estimating effort and take the PTW target to engineering to convert it into functional cost targets to at least the fourth level of the WBS. They help the estimators by identifying applicable cost history and estimating methodology. The business managers establish the cost and pricing ground rules such as learning curves, lot buys, and labor categories to help the functions create consistent estimates. They coordinate estimates so that preliminary and finals are completed on time. They develop a database to track the targets to the functional estimates as they come in. They work with functions to ensure that cost targets are met.

While finance, which works for business management, performs the actual analysis, business management takes the lead in creating the business case for the bid. The business case is the detailed financial component of the "Is it worth it?" question answered during the pursue/no pursue gate. The business case seeks to analyze the cost, profit, program schedule, terms and conditions, and program and technical risks to create the cash projection and a net present value for the project.

Contracts Administration

Contracts administration plays an important role on the capture team. They provide advice and counsel about how to fulfill the terms and conditions of potential contracts. They interpret RFPs, contract clauses and provisions. This means they play a critical role in identifying onerous terms and conditions early on and help to ensure the company does not enter into a program with requirements that they cannot deliver. Their role is to protect the business interests of the company. One of the ways they do this is to advise senior management of potential risks and provide mitigation alternatives.

Specifically, Contracts:

- Knows and analyzes past customer history
- Researches and quantifies all applicable taxes, licenses, royalties,

liabilities, and government regulations
- Ensures Proprietary Information Agreements are in place with all key potential suppliers
- Works with the subcontracts managers and legal department to conduct due diligence on potential teammates
- Assists in writing teaming arrangements and obtains approvals
- Establishes contacts with the customer's contracts representative
- Assists the customer in writing contract terms and conditions
- Provides general problem-solving in data rights and warranties
- Recommends contractual structure
- Works with business management to develop the business deal
- Conducts negotiations
- Is the focal point and repository for all customer communications – Request for Quotes, letters, customer questions and proposals

The personality of this individual is important. As the company advocate in contract negotiations, there is always the danger of offending the customer. Poor negotiation and interpersonal skills can be disastrous. During one U.S. Air Force contract negotiation with a company, the legal and contracts representatives were so contentious and intractable that the senior customer negotiator removed tens of millions of dollars from the company's work scope. This capture team leader did not get the obstinate negotiators removed and their company paid a high price. The leader must find a contracts representative with the skills necessary to be firm in their positions, but one who can mesh well with the customer.

The Proposal Manager

Depending on the customer and the RFP, proposals can range from a single page to tens of thousands of pages. The proposal development can cost hundreds of thousands or even millions of dollars. The proposal manager is responsible for developing and producing the proposal. Creating a large complex proposal is a unique and difficult experience. When a company delivers huge proposals, crafting the right document with all the supporting messages is a key factor in the win. The proposal manager acts like a day-to-day capture manager while managing this complex effort. They have significant input and influence on everything from win strategy and themes to cost management and teammate selection. In these cases, the manager must have significant prior proposal experience. Also, program management experience is a real plus, because creating a proposal is a complex program management job.

The proposal manager is responsible for preparing and approving the proposal including:
- Managing the proposal development
- Recruiting and organizing proposal and review teams
- Preparing the proposal budget, organization, and schedule
- Architecting the proposal and developing the proposal outline
- Helping develop the strategy and win themes

- Ensuring the strategy and win themes are incorporated into the proposal
- Coordinating the statement of work and contractual structuring
- Creating a mock draft RFP
- Developing author packages
- Reviewing and critiquing proposal inputs
- Reviewing proposal progress and obtaining assistance as needed

While the proposal manager is responsible for the proposal, many companies that regularly produce large complex proposals have a proposal process manager. This individual oversees and manages a company's proposal infrastructure. The top performers have formal dedicated proposal specialists who facilitate creation of the proposal. If the company produces large complex proposals regularly, this position is imperative. Developing proposals with hundreds or thousands of pages so that the customer can find and understand what they are looking for is no easy task. This position formalizes the proposal process so that lessons learned are collected and implemented from one proposal to the next. Without a formal process, a large proposal's complexity overwhelms a team. A team will expend large amounts of effort reworking their drafts after the team encounters all the dependencies and inconsistencies that a big group of writers create without detailed formal plans up-front.

Selecting the Team

Before the pursue/no pursue review, the capture team leader should develop a list of skills and criteria for the capture team members, based on the needs of the pursuit. The leader starts by clearly documenting each individual's roles and responsibilities on the capture team. From this, they develop a needs assessment, which identifies the skills, level, experience and personality required for each key slot. Special attention is given to what types of people the customer likes. Not only are different talents and skills are required for different roles, but different personalities are required for different customers. For example, selling to Microsoft demands different personalities and skills than selling to a more staid and formal company like IBM. Customers buy from people they trust. You must staff your team with people who can build a rapport with the customer.

The capture leader must work with functional management to find the right talent for these criteria. The capture team lead can ask function managers or vice presidents to identify individuals who meet their criteria. Vice presidents can identify experienced individuals with skills and contacts who might not be widely known. Functional managers can then provide the leader with the resumes, experience, and current job assignments of potential team members. While a capture team leader may know the people, frequently he or she has mistaken beliefs about an individual's experience. We often see capture team leaders make the mistake of assuming a longtime candidate has capture experience, when they do not. Major pursuits need people with capture experience. The proposal process manager should track capture experience of key personnel.

Once the leader selects a list of candidates for each key slot, they should interview and approve every member of the team. An important aspect of recruiting is giving the capture team leader an opportunity to select their vision team. Throughout the recruiting process, the leader wants to foster a desire to become part of the team and an enthusiasm for winning the pursuit. The capture leader should tell prospective team members about the customer's problem, how they plan to win and what the competition is doing. In addition, the capture team leader must establish clear and high expectations for each individual. People will live up or down to those expectations.

Often, an organization's culture promotes recruiting mediocrity because it is safe and comfortable. Finding the perfect package is difficult. It is often easy to be lulled into accepting the "available" personnel, but **there is no substitute for selecting good talent.** The leader must ensure that the team has people with the necessary individual skills and experience for every function.

It is critical for the company to recognize and reward people who staff capture teams. This is one of the key characteristics of top performing companies. Being on a capture team should be a good career move, and selection is a two-way street. It is as much a process of the candidates selecting the team, as it is the leader selecting them.

The capture leader should develop a candidate capture team list with back-ups. The company's executives then make the final decisions. Executives know how good the people on the list are. This process helps ensure the business review board selects the best people (frequently people who would not normally be thought of) from across the organization. The executives must make these decisions to create organizational "buy-in" to the assignments. Because capture teams usually need the company's "best" people, difficult trade-offs must be made between one capture team versus another, or the pursuit of new business versus the performance of existing contracts. How the company decides to handle these trade-offs often determines whether a company will win or lose a pursuit. **Getting the right team is paramount to victory.**

Training the Capture Team

The capture environment is unstructured. There are almost an unlimited number of actions one can take to influence a procurement – from advertising, demonstrations, writing articles, making sales calls, creating white papers and providing unsolicited proposals, to name a few. Which technique will be effective is difficult for even the most experienced to determine. Managing a capture effort is a complex and challenging assignment, and being on a capture team is usually a significant cultural change from the traditional business environment. It requires greater personnel interaction and more consensus decision-making than regularly practiced in most organizations.

Once the desired capture team is identified, top performing companies train their teams in a common capture process. This training should include such topics as win strategy development, creating the capture plan, communicating with the customer, capture team roles and responsibilities, and intelligence collection.

People learn far more from examples, case studies and exercises than from lectures. The training should include a mix of all of these things. The training should include capture plan-building exercises where the participants work together. This way the training has maximum impact on the team and starts them off in the right direction. The training can also serve as a team building exercise. The training should define the roles and responsibilities for each team member. This is imperative to ensure there are no holes.

By training the team in crafting their win strategy, the training process ensures that each team member understands that win strategy. A frequent problem we see on large efforts is that people often contradict one another in their discussions with the customer or in different parts of the proposal, because they lack a common understanding of their strategy.

While competitive intelligence is a critical to winning, most capture team members are unfamiliar with how to systematically collect and use it. Your capture team effectiveness improves with intelligence and your intelligence improves by enrolling all of the capture team members in the process. Prior to starting the pursuit, the capture team members should be introduced to the competitive intelligence process and instructed collection techniques. Then, as the capture team develops the intelligence plan (described in Chapter 9), all of the team members can become intelligence collectors.

Training builds confidence. Confidence helps a team take risks and tackle new challenges. Confidence also makes every customer interaction more persuasive. The customer senses a company's self-confidence and it builds confidence in your company's abilities. A capture team can spend millions chasing a large complex procurement; spending a small fraction of that on training that significantly improves the team's effectiveness is a wise investment.

Leading the Team

Team members should report directly or be a "dotted line report" to the team leader. If they are a "dotted line report," the team leader should still have recommended these team members and have significant input into their performance evaluations. Input into the performance evaluations of capture team members is critical to ensuring that the team members focus on the pursuit and not on assignments from their functional bosses.

The capture team leader must emphasize that the pursuit is a team effort and that everyone shares in the win or loss. Each team member brings functional discipline and provides inputs to team decisions that reflect the process managed by that functional discipline. While each team member brings skills of a particular discipline to the team, members must transcend their disciplines, blend their skills and integrate their efforts into the capture effort. The team and its members are not going to succeed unless they work together. They offer ideas or propose solutions outside their area of expertise and provide timely support to enable the team to progress to victory. Everyone must be convinced that it will be more rewarding to work for the team than for his or her own individual goals.

The capture team leader must motivate the team by making the pursuit enjoyable and instilling the desire to win across a large diverse team. The capture team leader is the program champion, and since sales campaigns can be long and hard, requiring great personal sacrifice, people need inspiration to maintain commitment. Enjoyment builds teamwork and brings out the best in people, and also builds energy. Team members who are having fun are more energized, creative, productive and motivated to win. A good leader creates an environment where people are committed to their job; enjoy performing their roles, bringing their talents to the assignment and achieving results that they feel good about.

There are many nonfinancial motivators a leader can use to energize the team. Being asked to join an important team is always a flattering and motivating event. Many times being a member of a team can be one of the most important events in our careers. Also, being at the genesis of a new project can also be very satisfying. A leader can motivate staff by allowing them to present their work to senior management, which gives them good exposure and enhances their career. The company can motivate capture team members by ensuring that being a member of a capture team is a career enhancer. It is a real plus if the company requires capture team participation to be considered for advancement into management. Capture team membership gives staff cross-functional exposure, making them more valuable employees. Teamwork is rewarding when people realize that they can learn a lot from their team members, so giving everyone a share of the responsibility for the result fosters teamwork. If the capture team leader focuses too much responsibility on certain functions – program management or engineering – it inadvertently fosters a lack of respect for the other functions and the people in them. This is destructive. A sense of fairness is essential to fostering shared responsibility. It requires that all functions pull their weight. Being on a fully functional team is like driving a car with all cylinders firing – it is operating at peak effectiveness.

Once the team is assigned, the company should co-locate them to the greatest extent possible. Co-location significantly improves teamwork, communication, and overall effectiveness. Being located with the rest of the team is important to creating a sense of belonging, which is a natural desire among humans. Even the nonconformist wants to be accepted. Developing the team requires reinforcement, so providing common training, vision, social time, rewards and team symbols (names, logos, mascots, etc.) can help coalesce the team. The leader should seek to foster an atmosphere where all members demonstrate respect, attentiveness and friendship between teammates.

The capture team leader must motivate the team, which starts with effective communication. No leader can achieve a vision alone. The capture team leader must impart their vision of how their company is going to win with their capture team. Once the capture is underway, the capture team leader is responsible for creating and maintaining the detailed capture schedule that meets the capture objectives. The capture team leader must assign, schedule and track specific tasks to capture team members and functional department managers. This requires structure. The capture team leader must define and communicate the tasks and responsibilities to the team members through individual assignments in one of the elements of the capture plan – communications plan, contact plan, intelligence plan or action plan.

To manage this complex undertaking, the capture team leader must conduct regular status meetings with the capture team to coordinate and communicate all capture activity. Frequent reviews are needed to ensure all of the planned actions are executed. One of the most common causes of losses is failure to execute the capture plan. Status meetings may happen twice a week or even daily as the competition reaches its climax.

At these meetings, the leader reviews the last meeting's action items and the next week's assignments in the capture plan's action plan. The team reviews progress and analyzes findings, and discusses new intelligence on the pursuit to provide a common understanding. The team leader reviews accomplishments, resolves conflicts, and obtains feedback. These reviews allow the leader to communicate the plan, collect new intelligence, track progress, resolve problems, track expenditures and iterate the plan. Attendance must be compulsory for all capture team members and minutes must be required to ensure team members and functional managers complete actions. As part of the process, the business development manager should update the capture plan. As a result, the team has one validated, up-to-date source of information for all team members.

Standing up the Follow-On Capture Team

After you win, you still need a capture team in addition to your program execution team. Each of these teams has different goals and a different personality. While the program execution teams focuses on delivering the promised system on time and on budget, the follow-on capture team is focused on shaping the customer to keep the opportunity sold and their customer satisfied. In addition, the capture team seeks to grow the opportunity. The follow-on capture team is a low intensity effort where the staff is small and part-time. You want to keep your winning team together because they are the most knowledgeable and have ownership of the program. However, skinners, and not hunters, should staff the follow-on team. So typically, you will transition out capture team hunters, such as the capture team leader and the business development manager, as you convert to program implementation.

To keep the project sold, meaning funded, the team should have a communications plan to advertise the project's successes. You want to keep investors abreast of progress and demonstrated benefits, or in the case of a government program, you want to publicize the project's job creation, local community involvement and importance of its mission. It is important to create advocacy for the program. Every year, a project can enter battle for precious budget dollars. You want your programs to win those funds. For government programs, that means selling your program to Congress, think tanks, industry thought leaders, the GAO and other influential groups. Plus, you want to enlist other interested parties, like suppliers, labor unions and trade groups with political influence to support your program. Building this political support is crucial to maintaining and growing the program's funding. You should work with the customer to ensure the program is in the customer's long-term strategic plans and is going to meet emerging needs.

The best customers to cultivate are your current customers, so part of your business acquisition process should be to ensure that your current customers are happy. Keeping programs healthy is very important, especially development programs, where problems dramatically increase the likelihood of termination. Problem programs also have significant impact on a company's reputation, endangering future business. It is the responsibility of your follow-on capture team to ensure customer satisfaction. Your team should hold regular customer satisfaction reviews to identify and correct problems in the relationship. If the customer collects metrics of your performance, then the team's job is to track those same metrics and see that these metrics are discussed in the company's program reviews and made part of the management process. This team should regularly report on customer satisfaction to your company executives for timely corrective action. They must monitor and document all changes in the contract baseline, to avert contractual disputes.

— Strategy in Action —

Northrop Grumman conducted quite an effective campaign to keep the B-2 program funded. They created advertisements showing the number of jobs they created in each Congressional district. They successfully lobbied the Air Force to conduct a demonstration where a single B-2 destroyed a simulated enemy armor column. This demo showed the amazing combat power of the weapon system. Northrop created white papers on new uses of the aircraft, and helped write articles with industry experts to publish in trade journals. They provided these articles and white papers to their Congressmen to wave around on the House floor. They named each one of the bombers after a state to try to arouse individual Congressman in funding additional bombers for their states. Northrop created much buzz on Capitol Hill. While Northrop was unsuccessful at selling 50 more bombers, Congress did throw them a "bone" of $493 million to convert the first test aircraft to an operational aircraft. The few million Northrop spent on the follow-on capture team had quite a good payback.

Part of keeping a program sold is managing the customer's contracting bureaucracy to ensure that your contract funding is not interrupted. At one customer, the projects are incrementally funded and contracted. To fund each increment, the customer must complete a statement of work while finance budgets the money. The customer's contracts manager must create an appropriations request. If the paperwork does not move, neither does the money. The supplier's follow-on team saw the customer continually fail to generate an appropriations request on time, which led to a costly break in the program. This resulted in needless fluctuations in the supplier's delivery schedule. As a result, the supplier's capture team established a procedure of proactively calling the customer individuals who processed the paperwork to remind them to move the paperwork. Keeping the funding stable was to everyone's benefit.

This team should always be on the lookout for ways to expand your work scope by finding new uses for your product, enhancing your product with changes or servicing your product for the customer. After you win, your team can start selling some of your engineering team's great ideas that were rejected as too risky in the pursuit phase. This team also prospects for new products or services your company can bring to the customer. As they work with the customer, your program execution team will learn about the customer's problems. The capture team should periodically interview your execution team members to understand these problems. They will look your company's capabilities for a match and identify solutions they can provide. The follow-on team then works to sell these solutions. Your follow-on capture team should seek identify and assess the customer's departmental plans, objectives, issues and budgets. Then, the capture team can work with the customer to prioritize potential solutions. The team works to get these product enhancements or modifications added into the customer's strategy plan. The key is to proactively identify user needs and technical problems, which is done by developing and maintaining relationships, and making a habit of being in the right place at the right time.

While logistics, maintenance, and training naturally fall out of many contracts, your team needs to ensure that when that happens the business is not lost to competitors. Your team should identify your intellectual property (IP) such as process technologies, methodologies, source code, databases, process instructions, patterns, plans, algorithms, methods, and techniques that have value beyond the current opportunity, or make it significantly more difficult to compete with your company downstream. The team can protect this IP by funding its development independently from a particular customer, or by using proprietary processes to develop it. It is important to plan ahead and negotiate IP rights in contracts, as well as to mark, label and protect these.

There are actions that your company can take to maintain their work and keep it from being competed. First, it is important to keep an acceptable cost posture so the customer does not have an incentive to compete your work. You can also negotiate incremental option quantities in all contracts, which makes it easy for the customer to extend your work. You can get new requirement quantities as immediate add-ons to prevent the customer from breaking out a new contract. Plus, you can make it harder to change to other vendors by stipulating that you retain the title to tooling or unique test fixtures. For example, Vought owned the tooling they used to fabricate large sections of the 747. This was leverage Vought held over Boeing as they argued over acrimonious issues such as change costs and delivery penalties for decades.

The follow-on capture team develops short capture plans of only a couple of pages in length. They have an extensive communication plan to keep selling the program to key constituencies, so that they stay committed to the program and its success. The team brings forward solutions to sell to the users and the budget controllers. If they do their job right, they can win most of these opportunities sole source.

If they have competitive follow-on opportunities, the incumbent team will still have an advantage over the competition by knowing the customer's problems better, having better access to customer and a greater ability to influence the customer.

Summary

Putting together the right team is critical to victory. This means bringing together a group with the right combination of skills, experience and personalities to win over the customer and construct the solution that the customer will like best. Each team member must be clear on his or her specific responsibilities. A team must have a good leader, but experienced capture team leaders are scarce, which is why putting together the right team is hard and requires sacrifice.

Chapter 8: Developing the Capture Plan

"Plans are nothing; planning is everything."

— Dwight David Eisenhower

Once you have your win strategy, the real challenge begins – converting your strategy into actions. The capture plan is the mechanism that converts the strategy into execution. ***Without execution, you have little chance of victory.*** The key to winning is positioning your offering prior to the proposal. This is the crucial time to collect intelligence, create your solution, enhance your capabilities, shape the acquisition and sell your solution to the customer.

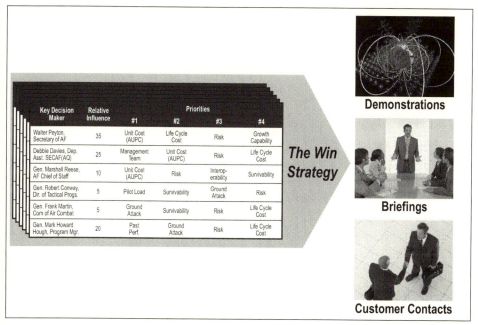

Key Decision Maker	Relative Influence	Priorities			
		#1	#2	#3	#4
Walter Peyton, Secretary of AF	35	Unit Cost (AUPC)	Life Cycle Cost	Risk	Growth Capability
Debbie Davies, Dep. Asst. SECAF(AQ)	25	Management Team	Unit Cost (AUPC)	Risk	Life Cycle Cost
Gen. Marshall Reese, AF Chief of Staff	10	Unit Cost (AUPC)	Risk	Interop-erability	Survivability
Gen. Robert Conway, Dir. of Tactical Progs.	5	Pilot Load	Survivability	Ground Attack	Risk
Gen. Frank Martin, Com of Air Combat	5	Ground Attack	Survivability	Risk	Life Cycle Cost
Gen. Mark Howard Hough, Program Mgr.	20	Past Perf.	Ground Attack	Risk	Life Cycle Cost

The Win Strategy

Demonstrations

Briefings

Customer Contacts

Exhibit 8-1: The Capture Plan Converts the Win Strategy into a Set of Actions

The capture plan is the formal document that details the "success path" – all of the actions the company must take to win. These actions include attending conferences, preparing white papers, winning specific R&D awards, establishing field marketing offices, demonstrating technologies, acquiring particular skills and briefing the customer. The capture team must schedule, estimate and organize the collection of intelligence, contact with the customer and the delivery of messages in order to position the company to win. The capture plan coordinates all pursuit activity into an event-driven schedule to ensure that the team delivers the right messages, and their substantiation, to the right customers at the right time for maximum persuasion. The most decisive feature of a capture effort is the shaping of the customer's acquisition, and the capture plan is the mechanism for implementing it. This plan identifies who is responsible for every action and tracks the completion of each task. It is a tool for management to use to oversee implementation of your strategy. Simply put, the capture plan allows you to plan the work and then work the plan.

The earlier a team starts developing and implementing the capture plan, the better they can align themselves with the customer's needs and maximize their influence. Therefore, creating the capture plan is one of the team's first duties after the pursuit decision is made. Developing the plan gives the capture team the opportunity to add details and make modifications, creating a sense of task ownership among all members. Once the capture team develops the plan, the team leader presents the plan to the company's senior management in a formal session where the executives review and approve the plan. This review ensures that management agrees with the steps the capture team is laying out and that there are sufficient resources to execute the plan. Once approved, executives can use the plan as a basis for monitoring the team's progress, ensuring that each step is being implemented. However, the plan is not stagnate. The plan is a living document that the capture team is constantly updating as they record customer reactions, collect new intelligence and adjust the strategy.

Contents of the Capture Plan

The capture plan documents the capture team's collective knowledge of the pursuit and puts it into the hands of each team member. This ensures that all capture team members have access to contact lists, customer funding assessments, competitor intelligence, messages to be sent and action plans. It should also provide a list and storage location for all of the customer briefings and documents, so that team members can readily access them. It should outline the opportunity, strategy, and all of the actions needed to position your team to win. The capture plan will describe what you know about the pursuit, how you are going to win and how you are going to get there. The plan can be a book or on an internal secure website; either way it is vital to protect this document because having a competitor compromise this information is fatal.

Specifically, the plan consists of:
- Information about the opportunity
    - Capture team members and contact information
    - Opportunity background
    - Customer profile
    - Competitive assessment
    - Key document list (important customer documents, strategy review documents, competitor marketing literature and location)

- Win strategy development (win templates as shown in Chapter 3, 4 & 5)
- Schedules and plans
    - Opportunity calendar (all key pursuit milestones)
    - Communications plan – influences strategy and message timing
    - Action plan – lists and monitors all the day-to-day assignments and their completion
    - Contact plan
    - Capture budget
    - Business case – the financial justification for the pursuit

A major flaw of many capture plans is their failure to focus on action, instead providing an inordinate amount of content on documenting the opportunity's background. The role of the capture plan is to translate the strategy into a set of coordinated, specific tasks. The capture team leader can then establish responsibility and accountability for each task. Management should use the capture plan as a means to manage status, and to track and oversee the pursuit. The key elements of the capture plan are: the communication plan, the contact plan, the intelligence plan, the action plan and the business case. All these elements will be described in detail later in this chapter.

It is important to note that every company must tailor the capture plan to their business. Commercial pursuits are different than government pursuits. International pursuits are different than domestic. In commercial pursuits, there is less opportunity to influence a company's acquisition structure and requirements than in a government pursuit. The same is true for selling a service versus a development contract; commercial companies do not require the extensive proposals that governments do. The capture process must be pliable to effectively and efficiently meet the needs of the different types of pursuits a company chases. As a result of that need, capture process activities are added, subtracted, changed or rescheduled to meet the needs of different customers and types of pursuits. In this chapter, we will describe the process in terms of a large government pursuit, because that is the most complex. If you pursue smaller commercial opportunities, the outlined principles still hold true, but you need to streamline the process described for your own business.

Shaping the Procurement

One of the most important objectives of the capture plan is to shape the procurement. Effective shaping is the surest way to win. The objective of shaping is to influence how the customer structures the procurement in favor of your solution. You would like to convince the customer to specify a product, service, delivery and experience requirement that only you can meet, or ask for information that only you have. Inclusion of these requirements will discriminate your offering, improving your evaluation score while driving up costs for the competition. As you contemplate this idea, you must recognize an important concept. A large complex sale does not consist of just one customer decision, but a series of decisions. The customer's acquisition decision-making process is a series of events, where an event is a scheduled decision-making occurrence that will influence the procurement outcome (setting the funding, writing the RFP, etc.). One objective of the capture plan is to position your team to influence the outcomes of these customer's decision-making events. You can influence these events by providing persuasive analysis to the customer before they set the requirements or develop the evaluation criteria. The analysis you deliver should logically describe why setting their requirements in your favor is to their advantage. You need to understand the customer's problems and needs plus what information they will use to make decisions. This knowledge will guide you in providing the appropriate analysis to sway their decisions.

For example, take the case of an Architecture & Engineering (A&E) firm trying to sell a contract to Exxon to design an exploration site. After Exxon initially identifies and explores a potential drilling site, these are the key procurement events:

- Event #1: During their capital planning cycle, Exxon must decide if they want to allocate a budget to develop the site and how much it should be.
- Event #2: Based on the site's depth, estimated reserves, existing pipeline locations, port facilities and expected recovery rate, Exxon determines the rig design requirements.
- Event #3: Exxon identifies potential A&E companies.
- Event #4: Exxon prepares a solicitation for an A&E firm.
- Event #5: Exxon evaluates bids and chooses a winner.

The shrewd A&E firm will attempt to influence every one of these events to their advantage. They will try to ensure that Exxon budgets enough money for their design concept. They will attempt to convince Exxon that their drilling approach – with which they have the greatest expertise – is the most economical for Exxon. They will also try to steer Exxon away from other competitors' offerings. The A&E firm will make suggestions about what requirements to include in the solicitation. They will try to influence Exxon's evaluation criteria to emphasize their strengths. If successful, the A&E firm will position itself as the natural winner of the competition before the customer ever solicits a bid. All of these events can be influenced. But the firm can only influence these events if they understand the who, what, when and how of Exxon's decision-making process and have a strategy for influencing it.

Your win strategy should define how you want to steer the outcomes of all of the customer's events. As we discussed in Chapter 3, you must start developing your strategy with the end in mind. You build your win strategy based on how you are going to get the key decision makers to select your offering. You envision success in the last step in the acquisition process – selecting the winner. Then, based on your win strategy, you identify how you want to influence each of the customer events leading up to the award decision as shown in Exhibit 8-2.

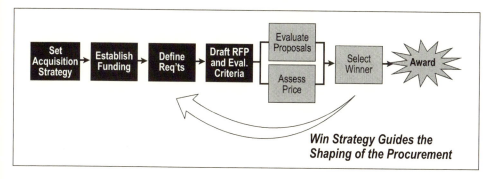

Exhibit 8-2: The Win Strategy Guides the Shaping

— *Strategy in Action* —

An engine and environmental controls supplier was competing for the contract to provide the Auxiliary Power Unit (APU) systems to an aircraft manufacturer for a new commercial jet. Traditionally, the aircraft manufacturer had purchased APUs, environmental control systems, cabin pressure and bleed air systems, and cooling systems and subsystems separately. The engine company had an integrated air management suite in development that was smaller, lighter and higher performing than any combination of competitor components. The price of the integrated solution would be lower than the sum of the components. Since their system was optimized as a system, some of their individual components would not be competitive with their competitors' components. They could win as a system, but if the aircraft manufacturer competed all of the individual components separately they were unlikely to win them all. The supplier's win strategy was to propose an integrated, much more capable system which provided greater value to the customer. However, they had to implement their win strategy in such a way that the customer would evaluate any solution as a system and not as a set of components.

Exhibit 8-3 shows how a company would try to influence customer events with this strategy.

The first step was to influence the customer's Platform Strategy Committee's acquisition strategy. This committee was to decide how the manufacturer would contract out the aircraft's work scope – whether each part of the air management system would be competed individually or as a group. The engine supplier wanted the manufacturer to change from their traditional approach and compete the whole air management suite as a system. If they were successful with overcoming that hurdle, then they would want the aircraft design team to specify more difficult requirements in their Request for Information to industry. More stringent requirements would be more difficult for the other competitors to comply with and force many of them to modify their existing products. In addition, if the requirements were easy, it would allow the supplier's competitors to offer significantly lower cost solutions. The supplier's newer solution had significantly better reliability than any of the competitor's products, which would provide life cycle cost (LCC) savings. The supplier took white papers to the manufacturer's program office as they were about to start writing the RFP, showing the importance the manufacturer's customers put on life cycle costs when making their buying decisions. Using this data, the supplier hoped to encourage the manufacturer to include life cycle cost in their proposal evaluation.

As this example demonstrates, the capture team attempted to influence different aspects of their customer's procurement across its evolution. The win strategy determined how the capture team would attempt to influence each customer event to improve the capture team's position.

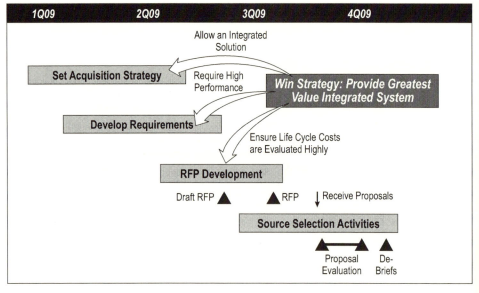

Exhibit 8-3: Shaping the Requirements

As you brainstorm ideas of how to influence the customer, foremost in your mind should be understanding and addressing your customer's problems. Ideally, you want your technical staff to be working with the customer's technical staff in order to define the problem and test concepts. The goal is to collaborate with the customer to shape the procurement and steer the requirements to emphasize your strengths, maximizing the value of your discriminators. You can amplify a discriminator if you can convince the customer to specify your strength in the RFP.

— *Strategy in Action* —

For example, two companies were vying for a contract with the Royal Navy to develop an air vehicle to land on a carrier deck. Company A worked hard to shape the Request for Tender (RFT). Company A designed their air vehicle with greater wing area, which provided much better flying qualities than their competitor. Company A knew that landing an aircraft on a pitching deck is one of the biggest challenges in flying. Having an aircraft with excellent handling characteristics at low speeds is vital. Company A emphasized this point over and over again to the customer and suggested that the customer evaluate each competitor's low speed flying characteristics as part of the proposal. Company A knew that their air vehicle would greatly outscore the competition on this factor. Company A knew that loss of a communications link to the precision landing system while on approach could result in a crash on to the carrier deck, so they designed a redundant communications architecture. The competitor lacked the same forethought. Company A convinced the customer that the safety of the ship depended on a highly redundant communications link. As a result, the customer inserted such a requirement into the RFT. This capability was inherent in Company A's design, but required an expensive rework for Company B. In addition, since the redesign of Company B's architecture was complex, the customer rated their approach as high risk in the evaluation. In addition to these examples, Company A had discriminators that provided significant value to the customer. They took advantage of these discriminators by selling the customer on their benefits and successfully convincing the customer to include them in the evaluation criteria. With actions like these, Company A had pretty much guaranteed their win before they even received the RFT.

A premise of this approach is not to wait for the RFP to create a solution, but to work with the customer to understand different ways to solve their problem. By walking their technical staff through your trade studies you can observe and record their reactions to your conclusions and perform a sensitivity analysis to show the customer the trade-offs between requirements and cost. As you discuss these results with the customer, you gain tremendous insight into the priority ranking of their requirements. You can then provide the customer with a draft specification and partner with them to finalize it. All of this must be done subtly. The specification must be generic enough so that other competitors can bid, but it should be slanted toward your approach. This builds rapport between the technical teams and gives your team a unique understanding of the rationale behind the requirements when you bid. Done well, your team will know the customer's needs as well as the customer does. You can then develop a solution that better matches the customer's needs and budget constraints than any other competitor. If you are successful in this shaping, the competitors will be playing catch up for the rest of the pursuit. If you are ahead of the competition in understanding the customer and developing your solution, you can encourage the customer to demand a quick response to the RFP. Being better prepared should allow you to submit a better response. You also want to suggest evaluation criteria to the customer. After all, if you help write the test, you should find it pretty easy to pass.

To illustrate these points, let's look at an armored vehicle sale to Southeast Asia.

— *Strategy in Action* —

In this case, an American company was trying to sell 65 armored vehicles to the Thai Marine Corps and they were pitted against a French company. The American company intended to sell their "combat-proven," low risk product. Meanwhile, the French company had a vehicle under development with many advanced features. When developing their win strategy, the American company realized that most of their discriminators, such as an established logistics network, low risk schedule, and commonality of production, resulted from proposing a proven vehicle that was currently in production. The American company concluded that if the Thais specified a vehicle with more advanced features, they would have to substantially modify their product and a new variant would deny them the ability to claim to be low risk or combat-proven. In addition, significant modifications would require new engineering investment and extensive testing; driving up costs and making meeting the customer's desired schedule delivery dates questionable. In meetings with the Thai Marine Corps, the capture team learned that although the draft requirements demanded few of the advanced features, the Thais desired many of the new capabilities promised by the French product.

The American company's strategy was to try to contain the Thai's requirement growth. In that way, they could propose their existing vehicle with minimum modifications. The American company knew the Thai Marine Corps suffered from chronic budget shortfalls, and as a result they were very price sensitive. After assessing all of this information, the American capture team strategized on how to keep the Thai Marines from changing their requirements. The American company cultivated a network of sources in Thailand who were close to the customer and would notify the Americans whenever the French company's representatives arrived in-country. By carefully listening to the customers after these meetings, the capture team's representatives could usually infer what features the French were pushing. After each French company visit, the American company visited the Thai Marine Corps Program Office and discussed the same product features. The Americans agreed that these features were beneficial, but worried that they were too costly. The American capture leader would illustrate how a feature could be added to the vehicle downstream as the technology matured and the price fell. In other cases, they provided analysis showing that the performance enhancement was not worth the additional cost. The American company repeated this process every time the French company's representatives visited over the next year. Just before the Thais began to write the RFT, the American capture leader visited the Thais and suggested the advanced features be priced as options. He argued that would give the Program Office maximum flexibility when they made their evaluation. When the Thais published their requirements, the Americans were thrilled to see the Thais did just that. The American company could bid their existing product with a few modifications at a very attractive price. And they won.

To successfully shape, as this story illustrates, you need to focus on your customer's key concerns in order to influence them. You also need excellent intelligence. The American company understood what was important to the customer, what the competition was offering and knew when they were going to be in-country. The capture team was then able to counter the competitor's moves.

The Ultimate in Shaping – Converting the Opportunity into a Sole Source

Avoiding a competition entirely is usually the best possible outcome of shaping. Executives love sole source contracts because the company forgoes spending dollars competing, lessens price pressure, and they can't lose. One straightforward approach to gaining a sole source contract is to enter into a long-term relationship with the customer through a risk sharing or joint development program.

— Strategy in Action —

We saw Company X implement this strategy beautifully on a large ship program. There were two competitors for designing and building the ship – Big Prime #1 and Big Prime #2. Two years before the ship source selection, Big Prime #1 sent out a Request for Information (RFI) to industry seeking data on the capabilities of propulsion system suppliers. While the other potential propulsion suppliers merely responded to the request, the Business Development executives at Company X recognized this as an enormous opportunity. The ship builders were already investing a huge amount of money in the ship pursuit and would relish the chance to offset some of their development costs. The Business Development executives at Company X convinced their executive team to offer a cost sharing development agreement to Big Prime #1. Company X approached Big Prime #1 and proposed making a multi-million dollar investment to begin working with their design team on the propulsion concept in return for a spot on their team. Big Prime #1 accepted Company X's proposal. Then, since that worked so well, Company X went to Big Prime #2 and made the same offer. Big Prime #2 accepted as well. Meanwhile, Company X's competitors were unaware of the cost sharing proposals and patiently waited for the primes to move forward. While Company X was working, their competitors were waiting. Company X set up two firewalled teams (there was no communication or exchange of data between the members of the two groups) each working with a different prime. While Company X conducted some common research and development applicable to both teams, each prime had different requirements and priorities for their firewalled teams which resulted in different solutions. It was more than a year later that Company X's competitors discovered that Company X had struck deals with both of the primes. However, by that time Company X was entrenched with both primes. Company X had locked up a multi-billion dollar, 20-year franchise with a relatively small investment and some effective shaping. The fortunes of other companies across the industry depended on who won the ship contract, but not Company X's, as they were on both teams from the beginning.

To get a sole source, you need to convince the customer that it is in their best interest to forgo a competition. As in the example above, the company was willing to invest money to reduce the prime's investment needs. Typically, you have to help the customer justify that decision. Once the customer has decided to compete a project, it is difficult to divert them to a sole source. Obviously, to be in this position, it is critical to be engaged with the customer early on when their thoughts on the project are forming. The easiest time to create a sole source award is when the customer is under extreme time pressure to implement a solution. If the customer is on a tight schedule and only your company can deliver in time, that is almost always an acceptable justification for going sole source. In these cases, the customer knows that skipping a competition will shortcut their schedule. If you find yourself in this position, the thrust of your messages should be to convince the customer that only your solution can meet their schedule. If you are successful with this argument, the customer will select your solution and they will have an easy case justifying a sole source. In fact, meeting schedule is one of only seven reasons for justifying a sole source award under U.S. Federal Acquisition Regulations.

You may have a viable solution to the customer's problem, but the competitors are proposing a paper concept or a solution that can only satisfy some of the customer's needs. The best approach to overcoming these challenges is to provide the customer with ample evidence that only your offering can satisfy the customer's mission. If the customer concludes that other competitors are viable, they usually go for a competition. Customers know that conducting a competition drives down prices. So, in spite of poor alternatives, many customers will still choose to hold a competition. The customer runs a risk with this strategy in that they may be forced to select the lower performing solution. If there is a big capability gap between the competitors, that can force the customer to water down the requirements so that the less capable company is eligible to bid and with those requirements the lower performing solution might win. You need to convince the customer that they do not want to take that chance. You must sell the customer on the value of your unique discriminators. The key is to be so successful at this selling that the customer decides they will not settle for any solution that does not have your discriminators.

Then you must subtly alert them to idea that the only way they can really ensure getting these discriminators is by issuing a sole source contract.

Another reason that a customer may wish to avoid a competition is that they lack the personnel to bring all the suppliers up to speed and to conduct the technical evaluations. However, customers will have trouble justifying a sole source based on a lack of internal staff, even though that may be the real motivator. A key tactic to heighten this issue is to monopolize the customer's technical staff, so that they don't have time to work with anyone else. The more time you spend working with the customer, the more time the customer will expect each competitor to require to create a compliant proposal. This increases the customer's anxiety over working with your competition.

To get a sole source contract, you must also convince the customer that they are getting a good deal. If they feel they are being price gouged, the customer will demand a competition to force your company's price down. This is what happened in 2002 when the U.S. Air Force was considering a plan to lease 100 767 air-refueling tankers from Boeing. Given the aerospace slump following September 11th, this seemed like a good way to support a large corporation and begin replacing the aging KC-135s. The deal began to unravel when the General Accounting Office and John McCain started questioning its high cost. Scrutiny of the lease deal led to a procurement scandal and the cancellation of the effort. When the Air Force competed the tanker program in 2008, Boeing's 767 per aircraft price dropped by 17 percent when adjusted for inflation and work scope, demonstrating that the 2002 lease deal was not, in fact, "a great deal," as Boeing's executives claimed at the time. Despite having the only viable tanker, the 2002 sole source lease deal unraveled because it was seen for what it was, a sweetheart deal for Boeing.

Building the Capture Plan

The capture of large pursuits is complex. To manage their complexity and coordinate all the actions necessary to win, a capture team builds a capture plan. Exhibit 8-4 shows how the elements of the capture plan work together. While the exhibit may look intimidating, this chapter lays out a simple, methodical approach for creating and integrating all of the elements of the capture plan. *The key to unraveling the pursuit's complexity is breaking down the capture plan into discreet tasks.* First, you decompose the capture plan into its major elements – an opportunity calendar, strategy templates, the intelligence plan, the communications plan, the contact plan, action plan and staffing and budget. Then, you start creating each of the elements. As we show in this book, these templates are relatively straightforward to create. You will observe that one template feeds the others and thereby integrates the planning. For example, as the team develops the win strategy templates, they identify intelligence requirements that are deployed to the intelligence plan. To implement tactics, the team plans actions, allocates resources and schedules messages. Each of these tasks is inputted into the appropriate template. The accumulation of all these templates is an extensive capture plan of manageable tasks all tied back to the win strategy.

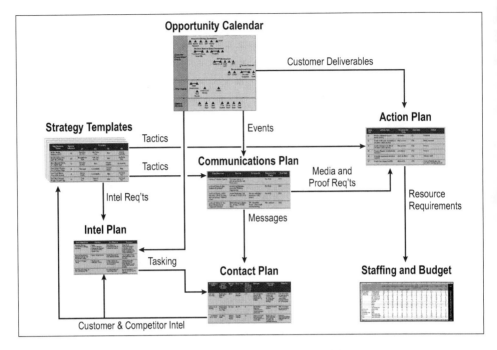

Exhibit 8-4: Building the Capture Plan

Building the Opportunity Calendar

After completing the win strategy templates, the first step to building your capture plan is to create an opportunity calendar (see Exhibit 8-5 for an example for a U.S. Army program). The calendar maps out all of the events that can impact the procurement. The capture team plans and schedules all of the capture activities around these events. The team puts all of the customer's procurement decision-making milestones on the schedule (Statement of Objectives (SOO), Acquisition Strategy Plan (ASP), Source Selection Plan (SSP), etc.). Not every date will be firm, but the capture team makes a best guess of the likely schedule. It is helpful to examine previous program schedules for this customer to understand their process and how long each step typically takes.

You also want to include any significant outside events that may impact the procurement. In Exhibit 8-5 some of the outside events are the Program Objective Memorandum (POM) development, this is when a Department of Defense program's funding is determined. On the opportunity calendar, you'll also identify key customer venues. Venues are situations that allow you to deliver messages to key decision makers, influence the technical experts, demonstrate your product or even negotiate the deal. These events are trade shows, industry award dinners, customer visits, conferences and technical meetings. In this example, there is an Armor conference and a key trade show called Association of the United States Army (AUSA) on the calendar because these are excellent venues for meeting with the customer. The schedule includes the ICC technical review which is an Army meeting where the Army labs will present their latest research and development results, much of which might be applicable to this pursuit. This meeting is an excellent opportunity to learn the customer's perceptions of emerging technologies that may apply to this opportunity.

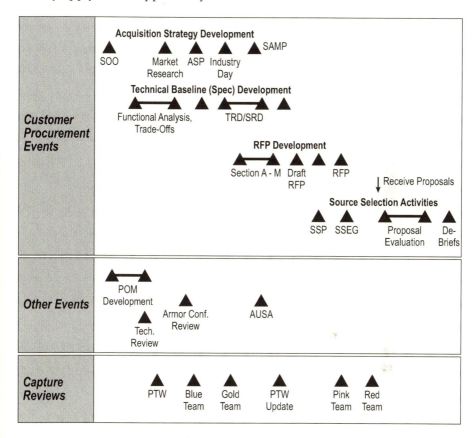

Exhibit 8-5: Sample Capture Calendar for an Army Program

External events can take a variety of forms. If your project requires Cabinet-level approval, it would be impacted by presidential elections. A project could depend on the World Bank or government funding, in which case, the budget preparation would be tracked. The President might visit the customer's country and could potentially lobby for your deal. These types of events can cause a project to slip or accelerate. You can potentially influence these events. Lastly, you can create events, like inviting the customer to your facility for a tour or demonstration. These self-made events allow you to pre-sell your solution to the customer.

Lastly, the internal capture reviews and pursuit milestones should be scheduled. This will help coordinate the reviews with the customer events. For example, there is usually an executive review every three months and it is best to have this review just before a major trade show that executives are planning to attend. That way, the executives will be up-to-date with the pursuit and be ready to make sales points or commitments when they meet with customer representatives at the show.

It is important to note that the opportunity calendar, as well as the whole capture plan, is an event-driven schedule, meaning that the start and completion of tasks are tied to particular events. And, as these events shift in time, all of the tasking is similarly adjusted. As the customer delays the program, tasks shift to the right.

Developing the Communications Plan to Shape the Procurement

Shaping the acquisition is one of the most important and decisive steps in any capture. During the win strategy development process described in Chapter 4, your team should have identified some specific tactics to shape the competition. When developing the communications plan, your team will hopefully expand that list of tactics and plan their execution. Shaping is one of the most cost effective and powerful techniques to winning, and it is limited only by your imagination. While many good capture team leaders intuitively develop a plan to shape the customer, most capture teams try only haphazardly to influence the customer, if they do it at all. The following tool facilitates systematically and comprehensively shaping the acquisition, and it is a powerful tool for helping novices as well as experienced capture team leaders. The communications plan establishes a formal process for influencing the customer's decision making. It helps you identify all of the influencing opportunities, the outcomes you want and the focused, timely messages to send to the decision makers for maximum impact.

The communications plan lays out the messages to be broadcast to the customer across the entire campaign. The plan, as shown in Exhibit 8-6, consists of four columns. In the first column, an event is listed, along with the participants and the timeline on which it will likely occur. The second column documents the outputs of this customer event. It is important to list all outputs of the customer's decision-making events, because even some innocuous ones can be converted into significant advantages. For example, suppose your competitor is planning to leverage a commercial software package in their solution and it is a significant discriminator. You could try to get the customer to include an onerous data rights clause that the commercial vendor would never accept. If you are successful, this data clause could force the competitor to drop that vendor from their solution and lose that advantage. Or, suppose your competitor is dealing with cash flow problems. You could suggest to the customer a payment schedule, which would exacerbate their short falls and probably result in the competitor bidding less aggressively. As these examples show, shaping opportunities abound.

After the team documents the event and its outputs, you'll brainstorm what would be the most desirable result for the outputs. The objective is what you want the customer to decide for that outcome. You carefully review the lists of discriminators, both yours and your competition's. The questions you ask the team are: What is the outcome that will best position your offering or hurt the competition the most? How can the acquisition be structured to gain the maximum advantage from our discriminators? How can the output be defined to put our competitor at a disadvantage?

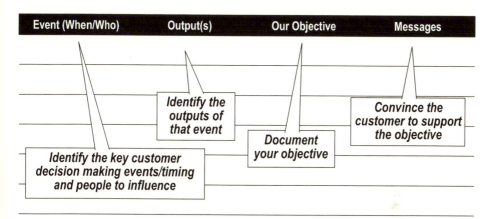

Exhibit 8-6: Setting up the Communications Plan

Next, you'll develop compelling reasons why the customer would benefit from providing the desired output. The messages describe the arguments and data that the team will provide to the customer to convince them to agree with your objective. Obviously, if there is no compelling benefit for the customer, there is no point in trying to influence them, and attempts to do so will likely cause the customer to see you as self-serving. A company should always strive to be perceived as trying to do what's best for the customer – that's the way you build trust and create deals that are winners for both parties.

We illustrate three different examples from three different pursuits in Exhibit 8-7. The first example refers back to the engine supplier discussed earlier in this chapter. The engine supplier wanted to influence the aircraft manufacturer's acquisition strategy, which is crafted by their Platform Strategy Committee. The acquisition strategy output defined the contract's scope and its structure. The engine company wanted the manufacturer to change their traditional approach of buying individual components to allow them to make a bid for the whole air management system. The engine supplier would provide analysis to the Platform Strategy Committee that showed how much precious weight an integrated system would save, as well as how this approach would save the aircraft manufacturer $20 million in their own air management system design and integration costs.

In the second example, the army was initiating a program to develop a defensive system for helicopters. The capture team's strategy was to employ newer and more expensive sensor technology. This new technology promised significant performance improvements in the future. The competitors would be bidding a mature technology, which was cheaper but had limited growth potential. The capture team knew that only the new technology could be evolved to defeat future missile threats, and they wanted those future threats to be considered in the procurement because of their advantage. The message the contractor wanted to send was that the program should require the system to address advanced threats. The capture team enlisted one of the Army's research and development labs to conduct an assessment of emerging threats. Then the capture team arranged a visit to the Requirements Office with the Army lab representatives who were anxious to discuss their assessment of those threats. The lab personnel convinced the Requirements Office that the warfighter would be seeing advanced threats within five years and that they should address advanced threats in their system requirements documents. Enrolling one part of the customer to influence another part is usually a very effective technique. The lab had none of the perceived bias that a contractor would, and the two departments were essentially comrades in arms, which added a level of trust to their discussions. If the influencing were successful, the competitor would have a big problem convincing the customer that they had a credible solution.

Event (When/Who)	Output(s)	Our Objective	Messages
Acquisition Strategy (1Q09/Platform Strategy Committee	• Scope • Contract Structure • Management Approach • Contract Incentives • Special T&Cs	Allow bidders to propose integrated air management system	Integrated air management system could save over 80 pounds in weight and $20M in manufacturer's development budget
Technical Requirements Document (Jan-Feb '10/ Requirements Office)	• System Requirements	Require the system to meet advanced threats	The warfighter will face advanced threats within five years
RFQ (Dec '11/Project Office)	• Requirements • Evaluation Factors	Include requirement for online management reporting system	Online management reporting improved insight helping to avoid an overrun on another program

Exhibit 8-7: Examples of Communications Plans

In the third example, a construction company had invested in an online management reporting system that tracked materials, inventory and supplier progress. The construction company had found that this system helped them to avoid budget and schedule overruns on a large project. Just before the developer's project office was about to write their Request for Quote (RFQ), the construction company visited their office and showed them a presentation about the benefits of their online management tracking system. They convinced the construction company to require all potential bidders to provide a similar system. The construction company knew that the other competitors had no such system and it would take a substantial investment to develop one, which would add cost to their bids.

In these examples, each company identified the customer decision-making event and their decision makers. They also identified the decision makers for this event. A common blunder is to send messages to the wrong people. For example, the capture team should not try to get the program manager to change the funding, when he has no control over the capital-planning group that establishes the budgets. The program manager does not want to hear about problems that he or she cannot fix, and approaching the wrong person makes you look inept. Sending messages and trying to influence the wrong people creates frustration for everyone.

A company must also identify the timing for the event. Timing is key to successfully influencing. Optimally, you want to present your case just as the customer is sitting down to begin working on the issue. In that way, you help establish their first impression, from which everything else will be judged. As you saw in the first example, the engine supplier needed to present the benefits of an integrated air management suite to members of the Platform Strategy Committee at the very beginning of 2009. This was just before the Committee would be deciding on the engine and air management acquisition strategy. The sales team would ask the Committee members to structure their acquisition so they could bid an integrated solution. If you try too early, the customer will most likely be uninterested as they are working on other issues. The worst situation is to develop a very persuasive analysis, and to provide it to the customer the day that they've finished their work. Too early or too late is too bad.

It is important to realize that influencing the customer usually takes a pretty comprehensive case; therefore, it takes a lot of customer face time to be successful. If your messages are controversial or complex, you should plan for multiple attempts with different analysis to ensure you sell the customer on your ideas. Since meeting time with the customer is limited, you must prioritize and focus on a small number of objectives for each customer event. As a result, the communications plan should be short, simple and concise, but it will prove to be a very powerful tool.

The above examples discuss the shaping of just one step in each acquisition, but a good capture team influences events across the whole procurement – funding decisions, contract structure, terms and conditions, and requirements. The effect of this influence can overwhelm all other competitive factors.

How the customer designs acquisition usually determines who wins. The KC-135 Tanker replacement program is a perfect example, as discussed in Chapter 5. In 2008, with one evaluation criteria, Northrop Grumman won. Then in 2011 when the customer's goal changed from a tanker that's best for the warfighter to a "protest proof" decision, they repeated the competition with a different evaluation criterion. Even though both competitors bid the same aircraft as before, Northrop Grumman decided not to bid because the game was so stacked against them that it ensured a Boeing win.

Pre-Selling Your Solution

The second role of the communications plan is to organize the pre-selling of your solution to the customer. Differentiation in the minds of the customer does not simply occur. You have to create it. This comes from pre-selling, prior to the proposal, the benefits of your solution. Usually, you don't want to surprise the customer in the proposal with new solutions or approaches. Every new solution brings new problems, and the first time your customer is presented with your new solution, they will first think of all of the problems it might create. You must address the customer's concerns by presenting your ideas to the customer and giving them the chance to critique them. Only by identifying and understanding their initial questions, concerns and objections can you fully address them. And if the customer's concerns are not addressed and their problems solved, the technical staff will assess you as "non-compliant" or "high risk." That outcome is avoided by pre-selling your approach.

To identify the messages you need to send, review your strategies and win themes. Themes provide the grist for your communications plan. Start by listing the key discriminators that you think the customer may perceive. It is important to identify all aspects of perceived differences – technical, management, past performance, cost and political. This list of discriminators should include key ghosts that you need to make about the competitor's solution, as well as the competitor's likely ghosts of your own solution.

You usually have a limited amount of time and venues to pre-sell the customer, so you'll need to prioritize your list of messages. You want to concentrate on the important few, instead of the trivial many.

Once you identify your top dozen or so messages, you'll need to identify to whom to send those messages. You cultivate the customer at all levels. **You want to sell up the organization** (as shown in Exhibit 8-8). You first sell the engineers and then their managers, and finally you sell the executives. The decision makers usually seek their staff's opinions about how well a solution is likely to work. After hearing a pitch, the executives will always ask their staff, "So what do you think?" You want them to say, "It's great," not, "It'll never work." Optimally, you sell the technical staff on your solution and then enroll them in selling their bosses. These influencers are the people that the key decision makers rely on for advice, counsel and assessments. They may not have a vote, but they have the ear of the people casting the votes. The technical may even end up being the proposal's technical evaluators. It is important to sell the customer's users too, as the decision makers are likely to ask their opinions on how well your solution is likely to work. These groups don't have the final authority to say "yes," but they can and do say "no." It is critical to pre-sell them on your technical approach, especially if the competition has a different approach or the customer organization is leaning toward an approach different than yours. If you bypass the technical staff and sell your solution to higher echelon personnel, you are usurping their role and authority. The technical staff will resent you and your solution. They will work overtime trying to find problems because uncovering shortcomings in your approach justifies their role in the process and proves to their executives that they should not be shut out.

Identify whom you'll need to meet with by using organization charts to go from the lowest point of contact to the final decision maker with procurement authority. You'll want to send your strategy messages to the key decision makers, influencers and evaluators. But look beyond those people directly involved in the source selection to see if there are any other customer organizations that are likely to weigh in, since you need to sell them too. These might include test organizations or strategic planners. If you are selling to a government, you'll want to sell your solution to the broader customer community and stakeholders, who will help neutralize political pressure to go with the competitor's solution. For government contracts, your capture team will also need to keep the program funded, so it is important to sell your solution to Congress, the Office of Management and Budget, the White House, and a think tank like RAND. Develop a "Hit List" of institutions and individuals with whom you need to communicate your themes. Then identify the messages your team needs to send.

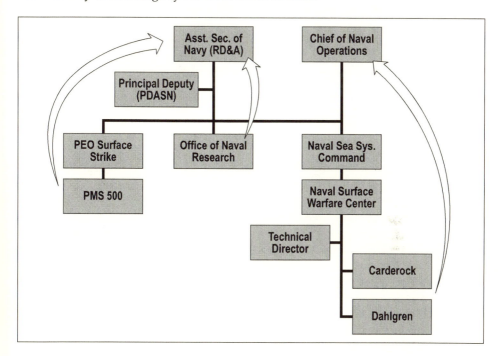

Exhibit 8-8: Sell up the Chain of Command

The more you understand and adapt your messages to the audience, the more likely you are to sell your idea. *You must start in agreement with your audience to be persuasive.* Every audience has a current position – an attitude, opinion or belief on every issue. It is critical to figure out what each individual's position is on an issue before you can be persuasive. By understanding their position, you know where to start your messaging. You must also know the depth of the audience's knowledge because they will need to know the generalities before you can motivate them to respond to specifics. You are trying to sell a solution to a customer problem by taking the customer down a logical mental path from the customer's problem to your solution.

You cannot shortcut the persuasion process. Each of these steps requires specific message(s). The persuasion steps for a new solution or feature are easy to understand, but implementation can be tricky. First, you must start in agreement with the customer about what their problem is. For example, suppose you are trying to sell a new navigation system to a satellite manufacturer. You identify a critical problem for the satellite manufacturer. In this case, it is that their satellites need improved signal reception. Next, you gain agreement with the customer about the root cause. In this case, you will work with the satellite manufacturer's technical staff so that they conclude that a two-degree improvement in navigation accuracy will improve the satellite's pointing accuracy and thereby solve the signal reception problem. Next, you get the customer to quantify the value of solving their problem, in this case the value of improving signal reception and thereby increase satellite data transmission. The satellite company determines that improved signal reception would be worth $10 million. Next, you get the customer to agree that your solution fixes the cause of their problem. In our case, you convince the satellite manufacturer that your new ring laser gyro will improve their navigation accuracy by two degrees. Lastly, you gain concurrence with the customer that your solution is worth the value of solving their problem. As a result, you convince the customer to conclude that your new gyro is worth $10 million to them.

If you miss a step, you derail your argument. It is important to understand what your customer's initial position on the issue is, so that you can start the sales pitch in agreement and then logically take them through your messages. Your sequence must follow the path described above or you will lose them as you make your arguments.

Graphically map messages to the individuals. You'll then refine these messages to best fit each audience. Messages "for everyone" appeal to no one. The key to effective persuasion is in understanding the audience. You choose messages of the greatest interest to the individual – the priorities of the key decision makers. Exhibit 8-9 shows mapping of messages to a customer. In this case, the capture team is selling an oilrig to an exploration company. Since the CEO, Don Ceglar, has stated that his number one priority is getting the rig operational, a message is sent that the capture team's rig would be producing oil in January '09, well before any competitor. The Vice President of Operations, Bill Green, has made it clear that his first priority is production capacity; so the message to him would describe how this design allows 12 percent greater capacity than any comparable rig.

Messages should also be sequenced so that they build on one another. One message should set the stage for the next. In the above example, the capture team would first sell Ceglar on their early delivery and the associated benefits. After this reinforcement, the capture team would provide messages showing that their competitor, Mason, had facility constraints that would delay the start of rig construction for six months. This message would raise doubts about Mason's ability to meet the exploration company's need date. You must heighten the customer's desire for a benefit before you expose the competitor's inability to provide it. Attacking the competitor's approach first would create skepticism and the perception of bias in the customer about your intentions.

Correctly sequencing your messages can make a world of difference. Pollster Frank Luntz discovered this lesson when he was conducting focus groups for Ross Perot's 1992 Presidential bid. Luntz found that people loved Perot when they first saw a video biography, then testimonials praising him, and finally a speech by Perot himself. However, one day the videotapes got out of sequence, and Perot's speech appeared first. The results were startling. The focus group thought he was a little kooky and lost interest in him as soon as they heard any adverse information. The order of the presentation can determine the reaction.

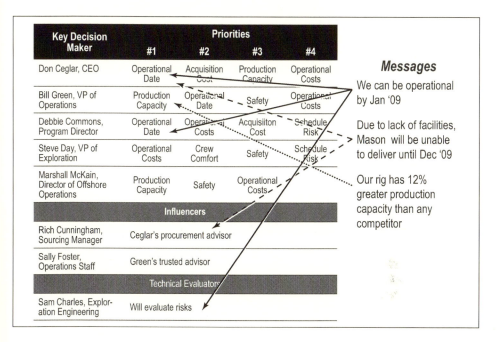

Key Decision Maker	Priorities			
	#1	#2	#3	#4
Don Ceglar, CEO	Operational Date	Acquisition Cost	Production Capacity	Operational Costs
Bill Green, VP of Operations	Production Capacity	Operational Date	Safety	Operational Costs
Debbie Commons, Program Director	Operational Date	Operational Costs	Acquisiiton Cost	Schedule Risk
Steve Day, VP of Exploration	Operational Costs	Crew Comfort	Safety	Schedule Risk
Marshall McKain, Director of Offshore Operations	Production Capacity	Safety	Operational Costs	
Influencers				
Rich Cunningham, Sourcing Manager	Ceglar's procurement advisor			
Sally Foster, Operations Staff	Green's trusted advisor			
Technical Evaluators				
Sam Charles, Exploration Engineering	Will evaluate risks			

Messages

We can be operational by Jan '09

Due to lack of facilities, Mason will be unable to deliver until Dec '09

Our rig has 12% greater production capacity than any competitor

Exhibit 8-9: Individual Tailor Messages for Key Decision Makers

Timing the delivery of messages is also critical. Ideally, you want to enroll the people who work for and influence the key decision makers in selling your messages to the key decision maker – use them to sell up the chain. But this takes time. You also want to allow time for multiple attempts. You should always go back to a customer after an unfavorable reaction. The more complex or controversial the message, the more attempts you may need to plan for the customer to be persuaded toward your point of view. A complex message can have one or more trade-offs, the customer's problem may have multiple root causes or you might have to uncover a previously unknown root cause. All of these instances are likely to invite controversy in the analysis.

In addition, selling up the organization adds steps and time to the selling process. Of critical importance when planning messages is considering the competitor's reaction to the pre-selling of your discriminators. If the competition has good sources within the customer, they will know what you've told the customer soon after you talk to them. You must expect this. Competitive knowledge goes through the customer to the competitors at different speeds, depending on the customer's respect for proprietary knowledge and the competitor's customer intimacy. While some customers are very tight lipped, with other customers it is as if you are briefing your competition. The earlier the competition knows your strategies, the more time they have to counter them. In addition, when you present a discriminator, the competition may have time to copy it.

While many customers adhere to strict ethical procedures to protect every competitor's discriminators, some customers do not. Some customers fail to control their urge to technically level competitors. It is natural for customers to want the best solutions, so if they see one competitor with a good idea, sometimes they cannot resist sharing it with another competitor. There are many ways that this can happen. Some customers do it directly by revealing the idea during discussions with other suppliers, changing their requirements or specifying a particular solution. They also technically level by asking leading questions which indicate that they are dissatisfied with your solution, or they may more blatantly ask if you have considered a particular approach – which just happens to be the competition's secret approach. You need to consider the customer's tendency to technically level as you plan the timing of your communications strategy.

— *Strategy in Action* —

With poor message timing, companies can blunder into losing their discriminators and competitions. For example, while bidding on a satellite, Contractor X was proposing an advanced solar panel array that would cut satellite weight and improve energy efficiency. However, Competitor Y believed the technology was too risky. As a result of having heavier arrays, Competitor Y had a smaller less capable satellite. Contractor X deluged the space agency with white papers and prototype production results showing the new arrays were ready for full-scale production. The space agency was won over by the merits of the new array. Unfortunately, Contractor X was too persuasive, too early – the space agency had not finalized their requirements and they decided to mandate the new array technology. Initially, Contractor X was ecstatic, having proven their engineering prowess. But ultimately, this contractor also lost their key discriminator, because both teams would now be bidding advanced arrays. Contractor X went on to lose this pursuit.

— *Strategy in Action* —

In another case, the OEM had developed a very cost efficient method for exchanging avionics boxes while competing for an aircraft avionics modernization program. The company wanted to pre-sell this approach to the customer, which they decided to do at the program's Industry Day (Industry Day brings together all potential contractors for briefings on the program). During their one-on-one sessions (no competitors were in the room) with the customer, they presented their approach. The customer was so excited by the innovative approach, he bragged about it at the end of the day wrap up session to all the attendees. All of the other contractors heard enough to copy the discriminator, and the company lost a key discriminator. Industry Day was the wrong venue for disclosing a discriminator that could be copied. Too many things can go wrong at an event like this. In this case, a naïve customer disclosed key information in public, but a competitor employee could just as easily have accidentally walked into the room at the wrong time. This discriminator should have been held back to the last minute, because it was simple, straight forward, unlikely to raise controversy with the customer and easy to copy.

With these examples in mind, you must assess the cost of disclosure versus the benefits. While you can be careful about what venues you use to disclose discriminators to the customer, you need to assume that the competitors will discover them eventually. You assess that risk. The more time the competitor has, the greater the chances that they will learn of a discriminator from the customer, and find out if the customer likes it. When competitors discover your discriminators, they have two choices: they can steal them or they can ghost them. The more time they have, the greater the chance they can copy your advantage or discredit it, so you must carefully consider message timing when developing your communications plan. You want to schedule disclosure so you'll have time for multiple passes, but the competition won't have time to copy your idea. As Exhibit 8-10 shows, if you have a discriminator that can be easily copied, you'll want to disclose it by pre-selling it to the customer at the last possible minute. This reduces the chances that the competitor will learn of it and copy it.

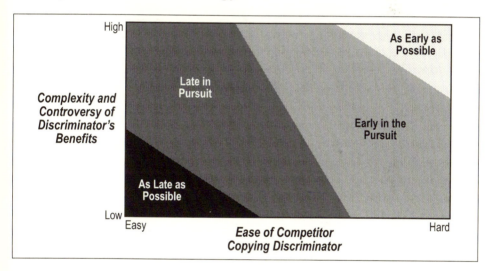

Exhibit 8-10: Timing of Messages Depends on Multiple Factors

Some discriminators are complex; the impact of their benefits is unclear, or they result in other trade-offs, raising concerns among the customer's technical staff. These discriminators take more time to sell their benefits, overcome the objections and allow for multiple passes. Some discriminators cannot be copied because they are patented or inherent from a different design choice, follow a different strategy than the competition or rely on some unique capability that the competition cannot match. All of these factors need to be assessed to determine the time requirements when scheduling messages in your communications plan.

Once you have identified the messages, the individuals and the timing, you'll need to identify the venues. Venues are opportunities to move your targeted audience from their current position on an issue to a new position chosen by you. You'll need to determine when and where you will meet with the customers. You can use an existing venue like a trade show, conference or Industry Day, or create your own by visiting the customer, inviting them to visit your facility or arranging for a visit for customers to see a demonstration of your products in action.

If you are creating a venue to meet with the customer, always have a legitimate business reason for every call and meeting. If you aren't giving the customer relevant inputs to his or her problem, stay away. You should always make good use of your customer's time as this will result in your call being a priority for your customer. It is important to continually touch your customers to refresh your contacts, to stay attuned to what is happening in the customer's organization, and to be aware of competitor customer initiatives.

Just as messages must fit their audience, so must they fit the venue. Context is everything – what works in a briefing won't work in a show booth. When you brief, you can deliver complex messages, but in a show booth, your messages need to be short and attention grabbing. Some messages are private and need to be delivered in person, one-on-one. Depending on the situation, you can also send multiple messages, but it is important to keep your team focused on only a few messages.

It is also critical that you carefully consider how you will get feedback from the customer in every venue. Dialogues sell; monologues do not. **You always want to learn while informing.** The goal is to test every strategy with the customer and get their reaction. That means that you have to be listening. In the immortal and grammatically challenged words of Lyndon Johnson, "I ain't never learned nothin' talkin'." You want to be brief – the less you talk the more you can listen. You want to make your venues response-oriented sessions, where you can encourage your customer to talk. Ideally, these venues provide the opportunity for the customer to give you feedback on your approach, and on each major point you make. You should specifically discuss why the customer rejected alternative approaches – with a special emphasis on the alternatives that the competition will propose. Look for rebuttals, because those give you clues to their feelings. You also want them to discuss technical concerns with you and share their ideas. Make this happen by asking the customer pertinent questions that encourage them to reveal their thoughts on the presentation and to discuss technical concerns with the group. Think of an optometrist. They ask, "Is it better like this or better like that?" They give the customer lots of choices and solicit feedback on every one. Using this approach, you can tease out the customer's reactions on everything you are thinking about. You learn their perceptions, biases and objections. Once uncovered, then you can address their objections. You can also hone on the solutions they like best and adjust your strategy and sales messages accordingly.

However, you must pick venues where you can get this kind of feedback when you need it. Giving a talk at a technical conference, for example, is a great way to give credibility to your ideas, but it does not allow you to get feedback from your targeted customers. Encourage the customer's feelings of importance by respecting their opinions. If you are wrong, admit it quickly. Try to make your solution seem like it was the customer's idea. Require a marketer to accompany every engineer and program manager when they visit the customer, so that they convey the right messages. For important messages, repeat them in multiple venues. As a capture team member, always remember the words of George Bernard Shaw, "The greatest problem in communication is the illusion that it has been accomplished."

When meeting the customer, you should listen for their key concerns. In your meetings with customers at all levels, not just the key decision makers, you need to record individuals' hot buttons. Hot buttons are particular issues that create an emotional response in that person. These are the issues that they have strong feelings and opinions about. Usually, they result from some very good or very bad prior experience. Customers will ask questions regarding their hot button and will return to the issue over and over again. When selling, it is important to identify and address hot buttons in your customer's key decision makers and their technical evaluators. You should compile a list of hot buttons for these people so that you can ensure that you address these in your pre-sell messages. You should ensure that you highlight their hot buttons in your proposal storyboards. That way, you ensure that these hot button issues are addressed specifically in the proposal. If you fail to address them, a key technical evaluator can latch on to your failure to address an issue that is very important to him or her and lower your proposal score.

Once you have identified your messages and venues, you'll plan the supporting media. The media should be structured to communicate the messages most effectively. For example, videos are great for trade shows, as long as they draw attention and are short. A well-produced video creates instant credibility. White papers can be given to the customer, but they need to be self-explanatory, interesting and brief. Extensive use of photos from field tests and demos are also very persuasive. Computer simulations make complex results easy to understand. They also provide significant credibility and allow customers to give very specific feedback. However, you'll need a venue where you can bring in the simulation and have the customer's undivided attention.

— *Strategy in Action* —

For example, while competing for a very large and complex battle management system for the Navy, Company X had already developed a great deal of software from other programs and would be able to reuse it for this application. They were unsure about how to prove to the Navy the maturity of their capability. Each of the bidders was going to perform a simulation of their proposed system for the customer at the bidder's facility. From their competitive analysis, Company X knew that their Competitor Y had substantially less software developed, but they could create outstanding simulations. However, because Competitor Y had yet to develop the software, their impressive simulations would merely take the Navy evaluators through various scripted scenarios portraying all of the system's future capabilities. To differentiate their simulation and show that their system already had much of the command and control logic implemented, Company X developed a simulation that brought the customer into the process. Company X decided to highlight that they actually had a working simulation environment and not just a set of scripted scenarios. For the Navy's on-site visit, the company brought their various software systems together and developed an interactive simulation. As the simulation progressed, one of the company's vice presidents gave the Navy program manager a menu from which to pick Scud launchers, downed pilots and surface-to-air missile sites to appear during the simulation. The simulation then adjusted the aircraft mission paths based on these new targets and threats. The simulation then showed the operators responding to these new threats and challenges and adapting their missions. The company's simulation gave the customer a role in the simulation, which made it more compelling, but most importantly, it clearly showed that the Company X's simulation had much of the required functionality already developed. This simulation went a long way to convince the customer that their system was lower risk and it justified their smaller proposed software effort. This simulation impressed the Navy evaluators, convincing them how far advanced and therefore, how low risk Company X's solution was. This successful demonstration was a key reason that Company X won the pursuit.

When strategizing your messages, always think about your audience. What is their position on the issues faced? What do they need to know? What will they find persuasive? Some decision makers are more visually than verbally focused, so you want good graphics and pictures, while people with the "intuitive feeler" personality type respond better to expert opinion, stories, anecdotes and metaphors, while the "detailed analytics" are more fact-oriented and statistical. The better you understand your audience and adapt your messages to their personality type the more persuasive your presentations to them will be.

Building the Action Plan

All of the media development, customer deliverables and proofs are scheduled and tracked in the action plan. This plan includes a unique item number for each action and a description of the item. You cannot successfully run a complex pursuit without an action plan to track all of the tasks the capture team leader needs to accomplish. The plan identifies who is responsible for completing the action item, the due date and status toward completion. Developing the specific actions needed to implement the identified tactics allows the capture team to estimate the cost of implementing their strategy. You'll need to ensure that the people you assign tasks to have the skills and capabilities to perform them. If not, you'll need a plan to get them that capability. The capture team leader will seek executive approval of the resources required and of the action plan.

When implementing the action plan it is critical to deal with the hard issues that people like to duck and that will keep the plan from being successfully implemented. Implementing the plan can also run afoul of a functional department's support or lack thereof. This is one of the key reasons for executive buy-in and review of the capture plan – to get the executives to ensure inter-departmental cooperation. Having executive approval allows the capture team leader to hold capture team members or functional department representatives accountable for completing their assigned tasks. Executives can then track the capture's progress by reviewing the status of the action, communication and contact plan tasking.

Creating the Intelligence Plan

Intelligence is key to winning every pursuit. ***Acquiring intelligence does not happen by accident.*** Top performers have a formal competitive intelligence process, because they know that ***the company with the most intelligence usually wins***. The team must develop a data collection plan to validate and iterate that strategy. The capture plan documents intelligence needs and makes an assignment list to obtain this intelligence. As we will discuss in Chapter 9, intelligence collection is a simple process. The capture team identifies what they need to know and they task someone to collect that information. The assigned person seeks out the information, which is then consolidated and analyzed. The analysis fits the intelligence into the bigger picture along with other pieces of information. Contained in the capture plan is an intelligence plan (which will be described in Chapter 9), which ensures that the necessary data for intelligence analysis is collected.

The Contact Plan

Think of awarding a large contract as getting married. It is a long-term commitment requiring trust and hopefully a win-win relationship. People buy from people they trust. You can propose marriage to a stranger and expect not to get a "yes." You have to build trusting relationships between your staff and the customer's. Trust comes from establishing rapport, selling conviction, and consistency. Having the right people on the team and having adequate face time with the customer is critical to building trust, and you manage that process with the contract plan.

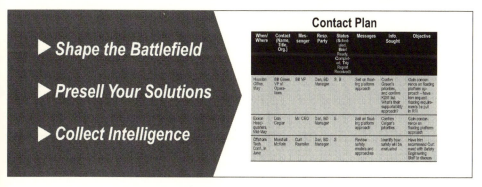

Exhibit 8-11: Creating the Contact Plan

Sales is a contact sport and the contact plan is one of the key tools used to manage progress down the field. While the communications plan lays out the campaign for sending messages across the entire pursuit, the contact plan focuses on the near term (e.g., two months out) specific customer meetings. The contact plan, as shown in Exhibit 8-12, adds detail to the communications plan and also brings in the intelligence required for the contact. This plan is used to set up all meetings with the customer. This is critical to ensure that the appropriate messages are being transmitted to the customer and that every customer meeting is used as an opportunity to collect information. Also, it ensures that the team is prepared for the meetings and that the results of meetings are recorded and analyzed.

When/ Where	Contact (Name, Title, Org.)	Mes- senger	Resp. Party	Status (Sched- uled, Brief Ready, Complet- ed, Trip Report Received)	Messages	Info. Sought	Objective
Houston Office, May	Bill Green, VP of Opera- tions	Bill VP	Dan, BD Manager	S, B	Sell on float- ing platform approach	Confim Green's priorities, and confirm KDM list. What's their supportability approach?	Gain concur- rence on floating platform ap- proach – have him request floating require- ments be put in RFI
Exxon Head- quarters, Mid-May	Don Ceglar	Mr. CEO	Dan, BD Manager	S	Sell on float- ing platform approach	Confirm Celgar's priorities	Gain concur- rence on floating platform approach
Offshore Tech. Conf., in June	Marshall McKain	Curt Rasteller	Dan, BD Manager	S	Review safety models and approaches	Identify how safety will be evaluated	Have him recommend Curt meet with Safety Engineering Staff to discuss

Exhibit 8-12: The Contact Plan

The communications plan typically identifies the venues and their target audiences – the "when and where," and the contact name in the contact plan. The contact plan then identifies a messenger and a responsible party. The messenger is the one actually making contact. Since the messenger may be a high level executive, a member of the capture team must coordinate the meeting, prepare any materials and brief the messenger for the interchange – this person is the "responsible party."

Typically, the responsible party is a member of the capture team and they schedule the meeting and set the agenda. They prepare any media required such as white papers and briefing materials. This person also prepares the talking points and briefs the messenger about the questions to be asked and the contact's background. The more your messenger knows about their contact, such as career history, family, personality type and perceived customer priorities, the more competent your messenger will look and the higher the probability of success. If an executive is making contact, the responsible party is accountable for debriefing the executive and writing the trip report.

When deciding whom the messenger will be, you should match the level of your executive to the comparable level of the contact. Your executives should meet contacts that have an equivalent stature from the customer's viewpoint. This is important in meetings as well as when writing letters. This is also crucial to showing and demonstrating respect. The messenger should have the credibility to deliver the message. For example, if the message is technical, one of your technologists should deliver it. Financial issues, or terms and conditions, should be discussed by the business managers.

One technique that we have seen very effectively employed by a company that sells services to state and local governments is "client matching." At this company, the capture team leads assigns a key executive "owner" of each customer key decision maker. This owner is responsible for building and managing the relationship with that individual. The company representative is responsible for developing a personal relationship, understanding their needs, desires for the program, and delivering bad news if necessary. Successful matching is an art and not a science. When pairing up executives, it is important to match them up by authority level as well as by similar background, interests and temperament. The match is usually based on finding common ground between the client and the representative that could include going to the same college, common hobbies or mutual friends. To enhance your customer rapport, you should always try to match personality types between your messengers and their contacts. For example, people with an analytical bent tend to communicate more effectively with other analytics and tend to clash with intuitive feelers. The intent is for the client to respect their match professionally and like them personally. Good things flow from good client relationships. This is all about building trust. People only buy from people they trust, and if you pass an individual around, having lots of people call on them, they will not feel valued or connected to your company. By developing a relationship with the key decision maker, you ensure that when you need to deliver an important message, the key decision maker will return phone calls and accept meetings.

When developing your contact plan, it is important to use all of your resources, such as field offices, executives, executives from teammates, personal friends of decision makers on your team and friendly politicians. We are frequently surprised by how many people across all the companies that make up a large team have staff with close existing relationships with key decision makers. Just as amazing is how rarely capture teams actually tap into these resources. This wide of expanse of people can provide excellent intelligence on the key decision makers and deliver messages.

A simple tool we use to help executives deliver messages and collect intelligence is a three by five index card. Prior to a customer meeting, we would give executives three by five cards. On one side are the messages that the capture team wants them to deliver and on the other side are the key intelligence questions they want them to ask. For example, one client was attempting to sell a health care information system to Poland and their delegation was coming to town. We planned the meeting and the dinner with the delegation like a wedding party. Each executive was assigned a "date" for the night. The vice president of engineering was paired with the Polish technology office official, while the vice president of programs was paired with their budgeting office official. Each of the cards was customized. While the head of engineering was talking up some of the key discriminators, he was also asking about the official's priorities for the system. The vice president of programs was telling the budget official about some of our financing options while asking him about the country's budgeting priorities. Then, by debriefing the executives after the dinner, the capture team was able to adapt their communications and intelligence plans accordingly.

All too often, capture teams create contact plans to show management their intentions, but the plans are then forgotten about and never implemented. Implementing the contact plan is essential to shaping the pursuit and collecting intelligence. Management must ensure that contact plans are implemented. Status is tracked so that the capture leader can ensure that meeting materials are ready for meetings and trip reports are completed and provided to the business development manager. The trip report should detail the results of the meeting, including any follow-up commitments and intelligence collected. It is critically important to document this information so that the team knows whether the sale is progressing or not – are they finding success at pre-selling the customer? **Not completing trip reports is a huge problem; few companies consistently complete them.** Without trip reports, valuable feedback is lost. For example, in a post mortem on a loss, one of the field sales force brought up that he had heard that the customer had received a Rough Order of Magnitude estimate from one of the competitors of $150 million. During the pursuit, this critical piece of information was not written down nor did it make to the team as they finalized their pricing. This price was significantly lower than expected and indicated the competitor was targeting a lower price than anticipated. Having this intelligence would have changed the company's approach and pricing. In addition, without a written record of what was said, customer comments can be reinterpreted and misconstrued. That leads a capture team to start making conclusions based on erroneous information.

Every contact should have an objective, and the objective is a call to action for the customer. You should ask yourself before every contact: Why is this contact a step toward winning? You should be progressing the sale at every meeting, which means you need to tell the contact in very specific terms what you want them to do. The contact plan is a living document that is constantly updated with new information and progress.

Developing the Capture Budget

Once the team has identified the tasks required by the action plan, they can estimate the staffing and budget of the pursuit. Start by estimating the cost of staffing the capture team. Then add in the cost of the discreet tasks, such as conducting demonstrations, developing simulations, conducting the Price-to-Win and writing the proposal. You need to identify how many trips your team will make based on how far away the customer is, how much time you have and how much influencing and pre-selling you must do. Plus, you need to include costs for attending conferences, teaming meetings and trade shows. Many costs are driven by the customer, such as how extensive a proposal they require and how long they typically spend conducting on-site customer negotiations.

The cost of estimating the capture effort should be closely scrutinized and the team should carefully prioritize all of the planned activities. They should evaluate all of the potential tactics, and spend money on activities that have highest impact on the probability of winning (Pwin). Frequently, a small team of the "right people" can be cheaper and more effective than a larger team with the wrong people, so it makes sense to fight for the right people. Once the capture budget is established, manage it like you would a contract – track and control expenditures, adjust as needed and create a management reserve.

Embrace a budget that the business can afford, but remember that you have to spend what it takes to win. The best way to approach management is in terms of a contract. The capture team proposes a win, which they believe they can achieve if they have the resources necessary. If those resources aren't available, don't pursue. Spending will vary based on the size of the award. If you have spending benchmarks for a pursuit, they need to be adjusted based on the nature of the pursuit. Larger awards cost significantly less per award dollar than smaller opportunities. Also, leveraging proven technology or competing for a service contract will cost less to propose. If there is new technology that has to be developed and sold you will spend more, and if you are selling a product to a government they usually require extensive and expensive proposals. International jobs require significantly more travel and living costs, plus translations and the cost of in-country experts. It also costs more, and is frequently underestimated, for you to pursue a new customer to your company, because past experience shows that it takes a huge effort to develop customer intimacy.

The Business Case

You bid to win – you operate to make money. The business case is your plan for how you are going to manage the business area once you win. ***You build the business case on your best assessment of the financial impact of winning the opportunity. It is not a financial evaluation of the discrete opportunity.*** The business case is not a literal interpretation of the customer's RFP, but considers how the contract is likely to be executed if you win. The business case also considers all of the likely downstream revenue impacts. These are two very different perspectives.

Developing the business case is a key part of the pursue/no pursue assessment. It is a key factor in determining if the opportunity is worth it. However, the business case is iterated as the pursuit evolves, so as to reaffirm your company's commitment.

To project the contract's impact, the business manager creating the business case examines the customer's trends. They assess what will happen within the scope of the contract – what options will be exercised and how the contract will change over its execution. Winning a large contract will increase your production base, which can reduce your fixed cost absorption. Is the customer likely to grow the contract by adding more volume or work scope, or is their workload shrinking and forcing them to bring more work inside? The opportunity may position you for support, spares, training or follow-on orders. In addition, a win can lead to foreign sales or entrance into adjacent markets. When analyzing the business case, the business manager assesses the impact of winning the job based on the probability of winning on other opportunities in the marketplace. They quantify this value. Winning may bring in licensing fees or other financial benefits. You must quantify the future revenue streams versus all of their accompanying costs. For example, one company was assessing a potential sale of 40 aircraft to a Latin American country. When they constructed the business case, they included the follow on training and support of the aircraft, which they would be the favorite to win. Their assessment of the customer indicated that the customer would likely need to buy more aircraft a few years later and the winner of this initial sale would be well positioned for that work. In addition, history showed that the other countries of Latin America frequently followed this country's lead in procurement choices. It was likely that the company would pick up another 15 aircraft sales from this country's neighbors. When the company's business manager developed the business case for this sale she considered all of these follow on opportunities in her analysis. It should be noted that all of these opportunities were discounted in the analysis by a probability of success. By using the business case, the capture team leader was able to justify more aggressive pricing and amortization of non-recurring expenses as part of their bid.

You must estimate the project's total cost and risk. You'll need to identify all of the capital, R&D and discretionary expenses for this particular opportunity as well as the follow on opportunities that you are forecasting in your business case. If you are going to be financing the project, that needs to be included.

You'll also need to identify and quantify the project's risks and include them in the business case. A winning pursuit usually contains risks that need to be identified to executive management along with an appropriate plan to mitigate them. Identifying and quantifying the opportunity's risks assists the capture team in developing approaches during the capture phase to mitigate them. They can use this insight to try to get the requirements or terms and conditions changed, or to bring in partners.

It should be understood that only one thing is certain when projecting future costs and benefits, and that is that the analysis will be wrong. That is why you must analyze the comparative risk of one project versus another. With this analysis, the executives can compare the opportunity cost of this project versus other choices to decide if this opportunity is one of the best few. It is a critical step to optimizing the balance of shareholder, customer and market forces. The business case answers the most important question: Is the return worth the risk?

Developing the business case is a team effort by business management, finance, business development and program management. This is normally the tricky part where managers make estimates of what will happen in the future and then take responsibility for achieving those results. The business case balances customer requirements, the terms and conditions, revenues and program schedule against your understanding of the program, customer, trends and the market environment. The business case is a calculation of the proposed project's true cash flow, Return on Investment, Internal Rate of Return and Return on Sales and their impact on the company's financials.

Developing the robust business case is a key best practice. If you narrowly define the opportunity, you put yourself at a disadvantage compared to the competitor. Since the business impact of winning is usually greater than just the financial return of the discrete opportunity, using the business case allows a company to justify greater investment, lower margins and more aggressive bidding. One division used business case extensively.

They bragged that they consistently bid the lowest margins in the company, but delivered the highest. And they had the data to prove it. One key approach they employed was to aggressively pursue opportunities they could grow. Developing the business case is critical to bidding the right price in some bids.

Summary

Some people think that the capture plan is merely a document where all of the relevant information regarding an opportunity is consolidated so that each team member has access to it. In reality, it is much more. Winners are usually decided before proposals are even submitted. It is almost always the company that is best positioned to win that walks away with the contract. The key to positioning lies in crafting a good capture plan and then implementing it. Getting the rules set to your advantage is one of the most important factors in winning. If you can influence the customer to write in requirements only your team can easily meet, or ask for information only your team already has, you create big advantages. None of this happens by accident. Crafting a great strategy is useless unless it is implemented, and the capture plan is an implementation tool. It identifies all of the proofs and data you'll need to persuade the customer that you have the best offer. Implementing the contact plan allows you to pre sell your solutions and influence the customer to shape the acquisition toward your strengths. The intelligence plan ensures that you systematically collect the information needed to understand and outmaneuver the competition. Implementing the plan ensures that the capture team collects intelligence to continuously iterate the plan throughout the pursuit. Simply put, the capture plan is critical to winning.

Chapter 9: Collecting Intelligence and Deciphering the Competition

> **"The reason the enlightened prince and the wise general conquer the enemy ... is foreknowledge."**
>
> — Sun Tzu, The Art of War

Pete West believes in obtaining and using competitive intelligence to win, but he calls it scouting. His girls' volleyball team won the Juniors Club National Championship. West says, "In order to exploit their weaknesses, you must know what they are." He always scouts the competitors to identify their star players and find out how they like to be set. This activity helps West teach his team how to avoid giving their competitors their favorite setups and how to keep the ball away from the best players. For example, West knew that at National Finals his team's toughest competition would be a team called Sports Performance Organization. To prepare, he had his second team mimic how Sports Performance Organization played, including how they adjusted their play for changes in tactics. This scouting focused his team. They avoided surprises and gave his players an extra boost of confidence that helped them win the tournament. In his words, "The payoff is huge." At that level of play, an edge of only a few points separates the winners from the losers.

While none of the top teen girls' volleyball coaches goes into a match without knowing their opponents' strengths and weaknesses, many captains of industry do. Executives often enter into costly competitions for vital business without considering the opponent's capabilities and possible strategies. Just as in sports, this lack of intelligence often leads to defeat. This was a key finding of our strategic benchmarking survey. Our studies uncovered a direct relationship between a company's knowledge of its competitor's approach and its success at winning new contracts.

For example, competitive intelligence was an important factor in helping Lockheed Martin defeat Boeing to win the Joint Strike Fighter (JSF) program.

— *Strategy in Action* —

While conducting the Price-to-Win analysis, we interviewed one of Lockheed's senior technologists – a gentleman who appeared as if he could have been sent directly from a Hollywood casting agency to play an eccentric scientist. When we asked what concerns he had about Boeing's JSF offering, he said, "this," and handed us a briefing some Boeing engineers had presented at a recent public technical conference. The briefing described a Boeing initiative called Bold Stroke. Following this tip, we researched Bold Stroke, uncovering many news articles, conference briefings and papers which described it. We understood why this scientist was concerned. We were, too.

Bold Stroke was a company-wide plan to develop an open avionics architecture that would facilitate the use of Commercial Off-the-Shelf (COTS) hardware and software. At that time, each new aircraft had a unique and proprietary architecture requiring the manufacturer to develop and support each component individually. Boeing's plan was to build common components like a mission computer and flight software for the F-18, and then reuse them on their F-15s, AV-8Bs, Wedgetail, and C-17 product lines. Boeing claimed their Bold Stroke approach would slash avionics flyaway costs by 50 percent, and operations and support costs by 60 percent. We discovered that they had 100-120 people working on this initiative, developing COTS architectures, program road maps, leveraged developments and tool sets. Plus, they had enrolled some of their key suppliers like Honeywell and Raytheon in the initiative. Avionics is one of the key elements in winning an aircraft development contract. Avionics performance is a large part of the technical evaluation, and its development is always one of the highest risk elements of a fighter's development. The latest U.S. fighter, the F-22, was years late due to avionics problems. The signals we uncovered showed a substantial Boeing corporate commitment to Bold Stroke. While Boeing publically only vaguely alluded to Bold Stroke during their efforts to win JSF, it was obvious that Bold Stroke would be a key element of their JSF win strategy.

On JSF, Lockheed was following their traditional avionics approach of building a proprietary architecture using military standard components. If Lockheed remained on that path, their solution would be more costly and riskier than Boeing's, and would likely result in a loss. When we presented this analysis to Lockheed's capture leadership, they reacted by assembling a cross-sector task force to assess their avionics approach. The team recommended the JSF team scrap their existing approach and leverage top expertise from across the corporation to develop an open system architecture for their solution. This effort enabled Lockheed to neutralize a key Boeing strength. Nothing stimulates action more than a rival, so when this competitive revelation hit Lockheed Martin's corporate headquarters, they decided to launch a cross-company open systems task force to leapfrog Boeing's Bold Stroke initiative.

Despite its importance, most companies gather competitor information in an ad hoc manner – they take what they can get, when and where they can get it. They think of business intelligence as an unaffordable luxury and regard its practice as a mystical art of dubious repute. As a result, the haphazard accumulation of data fails to provide insight that is of much value. Conversely, the companies with the highest win rates have found that business intelligence is not a mystical art; it is a mix of art and science whose ethical practice can be readily used to dramatically impact a company's top and bottom lines.

Intelligence is simply knowledge and foreknowledge of the world around us. The intelligence process collects, organizes and analyzes information about the external environment to create actionable information. The goal is to provide the right information at the right time to help management make better decisions and avoid surprises. Most of the data required is publicly available. Experts estimate that 80 to 90 percent of the information used in competitive intelligence analysis comes from public sources, which is consistent with our experience. The other 10 to 20 percent comes from internal team sources. Despite this, as we hope this chapter will show, *there is very little that one cannot discover about a competitor legally and ethically if one is willing to spend the resources to do so*.

Intelligence is Essential to Winning

To win, you devise a solution that differentiates you from the competition on those attributes most important to the customer. To accomplish this, you craft a strategy based on your capabilities compared to the competition. In fact, selecting your strategy should be based entirely on how your offering compares to the competition's for each of the customer's key values. It is not possible to craft strategies to heighten your strengths and neutralize your weaknesses if you don't know what the competition is going to offer. *A strategy is only as good as the information on which it is based.*

Everyone runs fastest against others, even Albert Einstein. While he was collaborating with the great mathematician David Hilbert, Einstein was also racing him. Hilbert was rushing to be the first to publish the mathematical foundations of the Theory of Relativity. It was that competition that spurred Einstein to focus, study, innovate and complete his work. It's no different in the corporate world – understanding what the competition will offer encourages you to provide the best solution. Too often, executives dismiss their competition until they discover just how good they really are. As mentioned before, arrogance is the void filled by ignorance. Opinions change when you learn about things like all competitor product features, the image a customer has of a competitor's past performance or the new technologies they are introducing. A clear understanding of the competition's approach and benefits encourages you to push the design envelope and develop the best possible solution. It forces you to develop a strategy that clearly differentiates your offering. Competitive intelligence is also important for the capture leader so that he or she can keep the executives abreast of the competition. This kind of intelligence encourages them to do the hard things that are often necessary to win, like redesigning a product as Lockheed did.

Customers perceive vendors as competent if they display significant market intelligence. When a capture team seems to know what's going on in the customer's community and among their competitors, the customer views them as competent and can't help but prejudge their performance accordingly. A program manager at one IT services company told us that his company had representatives at all of the customer's major facilities, including headquarters. His staff was so disciplined about writing trip and field reports, that he had great insight into the customer from field problems to the status of funding negotiations at headquarters and even the latest political gossip in the boardroom. As a result, he knew more about his customer's programs than his customer counterpart. Not only did this make him look very competent to his customer, it allowed his company to shape the customer's thinking.

An early understanding of the customer and the competition enables you to outmaneuver your rivals. In one competition, the capture team found that the customer had been spending millions of dollars on a small business to develop a software product on which the customer wanted to standardize. The pursuit required the use and functionality of this software product. As soon as the capture team realized this, they signed an exclusive teaming agreement with the small business, forcing the competitor to find a software supplier who lacked any prior relationship with the customer. The capture team won.

Intelligence allows your capture team to send clear, focused messages explaining how your company is approaching the pursuit and why. A proposal should address customer concerns and explain why a company chose certain approaches and rejected alternatives. Capture teams should "ghost" the competitor's approaches, explaining why their analysis led them to reject the competition's approach in favor of their own. The capture team provides data and direct comparisons between the approaches and describes why they logically rejected a competitor's approach. This is a very powerful story as long as the customer believes it to be objective.

It is important not to overestimate the competition. All competitors have real weaknesses that a capture team needs to understand in order to shape the game effectively. For example, one capture team influenced the customer to write requirements that the competition found difficult to meet, undermining their strategy. The competitor was proposing an off-the-shelf solution with limited growth capability. The capture team convinced the customer of the value of performance enhancements beyond the capabilities of the competition's product, and the new requirements forced the competition to redesign and re-qualify their product. They were no longer able to claim "proven performance" and "lowest risk."

As we discussed in Chapter 8, intelligence is critical to shaping the game. Sending the right messages to the right people at the right time to influence the course of the acquisition takes a significant amount of customer and competitor intelligence. One must thoroughly understand the customer and the competitor to achieve results. In fact, experience has shown that *one of the greatest benefits of intelligence is its ability to provide management with the confidence to take decisive action.*

Ignorance and doubt breed inaction. We once heard of a situation where an engineer had a very good idea what his competitor was going to propose. He deduced it, because a peer of his was an expert in a new technology and had just been hired by the competition. His peer bragged that he was hired to work on a big pursuit. The engineer realized that this expert was hired to bring this technology to a particular upcoming job, but because the engineer's company lacked a formal competitive intelligence process to validate his information or bring his case forward to the executives, his insight was dismissed. The company did not work to counter the new technology and lost. Simply put, the competitor with the most intelligence usually wins.

Intelligence Collection Must Be Done Ethically

All intelligence can, and must, be collected ethically. A company can also face very severe criminal and civil penalties under the Economic Espionage Act of 1996 for using illegal means, violating a contract or compromising a customer or another company's proprietary documents. The basic legal and ethical guidelines are:

- Do not break contracts or coerce suppliers to do so.
- Never misrepresent yourself in the pursuit of information by conducting false job interviews, setting up a fictitious company as a front, hiding or misleading someone regarding your identity or employer.
- Never obtain proprietary documents from a customer or competitor without their permission.
- Do not exploit new employees for proprietary information from their previous employer.

The consequences of unethical or illegal intelligence collection can be severe. Boeing obtained proprietary Lockheed Martin documents from a former Lockheed Martin employee to assist them in winning the Evolved Expendable Launch Vehicle (EELV) competition. This unethical and illegal use of these documents cost Boeing over a billion dollars in forfeit sales, disbarment from government competitions for a period of time, and significant damage to the company's reputation. A company's reputation is one of its most valuable assets and should never be compromised.

To prevent ethical lapses, a company's ethics department, working with the competitive intelligence group and legal departments, should create ethics guidelines to protect the company from unethical acts. The company should provide detailed and specific examples of both acceptable and unacceptable behavior so employees can understand where the boundaries lie. Most of the unethical competitive intelligence collection acts we have heard of have been committed out of ignorance about what constitutes unethical behavior. Every capture team member should review this guideline prior to collecting intelligence. Competitive intelligence analysts must be proactive in helping protect their company by monitoring for ethical missteps while seeking competitive intelligence.

Overview of the Business Intelligence Process

Providing your executives with knowledge or foreknowledge of a competitor's (or customer's, or regulator's) actions does not happen by accident, it is the result of executing a relatively simple, carefully structured process. As shown in Exhibit 9-1, the intelligence collection process is quite straightforward. The first step is to identify and document what you need to know. Then create a plan that identifies the specific data that will answer the question. The plan identifies the source that knows the answer and assigns someone to seek out this data. That individual will contact the source and report their findings. An analyst assesses the data, puts together the story and reports the answer. This chapter will explore each of those steps in detail.

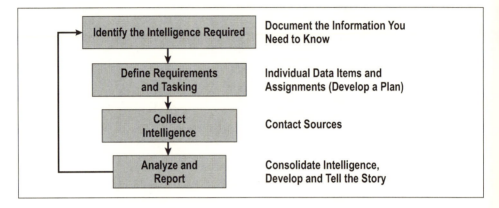

Exhibit 9-1: Steps to Gathering Intelligence

1. Identify the Intelligence Required

Untrained executives are a big obstacle to effective competitive intelligence. They frequently ask the wrong questions. Many executives ask questions just because they are curious. They ask for data so they can play analyst. Or their intelligence demands are too broad, for example, "I want everything you can find out about Bechtel." But, the reality is that they don't really what to know everything about Bechtel. What they want to know is what price will Bechtel bid on the Saudi gas development project. That is information they' can use to make better decisions. The mark of a good competitive analyst is to always ask the executives for what decision they would make if they were given the answer to the question they pose. The executives usually realize that if there is no decision to be made based on the desired information, then the intelligence is not actionable and it is useless. The competitive analyst should ask himself the same question as well, to help him focus on the critical data that will drive the company's business decisions and to help him avoid collecting lots of extraneous data and developing long reports that are not actionable. The purpose of intelligence is to make better decisions.

Purpose is the essence of effective intelligence, and intelligence is "need to know" information, not "nice to know" information. Therefore, the first step in any intelligence project is defining the business decision to be made and the information required to make that decision. For each critical business decision, an intelligence analyst must define exactly what information is required, when is it needed, who will use it and what its priority is. The more specific the question, the better. The narrower the question, the easier it is to answer. Executives must prioritize intelligence needs because one can find out almost anything if they are willing to spend the resources. Prioritizing forces a company to use resources wisely.

The first and most critical step in intelligence gathering is identifying information needs and uses. Exhibit 9-2 shows how the key intelligence needs evolve across the campaign. The needs become more specific as the campaign evolves.

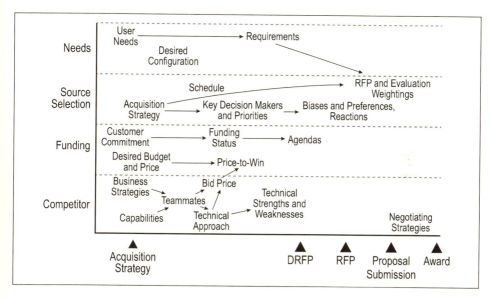

Exhibit 9-2: Evolution of Information Needs

In a pursuit, there are two principle focuses of intelligence collection – the customer and the competition. In fact, a capture team's first priority after developing the win strategy is to validate their key decision makers and their priority lists as described in Chapter 3. In addition, you need to understand their customer's acquisition and source selection processes. In parallel, you will need to understand the competition and their offerings. You should conduct an initial competitive analysis of all your competitors. Different competitors will bring different discriminators to the competition, which can affect customer's perceptions and desires. Even long shot competitors can have some good ideas or discriminators worth copying. However, it is our experience that it is more effective to analyze one competitor in depth than to spread resources thinner by analyzing two. You should conduct an analysis of all the competitors, but after expending about 25 percent of your effort, you should focus on the strongest one. For your top competitor, extensive knowledge is required:

- What is their bidding history?
  - What competitions have they bid on?
  - What strategies/approaches/discriminators have they employed?

- How aggressively have they bid?
- When have they bid aggressively?
- What lessons learned have they likely gained?
- What are they going to offer?
  - Who are their teammates and key suppliers?
  - What win strategies might they employ?
  - What is their likely technical approach?
  - What are their key discriminators -- strengths and weaknesses?
  - How well is their offering going to meet the evaluation criteria?
  - What is their likely bid price?
- How good is their relationship with the customer?
  - What is their reputation with this customer?
  - What is their ability to influence this customer?
  - How are they likely going to try to shape the procurement?

While customer and competitor questions will cover most of your needs, the intelligence plan must address any key missing information items listed as Red Flags, which were discussed in Chapter 2. Depending on your market and situation, these questions may address various other issues. For example, if you were going to bid on a railroad in Africa, you would probably have questions about the status of legislative or regulatory approvals. You might need to track a project's funding status if the World Bank financed it. The executives may want due diligence on a supplier. In one case, just before signing a teaming agreement, the executive team asked the competitive intelligence analyst to check on the background of a supplier. The analyst found that the supplier habitually sued everyone – customers, teammates and their own suppliers. In addition, newspapers linked the supplier to organized crime figures. The competitive analyst recommended that they not team with this supplier.

2. Define Requirements and Tasking

During the campaign, the team is constantly getting feedback from all parts of the customer – their logisticians, engineers, users, etc. Good capture teams are disciplined about documenting these customer conversations. The entire team needs to document and relate summaries to a single individual to archive and analyze. The capture team leader must assign an intelligence lead – someone responsible for coordinating the data collection, consolidating all of the intelligence, conducting the analysis and reporting the findings. If you do not have a competitive intelligence specialist, then the individual responsible for developing and coordinating the intelligence is the business development manager. Once the capture team has identified the intelligence questions, the intelligence lead decomposes these questions into data that capture team members can collect. The lead, working with the entire capture team, identifies where that data is or who has seen it. Then the intelligence lead creates an intelligence plan that assigns responsibility for collecting each data item to someone with a due date. This plan guides the intelligence effort by defining the sources and the questions to be asked.

The intelligence plan assigns accountability for data collection by identifying the specific data required, the data source, responsible individual and due date for each piece of information (see Exhibit 9-3). The intelligence lead works with business development to integrate these assignments into the customer contact plan. It is preferable if the person assigned responsibility for the information already knows the source and contacts them as a regular part of their job. If the source is a supplier, the plan designates a buyer; if it is a customer, the sales force will contact them. The comments column should note any concerns or suspected biases for a given source. It is important to present this plan to the capture team so that all members understand the intelligence requirements and can contribute to the plan. When reviewing the plan, capture team members frequently contribute intelligence that no one has ever asked about or good sources that the analysis hadn't thought of. The capture team constantly updates the intelligence plan with new questions and assignments across the pursuit.

Data Required	Source	Comments	Responsible Party	Due Date
Names of Industry Experts	Database search of AirLink articles for last three years		Kim Kelly	5/16
Is AirLink Trying to Hire Systems Engineers?	Advertising Manager, Journal of Systems Engineering		Kim Kelly	5/21
Is AirLink Buying a GPS Receiver? When Do They Want a Delivery? Without a Box?	Acme Electronics, Bill Lehman, 212-555-1213	Worked with Gary Larson on TSEC project	Kim Kelly	5/22
Is AirLink Talking to You about Developing an Integrated Solution?	Beth Wilkenson, Global Dir. of Eng., 714-555-8425	SW integration house. Likes to talk new technology	Alan Jackson	5/22

Detail and Map Questions to Sources

Exhibit 9-3: Excerpt from an Intelligence Plan

Before beginning to detail an intelligence plan to analyze a target, the capture team must develop a basic understanding of that target. The team should seek to understand the target's composition, history, perception in the marketplace, current environmental pressures, and products. The team should read the target's history, media reports, press releases and annual reports. They should focus not on the entire corporation, but on the business unit of interest.

Many times the data required will be simple to collect. For example, a critical question is: who will be the final customer decision maker for the job on which you are bidding? An important piece of data needed to determine the answer will be finding the final decision maker on the customer's last major buy. To answer this question, you identify someone who knows. This person may be a friendly customer executive or even one of your own staff who worked on the previous purchase. Assign someone to contact the individual who knows the answer.

For many of the questions you'll have, answers aren't so easy to find. Questions such as what the competitor will offer, and how much they will bid are more complex, and finding the answers requires a more sophisticated approach. The intelligence professional breaks down the information requirements into manageable questions with discrete answers or signals. To answer complex questions, such as what the competitor is going to offer, one must dissect the questions into a set of discrete, specific queries that lead one to deduce the answer. You must look for signals to suggest the answer to these questions. A signal is a fact that indicates what the target is doing. But a signal is only a piece of the puzzle and an analyst must assess how signals fit with the other pieces.

In situations where you are trying to decipher a complex question, you use a familiar framework. After studying the universe, a scientist develops a series of hypotheses to explain the behavior of nature. The scientist then constructs an experiment or series of experiments to test the hypotheses. Collecting this data either confirms or refutes the hypotheses. This is the scientific method. Intelligence analysts use the same process.

The capture team crafts an intelligence plan to prove (or by default, disprove) each hypothesis through planned and focused data collection of signals. The capture team systematically seeks out these signals, piecing together data to assemble a picture of their competitor's actions. They comb a vast array of diverse sources including past bid history, technical papers, marketing literature, financial statements and press releases, while interviewing suppliers, financial analysts, test lab personnel and trade officials to deduce what the competition is up to.

After analyzing the data, the intelligence professional synthesizes and packages the accumulated evidence into an intelligence product that allows management to reach a decision and take action. Implementing the intelligence plan for a complex intelligence question consists of the following steps:

A. Developing specific hypotheses
B. Identifying what signals the target would emit if the hypothesis were true
C. Identifying sources who would see these signals
D. Incorporating the search for these signals into the data collection plan

For each specific question, you analyze observations of the target and their available options to develop a hypothesis about the answer. For example, identifying your competitor's likely approach is one of the most important intelligence requirements in a pursuit. You start this analysis by identifying your competitor's current products and technologies. Companies, and people for that matter, never start with a blank sheet of paper. When a company starts working on a new project, they always begin by modifying an existing product or assembling their technologies, so you can examine the competitor's set of products and technologies, and those of their teammates, and pick the most likely combination for your project. You identify gaps in capabilities they must fill for the pursuit. The intelligence analyst, with the technical staff, should brainstorm a set of hypotheses about how the competitor will evolve their capabilities into a solution. Then the analyst can devise ways to test each hypothesis by seeking out marketplace signals consistent with that hypothesis.

Organizations are like people in that they have unique personalities. Key insight into a competitor's likely approach can be deduced by understanding the personality of the competitor – on what do they pride themselves and how do they usually compete? Do they focus on best technical solutions, quickest service or lowest cost? Companies, like people, try to reuse the same discriminators they have invested in and been successful with in the past. If you want to understand what has been done, collect facts. If you want to understand what can be done, collect facts and apply the rules of science. If you want to know what will be done, collect facts, apply the rules of science and understand the personality of the target. People and organizations are creatures of habit. Only rarely do companies, like people, break with the past. And just like people, usually it takes a severe emotional event like a major loss for them to break with what has worked. It is important to understand the target's personality when hypothesizing about their approach. Some companies try to win by providing the best technical solution. Others try to win by being the lowest cost. You use this understanding of their behavior to guide your choice of hypothesis. Projecting behavior is one of the arts of competitive intelligence.

By examining a company's marketing, a capture team can gain a good understanding of how the competition views itself and the market. For example, Apple Computers' "1984" television commercial portrayed a gritty future filled with zombie-like, gray-uniformed people with shaved heads. This compliant crowd sat staring blankly at a huge screen that dominated the enormous assembly hall as Big Brother spoke. As the crowd looked on, a young athletic woman in red shorts charged in and hurled a sledgehammer at the screen. The screen exploded in a blinding flash of light. The voice-over announced the introduction of the Macintosh and said, "You'll see why 1984 won't be like '1984.'" Apple's view of their market and their role in it was clear. Apple saw itself as David to IBM's Goliath and they intended to "liberate the masses." With an ad like that, one would expect Apple would act boldly, aggressively and disruptively in the marketplace. They did. They also developed stylish products that were user-friendly for the masses. They also demanded high prices and developed closed proprietary systems that would not work with other products.

Personality analysis is a powerful tool to predict decision-making. Personality analysis can verify or refute your analysis.

— *Strategy in Action* —

As an example, we were working to capture a ship contract. We believed we had excellent intelligence on the competitor's proposed ship, including its displacement, hull form (the competitor published an artist rendering), configuration, construction material and shipyard. We thought that the competitor was going to propose a unique ship design made of composites. Our research showed that no one had ever built a ship with their design as large as the one they were proposing, and they were planning to use an unproven and very expensive composite material to build the hull. The shipyard that they were going to use had never built this type of ship before, nor had they ever worked with composites. While our technical team projected that the comptetitor's solution would promise very good performance, it was also going to be high cost and high risk. And they were selling it to a very conservative and cost-conscious customer. Their strategy did not make any sense to us. We were mystified. To help us understand this competitor's behavior, we conducted a personality analysis of the competitor's key decision makers. We discovered that the competitor's chief engineer on this project was a domineering risk taker, who was high technology focused and arrogant, and he did not tend to listen well to customers or anyone else for that matter. Based on this personality analysis, we could now envision why this competitor was pursuing such a flawed strategy. The competitor lost. Years later, we met an engineer who had been on that competitor's capture team. He told us that the capture team figured out just weeks before submitting their proposal that their solution was hopeless. We did not have the heart to tell him that based on our competitive analysis we knew his offering was doomed a year before he did.

No organization operates in isolation. All companies broadcast their intentions to the marketplace through the signals they emit (see Exhibit 9-4). Every action that an organization takes broadcasts signals into its environment as it interacts and communicates with other organizations. Companies provide extensive information to organizations that they report to, and broadcast strategies and intentions to groups that they are trying to influence. They communicate information about their intentions as they try to sell themselves to potential customers, and they betray their intentions through choices about whom they buy from and what they purchase. These signals will help to form the basis for the capture team's hypothesis, but unlike the scientist, the capture team lacks the luxury of staging a controlled experiment. However, by using the scientific method to create an intelligence plan and by engaging in careful observation, a team can deduce what the competition is doing. The intelligence plan tasks the capture team to seek out those signals consistent with their hypotheses. These hypotheses cover the various marketing, technical, product line, manufacturing and service alternatives that the competition is likely to employ. The presence or absence of signals creates facts. Just like the scientist, by piecing these facts together, the intelligence analyst assembles the puzzle that is the competitor's offering.

The greater your initial knowledge of the target, the more accurate and detailed your initial hypotheses can be. However, experience has shown that having a correct initial hypothesis is not the key to success. The hypotheses, correct or not, lead you to identify a comprehensive set of signals, and the sources who will see them. If you execute the intelligence plan effectively, your sources will spot signals for every significant competitor action, even those that you don't anticipate. Uncovering conflicting data may disprove some of your hypotheses and lead you to formulate new ones to retest. This iterative process leads you to develop a comprehensive picture of the competition's strategy.

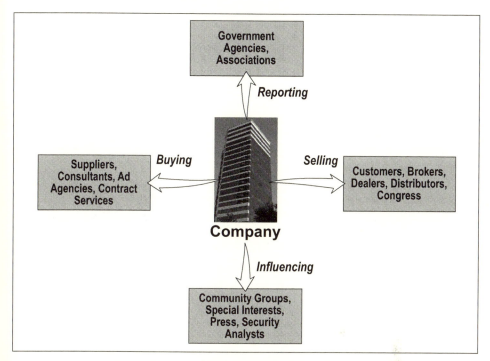

Exhibit 9-4: Targets Emit Signals to the Marketplace

The search for meaningful signals starts with identifying all the actions the target would take if your hypothesis were correct. Typically, the capture team employs a brainstorming meeting with a cross-section of functional experts – marketing, sales, engineering, human resources, quality, service personnel, purchasing, manufacturing and facilities for this process. It is productive and appropriate to involve outside partners in this effort – trusted consultants, teammates and supplier representatives. Each expert provides his or her perspective on the competitor's situation and possible actions. As you try to predict the competitor's actions, it is helpful to use your own company as a model. If your company were developing an integrated navigation system, what actions would you have to take? Then consider how your target is different. Using this process, you strive to identify all of their critical configuration points. These configuration points are those key product, technology, supplier, distribution and manufacturing choices that shape the offering to the customer.

For example, suppose your team wants to know if the competition is developing an integrated navigation system for commercial airlines. The hypothesis is that the target is developing an integrated navigation system. Currently the target company only manufactures two navigation components – an inertia-measuring unit (IMU) and accelerators. They do not manufacture Global Positioning System (GPS) receivers, which are a key component of an integrated navigation system. The intelligence analyst would sit down with the engineering and marketing staff to brainstorm the actions that the competitor would have to take to develop or acquire this new system. Exhibit 9-5 shows some of the key activities the target would need in order to begin. The target would have to assemble a navigation package with all of the components, so they would have to go out and buy a GPS receiver since they do not make one. They would need to buy a casting and have it machined into a housing, and they would need to buy a processor. The target would then need to develop software for the system. Given that they have only limited software development capability, they would either need to hire more specialized software programmers and construct a software test facility, or they would have to contract out the software. The company would also need to certify the system with the FAA as well as discuss its specific requirements with aircraft manufacturers. Before investing in developing a new product, the company would have conducted a market study of potential demand and needs, and would have also probably talked to some of their key airline customers to get feedback on the proposed system. In addition, if they were undertaking a strategy shift in the market they would likely announce the initiative to shareholders and financial analysts.

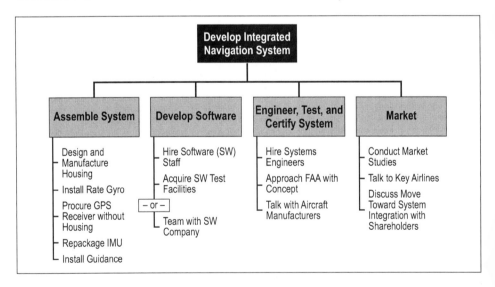

Exhibit 9-5: Actions that Verify a Hypothesis

This is not an exhaustive list, but merely a sampling of all the activities the target would probably undertake. Each of these activities creates signals in the marketplace, which an intelligence analyst can look for. After identifying these signals, the intelligence analyst would brainstorm with the team to identify the sources that would see these signals. Suppliers would know what components the target was buying. Key customers would participate in the market studies and know who was conducting them. The FAA would be consulted by the target about introducing a new navigation system.

The intelligence plan to validate this hypothesis would task the purchasing agents to talk to machining vendors, who might fabricate the housing. They would also talk to GPS suppliers and processor suppliers to see if the target has been buying any of the necessary components. The purchasing agent does not need to talk to every GPS or processor supplier. The capture team's engineering staff can usually narrow search to a couple of products that would likely fit the competitor's needs. Also, companies usually have favored customers, so the list of airlines they would discuss this offering with would be pretty short. To find out whether the target was hiring staff, the analyst would search their competitor's job openings, Monster.com or any other place that the competitor tended to recruit. Employment descriptions are great because they tend to be very specific. In this case, the target's job description might say something like: "desires software programmers experienced in developing integrated navigation systems for airlines."

If the intelligence plans identifies 15 potential signals and then the analyst finds 10 of those signals in the marketplace, you have pretty good confidence that the hypothesis is true. If you only find three, you have confidence the hypothesis is not true. The more varied the sources you task, the better your chance for effective crosschecks on the information and the deeper your perspective will be. You'll also have less chance of error or of falling for a successful deception.

When putting together the intelligence plan, the capture team tries to sequence the access of sources from the outside of the "intelligence onion" to the inside (see Exhibit 9-6). In this way the easiest and most accessible sources – literature searches and talking to your internal experts – are tapped first. As you implement the plan, your knowledge grows. The more knowledge you have, the more detail you can solicit from a source. Therefore, you are able to approach the most difficult and expensive sources for only the most valuable information. We will discuss each layer of the onion below.

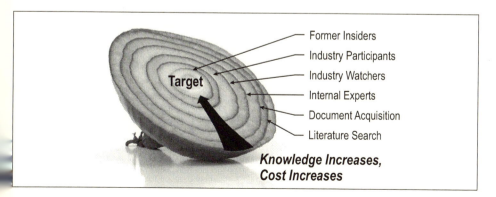

Former Insiders
Industry Participants
Industry Watchers
Internal Experts
Document Acquisition
Literature Search

Knowledge Increases,
Cost Increases

Exhibit 9-6: Peeling the Intelligence Onion

For example, you should not waste the time of the country's foremost authority on navigation systems by asking her what an inertial measuring (IMU) unit does. You might, however, ask her whether companies are moving toward developing integrated navigation systems for civilian aircraft. You use the most difficult or valuable sources (such as competitor employees at a conference booth) only for the most difficult information. However it is important to note that data easily obtained is not necessarily worth less than hard-to-get data. For example, when the Boeing Joint Strike Fighter capture team leader told the press that he planned to price his aircraft well below the customer's cost targets, that statement became the single most important piece of competitive intelligence collected on the pursuit. It gave us tremendous insight into Boeing's price strategy.

There are primary and secondary sources of information. Primary sources are people who have been directly contacted, while secondary sources are those that report the findings of others, such as books, newspapers, and TV broadcasts. Secondary sources are the easiest and cheapest sources to access, but secondary sources have drawbacks. They provide old news. Information in books can be dated by years, regulatory filings by months to years, conference proceedings by several months, technical journals by months and newspapers by weeks. It is also not uncommon for newspapers, magazines and directories to make factual errors. Reporters often misinterpret things or have bad information.

Literature searches include public or published sources such as newspapers, books, marketing materials, government publications, court documents, professional journals, and more types of easily found information such as:

- Web sites (you can e-mail the target with questions)
- Chat rooms and blogs
- Press kits
- Journals
- Trade and financial publications
- Directories
- Databases
- Conference proceedings
- Competitor executive biographies and speeches

The next layer of the onion is documentation acquisition. The competitors publish product brochures that contain their product's technical capabilities. Their annual reports can tell you their financial condition, business strategies and market focus. Their company newspapers can provide insight on developments and key personnel. Your company has vast amounts of documentation about their customers and competitors spread across the company in desks, filing cabinets and on hard drives. This data can include internal memos, trip reports, previous competitive analyses, past competition lessons learned, competitor presentations (from conferences, investor meetings, or teaming discussions (if not marked "proprietary")), past source selection debriefings and competitor marketing literature. When interviewing marketing or technical personnel, you should always ask for any publically available documentation on the competition you are chasing. Many times while working on an assignment, after interviewing a source, we ask for any competitor briefings before we leave. More often than not, the source will pull out a briefing he picked up at a conference and will say, "Won't tell you much." But to the competitive analyst, the document reveals the centerpiece of the competition's technical approach.

From the State and Local Government you can get all kinds of documents that are gold mines for competitive intelligence. For example, one competitive analyst found court documents where a woman was suing a company for sexual harassment. She worked on the plating line and the court documents contained all kinds of information about their production process and capacity. An auto company's competitive intelligence analyst once revealed how he got blueprints of his competitor's facilities from the local fire department. He got Occupational Safety and Health Administration inspection report which basically walked the reader through the competitor's production process. He obtained the Uniform Commercial Code (UCC) filings that are prepared for insurance purposes and list the competitor's equipment. Knowing the competitor's equipment, layout and process flow, he then estimated their production capabilities and costs to benchmark the same things for his own company.

State governments often publish bidders' proposals after competitions. If a competitor bids on state business, you can obtain copies of their proposals, which are packed with competitive intelligence. The impact of having your proposals published should be one of a company's key considerations in whether they bid for a state job or not. These proposals give away pricing and discriminators, which can negatively impact other markets.

If your competitor has federal work, you can request copies of their past winning contracts under the Freedom of Information Act (FOIA). If you are pursuing a job using new technology, try searching the science and engineering doctoral and master thesis list of universities within fifty miles of your competitor's research facility. Many company researchers go to night school for advanced degrees and it isn't hard to guess what they write their school projects about – the research they are working on during the day.

Other documents can include market studies, research papers, books and case studies. For example, working on one campaign we needed to understand how aggressively Eurofighter GmbH, a consortium that built the Typhoon, would price their offering. Three European companies own Eurofighter – BAE, Alenia and EADS. We talked to European financial analysts to understand their current financial outlook and near term goals. We learned that these companies have lower profit and return on investment targets than American companies. We knew that Eurofighter had defined pricing policies in their consortium contract, but could not find anything describing these policies in the public domain. However, we were able to find a case study and a book written about Airbus, which described key elements of their pricing policies. Airbus, like Eurofighter, is a consortium owned by BAE and EADS. We used insights from this book and case study to analyze Eurofighter's bidding history. We found a pattern, which allowed us to predict their future bid prices.

The next layer of the onion is primary sources. Primary sources are people you contact directly. Many researchers, capture teams and competitive analysts mistakenly rely almost exclusively on secondary sources. The failure of researchers to use even their own internal experts is a key shortcoming of the industry. Primary sources are critical. They provide a richness unavailable in general interest articles. Primary sources provide highly specific information about the customer and competition that is usually not available in print.

The intelligence lead should survey and tap internal experts. Engineers and marketers can explain all of the intricacies of the pursuit and they often have insight into what the customer and competitors are working on. Many times it is a company's own internal experts who have seen the signals that the intelligence plan seeks. The sales force hears of competitor marketing studies and picks up the competitor's product literature. The business development professionals are typically excellent sources of intelligence, especially concerning a competitor's approaches and sales messages. Engineers often learn what technologies the competition is working on from conferences, personal networks and discussions with suppliers or customers. Engineers can also provide the capture team with insight on the trade-offs between different approaches, signals to look for and the names of industry experts and suppliers who know what's going on in the industry.

It is tremendously valuable to interview the engineers and marketers of your teammates. They know their niche of the market better than you – the technologies and competitors. They may have even worked with your competition on a prior pursuit. They can offer a different perspective on the customer. And they can provide lots of insight on competitions with the customer or competitors that they were party to and you were not. This information can significantly increase your customer and competitor knowledge base.

Procurement specialists usually hear a great deal about the competitors, because many suppliers are sieves for information. They hear what suppliers the competitor is using, which components they are buying and in what rough quantities (which can tell you how big the competitor believes the market is and what their bidding quantities are). Identifying the competitor's suppliers is one of the most important information gathering tasks on the pursuit. Supplier choices broadcast what product features they are going to sell, reveal key subsystem costs and reflect their strategy. Because suppliers provide products to the open market, their prices and product specifications may be widely distributed in the public domain. Generally, equipment and component suppliers like to discuss what their other customers are doing with their products. However, they are just as likely to disclose your information, so you must be very careful what you tell them.

Even human resources (HR) can be a valuable source of competitive intelligence. HR can identify the competitor's pay scales and benefit costs, hiring patterns and skill needs, management backgrounds, names of ex-employees and knowledgeable recruiters. They can tell you where the competitor is likely to be advertising for new employees. And, as mentioned previously, employment openings are great sources of intelligence.

There are also many people who focus on your industry that can make great primary sources. These "industry watchers" include academics, leaders of professional organizations, financial analysts, trade officials and journalists. They follow an industry and know market and technology trends, key players and industry history. They are usually easy to reach and enjoy talking about their field.

The next layer of the onion is made up of industry participants who include:

• Suppliers	• Distributors
• Executive recruiters	• Test lab personnel
• Teammates	• Congressional staff
• Union officials	• Trade Association officials
• Consultants	• Lobbyists
• Bankers	• Regulators

While many team members interact with these industry participants as a normal part of doing business, many are reluctant to ask intelligence questions. To overcome reluctance, you can prepare team members by instructing them in what questions to ask and by explaining the importance of the information. You can rehearse and role-play with them, identifying possible objections and responses to give them practice and build their self-confidence. Make sure these team members are willing to gather intelligence and that they feel comfortable doing so, and always brief everyone who is going to contact anyone outside your company about what constitutes ethical and unethical behavior. When giving out intelligence assignments, set short-term due dates and then check progress.

You can talk to ex-employees of the competition, as long as you make it clear that you don't want any proprietary information. Ex-competitor employees are usually excellent sources of information. You can find them in your own company and at your teammates' companies. You can even search for retirements or call headhunters for referrals. These former employees can tell you how the competitor views the marketplace and your company. The competitor will compete with you differently if they see your company as a high-end technology company versus an aggressive low price supplier. An ex-employee can also describe the personalities of the competitor's key executives. Just as you don't sell to organizations, you do not compete against companies. You sell to people, and you compete with your competitions' capture team leader and divisional president. Knowing whether the capture team leader is an experienced aggressive capture leader or a conservative program manager helps you understand competitive moves and anticipate decisions. When talking with former employees, keep in mind that former competitor employees tend to have strong biases. For example, disgruntled former employees will frequently overemphasize their former company's weaknesses and underestimate their strengths.

You can also ask the target for information directly. You can call current competitor employees (make sure that you accurately identify yourself and your company, and never discuss pricing), and by talking about common concerns, like common competitors, you can gain significant insight. Developing a relationship with your competitor counterparts can be very valuable for both parties. You can exchange information on the customer or mutual competitors. In Sunnyvale, California, Loral and Lockheed Martin's rival satellite manufacturers are less than six miles apart. Husbands, wives and sons work at the competing companies and each staff belongs to the same chapters of professional societies and college alumni organizations. Both companies have hired engineers, technicians, buyers and executives from one another over the years. As a result, each company has excellent insight into the other. To collect competitive intelligence, one business development manager at a rival satellite manufacturer cultivated contacts with his counterparts at Loral and Lockheed Martin. He would call up his counterpart at Loral and discuss the latest developments at Lockheed. As soon as he hung up, he would call his counterpart at Lockheed and discuss the latest developments at Loral. This allowed him to closely follow developments at both companies.

Information exchanges between competitors are legal as long as the purpose is not to restrain competition. **Never** discuss fixing prices, coordinating purchasing decisions or allocating customers or sales territories. The Justice Department might consider this collusion, which is a violation of the Sherman Antitrust Act. Since interview time is usually limited, don't expect to ask too much from any individual – collect small but valuable pieces.

Engineers love to brag about their technical solutions to anyone who will listen, while salespeople love to talk about new products and mutual competitors. If you plan well, you can "run into" your competitors at a conference, or be in the same golf foursome. In fact, the authors of this book originally met in exactly this way. Michael O'Guin wanted to collect competitive intelligence on Kim Kelly's work. Kelly worked at one of O'Guin's client's competitors and they wanted to understand how Kelly performed PTW analysis. O'Guin called the chair of upcoming competitive intelligence professionals conference and suggested that she invite Kelly to present. Kelly presented an overview of his process and O'Guin got to ask him questions as an audience member (unfortunately for O'Guin, Kelly is smart and revealed little).

You never know what people will be willing to tell you unless you ask. You can see an example of this in a scene from the movie, *We Are Marshall.* The film tells the true story of how after a plane crash that claimed the lives of members of the Marshall University football team and its biggest boosters, the team's new coach, Jack Lengyel, and his surviving players, tried to keep the football program alive. Jack Lengyel decided that his inexperienced players needed to play the simple veer offense. Unfortunately, Lengyel and his coaching staff had no experience with the veer. However, their archrival West Virginia University did. So, Lengyel and his assistant coach, Red Dawson, visited West Virginia's head coach Bobby Bowden and asked him for tips on the veer offense. While Bowden was surprised by the request, he proceeded to point out where they could watch his game films and allowed Lengyel and Dawson to make copies of his playbooks so they could acquaint themselves with the veer offense. As Red Dawson was, you may be surprised what information people are willing to provide if you simply ask.

Be imaginative and try many sources in your quest for intelligence. You will find a wealth of information in surprising places and some promising sources will yield very little. The more varied the sources, facts and data, the less likely you will be to draw an erroneous conclusion. The more sources you access, the richer your data will be, and the less chance you will have of making a mistake or falling for a deception. When searching for sources on a target, consider to whom the target is important. Where are they a big fish in a small pond? Big fish get much interest, and therefore, much reporting. Most companies are important somewhere – in their industry, local neighborhood or in their trade groups. For example, you can find information on developments at a local factory through their local paper. You can also take public tours of facilities, send e-mail questions to the corporate web site and ask the president questions at financial analyst or shareholder meetings. Trade shows are the supermarket of intelligence. You get a "shopping bag" and walk from booth to booth picking up marketing brochures and intelligence.

You can collect intelligence at training classes, seminars, customer dinners, and design and program reviews – any place where customers, competitors, suppliers or industry watchers are likely to be.

— *Strategy in Action* —

For example, an armored vehicle supplier wanted to know how their competitor had recently performed on their in-country demonstration to the Kuwaiti National Guard. Each competitor brought their vehicles in-country to run them through a series of firing, endurance, speed and maneuverability tests at the Kuwaiti's test range. These demonstrations were a key part of the customer's evaluation process. By understanding their competitor's demonstration performance, the supplier could raise or lower their price as well as ghost their performance. The capture team brainstormed about who would know how the competitor had performed in the demos. They realized that the Kuwaiti technicians who manned the test range would see their competitor's results. The capture team leader called together his demo team and announced a contest. His vehicle technicians would compete to see who could come up the best competitive intelligence while they were in Kuwait preparing for their test. The winner would receive a free dinner for two at the best restaurant in town. Their competitive intelligence analyst briefed the technicians on the basics of intelligence collection and gave them a list of questions. The technicians enjoyed the challenge and asked the Kuwaiti sergeants and corporals' questions as they ate and worked together setting up the demo. Upon the demo team's return, the competitive intelligence analyst debriefed each technician individually. The capture team learned how many shots the competitor had on target, found out that the competitor had thrown a track on the second day, and discovered which customers had attended the demo and what the Kuwaiti's reactions were. With a little planning and $150 dinner tab, this capture team was able to confidently raise their bid price by $15 million based on their knowledge of their competitor's poor demonstration performance.

It is important to keep intelligence efforts focused. The more information collected, the more difficult it becomes to filter, organize, assess and use it. Intelligence planning and collection can be time-consuming, so you must concentrate on intelligence that will be actionable.

3. Collect Intelligence

You contact sources looking for the presence or absence of signals. Planning a contact is critical to optimizing the source. Before calling or meeting with a source, you should define exactly what information you need and what you will share. You should also sequence the questions and develop the exact phrasing for each. Better questions produce better answers. Limit the contact plan to only five to ten questions, but be ready to improvise to pursue important points.

Trained data collectors ask open-ended questions that prompt descriptive and detailed responses, offering the source the maximum opportunity to reveal their knowledge. Similarly, seasoned interviewers typically drive the conversation from more general questions to more specific ones. In this way the interviewer has the chance to build rapport before asking more specific and potentially sensitive questions. Skilled interviewers feed the source information to keep them talking. These trained interviewers use information they gathered during their review of the contact's background. The more you know about a contact, the better the rapport you can build. By referring to a person's position, background and hobbies, you can help to open up the source.

When a source gives a valuable piece of information, the interviewer should try to identify how they obtained that information – did they see it for themselves, hear it from someone else, or guess it based on other evidence? If your first questions don't produce the information you want, reword your questions and ask them again later in the conversation. It is also important to note that the more you know about the potential answer to your questions going into the conversation, the greater the knowledge you can pull out of a source. Sources are freer with their information if they think you already know the answer. You can try the old reporter's trick of making a bold assertion about what the competition is doing. "I hear you are pulling the J-12 out of the market next month." The surprise declaration always tempts the source to refute or verify it.

It is important to assess the truthfulness and accuracy of your sources. They may think they know more than they do or they may have their own agenda. If you are suspicious about the honesty of a source, you should ask them a question that you already know the answer to. This test works best if you pick a question about which they have some incentive to exaggerate. For example, we had one situation where an engineer was trying a little too hard to convince us that a particular technical approach offered significant performance improvement at little risk or cost. This technology was his specialty and he wanted it proposed in the bid we were working on. We tested him, by asking if he thought the competition was pursuing this technology, even though we knew the competitor was not. He told us, "I am certain they are and we do not want to be left behind." Based on this response we discounted much of what he had told us. When the source gives an opinion, the data collector should attempt to prompt the source for underlying facts upon which their opinions are based by asking for examples and details. Learning the specifics allows the analyst to make their own judgments.

Information is valuable – trade it with others. People like to share information for recognition or to enhance their position or status, and good sources require interchange. You need to provide a valid reason for a source to help you. By exchanging information, you can help the source do their job, while gaining intelligence. However, it is critically important that before you have your people talk to anyone, decide what information you do not want disclosed. You can exchange information, but you do not want to give away any of your critical strategies or discriminators.

Create new information assignments to fill knowledge gaps and verify conclusions. Continually reassess what you know. As Edward Youmans, founder of Popular Science magazine, said, "Every fact that is learned becomes a key to other facts." The intelligence plan is a living document, with new sources and questions being continuously added or subtracted.

Intelligence errors almost always come from too few facts and too many assumptions. It is important to remember that the objective of the data collection process is not to prove your hypotheses. The objective is to collect facts – not opinions or proof about some preconceived notion. A professional draws conclusions by analyzing a set of facts, not opinions. Intelligence professionals rely on the maxim: **weigh facts, not experts**. Hopefully at this point, you can imagine what the result would be if you used trained professionals to conduct over 100 substantive interviews in and around a business intelligence target. There is very little that they wouldn't be able to find out legally and ethically. However, we rarely need to go to such lengths. We find 75 percent of the information that we need to develop a competitive analysis and Price-to-Win with an 85 percent win rate within the walls of the company and its teammates.

4. Analyze and Report

It is critical in intelligence analysis to consolidate your data. One person on the capture team must prioritize, coordinate and consolidate all gathered intelligence. Typically this will be either a business intelligence professional or the business development manager. Team members summarize and document customer meetings and verbal exchanges and funnel these to this person. Consistent reporting is critical, so the capture team can develop the best possible picture of the competition. Some people believe that knowledge is power and that to be valued they must keep intelligence to themselves. This attitude is unacceptable.

This avoids the "Pearl Harbor Syndrome." Before the Japanese attack, there was ample evidence that the Japanese were about to strike – Japan was running out of oil, the U.S. Navy lost track of six Japanese carriers, the Imperial Navy had started their last war with a surprise attack on the Russian fleet at anchor, U.S. code breakers had discovered that the Japanese embassy was destroying their encoding machines, Army radar operators spotted a large blip heading south to Oahu, and a Navy destroyer attacked a submarine trying to gain entrance to the harbor that morning. However, the American military failed to assemble all this data in one place to create a comprehensive picture of the situation.

Some companies make the fundamental mistake of not consolidating intelligence by establishing multiple teams to analyze their competitor. Because they want these teams to be independent, the teams do not have access to all the same intelligence and are not allowed to share the intelligence they uncover. This means that intelligence is not consolidated, which significantly degrades the accuracy of the results. Just as damaging, independent teams using different intelligence typically come back with different conclusions. This invariably leads the executives and the capture team to not have confidence in any of the results. Lack of confidence leads to inaction. The capture team fails to ghost, bid aggressively, or take advantage of their competitors' blunders because they are not sure what the competitors are doing.

Another problem capture teams run into is that they get contradictory messages from different parts of the customer. For example, the program office is telling the capture team to raise the requirements, while their budgeters are telling the team they are cutting the funding. These messages are contradictory; higher requirements need more funding. What is the customer trying to communicate? What is the customer's strategy in sending us these different messages? After years of attending meetings, spending countless hours trying to decipher the "grand conspiracy," we have figured it out. Our customers are big bureaucracies and the right hand frequently has no idea what the left hand is doing. Different constituencies within the customer have different ideas and they do not necessarily resolve them. The capture team just needs to figure out who is likely to come out on top in the end and plan accordingly.

Information is useless unless you know how to interpret it. One must also assess the validity of the information received. People sometimes have bad information and make mistakes, and there is always the potential for common communication problems – what he meant to say, what he thought he said, etc. As a result, data will conflict. Just as scientists base their methodology and findings on facts, so do business intelligence professionals. The data collector must provide the analyst with details about how the source obtained their information. Did the source see it firsthand, hear about it from a reliable source or hear a third hand rumor? It is important to evaluate the raw inputs to get the most likely story, and it is critical to reconcile conflicting opinions and put the puzzle pieces together. The four tests of a signal are:

1. Signals are only as good as their sources. What is the vested interest and reliability of this source? Why is the source giving you this information? Do they have an incentive, such as a supplier trying to interest you in a sale by telling you that your competitor is

buying their product? How reliable is the source that provided the signal? Assume that every source's own point of view permeates their data.

2. How far is the source from seeing the actual signal (the greater the distance the more distortion)? Did the source hear or see it firsthand? How many people did the signal go through before it reached your capture team? Did your chief engineer see the competitor's product demonstrated, or did your uncle's barber hear about it from a friend? The more steps in the process, the more likely that there is distortion in the message.

3. How expensive was it to create the signal? The expense can be measured in cost or reputation, and the more expense, the more credible the signal. It is important to recognize, however, that the expense is relative to the magnitude of the decision.

4. Is the signal consistent with other intelligence?

You will always have some conflicting data. That is why assessing the sources while you are interviewing them is so important. Following good intelligence tradecraft, one should consider a data point valid only if confirmed by two independent sources, if it has been confirmed by a proven source of high reliability that has firsthand knowledge, or if the data has legal liability, like testimony in a court case. Working on one assignment, we interviewed a former senior executive at the customer who was now an executive with our teammate. From his prior customer position, he knew the customer's source selection process and buying behaviors intimately. During the interview, he was well informed and candid. However, other data contradicted many of his key assertions. For example, he said the customer always went with the lowest price and we found only two instances out of eight where this was true. This was baffling. He was on our team and had every incentive to help us. Further analysis uncovered that since he had left five years ago, the customer had undergone significant management change which had radically changed their behavior and that his information was out-of-date.

Analysis involves consolidating the facts and trying to develop a story about what the competitor is doing or will be doing. As the capture team receives, analyzes and consolidates the data, they assess each hypothesis. Often, the facts they uncover will conclusively prove their hypothesis is true. In other cases, they'll find an absence of the signals consistent with their hypothesis, indicating that the hypothesis is false. Sometimes, they'll discover a mix of confirming and disconfirming signals. Where conflicting data exist, the capture team applies the analytical standard called "a preponderance of the evidence," which is the same standard lawyers use in civil proceedings. Specifically, they make a decision with the rationale that it is more likely than not that the hypothesis is true.

A key step in the competitive analysis is to identify the competitor's teammates and key suppliers, and their role on the competitor's team. Companies frequently publish press releases with this information, and a good clue is to look at whom the competitor has teamed with before. You'll also find that when you're searching for teammates, certain companies aren't interested in talking to you because they are already committed to other teams. In addition, there is usually a lot of talk around the industry about who is teaming with whom on big jobs. Suppliers frequently brag about their roles on major projects. Once you identify the teammates and key suppliers, research them through their web sites, articles and interviews with industry experts. The supplier's own web sites will highlight their key capabilities and discriminators, which reveal the reasons that the competitor has hired them. The choice of suppliers communicates a great deal about the company's win strategy. Did they pick a supplier because they are low cost, know the customer or provide quick service? The choice of supplier reflects a company's strategy.

One of the most important outputs of a competitive analysis is your estimation of the competitor's technical architecture. To deduce what the competition is offering, you focus on identifying the differences between your offering and your competitor's. Because both your offering and the competitors are trying to satisfy the same customer requirements, they will have much in common. You seek to identify signals that indicate which different design choices the competitor made. By analyzing marketing materials, teammate selections, press releases, photos and artist renderings you can seek these clues. These differences in weight, throughput, size, or performance allow you to present this information to your engineering staff and question them about how the competitor's design is different. The engineers can spot the differences and can tell you how the competitor's choices impact their cost and desirability to the customer. One key to deducing the competitor's approach is to understand the design trade-offs that your own team made in solving the customer's problem. Then look for signals that the competitor made the same or a different choice. For example, if you were developing an integrated navigation system, your team could chose to incorporate a ring laser gyro or an inertial measuring unit. These two different technologies can provide similar performance with different weight, cost and reliability. Which choice each competitor makes says a lot about their strategy. From a competitive intelligence standpoint, most companies will say in a marketing overview which technology they are using. Or, if you see a picture of the competitor's unit, you can spot a ring laser gyro because it's a short rectangular box versus a cube for an inertial measuring unit. In today's environment, few prime companies have captive suppliers or unique components. In most cases all technologies are available from merchant suppliers – some are just a little better than the others.

Once you identify a competitor's technical approach, the next step is to estimate how that technical approach would impact their costs. What components would their approach require, which your solution does not? Would they need more parts than you have? Would their approach allow them to have more expensive or less expensive components? These differences are then costed out. For example, working on a competitive analysis of a radar system, we knew that the competitor was using a centralized processing system versus our decentralized one. Our solution converted the signal processing out at the antennas while the competitor did all of their processing at a centralized computer. As a result, their solution was able to use one-fourth the number of processors. However, their processors were more expensive than ours because they had significantly greater processing requirements. More importantly, their solution required signal amplifiers on each cable from the antennas to the computer and very expensive high frequency cables. When we compared the costs, we found the decentralized approach was cheaper.

There are other analysis techniques, such as content analysis, from which one gets a sense of the competitor's personality. This process assesses the competitor's annual reports, executive speeches, marketing literature, advertising, press releases and company newspapers. It examines what the competitor says about itself and where they are headed. This can tell you what is important to them and what are they pushing, and can tell you about their opinion of themselves and the competition. Do they emphasize growth, profits, or employment? They will behave differently depending on their goals. You can put competitor events like reorganizations, buy-outs, key wins or losses and executive changes on a timeline. Then you can compare that to what the competitor is saying in the media over time and identify changes.

— *Strategy in Action* —

In the early stages of one pursuit for a ship defense jamming system, we wanted to know what type of system the client's rival was developing. From a literature search of the competitor's past contracts and marketing literature, we identified two very different potential approaches. It seemed unlikely that the competitor would be investing in two competing technologies. A few years before, the Army had paid the competitor to demonstrate a new chip technology that could potentially evolve into a small and inexpensive jamming system. This demonstration was very limited in scope and the technology immature. As such, it would require significant investment to scale up and mature it to be applicable to the upcoming program. The other approach the competitor was working on was a multi-function system. They were touting in the marketplace a system that would not only jam, but also collect signals and provide communications. This system's cost, by using a common antenna and processor, would potentially cost significantly less than the total of the three systems it would replace. However, the multi-function system would be very sophisticated and high-cost when compared to just a jamming system.

The competitor had presented product roadmaps at technical conferences, which clearly showed that the company was pushing their multi-function system as a solution to many of the customer's problems. In addition, in a recent briefing to financial analysts the company's CEO had mentioned the importance of his company's investments in systems to reduce system ship footprint. The multi-function system, by combining multiple antennas, would significantly cut the amount of above deck space needed on a ship and seemed to be the investment he was alluding to. Looking at the company's history, we uncovered a pattern of investing in unique products that allowed this competitor to carve out sole source positions with their customers. This multi-function system certainly looked like that type of investment. On the other hand, we could find no evidence that their chip supplier had continued maturing the jamming technology after the Army demonstration. Researching a technical paper on the chip technology, we identified the competitor's two key scientists who had spearheaded the demonstration. It would make sense to us that if the competitor was working on the chip technology, they would involve one or both of these scientists. We searched for the scientist's recent publications and examined their Facebook pages. We discovered that both scientists were busy working on unrelated projects. From this analysis, we concluded that the competitor was going to push the multi-function system as their jamming solution, so the key battleground for the upcoming pursuit was to influence the customer's acquisition strategy. If the customer chose to develop a standalone jamming system, our client's solution would be well positioned. However, if the competitor successfully sold the benefits of a multi-functional system and convinced the customer to construct a combined jamming, signals and communications program, our client would have little to offer. This intelligence enabled our client to develop a campaign to ensure a standalone system.

The axiom of business intelligence is that it should be timely truth, well told. Analysis of your hypotheses should tell a story. The presentation of your analysis should drive to a conclusion and include nothing unnecessary. You must make your conclusions fact-based and structured so that the intelligence drives management to take action, and the results of the competitive analysis must be briefed to the capture team. When reporting on the competitor in a campaign, the results presentation typically includes an overview of the competitor that describes the competitor's core competencies and how they like to compete. The analysis should also include a description of bidding behavior detailing what factors they have attempted to use to win jobs in the past, and how aggressively they have bid. The analysis attempts to give the capture team or the executives a feel for how this competitor behaves.

The analysis should go on to describe the competitor's likely win strategy, technical approach and key discriminators (both strengths and weaknesses). Next, the analysis should include a comparison of relative scores against the customer's source evaluation. Lastly, the competitive analysis should feed into the PTW, which will include a cost analysis of the competitor's bid price and a recommendation of where your price should be set to confidently win the opportunity. This competitive analysis and PTW should be used to test the soundness of your win strategies and to update them if necessary.

Lastly, to ensure future cooperation, protect your sources. For example, if someone gave you sensitive information or politically controversial information, don't speak their name in a meeting. It is rare for someone to ask for the identity of a source, and we avoid naming sources. If you have to disclose it, do so privately. If you are loose with names, they will hear about it and you will lose their trust.

Counter-Intelligence

Competitive intelligence is offense, counterintelligence is defense. Counterintelligence is the process of thwarting your competitors to keep them from learning your strategies and secrets. While most company's security groups focus on fences, locks and badges – your physical property and assets – many times the wealth of your organization is in its information. Every company faces an intelligence threat to its secrets and technologies – nothing is safe. We have seen pursuits lost because competitors have unethically discovered our prices – those are very painful losses. However, competitors are not the only threat, others include customers, suppliers, consultants and lawyers. These threats want your technologies, source code, designs, strategic plans, capture, bid and negotiation strategies, pricing and cost data and proprietary processes.

Industrial espionage is a prevalent problem today. It has been increasing in the last twenty years for two principle reasons. First, as part of the Cold War Peace Dividend there are many unemployed spies looking for work. Second, espionage works. Many companies and countries figure, what is a little ethics shortfall when billions of dollars are at stake? And some countries have a different view of espionage. The Chinese consider spying to be a noble profession. The notion of intellectual property is also different in other parts of world. Behavior in the United States that is not only unethical, but illegal, is considered normal business practice overseas. While in the U.S. there is the Corrupt Foreign Practices Act, holding company officers liable for bribery and other crimes, until 1998, French companies could write off bribes as an allowable expense on their taxes.

Competitive intelligence professionals, security, investor relations, communications and other internal organizations that provide data to outside entities should work together to put controls and safeguards in place to protect your company. A company cannot protect everything, so you must prioritize. You must identify those pieces of information that you do not want your competitor to uncover. This should be information that, if gained by an outsider, could damage your business – such as capture plans, technical approaches, pricing data and proprietary technology.

Once a company identifies its critical information, they identify the likely threats that could take this proprietary information. This list includes the obvious candidates like competitors and teammates, but could also include people such as real estate agents, for instance, if you are planning to purchase some land after a win. An unscrupulous real estate agent might purchase an option on the land ahead of you, which would drive up the price your company ends up paying. Customers can also be a threat. We saw one company fail to put controls in place on their drawings, and the customer provided their drawings to a local manufacturer to produce spare parts, and the company lost this lucrative business.

Once threats are identified, you need to assess the threats for their intelligence collection capabilities and methodologies. Does the threat have a competitive intelligence staff and how do they collect intelligence? Do they conduct web searches, hire your ex-employees, bug phones, bribe current employees or hack into computers? The company should assess how important its information is to the threat. A desperate entrepreneur acts very differently than a loyal corporate officer. When competing internationally, a capture team may find French, Israeli, or Chinese intelligence services helping their competitors. They have been known to:

- Bribe employees
- Plant moles
- Intercept phone calls and faxes (estimated at 40 percent worldwide)
- Search hotel luggage
- Hack into computers
- Steal laptop computers

Company security should perform a vulnerability analysis to assess how secure their critical information is. Identify where the information is stored, who controls it, who has access, how it is marked, whether it is under lock and key and how is it transmitted. By comparing the threats' capabilities to how your data is stored and transmitted, you identify vulnerabilities. Then, you develop countermeasures. Some typical countermeasures for a capture team include:

- When visiting potential suppliers and teammates mark all documents "proprietary" and make them sign non-disclosure agreements.
- Consistently mark all proprietary documents as proprietary.
- Do not send any sensitive data across the Internet without appropriate encryption.
- Do not fax any sensitive data overseas.
- Do not discuss sensitive information on the phone while overseas.
- Avoid announcing teammate and supplier relationships in the press.
- Restrict cost roll-ups, negotiating strategies, pricing summaries and Price-to-Win analysis to only those with a need to know. The more people who know your price, the less security conscious people become and the more likely information is to leak.
- Require confidentiality agreements of all employees to discourage employee theft, which is the most frequent threat.
- Screen all technical briefings to ensure your engineering staff focuses on what your company is capable of doing and not how they do it. The "how to" is your secret. There are few worse feelings than realizing that your engineering team helped your competitor solve their technical problems by giving away your insights.
- Develop an employee awareness and education program on counterintelligence for your capture team and technical staff.

- Edit all of your company's publications to avoid disclosing competitive insight including your help wanted ads, technical briefings, company newspapers and company web site.

Protecting your critical information is crucial to winning. If the competitors know your plans to influence the customer, they can thwart them. If they know your discriminators, they can copy or ghost them. If they know your price, they can underbid you. The more intelligence the competitors have the more effective their strategies will be. So, don't give away your secrets. For example, before meeting to negotiate with a potential teammate, your capture team leadership and your competitive analyst should clearly identify what you want and what you need to know about your potential teammates. Some companies make a habit of entering teammate discussions when they have no intention of teaming. They meet strictly to collect intelligence from their future competitors. You must take steps to protect your competitive sensitive information. Though you should always have potential teammates sign a confidentiality agreement, but that does not really protect you. The best protection is to not divulge your secrets. You must decide what information, such as strategies, and research and development programs, that you want to disclose. Naturally, you want to entice a company to join your team, but you must by wary because they may become a competitor if the negotiations fail! Most importantly, brief everyone who will be in contact with the potential teammate on what is allowable to share and what is not, and why it is important.

Deception

Companies that practice deception view it like a trick play in sports and use it to help them win campaigns. The objective of a deception campaign is to decide what you want the competition to do, and then to get them to do it. To do this, you devise a plausible story to plant in the marketplace. The implanted story is intended to get the competitor to react as you want them to react. You create a meticulously detailed scenario and timetable from the story. From this scenario you identify signals that this scenario would be likely to create. Then you transmit these signals into the marketplace for the competitor to pick up. This allows the competition to learn bits and pieces of the story – largely true, but false in crucial particulars. Then the competitor will react to the story and take the desired action.

For example, your capture team might want to induce a competitor to bid less aggressively, so they could devise a deception campaign to lull the competitor into thinking that the capture team's offering is not competitive. The capture team could implant a story that they were going to build a solution requiring a million lines of code, which would be many times what they really intended to bid. A million lines of new code would bust any customer's budget and be a high-risk solution. The capture team could invent a scenario where they would create a number of new software modules with greatly enhanced performance for the customer. They could develop a mock project plan for the project and a story line, which would include the capture team figuring out that their solution was too big and trying to fix it just before the proposal went in. Next, they would identify signals that they would emit if they were in fact implementing this fictional software development. To make a story believable to the competitor, it is important that it feeds their preconceived notions. It is important to remember that the most effective deceptions involve the competition fooling themselves. They have to learn what you want them to learn, and it has to conform to their expectations or their hopes or fears. So, the story would need to be consistent with how the competitor views the company trying to deceive it. In the above case, the competitor would more likely believe the story if the industry considered the capture team's company to be one that took big technical risks and prided themselves on being one of the country's top software developers. Therefore, if anyone were going to propose an enormous software solution, it would be the capture team's company.

One of the key challenges facing companies attempting deception is that many competitors are unsophisticated in intelligence collection. This can result in them missing even the most obvious signals you are trying to broadcast to them. We call this the "Israeli Problem." During the 1980's, the Mossad ran several deception campaigns against their Arab adversaries and, unfortunately, found out later that these campaigns were all ineffective. The Arab intelligence services failed to pick up on the Mossad's subtle signals. In the business world, most companies have limited or no competitive intelligence capability, so there often is no one tasked to consolidate and analyze intelligence – they live in blissful ignorance of what their competitors are doing (blissful right up until they lose). It is very difficult to deceive these companies because they are not paying attention. Optimally, a company trying to deceive another will identify what channels the competitor systematically monitors for intelligence and then feed those channels true information and select disinformation. In addition, it is helpful to get feedback from the competition regarding what they are learning, so you can adjust and amplify signals where needed, to reinforce what they are coming to believe. But if the competitor is not sophisticated enough to consistently monitor any channels, it is difficult to implement a deception campaign.

That said, the following story illustrates what a deception campaign could do.

— *Strategy in Action* —

In 1985, Boeing started developing a small, fuel efficient aircraft called the 7J7. Boeing conceived the 7J7 as a short-haul aircraft to avoid cannibalizing the sales of their long haul and highly successful 737. The 7J7 was going to use a radical new propfan engine, called the GE36. This engine featured large external fan blades that were swept and shaped in such a way that an airliner could fly at jet-like speeds, but achieve fuel savings of up to 30 percent. Boeing had 600 engineers working on the 7J7 program and they sold a 25 percent equity stake to a Japanese consortium of Fuji Heavy Industries, Kawasaki Heavy Industries and Mitsubishi Heavy Industries. Yet, when McDonnell Douglas's executive team tasked their competitive intelligence (CI) unit for their assessment of the project, the CI unit came back with a shocking assessment. Mc-

Donnell Douglas's CI unit concluded that Boeing had no intention of actually bringing the aircraft to market. The CI unit believed that the 7J7 program was a cover for Boeing to modernize their engineering and production processes with digital design and computer controlled machine tools. The CI unit's key rationale was that Boeing's concept did not make economic sense. A large portion of an aircraft's fuel burn is expended climbing to and from altitude, so highly fuel efficient engines on a short-haul aircraft made little economic sense. Sure enough, in 1988 after two delays, Boeing claimed there was no market for a propfan aircraft and canceled the 7J7.

At the same time, Boeing was developing the 7J7, their competitor McDonnell Douglas was developing an all-new twin propfan; designated the MD-94X. This long-haul aircraft was to seat 160-180 passengers and compete with Boeing's 737. The 737 was the most produced commercial passenger jet of all-time and a Boeing cash cow. In addition, McDonnell had plans to retrofit their MD-80 aircraft series and was designing two new MD-80 derivatives with the GE36. McDonnell Douglas was planning to have all these designs in service by 1992. Unfortunately for McDonnell Douglas, Boeing was able to tie their 7J7 program to the GE36 so when the 7J7 was delayed, delayed again and canceled, so was the GE36. McDonnell Douglas had an aircraft designed but no engines for it. McDonnell Douglas was in deep financial trouble at the time and could ill afford to squander their meager development funds on a bunch of aircraft designs that had no engines. With their stale product line, McDonnell Douglas continued to lose market share to Boeing, dropping to just four percent of the world's commercial aircraft orders in 1996. In 1997, Boeing bought out McDonnell Douglas. Either Boeing conducted a masterful deception campaign, or they were very, very lucky.

A deception campaign can have a big return, but can be difficult to successfully implement. In addition, you need to work with your legal and ethics staff to avoid legal and ethical missteps such as committing shareholder fraud.

Summary

The intelligence process starts with a company's management articulating the need for information from which they can make an important decision. Acquiring and cultivating sources and intelligence takes time, so forward planning is crucial. Effective business intelligence results not from luck, but from the same careful planning, discipline and systematic processes that scientists employ. Like a scientist, the intelligence analyst deduces a target's most likely actions or intentions using the scientific method. The analyst forms and tests a theory about the target's actions, complete with a set of hypotheses that are consistent with the overall theory. However, instead of crafting an experiment like a scientist would, the business intelligence analyst looks for observations consistent or inconsistent with the hypotheses. The analyst then constructs an intelligence plan to seek signals about the target's actions in the marketplace. The presence or absence of these signals betrays a target's intentions. And the best place to start this analysis is by understanding what core capabilities the competitor brings to the competition. It is this core set of capabilities that the competitor will build on, and the messages they broadcast into the marketplace will reveal their strategy. By understanding the competitor's strategy, you can deduce how they will adapt and leverage their capabilities to this pursuit.

It is important to start formal intelligence collection early in the capture process. Sources are more open early in a pursuit when the competitive pressure is lower and many unknowns exist. People get more and more concerned about competitive advantage as the RFP submittal becomes imminent. In addition, it is important to leverage the whole team and instill a culture that embraces the importance of collecting and reporting customer and competitor intelligence.

One critical byproduct of competitive intelligence is focus. Gathering intelligence forces a company to cull through all of the data about a competitor and concentrate on the most important elements, to focus information capture efforts on learning the customer's values and how the competition stacks up against them. It concentrates the company on sending a few key messages to the customer. Competitive intelligence provides the data and structure to communicate persuasively and win substantially more business.

This process is so effective that there is very little that the skilled business intelligence professional cannot find out legally and ethically. The only requirements are the will to win and willingness to commit the resources. While such intelligence is not inexpensive, it does result in a decisive competitive advantage.

Chapter 10: Avoiding the Common Pitfalls

"The fault, dear Brutus, is not in our stars,
But in ourselves, that we are underlings."

-- William Shakespeare, Julius Caesar Act 1, Scene 2

No matter how brilliant your strategy, a flawed implementation is fatal. Therefore, one of the secrets to winning is not losing. Chasing every opportunity provides a team with ample chances to make mistakes, and many mistakes can be devastating. We have seen companies lose billion dollar opportunities by making fundamental errors. In this chapter we will discuss some of the more common and disastrous pitfalls, as well as how to avoid them. These pitfalls include:

- Losing commitment
- Catering to the wrong customer
- Bidding the wrong technical solution
- Teaming poorly
- Lacking cost discipline
- Using an undisciplined proposal process

Losing Commitment

No executive ever says that they are not committed to winning, but that is exactly how some behave. We have seen capture efforts on critical programs that start off with great initial positions and then fail because management attention falters as the pursuit advances. The key to winning is to develop and then execute a good capture plan. It is management's responsibility to pick the opportunities to win, develop effective capture plans and ensure that all of the company's functions support the plan. Most importantly, to successfully execute the plan, management must assign the necessary resources to implement it and keep them assigned. It is the capture team leader's responsibility to meet regularly with senior management, keep them abreast of the team's progress and demand the resources necessary to win. If management loses their focus and is unwilling to pry loose the right people from other jobs to make the win happen, a company can squander a great opportunity.

A fatal problem we have seen is management tolerating a key member of the capture team who is not up to the job or does not accept the team's win strategy. Sometimes, people are put in place and they lack the experience or judgment to win. If this person is in a key position like capture team lead or chief engineer, they can cost you the pursuit. We have seen chief engineers continue to design in innovations that violated the win strategy and had been rejected by the capture team.

The choice for management was simple; the chief engineer had to go. But that was too difficult a decision for them to make, so he stayed and the team lost. We've also seen key functional leads ignore cost targets, undermining the win strategy, and we've seen contracts managers so abrasive that the customer refuses to work with them. In each of these cases, the company must remove individuals or lose. Winners do the hard things, and losers don't.

Management must make timely decisions. Recently, we were reminded of this while watching a market leader attempt to win a next generation product.

— *Strategy in Action* —

In this specific market, every ten years or so there is a big customer who undertakes a major pursuit, the winner of which ends up dominating the worldwide market for the next decade. This company in this example had won the last time around, and was working to win again, but there were several factors working against them. Their first problem was that they squandered their R&D investments building a product against a poor set of requirements, which represented a compromise across several different customer market segments. As a result, the solution they developed did not fit any of the customers' platforms well. As the lead customer starting planning the next generation product acquisition, it became clear that the incumbent's technical solution was seriously flawed. Even worse, the customer was specifying that they wanted an off-the-shelf product and not a new development. Luckily, the company had an excellent technical staff and they quickly developed a plan for an innovative product concept well suited to the lead customer's needs. Unfortunately, the company's executives dithered. They had difficulty approaching corporate with the admission that the initial R&D product was flawed and asking for more investment. They squandered six months with indecision. When the customer released the RFP, they reiterated that they wanted an off-the-shelf product with supporting reliability data as part of the evaluation process. At this point, the company spared no expense and assigned their best engineers to the new product, but lost time is impossible to make up.

In the above example, the company's executives were unwilling to make timely decisions, and in four years this business unit could be nothing more than a shadow of itself as a result. The moral? When difficult decisions are required, management must be willing to make them.

Key executives must stay engaged throughout the life of the pursuit. They must continually assess the strategy and determine whether it is on track. The executive staff needs to review the win strategy because it is critical for the executives to ensure that the capture team has a valid plan. In other words, the win strategy must fit with the company's business strategy overall, and it must accomplish the executives' goal. If it meets these criteria, it is a winner. It is management's prerogative to ask the tough questions and suggest changes to the capture plan.

Frequently, with their broad perspective, executives recommend capabilities that can be leveraged from other parts of the company. These capabilities can create new discriminators or save the capture team time and money. Executives should also be fully engaged in selling the customer. When so engaged, they typically pick up excellent insight on the customer's needs and perspectives on the pursuit – invaluable intelligence. It is also important that executives pass any intelligence on to the capture team. All too often they forget.

Executives must assess whether the capture team has balanced their resource allocation across the customer values appropriately. The team needs to spend their time and money on all of the customer values to maximize the company's impact on the customer's desires. You do not want the team over overspending on fun and exciting technology, but ignoring critically important but tedious tasks such as developing program plans, offset packages, or logistics systems.

The executives must monitor the capture team to ensure that they are implementing the plan and have the necessary resources to do the job. Executives should know whether the resources requested have the necessary knowledge, skills and experience to carry out the actions assigned to them. These leaders must hold the capture team leader accountable for performance, monitoring implementation of the capture plan by routinely reviewing accomplishments and concerns. Once approved, the capture plan becomes the baseline for tracking and monitoring the actions to win. Similarly, the team leader must report on team member and functional department performance. The capture team leader uses the plan to ensure the functional organizations are accomplishing their assignments. Collaboration between the capture leader and the departmental managers is imperative. If conflicts arise, the leader must raise them to the executives immediately. Capture efforts lack the luxury of time for departmental politics. Company leadership must demonstrate commitment to keep pursuits on track and win.

Catering to the Wrong Customer

Companies often fall into the trap of designing their solution for the wrong customer. Sometimes capture teams develop their solution to satisfy the most vocal of the customer's constituencies. Unfortunately, many bidders confuse volume for influence. Frequently, the users or the technical staff may be very blunt and forceful in stating their desires and dislikes, but this does not mean they will even have a vote in picking the winner. Procurement, contracts, or a key economic buyer usually dominates the selection process. By failing to identify the key decision makers, these bidders optimize their solution for one set of customers who have a different set of priorities than those awarding the work.

— *Strategy in Action* —

For example, initially both Raytheon and Lockheed were focusing on the wrong customer pursuing the program to develop and install a combat system on an aircraft carrier – CVN-77. Traditionally, the U.S. Navy had always integrated the combat system into its aircraft carriers, but for this program the Navy had delegated the responsibility to Newport News, the aircraft carrier manufacturer. When Newport News held Industry Day to acquaint potential suppliers with the program, Navy representatives conducted almost all of the briefings. The Navy invited bidders to discuss the program requirements. When Newport News called in the bidders to discuss the RFP, the Navy program managers did almost all of the talking. Raytheon believed that the Navy was the true customer; after all, they were dominating all of the program discussions. Lockheed believed that the Navy was the customer, until they went through one of our win strategy development sessions and realized that the decision makers would all be from Newport News.

So while Raytheon focused their win strategy on the Navy, whose priorities were greater technical capability and lower cost, Lockheed concentrated on Newport News and their priority of minimal schedule risk. Lockheed chose strategies to mitigate risk and ensure an on-time finish. A delay in the combat system installation would cause the carrier's delivery to slip, which would be financially catastrophic for Newport News. Lockheed won because they focused their strategy on satisfying the right customer.

Bidding the Wrong Solution

Winning solutions are created, they don't just happen. You have to focus on what's important to the customer. Having the best solution will not always win business, especially if the customer is convinced that they want something else. As in the following example, you must make the customer want your solution, or offer something that matches their preconceived notion of what they want.

— Strategy in Action —

When one company was chasing an overseas surveillance aircraft program, a senior government official told the contractor that they had, by far, the most qualified team and experience for the job. While the company had vast surveillance system experience, they were enamored with a tiltrotor (aircraft which has engines which rotate to provide vertical lift like a helicopter) air vehicle, which they had recently developed for another customer. Their competitor, on the other hand, proposed a fixed wing vehicle. Since the company's tiltrotor aircraft did not require a runway and could operate from any open field, it had many operational advantages. On the other hand, tiltrotors are more costly to operate and maintain.

Unfortunately, the customer's pre-conceived notion about what they wanted involved a fixed wing aircraft, and the company failed to effectively sell the unique advantages of their rotary solution to the customer. As a result, the customer did not want their solution and they lost.

Your solution should avoid approaches that the customer does not want. Engineers like to work on fun, interesting and challenging technical solutions. Unfortunately, many customers want low cost, low risk, proven solutions. We have seen companies lose bids because they just had to bid a technical "pet rock." A pet rock is a feature that your engineers are dying to bid, but that the customer doesn't want. Companies propose "pet rocks" because they want to sell them, not because the customer wants to buy them. Typically, these new features represent an exciting new technology; unfortunately they also tend to be expensive and risky. We have heard the following reasons to bid risky and high cost "pet rocks:"

- The solution will really help the customer – once they understand it.
- Developing and proving this technology on this program will position us perfectly for other programs with other customers.
- Winning this contract will justify our investment in this technology. This technology represents what our company is good at – how could the customer not want that?

If you discuss your technical approach with the customer and they do not like it, you have two choices. You can change the approach or change the customer's mind. The wiser choice is usually changing the approach. Convincing the customer that their first reaction to a solution is wrong is challenging. If you opt to try to change the customer's mind, the first step would be to understand why they did not like the suggested approach. Any concerns must then be fully addressed. This must be accomplished in the pre-proposal phase. If you cannot sell a customer on your approach during the interactive discussion of the pre-proposal process, you are extremely unlikely to succeed by sending them written arguments (e.g., the proposal).

— *Strategy in Action* —

On one ship program, the Navy specified a plethora of demanding developments including an automated gun system, a 50 percent cut in ship manning, a new combat management system and a reduced signature (thermal, radar and acoustical). Since there was so much inherent risk in the program, one bidder believed that low risk was the most important customer value, so this bidder's win strategy was to offer the low risk solution. Unfortunately, their chief designer wanted to add another major innovation. He wanted to go down in history as the naval architect who fundamentally changed military ship design. Instead of choosing the conventional shaft and propeller system for propulsion, he decided to propose podded propulsors. Podded propulsors are steerable motors with propellors that hang down from the hull. By rotating the pods they change the ship's direction, offering many advantages over rudders and shafted propellers, including better sea keeping, improved maneuverability, and lower fuel costs. While cruise liners have used podded propulsors for years, no navy had designed them into a major military vessel. This technology was unproven as far as the Navy was concerned, yet the chief engineer decided to propose podded propulsors. This was a high-risk choice. This decision conflicted with their win strategy. The high-risk choice, irrespective of its many merits, undermined their whole strategy of being low risk. As a result, they were no longer the low risk solution and the customer no longer knew what this team stood for. Most importantly the customer did not want podded propulsors. This team offered a solution with a key feature the customer did not want and they lost. The lesson is clear: don't bid things the customer does not want to buy!

There are many ways to solve a customer's problems. Follow your win strategy. The win strategy defines the attributes on which you intend to win. It is also the capture team's job to develop discriminators that strengthen their position. Your win strategy must be bounded by the Price-to-Win targets, so your solution is affordable. From your win strategy, develop a supporting technical, management, and pricing strategy. Then translate those strategies into your approach, or more specifically, a description of how you are actually going to do the work. This process ensures that your offering conforms to your overall strategy, which is driven by the customer's most important values.

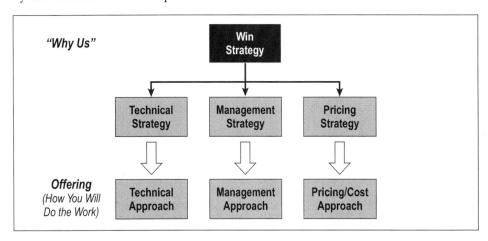

Exhibit 10-1: Translating the Win Strategy into the Offering

The capture team defines the approach and documents it. The objective is to define the solution in the form of a system concept that fulfills the customer's requirements. When designing the offering, apply the win strategy to every element of the Work Breakdown Structure and describe the approach. Consider the strategy when deciding how to perform every activity, so that the approach, estimating rationale, and strategy are all in alignment. For example see Exhibit 10-2, for the activity "Configuration Management," if the strategy is to *"Leverage existing programs wherever possible to minimize risk,"* then the configuration management approach will be, "use existing procedures as successfully demonstrated on previous programs." However, if the strategy is to "provide innovations to reduce cost," then the approach could be to *"propose a single paperless database sys-*

tem to slash administration costs." The capture team leadership provides this description to cost estimating and to the proposal writers, ensuring consistency between the technical volume and cost estimating. Your solution should follow and support your win strategy.

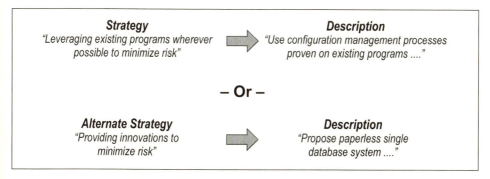

Strategy
"Leveraging existing programs wherever possible to minimize risk"

Description
"Use configuration management processes proven on existing programs ...."

– Or –

Alternate Strategy
"Providing innovations to minimize risk"

Description
"Propose paperless single database system ...."

Exhibit 10-2: Example strategy and approach

To optimize their position, top performers use trade-offs to win. All good engineers and managers conduct trade-offs, where trade studies are an analytical comparison of cost and performance between two or more system design alternatives. Capture teams should assess all of the feasible technical, organizational and management alternatives and then evaluate those alternatives against the customer requirements as well as system effectiveness, affordability, risk and cost. Unfortunately, many engineers do this intuitively and don't document their results. Proposed concepts without supporting details and data may be considered unsubstantiated and lacking credibility, even though they have technical merit. Omitting trade-offs from your customer presentations and proposal has dire consequences – your approach appears unjustified. Only by documenting this analysis does it become available as proof, and proof sells. You want to prove to the customer that they are making the best choice. Trade-offs and performance analysis justify the proposed approach and are substantiated by the specific details and data of the design, implementation, and management plans.

It is the technical team's job to develop this supporting analysis. Engineering can only generate specific details by conducting engineering homework and actual management planning. Hence, evaluators look for details to confirm that your approach has been proven and you are really prepared to do the work. By showing the customer your trade-offs, you help them do their job and justify why they should pick your solution. It is important to remember that many customers, especially key decision makers, are not technical people, so make the presentation of data simple and easy to understand. If you want to win, you must provide the customer with the rationale for selecting you and not the competition. Showing the customer trade-offs is an excellent way to make that case. It also shows that you are objective, thorough and do your homework.

Exhibit 10-3 shows a typical trade study output. This example shows the optimal solution with significantly better performance at slightly higher cost than the competition's lower performing solution (Alternative #1). It is important to specifically address those options adopted or likely to be adopted by the competition. Writing up this analysis also gives your proposal writers an opportunity to directly address why your company logically and objectively rejected your competitor's approach. You can plant doubts in the evaluators' minds about whether the competitor's solution will perform as promised or be delivered on-time.

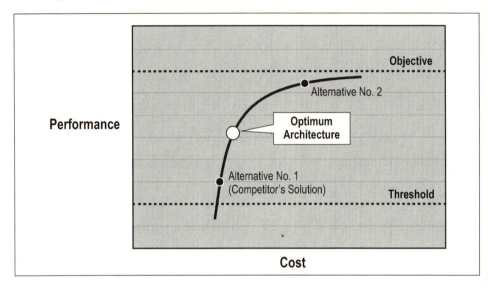

Exhibit 10-3: Demonstrating Trade-offs

If the customer specifies a requirement that you believe is unachievable, you have a quandary. To solve this dilemma, you need to understand your customer. *Some* customers don't require compliance with all requirements. Many foreign governments, for example, will award to a supplier who is *strategically* compliant. Some customers ask for the moon, and when they find that the moon is too expensive, they settle for a trip to Paris. With these customers, taking exception to expensive and risky requirements is usually the best strategy. You don't have to meet all their requirements, but you must clearly identify your exceptions. Other customers, like U.S. Department of Energy and the United Arab Emirates want bidders to meet all of their requirements, and they strictly enforce all contractual commitments. This has resulted in catastrophic financial consequences for more than a few companies who did not understand this customer behavior.

Most customers will reject an offering that fails to meet their requirements. However, customers do not include requirements that they do not think the suppliers can achieve. After all, they want a competition and to award a program. So the question that must be answered is this: Can your competitor meet the requirement? If they clearly can and you can't, the customer has fixed the competition for your opponent. If this is the case, you need to either disrupt the competition by appealing to a higher authority to change the procurement or choose to "no bid."

If the competition is no more capable of meeting the requirement than you are, then either the customer's technical staff does not fully understand the issue, or you are incorrectly interpreting the requirement.

— *Strategy in Action* —

"Company A" had a dilemma on a NASA pursuit. NASA was requiring the rocket bidders to indemnify their launch of a space probe to the outer reaches of the solar system. In this case, the rocket was carrying a nuclear reactor and if the rocket exploded it could potentially rain radioactive debris across south Florida. While the probability of occurrence was literally a million to one, Company A's management was unwilling to accept this multi-billion dollar liability. When Company A's executives met to decide what to bid, their competitive intelligence analyst pointed out that Competitor B was willing to the accept the liability. If Company A submitted their proposal with an exception to the indemnification requirement, NASA would evaluate them as non-compliant and Competitor B would win. This intelligence forced Company A's executives to make the hard decision and accept the indemnification, which resulted in them winning the NASA launch. This situation demonstrates the power of competitive intelligence to change minds.

However, if you believe you have an unachievable requirement, usually what you really have is an interpretation problem. The requirement means one thing to the customer and another to your engineering staff. You can ask for a clarification of the requirement before you submit your proposal. However, the problem with this approach is that you may get an answer you would rather not have. Another approach is to clarify your interpretation of the requirement in your proposal. Describe your interpretation of the requirement and how your product meets it, allowing you to argue that your solution is technically compliant.

If you want to win, bid what the customer asks for, even if it is wrong. Sometimes, customers specify very difficult or costly requirements, which make no sense to a proposal team. When this happens, the best strategy is to convince them of their error before the RFP. But if you are unsuccessful, bid what they ask for. After winning the contract, a team can propose that they continue to conduct cost tradeoffs to improve the solution. This leaves the opportunity to readdress the issue after the win, and can remove a contentious issue from the evaluation. This gives a proposal team time to work on changing the customer's opinion after the award. Amazing as it is, we have seen companies fail to change the customer's mind for months prior to the RFP, and still try to accomplish this in the space of four pages within the proposal. This can result in little more than alienating the customer.

— *Strategy in Action* —

One company was bidding on a contract to build a satellite constellation and ground stations to provide space-based reconnaissance. The company tried to convince the government that they needed to specify bigger ground stations. Up until that time, this company had built every single reconnaissance satellite for the United States so the company knew what they were talking about. Based on their experience, the company knew that the government would need large ground stations capable of processing the terabytes of data that would be collected by the next generation of satellites. Despite the company's expertise and arguments, the government specified small, lower capability ground stations. The company's engineers were so certain they were right that they bid big, more expensive ground stations. They lost. Their big ground station solution was too expensive, and they accomplished little besides impressing the customer with their arrogance. Within two years of winning, their competitor received a multi-hundred million-dollar engineering change order to build bigger ground stations. The company's engineers were right, but that was little comfort for forfeiting a multibillion-dollar business franchise.

Beware when a customer says, "It wasn't written in the RFP, but you must...." A common blunder to avoid is to assume that what they say is more important than what they write. It is not. Often, technical staff or even high-level customers will tell a potential supplier about a "requirement" that is not in the RFP. Evaluators can only evaluate proposals against the RFP, so if it isn't in the RFP it isn't evaluated. And if this requirement is so important, why isn't it in the RFP? While there may be a constituency for the requirement within the customer, this constituency lost the internal battle, because the requirement was not in the final proposal. Follow what's written, not what's said.

Another common blunder the technical team can make that can ruin an otherwise successful campaign is failing to decide on what specifically to propose until they are in middle of writing the proposal. During one program we worked on, the chief engineer was still changing the design as the company was putting their final edits in their multibillion-dollar proposal. Chaos reigned as last minute changes ripple through the proposal and cost estimates. The team became so focused on incorporating changes that the proposal quality suffered with poor messaging, inconsistent formatting and even grammatical errors, which slip through the review process into the submitted proposal. This can make the difference between winning and losing.

To submit an on-time proposal, the proposal writers and estimators need a lot of time. If the technical team has not decided on the exact configuration of the offering, the proposal writers and estimators must guess. This design freeze means the technical team completes the supporting documentation and fully describes the system so it can be written to and its cost estimated. Once the baselines are defined, they should be put under configuration control. That way, when a change is made, everyone on the team is notified. On long duration pursuits, the baseline can be frozen and iterated at different times to stabilize and control the design process. Defining what you are selling facilitates discussions with potential customers. This helps you iterate the solution.

Teaming Poorly

Most large pursuits require teaming with other companies to win and perform the job. Exclusive teaming is most common. Team members agree to share work and investment commitments when a contract is awarded, on a pre-agreed basis. Non-exclusive teaming allows team members to offer their capabilities to other bidders, but to establish a firewall to protect the proprietary information from reaching the competitors. Teaming reduces the cost of bidding, investment, and risk in the program. It can strengthen customer relationships and intelligence gathering in areas where the prime has not worked. However, it also lessens solution flexibility and adds to management complexity.

Who one partners with has significant influence on the capabilities your team offers and how the customer perceives your team. Effective teaming is important. Choosing the wrong teammate can cost a company the bid.

— *Strategy in Action* —

One large aerospace company lost a billion dollar bid to NASA with a 16 percent lower price than the competition. How? One of the company's key subcontractors was unable to deliver a critical component on another high profile job to NASA. On this bid, that same subcontractor was supposed to provide a derivative of the same problematic subsystem. The NASA evaluators had little confidence that the subcontractor could deliver on time, so NASA thought the contractor's proposal was high risk and chose the other bidder despite their substantially higher price. This prime lost because they failed to do their homework. The capture team did not fully understand the subcontractor's track record and NASA reputation until after they were signed up. The lesson is clear, do your due diligence on teammates and key suppliers to avoid joining forces with an albatross.

A lot of executives seem to enjoy making deals. Too frequently, the executives select the teammates based on their industry knowledge or some previous agreement and not on the capture team's win strategy. Then, because they don't do their homework, they negotiate work share to guarantee the other company a certain percent of the contract value. While executives seem to find it easier to negotiate percentages than work scope, guaranteed work share has proven to be a huge problem in numerous pursuits. While percentages are straightforward for executives to negotiate, they can lock companies into uncompetitive cost structures and make adapting to customer scope changes difficult. For example, two companies teamed on a large communications system. One company excelled at production and the other at logistical support. The anticipated work scope of the contract was 70 percent production and 30 percent support, so that was the agreed percentage split between the companies. Unfortunately, after the teaming agreement was signed, the customer decided to incorporate most of the logistical support into another contract cutting the logistics portion of this contract to 18 percent. The logistics company demanded that their agreement be honored, so they got to bid a substantial piece of the manufacturing. Manufacturing was not their core competency; they were too risky and expensive. The team lost. If the companies had agreed to divide up the opportunity based on work scope instead of work share, this problem would have been avoided. With the size of their opportunity slashed, the logistics bidder would certainly have cut back on their investment in the pursuit, but both companies would still be proposing the tasks that they were best suited for. This agreement resulted in a less competitive offering overall, as well as resentment across the pursuit team as everyone else had to compensate for the less competent team member.

Good negotiating approaches profit first. Next, they negotiate work share based on core competencies and past performance. One can use formal trade studies to determine who gets what work scope. It sends a powerful message to your teammates if the prime treats everyone, even sister divisions of their own company, the same way, with no preferential treatment. This can instill goodwill and trust. It takes significant analysis to determine the optimum work share split across different companies so that the best team member is assigned to each work package. Capture teams build the most successful teammate relationships by dividing a project based on work scope. Each company gets the work scope they are most qualified for. Each teammate takes on the risk of customer work scope changes as part of their initial agreement. You should try to develop and clearly define risk sharing, investments, terms and conditions. A poorly thought out teaming agreement is a disservice to everyone.

The selection of teammates should flow from the win strategy. Many times the primary reason for teaming is to use your team members' strengths to bolster your weaknesses.

— *Strategy in Action* —

Effective teaming was the key reason that ITT won the FAA's $1.8 billion dollar Automatic Dependent Surveillance-Broadcast (ADS-B) in 2007. ADS-B is a revolutionary system and key to the FAA's plans to dramatically expand air traffic capacity. The system is going to use GPS signals to provide air traffic controllers with data much more rapidly and nearly ten times more accurately than the current radar-based system. Of the three bidders, Lockheed Martin and Raytheon dominated FAA contracts while ITT was a second tier air traffic control player. ITT knew the FAA was technically sophisticated, risk averse and liked low cost. So besides developing a good technical solution, ITT teamed with ATT and Thales. ATT had an existing telecommunications network and hardened facilities all across the country. ITT proposed hosting the ADS-B equipment at these existing hardened sites, which significantly cut facilities costs. They overcame their lack of large system implementation experience by teaming with Thales. Thales had recently implemented a similar system to ADS-B for Australia. Plus, Thales had a great track record with the FAA and provided nearly all of the FAA's navigation aids. This experience substantially mitigated their implementation risk. ITT took their initially poor competitive position and turned it around to win a very prestigious job through effective teammate selection which mitigated their weaknesses. This is why FAA awarded to ITT as the best value and lowest risk. Interestingly, Raytheon proposed leveraging existing satellite capabilities and standardizing on a single link nationwide, thereby reducing costs by dispensing with the translator and the extra frequency. Unfortunately, the FAA considered Raytheon's approach "just too innovative." Which was not surprising; they failed to understand the FAA's risk aversion.

Before selecting a teammate, a company should develop at least a first pass win strategy. You have to know how you intend to win, and what capabilities your strategy requires before making commitments. In a typical example, a company signed on a teammate because they had been battling for the same business for years. The prime felt that the two of them together would dominate the pursuit. However, when the company conducted their strategy development, the capture team came to realize that the teammate had pretty much all the same strengths and weaknesses as they did. Not only did the teammate not add many new discriminators, they also wanted all the same work share as the prime. This match was a disaster.

When selecting teammates, the capture team should compare their strengths and weaknesses for each customer value to understand how they will integrate into their offering. A capture team should assess every potential teammate by identifying their strengths and weaknesses against the customer values. While most people know to never underestimate a competitor, they should also know to never overestimate a teammate. **Selecting a team is one of your most important strategic decisions – do your homework.** When selecting teammates, one must understand their goals and what they bring to the program – both good and bad. This includes understanding how the customer perceives potential teammates.

One key to effective teaming is to conduct a preliminary Price-to-Win analysis before finalizing any work share agreements. The PTW analyst will determine the competitor's cost for all of the major parts of the bid. This allows the analyst to set cost targets for the major work scope elements, so that the capture team leader knows just how much they can afford for each teammate. Interestingly, we frequently find the proposed teammates and subcontractors have lower costs than the prime. In those cases, the PTW analyst can recommend that the teammates receive more work scope than originally planned, for the team to be more competitive.

Top performers typically reach teaming agreements early. This allows them to get their first choice of teammates and gives them more time to innovate together. Working one pursuit, the PTW analyst discovered that for a critical component there were only two possible sources, both small businesses. Their competitor had already signed up one exclusively. As the analyst did more research he discovered that the customer had recently given the competitor's small business a major R&D contract to advance their technology for the application his company was bidding. This told the analyst that they were going to lose. It would take a miracle for the customer's technical staff to suddenly reject the technology that they were funding and go with another team's solution. They lost by teaming too late.

Once signed up, many companies do not treat teammates as valuable partners, but as subcontractors whose opinions are quickly dismissed, despite the fact that teammates were brought on for their unique expertise and knowledge. A teammate's knowledge base can be a powerful discriminator if leveraged. Capture teams should include teammates in the strategy development process. You will find that they are invaluable in helping develop the strategy and in analyzing the competition. The better the partnering, the more successful the pursuit and the program. You maximize a teammate's value if you involve them in conducting the trade studies, and engineering analysis up-front. You build trust if you invite them to join you in working with the customer and lead Integrated Product Teams (IPTs) as appropriate. Granted, teammates and the prime have different agendas. But one of the keys to a successful relationship is to ensure that there is minimal goal conflict, so each player is incentivized to sacrifice to some extent to win.

Strong team management leverages the combined resources to win and perform business without increasing risk. While conducting our benchmarking study, we uncovered one key to successful teaming. We assessed two companies with billion-dollar contracts. The first company complained about budget overruns and late deliveries on their major subcontracts, while the second basked in awards for their superior subcontract management. When we looked at their respective organizational structures, the root cause was obvious. The company with outstanding subcontract performance had tasked their assistant program manager to manage all the major subcontracts. At the poorer performing company, the individual responsible for subcontract management was buried six levels down in the procurement organization. These procurement managers had little decision-making authority. Companies that empower their key subcontracts managers are much more successful than those that don't. The assistant program manager had significantly more authority and control over resources than subcontracts manager buried in the procurement organization. As a result, the assistant program manager could quickly respond to subcontractor problems with engineering assistance or renegotiate a contract to relieve troublesome requirements. Also, they could approve and allocate more money to the subcontractor to take advantage of unanticipated new capabilities. Teammates and major subcontracts typically amount to forty percent of a program's value. Not surprisingly, our benchmarking studies found a very high correlation between subcontracts being received on-time and on-time customer deliveries. The person managing your teammates and major subcontracts needs to be empowered – this is critical to having a successful program.

These findings are consistent with our benchmarking results for superior program management. Companies that had higher on-time deliveries also had empowered program managers. These companies gave their program managers significant input into the selection and job evaluation of their program staff. They also had significant control over program resources and access to executive leadership so they could tap the whole company's expertise when needed. At companies with poor delivery performance, program managers had little clout and were little more than status reporters. Empowering managers was a key to better delivery and cost performance.

Lacking Cost Discipline

While working on a large aircraft program, we discovered that hundreds of engineers were working on estimating the development program. However, program management had assigned a single individual to estimate the initial ground support equipment (sparing, training aids and ground equipment). The initial ground support cost almost as much as the $11 billion development program. And, one dollar of the initial ground support was worth just as much in the bid evaluation as a dollar of development. The capture team was not effectively allocating their estimating resources!

Poor cost management causes companies to lose many pursuits, as well as billions of dollars in budget over-runs after award. During the pursuit, most companies devote a fraction of their time and attention to estimating and managing costs compared to technical performance. As a result, while capture teams have an excellent understanding of how changes in the technical approach affect performance, they have a poor understanding of how the same factors affect cost. They know the direction of change, but not the magnitude.

Many companies rely on engineers to create cost estimates instead of using cost analysts. Engineers, untrained as cost estimators, compound errors from incomplete bills of material, notational estimates and rough order of magnitudes quotes, by failing to burden the estimates with the proper material handling, general and administrative costs and profit. In addition, they frequently forget about including internal functional costs like program management, configuration management, data management and quality. They overlook, forget or ignore some of the customer's expensive terms and conditions.

We have seen trade studies developed where a major subsystem's cost estimates were later to be found to be understated by a factor of four, or overstated by two. As a result, the cost/performance trade studies, which the capture team spends months and hundreds of thousands of dollars developing, are so flawed that, in retrospect, they were useless. If a capture team has poor estimates, it can cause their cost-benefit trade-offs to be wrong. While engineers have used extensive analysis to validate the system's performance to plus or minus three percent, we have seen cost estimates off by a factor of two or three. As a result, they are liable to unwittingly choose a subsystem that is higher in cost and lower in performance because their base cost data is wrong. When developing their first cost roll-up, its results shock the capture team leaders when they see their total bid price for the first time. This often occurs after receiving the RFP, when the team has begun to write their proposal. At this point, they have already locked in many design choices, confirmed the work scope with teammates and frozen large elements of cost. The capture team leader would probably have reconsidered some of these choices if he or she had understood their true costs earlier.

In other situations, we have seen cases where the initial cost estimates were too low, which led the capture team to quote prices to the customer that were also too low. As a result, the customer used unrealistic cost expectations to set their budgets. This leads the customer to be disappointed and angry when true costs are revealed and they have insufficient budget for their program.

Developing good cost estimating skills is undervalued at most companies. But it is very important – it is one of the keys to bidding successfully and performing effectively. To avoid the problems with engineering estimates, a company must either train engineers in estimating or have estimators work with engineers to create cost estimates. One company developed superb cost estimating by hiring engineers, extensively training them in estimating and then forming a group called cost engineering. Estimators believe that everything has been done before. Engineers must learn that if the overall task has not been done before, at least the vast majority of its subtasks have been, when sufficiently segmented and defined. The engineers need access to an estimating database that is consistent, traceable and accurate. They need to learn how to apply the database to explain their estimating rationale, as well as when and how to adjust for quantities, scope, inflation and production rates. Also, executives need to delve into the estimates to ensure they are accurate. Executive attention ensures the estimates receive scrutiny. Developing better estimates is the key to developing more effective pricing.

Companies need to start working on cost early with market-driven top-down cost targets as discussed in Chapter 6. It takes time, management attention and effort to question, adjust and verify estimates. While it is everyone's job to develop the most accurate estimates possible, it is not human nature. If people are tasked with bottom up estimates, they will tend to overestimate their work and then become reluctant to change their position. Functional managers frequently pad their estimates to build their empires or buffer themselves from executives' arbitrary cuts to their estimates later. When asked later to lower their price, they think they are being squeezed out of profit, hours or work share. While considering costs for one proposal, a training department inferred lots of training work scope in the RFP. They saw the program as a training program. They "aggressively" estimated the costs to be $84 million. Their executives had to point out to them that the whole program was only budgeted at $65 million, so they needed to take a second look at their estimates or the company would have to no bid.

Developing top-down numbers quickly uncovers scope differences and other disconnects. If bottom-up cost preparation yields higher budget values than the initial top-down bogies, then you should reconcile what is driving the differences. After identifying the root causes of differences, one should continue bottom-up iterations, reassess allocations of "bogies" to the WBS and revise the technical and management approach as necessary.

In addition, as differences are identified, a team can conduct independent cost assessments (as they frequently do on performance) using top-down parametrics, "should cost" analysis, and comparison with previous programs. The team should use this information to verify the total PTW and reassess the allocation of the overall PTW target to the WBS. If reconciliation with the overall PTW target is not achievable, it may be time to quit the pursuit, or a team must get innovative – change the procurement rules, or reassess assumptions. Aggressive top-down targets can force engineers to break paradigms. You should work the "what ifs" to understand the trade-offs between the requirements and cost amongst your engineers, functions, suppliers and even the customer. This dialog does not end, but is a continual process, trading off design features, schedule, risks, and costs throughout the capture effort to evolve the most cost efficient solution possible. As a result, the capture team leader should negotiate design and program changes to develop the winning offering and iterate the results two to three times. Only with relentless effort can costs be driven down to a good concise estimate.

The team refines the preliminary estimate over time and eventually evolves it into the cost volume, if the customer requires one. If the customer requires a cost volume, it must be realistic, believable, and supported by a credible rationale or basis of estimate (BOE). If not, the customer will rate a proposal as risky and add cost risk dollars to the price. With some customers, we have seen a price "plussed up" by more than a billion dollars for cost risk. To avoid this, cost rationale must be thoroughly documented. The task descriptions used in the technical volume must match the estimating rationale.

Using an Undisciplined Proposal Process

While some customers merely want a letter with a price as their proposal, other customers provide complex RFPs with loads of requirements and an extensive evaluation scoring. As a result, the proposal response becomes a very complex document and its quality is a critical factor in deciding the winner. We agree with the conventional wisdom that a good proposal cannot win a job, but a bad proposal can lose it. A well-written proposal can put your offering in a good light, but it will not overcome a flawed offering. A company also may have helped the customer write the requirements, developed a persuasive strategy, and ghosted the competition, but a poor proposal undermines all that work.

The story of how an undisciplined company cobbles together a proposal when they lack a formal process always seems to be the same. They start working the proposal in earnest only after the RFP is released. They dump all of the proposal responsibilities on a few key people, overwhelming them, as these folks are busy inventing a proposal process from scratch. The proposal leaders scramble to staff up their effort. The company's management provides the proposal team with a bunch of people who are in-between assignments or otherwise not too busy. Due to the quick turnaround required, the proposal leaders immediately assign these people to start writing proposal sections as they become available. The writers are not sure what exactly they are bidding, so they make their best guesses. These writers struggle to find substantiating data for their proposal, which in most cases was never created. The proposal staff scrambles to bring all of the sections together. It is difficult to collect the written material for proposal reviews. When the proposal reviews eventually take place, the general manager discovers that their very important proposal is in deep trouble. Draft sections of the proposal do not address all of the requirements; there is redundancy and inconsistency among sections and volumes, and even different formatting. The draft proposal lacks sales messages – no one reading the proposal would see why the customer should pick this solution. Lacking a formal process, these companies neglect giving senior management an early preview of their proposal strategy. Consequently, the general manager discovers the abysmal quality during a late proposal review. In desperation, he throws in their top talent, disrupting other pursuits and ongoing programs alike. The proposal team is flooded with new people and everyone begins furiously to rework the proposal. Confusion reigns. Since management did not review the proposal strategy early, they frequently redirect the effort with a new win or pricing strategy. Finally, the proposal is rushed into production. The proposal budget is significantly overrun. Only after the proposal is delivered does the exhausted and demoralized proposal team discover embarrassing errors in the proposal.

What makes a good proposal? The most important fact to always keep in mind when writing a proposal is that it is a sales document. It must sell your solution approach, your management team and your business case. A good proposal is a collection of substantiated claims that respond to the request for proposal. It clearly states how you solve your customer's needs and why you offer the best value solution. The proposal is the culmination of all your capture work, but the proposal does not win the contract, it only avoids losing it. A high scoring proposal must be based on and consistent with the win strategy. A good proposal is a sales document, which meets the following five requirements:

1) **Be Compliant.** As amazing as it seems, we have seen companies lose multi-billion dollar bids despite spending millions of dollars on proposal preparation because they still submit a non-compliant proposal. The proposal team becomes so wed to their solution and so insular that they cannot believe that the customer will not accept their approach. In these cases, the proposal leaders are shocked when the customer fails their proposal. If you are not compliant you will not win.

   Follow the customer's instructions. If a bidder does not follow the customer's proposal directions, the customer knows the supplier will not be following their directions after the contract award. Customers want their needs met, and they know that those needs will not be met if the bidder does not listen to them. One of our clients was the incumbent, recompeting for a contract to provide maintenance services to a set of facilities around the world. The RFP called out service levels well below the work currently being performed. The client knew the RFP's workload data was greatly understated. In fact, the client knew that service levels were going to increase. Should they bid what the customer asked for or what they knew the customer really needed? Just a year earlier, the company had had a similar situation, and they choose to bid what the customer really needed and not what was asked for. They lost, but they learned their lesson. They overcame the temptation to show off their knowledge of the existing contract and bid what the RFP asked for and won. ***Be compliant;***

always bid what the customer asks for in the RFP. The customer's acquisition organization may not be listening to the operators; they may have made a mistake or may have another agenda. Either way, you lose if you bid something they did not ask for. Their mistake is not your problem. They will have to fix their own problem after award.

2) **Make your proposal response easy to evaluate and score.** Sacrifice the desire to make the proposal read like a novel and instead make it easy to score. Customers appreciate this effort. If the evaluators become frustrated trying to score your proposal, they will unleash their frustration on your evaluation. Always include a compliance matrix in your proposal, so that the evaluators can easily find in your proposal your approach to meeting every requirement.

3) **Provide clear justification of the approaches taken.** There are many ways to solve a customer's problems. A good proposal explains why you chose the approach you did. In your proposal, you want to show that you systematically and objectively selected your approach; in the way you hope your customer selects the winner. You want your proposal to describe how your team carefully balanced the customer's needs against what is realistically achievable and affordable, to pick the best solution. You demonstrate this by tasking your engineering team with conducting a trade-off analysis of alternatives during the capture phase. The customer can use your thorough analysis in justifying your selection.

4) **Have all of your claims well substantiated with supporting data, facts, and proofs.** Data sells. An approach is justified by tradeoffs and performance analysis, but it is substantiated by specific details and data. Proposed contents without supporting details and data are empty and lack credibility, even though they may have technical merit. This is because specific details can only be generated by planning, engineering, and test results. Hence, evaluators look for details to confirm that you have proven your approach and that you are really prepared to do the job.

5) **Clearly communicate your benefits to the customer.** A proposal is a sales document. It must sell your solution's benefits to the customer. Benefits are what the buyer gains from the solution – they satisfy a buyer's needs. Benefits motivate people to buy, but features prove the benefit is true. A good proposal is engineered so that every feature presented includes a benefit to the customer. Every writer and reviewer should ask themselves, "So what?" and "Why is this good?"

Dividing up different sections of the proposal across twenty people or more, ensuring that everything they write is consistent, while sending a persuasive set of sales messages and addressing all the requirements is not easy. If a company lacks the discipline to adhere to a consistent process or fails to invest time, money and people into developing a dedicated and formal proposal process, they set themselves up for producing a poor quality proposal.

The key to efficiently and effectively creating a persuasive proposal is planning. Just as a contractor does not start building a home without a plan, neither should a proposal manager. Just like a house, you architect a proposal. You design your proposal so that it is compliant to the customer's instructions and deploys your strategies and themes across the proposal, ensuring that your strategies and themes are communicated clearly. The whole proposal development process must be well planned and executed. The proposal manager must coordinate and schedule events including: analyzing the RFP, finalizing and training the team, developing storyboards, estimating the offering, conducting reviews, and following all the other steps to produce the document as shown in Exhibit 10-4.

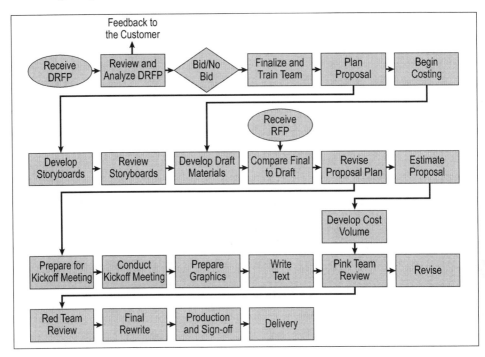

Exhibit 10-4: The Proposal Process

Front-loading the proposal staffing goes with up-front proposal planning. The most successful companies assign their proposal staff early on in the proposal process and peak halfway through the effort as shown in Exhibit 10-5, while undisciplined companies backload their proposals. Front-loading allows the proposal team ample time to train the staff, plan the proposal and build storyboards before anyone starts writing. The team can work to ensure storyboards are completed and reviewed before writing starts and the team has time to develop "proof" of claims. Having the proofs available leads to less "creative writing" in the proposal. The executives can conduct early reviews to ensure the proposal is aligned with their strategy. And most importantly the proposal work packages are "ready" for assigned personnel when the time comes to start writing. As a result, the proposal process allows for multiple iterations, which build quality. This process leads to better written and more persuasive proposals at a lower cost.

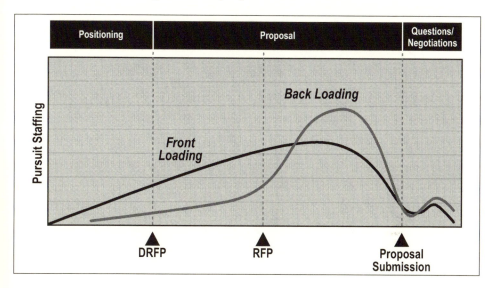

Exhibit 10-5: Front-Loading a Proposal Effort

The first step in the proposal process should be reviewing and analyzing the draft RFP. To analyze the draft RFP, the core team should first individually read the RFP and take notes of questions and comments. Then, we recommend that the core team read through the key sections together to discuss and analyze. The team goes through the draft, identifying evaluation factors, requirements, and contract deliverables, which they then parse out into a work breakdown structure and statements of work. These elements will be driven into the design of the proposal.

Next, functional specialists are assigned to perform detailed analysis of the requirements to fully understand their implications for the solution. One of the most important tasks is to suggest improvements in the draft to the customer. This is the customer's key reason for sending the draft out in the first place, and one of the few times when they are actively soliciting suggestions. This is a critical opportunity to shape the RFP. In addition, the team develops questions for the customer to clarify issues. This allows you to actively engage with the customer to improve their product and resolve procurement issues. Examine the draft with a skeptical eye looking for evidence of the competitor's influence. Did one of your competitors get a requirement placed in the draft that gives them an advantage? If so, what does this say about the competitor's customer relationship and their position? Next, the team develops the compliance matrix and prepares for the bid/no bid meeting.

As discussed in Chapter 2, the bid/no bid meeting is a critical decision making point. At this meeting, the executives decide whether the opportunity is shaping up as one of their best few. The meeting starts with the executives reviewing any unanticipated requirements, terms and conditions, evaluation criteria or other issues that impact the competitiveness of your offering. You assess these issues and determine if your company should still bid. Then the executives review and adjust their capture team's win strategy, pricing and negotiation strategy in light of the RFP. It is crucial that these strategies be defined and agreed upon before the proposal development starts in earnest. If these decisions are not made or adhered to, it can result in the executives redirecting the proposal effort late in the process, which can have a disastrous impact on the proposal quality; demoralizing the proposal team, upsetting the proposal schedule and eroding the chances of winning. While a proposal effort is one of constant refinement and improvement, it should avoid wholesale redirection to change strategy, technical approach, or even format. A good proposal process avoids unnecessary rework. That's why it is so important for the capture team to gain executive concurrence with their strategies prior to initiating the writing effort.

As a pursuit enters the proposal phase, the company forms the proposal team. The proposal team is responsible for creating the proposal. The proposal team should include a cadre of capture team members along with the company's core staff of proposal specialists and functional experts. This continuity also helps ensure successful knowledge transfer. A proposal team is organized around end products. To have clear accountability, the proposal manager assigns captains or book bosses to each major deliverable. Each person is responsible for his or her deliverable's quality and successful completion.

It is critical to train all of the proposal staff just before working on the proposal. Top performers always train their proposal teams how to create an effect proposal. Proposals are so complicated that even experienced hands learn something new or are reminded of key practices they should not forget to use. We often hear how surprised executives are toward the end of a major proposal effort when they discover how much of their staff is working on their first proposal. These training sessions range from two hours to a full day depending on the size and complexity of the bid to brief them on the pursuit. During this training, the capture team leaders should review the pursuit history, customer needs, competitors, their offerings, their solution, their discriminators, their win themes and strategy. This information helps ensure that all strategies are embedded throughout the proposal. The core specialists train the rest of the proposal team in the proposal development methodology. The team should be instructed in the proposal process, storyboarding, creating win themes and writing tips.

The next step is to plan the proposal. This is where they organize the creation of the proposal. During this step the proposal manager assigns sections, secures the facilities and schedules the work. Then the team maps the RFP requirements to an outline and develops a compliance matrix. The compliance matrix shows where in the proposal every one of the customer's requirements is met. Every proposal should include one at submission.

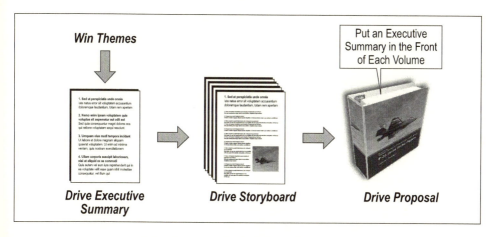

Win Themes

Put an Executive Summary in the Front of Each Volume

Drive Executive Summary   **Drive Storyboard**   **Drive Proposal**

Exhibit 10-6: Architecting the Proposal

To ensure that the proposal delivers your sales messages to the customer, you must take steps to plant the win strategy clearly throughout the proposal. Write your proposal based on a top-down structure starting with your win themes as shown in Exhibit 10-6. Using the win themes, compose the story to describe why the customer should select you. These win themes will help sell the benefits of features to maximize your proposal evaluation score. Since the customer values are the most important customer concerns, you organize your proposal executive summary around the customer values. Then you provide any additional win themes you developed from the proposal evaluation criteria. In this way you are going from the most important customer issues to the least. This story is the executive summary. The executive summary tells the customer "why you" and it drives the rest of the proposal. Some people make the mistake of writing the executive summary last, and it should always be written first. Whether the customer asks for an executive summary or not, provide one.

The executive summary is usually not graded, but it is your opportunity to tell your story and sell your solution. The key to a well-written executive summary is to focus it on the key decision makers. Make assertions to address their needs, desires and prejudices. Make it simple – why the customer should pick you. Put in good graphics. Everyone – especially busy high-level people – read pictures and captions first. Introduce your major themes. This is the one part of the proposal that everyone reads.

The next step in the proposal process is storyboarding. Storyboards were invented by movie directors, with their earliest use attributed to D. W. Griffith, who directed "Birth of a Nation." An artist would make a series of sketches where every basic scene and camera setup was illustrated. The preproduction staff would post these comic book-like "story sketches" on the wall to illustrate the story. This allowed all the director and production staff to understand and critique the stories. In the 1960s, proposal staff at Hughes Aircraft adapted this technique for proposals. Proposal storyboarding consists of posting the different sections on the wall, so the proposal team and management can review the story. It allows the whole team to get an early glimpse of how the whole proposal is going to fit together.

Exhibit 10-7 shows a standard storyboard sheet. It lists the requirements, section title, and strategy, explaining what you want the customer to get out of each page. Plus, the storyboard should have one win theme that describes one feature, proof and benefit of what you are proposing. The storyboard authors sketch at least one graphic and list their key points. The sketch should include an action title and describe the rationale for the approach and its benefits.

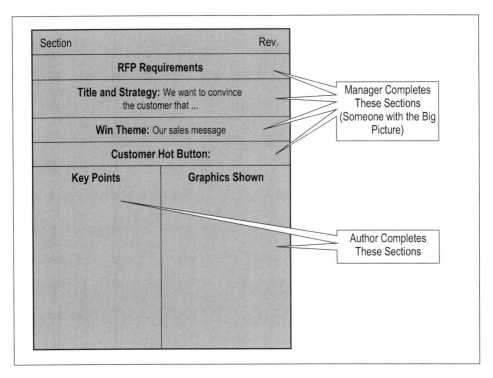

Exhibit 10-7: Sample Storyboard Form

A picture is worth a thousand words. Graphics stimulate the reader's interest and break up text. Charts and pictures can communicate much more information than text, that's why graphics come before text. But it is very important that any graphics you develop be easy to understand. The message should be clear within a few seconds. Authors must focus on trying to create visuals that communicate their arguments. The authors then organize their key points to support the thesis of their storyboard.

With the storyboards complete, a review team conducts a formal group review by walking the wall. The proposal review team can then see how the visuals and key points progress the story. They look to ensure:

- Requirements are covered
- Claims are valid

- Win themes are clear
- Win themes follow and support the win strategy
- Win themes do not conflict

This process helps allocate and clarify sales messages. In addition, it helps the team ensure that themes reflect the proposed approach and that the proposal highlights the discriminators. If there are holes, the team can then add in or create new themes to make the story complete before writing. This process helps uncover deficiencies and eliminates major rewrites. It also establishes configuration control over the whole proposal prior to writing.

After holding reviews and incorporating feedback into the storyboards, the next step is to break down the storyboards into author packages. It is important to give the authors only what they need, which will be a lot. The author packages include: ground rules, standard presentation formats, the work breakdown structure, acronym guide and page counts plus the graphics, key points, win themes, and customer requirements from the storyboards. All of this information helps the writers know what to write about in each section. This organization allows the proposal writers to focus on telling their story persuasively. When the technical team adds substantiation to the themes, it creates a powerful section.

Through your contacts with the customer, you should identify customer hot buttons. As covered previously in Chapter 8, hot buttons are particular issues that create an emotional response in an individual. If your customer has a hot button, especially a strong opinion on a technical approach, you want to address this issue in the proposal. Hopefully, you have successfully presold your approach, but it is helpful to reinforce your position in the proposal versus ignoring a key issue of importance to a customer.

Concurrent with planning the proposal, the team should begin the costing effort if it has not already done so. You need to start validating costs and collecting preliminary material quotes. To validate costs, you need to develop the WBS, responsibility matrix, preliminary material requirements, and define overhead and fee structure. You will also need to define the investment strategy, task descriptions and send out a preliminary basis of estimates. An important but often overlooked step is developing a comprehensive set of estimating ground rules, which are all the necessary assumptions to estimate a job – covering everything from production quantities and delivery dates to inflation assumptions. This database is an important tool to enable the proposal's finance lead to effectively manage the cost and estimating process to ensure an accurate cost estimate is developed and appropriate cost trade-off decisions are made.

After these preparatory steps are complete, the core proposal team can assemble the draft material in anticipation of the final RFP arrival. The team consolidates and organizes all of the edited storyboards, proposal outline and initial cost estimates. In this way, the team has all of the materials ready once the RFP is received.

Once you receive the final RFP, your team needs to compare the original document to the final one. After identifying and analyzing the changes, your team can revise the proposal plan and refine the strategy. If the changes are significant, the team may need to conduct another bid/no bid review. Your team then needs to freeze the technical baseline, finalize the make/buy and update the executive summary and cost targets, as well as revise the proposal outline, RFP requirements and page counts. The core proposal team will prepare the author packages. The author packages are designed to provide everything the authors need and only what they need.

Next, your team needs to hold the proposal kickoff meeting. During this briefing of the proposal team, the proposal lead will describe the customer's requirements and how their offering satisfies them. They will review changes from the draft, work packages and the proposal schedules. The overall win strategy will be presented and discussed to ensure that everyone understands it and how it impacts their portion of the proposal that they are responsible for.

Obviously, it is important to write clearly with no grammatical errors. Your writing will reflect your technical competency to the customer. Putting effort into writing well reduces the customer's reading effort. Be positive and honest, frank and specific – speak the customer's language. It is important to remember that what you say is more important than how you say it. Get your intellectual content down on paper and editors can then fix it.

Concurrent to writing the proposal, the proposal leaders must be estimating the cost of the proposal. Winning is just as dependent on effective pricing as it is on a good technical proposal. A company should not treat the cost estimating as any less important than writing the technical volume. If you are selling a cost-plus project, you have to provide a cost proposal that describes all of your costs and their basis of estimate. And creating cost proposals is hard. There can be hundreds of pages of data, which must be consistent, and it is easy to make mistakes. It is difficult to check for inconsistencies across volumes while technical volumes are still being written. If there are mistakes in the cost volume that the customer uncovers, it gives the customer an overall impression of sloppiness and haste.

Early on, management should conduct thorough reviews of the proposal. Early reviews coupled with a consistent approach and format allow the proposal team to avoid rework. The purpose of team reviews is to ensure that the win strategy is clearly integrated in the proposal, thereby improving the probability of winning. The reviews need to be timed so that the proposal team will have enough time to incorporate the reviewers' recommendations.

As the writing process progresses, companies conduct two major reviews – the Pink team early on, and then the Red team review of the complete draft including both text and art. The Pink team review is conducted first, usually by functional management. The Pink team is the first review of the authors' draft art and text. The top priority of this review is to ensure the draft is compliant with the RFP. The draft text must be responsive to the requirements. If the text doesn't answer the requirements, it is critical to catch this failing early and correct it. Secondly, the team focuses on ensuring that the story matches and communicates the strategy.

The Pink Team review checks for clarity, compliance with the RFP, and the persuasiveness of the themes and messages. We always tell our reviewers to look in every section for features, proofs and benefits to do a great review. Authors are so busy describing their features that they forget to tell the customer about benefits or assume that the benefits are obvious and don't need to be identified, but benefits are what sell. Additionally, authors rarely include proof that their benefits are true. Without proof, benefits are just empty claims. Driving in proofs and benefits greatly enhances a proposal. After the Pink Team completes their work and the proposal is revised by the specialists, these reviewers are released to their day jobs.

About two thirds of the way through the proposal cycle, the company conducts a Red Team review. The Red Team acts like the customer and conducts a proposal evaluation, including scoring of the proposal. A successful proposal is understood by the customer the first time they read it. The reviewers score sections by book or volume and offer feedback for general assessment. They check for compliance, consistency and persuasiveness. It is important that they only check what is in the document and assume nothing. At this stage, hopefully the review team spends 90 percent of their time assessing how well requirements are addressed, and only 10 percent assessing whether they actually are.

The Red Team consists of your best experts not working on the proposal – senior executives, senior technical experts, and knowledgeable objective outsiders, plus business development and field marketers intimately familiar with the customer. The key to an effective review is to enlist the right people as reviewers. The right people are a cross section of individuals with different views on the pursuit. The Red Team should be led by an experienced Red Team leader who has sufficient stature within the organization to provide an independent check and balance on the proposal team and push unpleasant recommendations to senior management if necessary. Most importantly, you need seasoned hunters as reviewers – those who have competed often. These people, through their experience, know what strategies tend to work and which do not. Also it is important to have customer experts who understand how the customer thinks and behaves. These people should help keep you focused on what works with this customer. If the project involves new technologies, you should have one or two senior scientists who have good business sense. The technologists can ensure that your solution will work, whether the competitor's approach is likely to work and whether your vision fits with technology trends. Lastly, you need people with good insight into your top one or two competitors to ensure your strategies will outmaneuver the competition.

The final steps of the proposal process are production and delivery. Some proposals are 10,000 pages long with tabs, and fold outs. Just printing, collating and shipping a document of that magnitude is a big logistical undertaking. The proposal must be turned over to the production personnel with a safety margin of time. Do not spend months and millions of dollars only to have your proposal rejected at the last minute, as U.S. Aerospace did for the $35 Billion KC-X bid. They were disqualified by the Air Force because their courier got lost and was clocked in by the customer three minutes late.

To ensure an effective proposal process, the best-in-class companies co-locate their proposal teams whenever possible. Having the team co-located provides for significantly better communication among the members. It also makes overseeing and coordinating their work easier. Top companies have dedicated proposal facilities. This avoids having the proposal manager deal with getting a local area network installed, arranging desks, establishing security procedures and a whole host of administrative issues which would just be added to their already extensive duties preparing for the proposal, and avoids distracting the proposal manager from focusing on creating a high quality proposal.

Summary

Big jobs are always very competitive. We recommend our clients to implement excellent strategies that result in overwhelming victory. However, we have seen companies awarded contracts not because they won, but because their competitors lost. Capture efforts are usually long, complex endeavors. During this process, it is possible for a competitor to commit such big mistakes that a company wins by merely avoiding huge mistakes. Frequently, competitors stumble, so even if you do not have a brilliant strategy, you can still win. A company's great strategy can be undone by a costly error. It is best to avoid the mistakes described in this chapter:

- Keep committing to winning, even if it is hard.
- Make sure you are catering to the right customer.
- Provide a solution the customer desires.
- Be careful when teaming. Make sure you and your teammate have complimentary goals and that the teammate has a favorable relationship with the customer.
- Develop an early Price-to-Win target and manage your costs to meet it.
- Use a disciplined proposal process to ensure you present your company and your solution in the best possible light.

If you only avoid the mistakes discussed in this chapter, you will improve your win rate.

Chapter 11: Closing the Deal

"It's not over 'til it's over."

— John Connor, rebel commander, *The Terminator*

You just shipped out the proposal and are breathing a huge sigh of relief, but it is not over. Now, negotiations begin. You are entering another critical phase, where you have the chance to snatch victory from the jaws of defeat or vice versa.

The post-proposal submittal process varies widely by customer. The process can include price concessions, technical discussions, negotiations, orals, site visits, price updates, cost negotiations and proposal updates with large variances in behavior. It can run the gamut from seemingly endless rounds of price concessions to squeeze out the last penny, to a formal structured negotiation of rounds of questions and answers that result in raising prices. And by failing to understand and plan for this process, companies lose.

The objective of a post-proposal negotiation is to establish a mutual agreement about the statement of work, delivery schedule, terms and price. The agreement should represent a fair and reasonable overall settlement of these terms to satisfy both parties. However, that may not be the attitude of your customer. Some customers want the best deal, so seller beware.

Negotiations

When the customer reviews your proposal, they identify questions. Most customers request answers from bidders to formal written questions after the proposal is submitted. In some cases they will find elements of your proposal unacceptable and they will ask for changes, and in other cases there will be some proposal language that simply needs clarification. Customers then invite the bidder to respond to the deficiency or clarification questions.

It is good practice to get ahead of this process by performing your own after-the-fact review of your submitted proposal in anticipation of receiving customer questions. The core proposal team reads the entire proposal to identify errors and ambiguities, which will likely lead to questions or allow you to proactively tell the customer of problems. You may find you want to clarify issues that seem unclear before the customer asks.

The individual responsible for negotiating all contracts is the contracts manager. Based on the size and nature of the contract, the contracts manager recommends to the executive team who should be on the negotiation team and what their responsibilities will be. After the customer provides their questions, this team analyzes them and prepares responses. They treat these responses just like mini-proposals – following the same proposal process described in Chapter 10. The proposal team should process the responses just like the proposal, including storyboarding and formal reviews. The capture team leader is responsible for responding with the best information available and ensuring that the answers are reviewed. A Red Team should review all responses and ensure that responses don't add any new company liability – that they are in compliance with the RFP and don't impact the win strategy.

All questions asked by the customer during the post-proposal submittal period are critical. The proposal may have left some customer need unsatisfied. It is important to understand the message that the customer is trying to convey, because the wrong answer may be cause for disqualification. To manage customer questions, it is critical to:

- Log all questions and maintain a central file with the questions and all of your responses
- Analyze and strategize the answers to each question carefully to be fully compliant and responsive
- Ensure that the business manager reviews all technical responses for possible cost impact
- Subject all responses to formal management review

As customer questions are answered and clarifications go back and forth, it is common to make changes to your offering from the submitted proposal. It is critical to carefully manage and document all of these changes. Be sure to understand the changes and their impact on cost, schedule, performance and risk. Answers must be clear and concise. The responses provide your company with the opportunity to clarify issues the customer did not question, but that you consider important. This is your last chance to clear up what could become contentious program issues later.

When responding to customer questions, you need to listen well. When the customer hones in on details about some specific aspect of your proposal, it may be because they are very uncomfortable with that aspect. If your customer's technical team sends you questions, it typically means one of two things. Either they do not understand what you are promising or they are trying to subtly suggest that you change your approach. If it is the former, you just need to send some clarifying information. However, if it is the latter, you'd probably better change your approach if you want to win. *You have to be alert to customer concerns. You need to analyze all of their questions and comments so you can know when to provide clarification and when to switch approaches.* As always, you are trying to evolve your solution into the best solution possible for the customer. If the customer wants you to change, and you listen and change, you usually gain great favor and the customer sees you as responsive. The problem lies in knowing which situation it is. Hopefully, when you were communicating openly with the customer before the RFP, you got some sense of their pre-proposal position. That is a big clue to their current position. But the situation may have changed since the dialogue closed off. New people may have entered the scene or the competitor may have successfully influenced them.

Some customers, like the U.S. Government, give suppliers an interim assessment of their proposal evaluation as part of the negotiations. This can be a shocking experience. It is not uncommon to find that the customer has rated a section of your proposal "unacceptable" or "high risk." Despite your best efforts, much of the time, this is the result of a poorly communicated proposal section. Do not overreact to these assessments. The customer is merely going through the mechanical process of proposal evaluation. If they do not understand what you are committing to, they rate you poorly. But you have the opportunity to fix the issue. The customer will often ask a very specific question allowing you to respond with a detailed explanation. The customer's concern is cleared up and suddenly your score goes from red (unacceptable) to blue (exceptional).

If you change your approach when the customer was not trying to subtly tell you to do so, you can significantly worsen your position. Suddenly changing your position, if the customer doesn't want you to, will cause them to lose confidence in you. In one example, a company was bidding on a contract to take over the operations, maintenance and upgrade of several customer facilities across the country. The customer asked some questions about their contractor's proposed roll out schedule. The contractor interpreted the customer's questions to indicate that they did not like the company's upgrade roll out schedule, when in fact the customer just did not understand their proposal – certain parts seemed contradictory. The bidder responded to these questions by breaking out another block of tasks, which seemed to introduce more risk and confusion into the program. After the company lost, in their debriefing, the customer said that this change significantly hurt their position by raising all kinds of new questions.

If you don't understand which situation you are in, you can usually ask for a face-to-face meeting. Then you can look the customer in the eye and observe their body language. If you are given a face-to-face meeting, we recommend that you have someone attend from your team who has no bias on the issue and reads body language well. This person can interpret what the customer is feeling about the issue and what they are trying to communicate. Hopefully, by carefully assessing the facts and through observation you can deduce whether the customer is just looking for clarification or really wants you to change your approach. Whether or not you change can cause you to win or lose.

Orals

After submitting the proposal, some customers require an oral presentation or demonstration. Oral presentations are weighed as part of the source selection evaluation and are therefore very important. The customer is, to a large extent, buying your team and this is an excellent opportunity to showcase it. Orals provide the customer with the face-to-face opportunity to assess the quality and competency of your proposed key personnel. Often, the award is heavily dependent on the customer's evaluation of the ability of your proposed staff to act as a team and perform the work. Through an oral presentation, the evaluators can witness how the offeror's key personnel present themselves, work together, solve problems and communicate technical information. Orals give your team the opportunity to demonstrate their knowledge of the customer's problems and of your solutions.

The proposal and program managers must fully prepare the formal oral presentation, including rehearsal after rehearsal. It is important that the presentation detail be consistent with the proposal as updated by the negotiation responses; yet not replicate the information already provided in the written proposal. As you create the presentation, it is critical to design the presentation so that it tells the customer both what they must know and what you want them to know. Your best approach is to stick with your win strategies and win themes. Maintaining consistency in your messages is the key to getting them delivered and accepted. The evaluators will be looking to confirm your claims, so build your presentation around your win themes, which provide the proof they seek. If you were to change your strategy and try to sell a new set of benefits, chances are you would undermine all of the work that has gone on in developing your offering. You must pre-sell your approaches to the customer all the way through the process including orals.

The oral presentation attempts to overcome any proposal weaknesses, and support and validate your strengths. Senior staff should participate to show the importance of the program to your company. Everyone involved must understand the key messages and themes so that they can be repeated and reinforced. Also, practice all presentations a number of times to ensure they are effective, that everyone is prepared and that any problems are resolved before the customer hears them. Rehearsals are critical, as is choosing the right presenters. Surprisingly, some of your best people may not be your best presenters. You need a top team to win, so exclude poor presenters, if possible. You can also provide individual speaking coaches to key individuals to boost their presentation skills.

A key opportunity provided by orals is the chance to provide objective proof to support your benefits. During orals or a site visit you have a lot of flexibility in what you can show. Since seeing is believing, show your prototypes, labs, test facilities and demonstration results to validate your claims. By displaying your facilities, you demonstrate that you are ready to go and can deliver on your promises. There are things you can communicate in the demonstration that you cannot in a proposal. A well-produced video can create instant credibility. You can show how easy your information systems are to use or how responsive they are. The evaluators are looking for objective evidence that you understand their problems and have real, workable solutions for them.

The customer may also request a demonstration of the hardware or software that is described in the proposal. They may request a sample of your offering for testing as part of the evaluation. Performing well on these tests is critical to victory. If your demonstration fails, it can disqualify your offering, so it is important to invest in developing these samples. You should try to schedule your sample development so that you can pre-test your samples under the same conditions as the customer will, and then debug your samples prior to sending them to the customer. Packaging and presentation are also important. Your customer cannot help but prejudge your demo's capability based on the care with which it is handled and even the box it comes in.

The other key opportunity during orals is to get feedback from the evaluators. While presenting your themes and showing proof of your claims, you need to carefully listen to the evaluator's questions and observe their reactions. Document the questions they ask and observe what they choose to review; this may reveal where their priorities and concerns lie. You may receive subtle clues about how to improve your approach. There is something to be learned from every interaction with an evaluator, even if the discussion is one-sided. This is invaluable feedback about how well your approaches are being received. You then can use this information to decide how to update your final proposal revision.

Cost Realism Assessment

Some customers, when awarding cost-plus contracts, evaluate the offeror's proposal for cost realism. They usually add dollars to one's bid price to calculate what they call a "most probable" cost. The customer then evaluates each competitor, not on their proposed price, but on their most probable cost. This assessment of cost risk adds another dimension to the post-proposal strategy. In this case, you need to estimate the relative cost adjustment that your team will receive compared with the competition as part of the Price-to-Win analysis to identify your optimum bid price. Then, during the proposal evaluation, the customer usually informs the companies of the amount of adjustment and reasons for their specific cost risk adjustments. The company then has the opportunity to persuade the customer as to whether these cost adjustments are justified or not. After the discussions, the offerors must submit their final proposal. In that final proposal they can add into their cost proposal the cost adjustments that are merited. A key issue is that you may reduce the adjustment if you raise your price somewhat. For example, imagine the customer originally estimated that you had underbid $20 million in software. Since the customer is going to evaluate your price $20 million higher, you are better off from a program execution perspective bidding a higher price instead of bidding a low price that will receive a cost plus up. If you add no money to your software cost estimate, they may add as much as $20 million to your price. But if you add $15 million, the customer may decide that they do not want to contest that extra $5 million and accept your new bid. Or, depending on the customer, they may still raise your price for the additional $5 million. Much strategizing and understanding of the customer comes into play.

Cost realism assessments affect your Best and Final Offer (BAFO) strategy. When the customer evaluates cost realism, it is risky to drop your price significantly at BAFO. It raises cost realism questions. You will have to explain why your new price is lower and justified, as well as bridge it to your initial price. This reduces your pricing flexibility.

Develop a Post-Submittal Strategy

It is our experience that the most common and disastrous mistake most companies make before negotiations is failure to plan for them. You should start planning for negotiations as part of your proposal strategy. The PTW targets are set to be the final price after all rounds of the post-proposal submittal negotiation, so you must develop your negotiation strategy and set your proposal price accordingly. A common blunder for novices entering foreign markets is to set their prices with incorrect or no negotiation margins. This usually forces the companies to give up much of their margin to close the deal, as most overseas customers demand price concessions.

Knowledge is power. It is the lifeblood of every negotiation. Before any negotiation you must do your homework. You need to understand the customer and their negotiating behavior – it is critical to making a good deal. The more you understand the customer's needs and constraints, the more effectively you can negotiate. For example, when asked if he knew what the Soviets would offer at an upcoming arms control summit, Henry Kissinger replied, "Oh, absolutely, no question about it. It would be absolutely disastrous for us to go into a negotiation not knowing in advance what the other side was going to propose." The better you understand what your counterparts are willing to give up and what they are not, the better you can optimize your demands. More intelligence instills greater self-confidence in the negotiating team, which improves the deal they can command. And proving to the customer that you've done your homework demonstrates competence, which improves your stature and respect with the customer, making them less likely to try to deceive or manipulate you. It is vital to the success of your bid that you understand your customer's negotiating behavior.

You must include in your proposal submittal a negotiation margin based on how the customer conducts post-submittal negotiations. A negotiation margin can be as high as 40 percent on top of your intended final price, but typically it is much smaller than that. This negotiation margin allows you to negotiate your price down through multiple iterations and still maintain your profit margins. Never tell a customer that you put a negotiation margin into your bid. They will immediately argue it away and still want to negotiate more. You should plan the timing of concessions up-front. When one is in the heat of negotiations, perspective can be lost. Developing a strategy up-front gives the negotiators more confidence and helps control the concessions.

It is also important that you budget for negotiations and for the proposal update in your capture budget. All too often capture teams dismiss the cost and length of time negotiations take. Responding to questions, conducting orals and preparing for the best and final offer can be expensive and time consuming. This results in overrunning the capture budget and disrupting staffing as you scramble to bring together a response team. The more prepared you are, the more confidence your executive leadership, your team and the customer will have in you. This confidence helps you win.

Understanding the Customer

You learn your customer's negotiating process through intelligence collection. If you are negotiating with a foreign company, you need to understand the negotiating behavior of their nation. Negotiating behavior follows the cultural norms of the host country. Some cultures, like the U.S., try to minimize negotiations, which is why General Motors' Saturn's "no-haggle" sales policy was such a popular innovation when introduced in their dealerships. However, other customers may come from a culture that expects negotiation like the United Arab Emirates. The Emirates have negotiated to survive for thousands of years – they never take the first price, and everything is negotiable. Some cultures use hierarchical negotiating, where the negotiations start with a lower level employee and then, after they receive concessions, their boss takes up where they left off. Each management layer builds on the last customer position as they push for more and more concessions. You must go through multiple rounds at one organizational level and then graduate to negotiate with their boss and then their boss, all the way up the customer hierarchy. Some cultures are known for their red faced, table banging behavior in negotiation. Some customers will walk out on negotiations as a ploy. Some will attack every piece of your proposal.

— *Strategy in Action* —

For example, while negotiating with one of these difficult customers on the upgrade of a ship, the shipyard ran into difficulties when the proposal stated that they would remove and replace old equipment. The customer negotiator noted that they were not getting reimbursement for the equipment being removed from the ship. The shipyard told them that the removed equipment was junk. The customer negotiator argued that the equipment was worth something and they should be refunded for it. The shipyard held firm, pointing out that the equipment had to be disassembled and cut up to get through the hatches and off the ship. After hearing this explanation, the negotiator wanted credit for the equipment and for the damage that would be inflicted on the equipment as it was removed. These negotiations went on and on with the shipyard ending up with a very slim margin on the contract.

Once you understand your customer's culture of origin, you need to identify the official post-proposal process of your customer and their usual behavior. Customers will often use the same negotiation techniques over many years across all of their purchases. You should identify similar contract awards from this customer. Once identified, you can interview people who were party to the negotiations or who closely followed them. You should strive for as much detail as possible about the past negotiations. What was the customer's process? How many rounds did they conduct? How far did the price fall from the start until the end of negotiations? What tactics did the customer employ? You will see negotiating patterns emerge. Some negotiators are fond of forcing others to negotiate, make commitments or respond to queries under intense time pressure. For example, one customer encouraged suppliers to drop their price significantly by misleading them into believing that a decision must be made immediately so the customer could announce the deal at the upcoming international conference. However, history showed that this was just a ploy and that the customer was willing to miss the conference or even wait until the following year. Since negotiating is a skill, individuals tend to use the same negotiation techniques over and over again, so identifying individual negotiators and profiling their specific negotiating techniques can really help prepare your negotiating team.

— *Strategy in Action* —

For example, former Secretary of State Henry Kissinger was a master of negotiations and he used one technique repeatedly. He would take his time at the beginning of negotiations discussing trivial matters. He would lull his counterparts into a sense of resignation and low expectations. Then, as the deadline for the end of the talks loomed he would suddenly hit them with a comprehensive list of demands. This tactic would surprise and unnerve his counterparts. This would frequently result in the other diplomats giving in to his proposals or cause them to become emotional and make mistakes. If his counterparts had studied his past behavior they would have anticipated this technique and been ready to respond.

You also want to understand the customer's needs, priorities, constraints and perspectives. Understanding these points allows you to concede your low priority negotiating positions for their high priority positions. You should continue to collect intelligence throughout the negotiating process. If you have a face-to-face meeting with the customer, it is important to ask them questions to ferret out their negotiating priorities. This knowledge can help identify issues for trading. *Negotiation is a game of information. Those who know how to obtain the most information outperform others. The better you understand your customer's situation and negotiating approach, the higher your probability of a win and the more successful your negotiations are likely to be.* Because each customer is different and negotiations can be critical to maintaining margins, your team needs to know the customer's negotiation process very well.

Understanding Competition

You also need to understand the competition's negotiating strategy in order to game against them. Customers can play one competitor against another. They will get a concession from one competitor and then use it as negotiating leverage with the other, so it is important to understand how the competitor is doing in their negotiations because it impacts your relative position. You must understand the competitor's typical negotiating behavior. How much of a negotiating margin are they likely to bid? Will they accept bribes from the competition? It's important to understand the competitor's past negotiation history – who have they sold to before? It is also important to assess how much experience your competitor has with this customer or customers like this one. You must also learn if they have someone, like a consultant, working for them, that knows how this customer negotiates.

Price Negotiations

For some customers, price negotiations are rather perfunctory, but for other customers it is an integral part of the selection process. For the first set of customers, price is just one element of negotiation, they will, of course, take a price concession when they can, but they are more focused on finding a well balanced solution. The second set of customers we will discuss in detail.

These customers tend to technically level their bidders so that price becomes the major discriminator. With these customers one of the most important pieces of information in developing your negotiation strategy is how many rounds of price concessions are they likely to attempt. One key indicator is whether they have a firm implementation schedule or not. Customers with real schedules adhere to them because they have a legitimate business reason for getting their project on-line. Others adhere to their schedule because that is their culture. When these customers solicit your Best and Final Offer, it is truly time for a BAFO. They make a decision based on your BAFO and select a winner.

Other customers do not have real schedules. These "flaky" customers tend to be nationally owned monopolies, companies entering new markets or others that do not face a pressing schedule need. These customers usually don't have a formal acquisition process or evaluation criteria. They develop a set of requirements and then go with the lowest price solution that meets most of them. Since these customers do not have a pressing need to sign a contract, they will request your BAFO over and over again as part of their strategy to squeeze the last penny out of every negotiation. At every BAFO this is what they expect, and they are insulted if they don't receive a price concession. Failure to provide a concession throws your company out of the competition, so each round lowers your price. They may even announce you as the winner, but keep a backup supplier. Then they will still try to negotiate price concessions, because the award announcement means little. This type of customer does not close the deal until they ink the contract.

In most negotiations, concession rates tend to follow a pattern of diminishing concessions at each subsequent round. In the first round, one decreases the price by 10 percent. In the next round it is five percent, and then three percent. The key to selling successfully to these "flaky" customers is to provide them with high prices until the final round of pricing. Figure 11-1 shows the impact of a poor negotiation strategy where a supplier made large reductions at the first pricing round. And then they make relatively large, but smaller price reductions on the later rounds. If one makes a large price concession at the first round, the customer will expect a similar drop on the next round and the next. If one makes little or no pricing concession on any round, the customer will reject the offer as insulting. Therefore, once a company starts making significant price cuts, it is difficult to stop without the negotiations breaking down. The result, as shown in Figure 11-1, is that an effective negotiation strategy of small early drops can result in a total price reduction from initial proposal submittal of 20 percent, while a poor negotiation strategy can drive down the price nearly twice that much. Studies have shown that making many small price concessions is much more psychologically satisfying to people then one equally large price cut. By making small initial price concessions, you protect your margins until you need to, and your true pricing does not leak to the market until later.

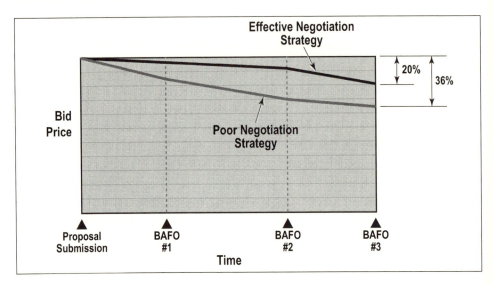

Exhibit 11-1: How Post-Proposal Negotiations can Affect Price

Of course, the trick is figuring out when the final round will be. You usually have to rely on your intuition to figure out the "real BAFO." But there are some signs. You will usually be on the third round, and when you notice an increase in the frequency and level of the customer interactions. Your salesman will also become highly agitated – that is a good sign of the sale reaching a climax.

Coming in with a high first price has it dangers, too. Too high and your bid may not be credible. Asking for too much can cause the customer to open or focus their negotiations with the competition. If the customer negotiates with multiple competitors simultaneously, you have less risk when coming in high than in the cases where the customer focuses on only the best offer. You need to consider where your final price will be and where you think the competitor is currently. It is important that you justify whatever price you come in at to the customer. Providing justification for your price will improve your negotiation position.

Unfortunately, in some businesses and parts of the world, you company may face situations where bribery can occur. If your competitor uses bribes, timing and intelligence are critical to blocking this challenge. There are three common approaches to neutralizing bribing. First, you can turn in the individual who is soliciting the bribe to the customer's leadership. This approach has a host of potential problems. You may not have proof. The customer may not want to take any action against the individual. You embarrass the customer and can cause significant resentment, which often derails the sale. The second approach is to compensate for the bribe by providing such an attractive offer that the person or persons being bribed cannot swing the decision to the competitor. The third approach is illustrated below.

— *Strategy in Action* —

Company X was in a competition where they strongly suspected that an individual at the customer was being bribed and passing on their pricing to Competitor Y. To prove it Company X waited until the last possible opportunity to put in the BAFO, which was significantly lower than their previous bid. The bribed customer individual told the Competitor Y's salesperson about the significantly lower price. The salesman in turn notified his management. The price reduction was so large that Competitor Y's executives probably did not believe the customer, thinking it just another one of the customer's negotiating ploys. In addition, their counter would have to be so significant that Competitor Y would need their senior executives to approve a matching price cut. This price change would be a significant policy shift. Competitor Y's bureaucracy debated the policy change while their executives and their sales force tried to determine if the price cut was legitimate. In the end, Competitor Y froze with indecision. The customer became impatient and agitated with the competitor's stalling and awarded to Company X.

Company X neutralized the bribe with an effective strategy and timing. They understood the customer's selection process well enough to know when to give their price concession so that Competitor Y did not have time to respond.

Your prices will sometimes leak out. On one occasion, the customer faxed a summary of our client's bid costs back to the client's facility to clarify some numbers. Unfortunately, they accidentally faxed the information to the wrong company – the competition. From these numbers the competitor could deduce the company's bid price. When the customer realized what had happened, they contacted both companies and apologized. The competitor promised not to look at the numbers and adjust their final proposal revision any differently from what they already intended. However, the capture team did not believe the competition and had to adjust their bid down based on the assumption that the competitor knew their bid price.

In another case, a senior customer executive did not think he was doing anything wrong by telling both competitors which company was lower in price. While the competitor did not know how much higher their bid was, the information did tell them that they had to lower their price significantly.

When you suspect that your prices have leaked to the competition, you need to reassess your PTW based on how much you think the competitor's price will come down. The first question is: do they know simply who is higher and who is lower, or do they know your absolute price? Secondly, you need to know how much lower the competitor can bid if they have to. To answer the second question, you must revisit the PTW analysis and adjust the projected costs with their minimum margin and maximum investment. They may know your price, but they may not be able to match it. The results of this assessment will tell you how you should adjust your price.

It is important to remember that selling a large contract is akin to marriage. Long-term commitment, trust and respect are keys to success. You don't want to lose the job or damage the relationship by hard-nosed bargaining. ***People are satisfied at the end of negotiations, not if they got a good deal, but if they feel that they were respected and believe they got a good deal.*** One's success at negotiating depends on how well one manages the customer's perceptions. In any negotiation you need two goals – get a good deal for your company and strengthen the relationship with the customer. Success in negotiation has everything to do with how well someone thinks they did, and often has little or nothing to do with how well they actually did.

Intelligence about Where You Stand

Theoretically, you should not get feedback on your relative position during this phase. But sometimes you will get informal feedback from your customer or the marketplace about your position. This intelligence can guide you to adjust your strategy. It is critical to assess this intelligence and the person who uncovered it.

— *Strategy in Action* —

For example, during the negotiating process, one company learned that the customer had their budget reduced and were unable to make an award because they could not afford anyone's proposal. While the customer needed to buy 200 aircraft over the next eight years, it was impossible with their current budget. Given this intelligence, the company submitted a new proposal. The company reduced the number of aircraft to 150 with a balloon payment toward the end of the program. The balloon payment could also be used to offset the cost of exercising an option for 50 more aircraft. In this way the customer could order 150 aircraft with all the money they had, but position themselves with their budgeters for the additional money in later years. For the company, selling the 150 aircraft would lock the customer into buying their aircraft, and potentially another 50. In addition, the company bid the per unit aircraft price as if were a quantity of 200, with the cost savings of the quantity discount equal to the balloon payment. In that way, they gave the customer an attractive price concession, which sealed the deal, acing out their competitor.

— *Strategy in Action* —

In another case, Mr. X, a senior executive at one supplier bidding on a large job, reported that he had talked to a close friend of his who was a senior customer executive. Mr. X reported that this close friend told him that the competition was a "dead heat." The customer said that Mr. X's company needed to provide a reason to select them in the BAFO to win. Mr. X previously worked at the customer and had many close friends there, so he had the relationships to get this type of feedback. He had also led two losing pursuits within the last two years and believed his executives would fire him if they lost this bid. The supplier had undertaken a detailed and thorough PTW and competitive analysis. The analysis concluded that the supplier had a large cost advantage and could keep their current price. The supplier's executive team discounted the PTW and took Mr. X's word. They went with their intuition and dived on price at BAFO, cutting their price by more than 15 percent and won. In the end, the customer's debriefing shocked the supplier's executives. It revealed that their pre-BAFO price was well below the competition's and final price was more than $50 million less. Mr. X's intelligence was either wrong or he wanted to ensure that this company won so he could keep his job.

Beware of unconfirmed intelligence, especially intelligence from a source with a vested interest in changing your pricing. As these situations show, it is critical to assess any post-submittal intelligence before making decisions. You must assess not only what was heard, but also who heard it. Could your source be misinterpreting the conversation? Is the intelligence corroborated? What are the motivations of the source? What is the motivation of the person reporting the intelligence? Only after a thorough and dispassionate assessment of your intelligence should you make a decision about changing your bid.

No matter how well prepared your negotiation team; you will always be surprised by some customer issues and tactics. It is important to structure your negotiation process to allow time to analyze customer responses and develop appropriate strategies. Too often, customers use false deadlines to force sellers to make rash decisions. You should query the customer about what is driving their schedule and assess whether it is real, and what the consequences would be of failing to meet it. Unless you know that the customer is facing a legitimate deadline, you should avoid giving in to these tactics. Usually, you can postpone your response for a little while. This delay can allow you time to carefully assess the situation, without being forced to make a decision without analysis.

Show Commitment

You can conduct activities during the post-submittal phase that are visible to the customer and demonstrate your commitment to the pursuit. For example, Boeing bought long lead materials for their Korean fighter pursuit to assure the Korean Air Force that they could meet their schedule. As part of one pursuit, a contractor initiated a program called "Head Start." As part of this program, the contractor flew test flights on their own aircraft carrying the new radar they were offering. This demonstration was impressive to the customer because it directly addressed and helped mitigate the customer's concerns about the maturity of the contractor's sensor. Activities such as these allow suppliers to improve their schedule position or reduce risk in their proposals, by conducting activities that they could not complete prior to the proposal submittal. Investing a company's own money in these activities impresses customers by demonstrating commitment to the customer's success and garners tremendous feelings of goodwill. Similarly, a contractor can seek to enroll the local community in their sales effort. They can place advertisements in local media, sign up local suppliers, conduct job fairs and have executives give speeches to local organizations to create community support for the company.

Political Insertion

We have watched selection decisions reversed in the final days by political insertion. This happens after the acquisition committee has made their recommendation. Just before the final approver is to sign off on the decision, an advocate of the losing competitor approaches the final approver and makes an appeal. The appeal to the final decision maker may be a deal on an unrelated issue, or a personal favor. They always argue that the evaluation was unfair, despite the source selection being designed to assess the merits of each competitor. For example, one source selection switched when news of the winner was leaked. A powerful politician learned that "his team" was going to lose. He had one of his people call the source selection official and threaten to destroy the careers of everyone involved unless his team won. Given that he had destroyed the careers of the last source selection group that had gone against his team, his team won.

— *Strategy in Action* —

In another example, the competitors learned that the buyer country had selected Country A's product for a large government procurement. Reacting quickly, the leader of Country B flew into the capital of the buying country a week before the award announcement. The following week, the customer announced that Country B was the winner. In one week, the decision flipped. To change the decision, sometimes a politician will offer some geopolitical benefit to the customer, like advocating the buyer's entry into the European Union in return for selecting their country's company. We have also seen a former high-level government official make such a trip and ask the President of a country to change the decision as a personal favor. Usually, advocates that can make this type of approach are friends of the decision maker or politicians from the competitor's country.

If you are worried about political insertion, there are three effective ways to block it. The first is to make your offering sufficiently better than the competition so that the final decision maker does not want the political heat of overturning the decision. Typically, this means lowering the PTW to ensure a healthy difference between your bid and the challenger's. In the same way you would adjust your PTW target down if you believed that bribery might take place, you should adjust your price to block a political insertion. The second approach, which is much more difficult, is to block the political diversion as it happens. In those cases, you have to have good intelligence and know if and when the competitor is going to try to use their political contacts to flip the winner. As soon as the competitor makes their move, you need to have a comparable political operative go to the final decision maker and appeal to them. This can neutralize the political insertion. Once again, this approach depends on having excellent intelligence about what's going on at the customer. With the third approach, you leak the news early that you have won. This puts more visibility on the decision and can increase the political cost of the final decision maker overturning the acquisition process's recommendation.

Protests

The customer has announced you've won, gotten your debrief and scheduled your win party. Are you done? Maybe, maybe not. Many government agencies (federal, state and some foreign) allow bidders to protest the award decision. So, even after award, you may not be finished with the pursuit.

A lot of the time when a company loses, they think a grave injustice has occurred. The loser believes the customer did not score them fairly. The competitor must have bought in, or the customer was biased. After all, they would not have bid if they did not think they had the best solution for the customer. So, it is easy to see injustice even if none exists.

The reality is that a customer is not evaluating your company or even your proposed solution, they are evaluating a proposal. If your capabilities are not in the proposal or were poorly communicated, it can score poorly.

Protesting a loss has its pros and cons. A protest can overturn a decision, but the odds are less than one in five at the federal level. So, your chances of success are pretty small. The protest can hurt your competitors by delaying the award. Also, we have seen companies appear to use protests to intimidate the customer. They protest every significant decision that goes against them so that the customer will fear awarding to anyone else. The company in question becomes so well known for protesting, that customers will try to award to them to avoid a near certain protest if the customer chooses another contractor. Also, we have seen companies successfully protest by coupling their protests with significant political pressure from powerful congressional advocates.

By protesting, you are questioning either your customer's competence or ethics, which tends to not endear you to your customer. Another frequently overlooked con is that both sides disclose into the public domain quite a bit of information about their bidding behavior, and relative strengths and weaknesses. At most agencies, protests are published on the web, and depending on the agency this may include disclosing your prices among other things.

Agencies have plenty of discretion in evaluating proposals and making decisions. The key question the arbiter will seek to answer during a protest is whether the agency followed their proposal evaluation procedures. Typically, a successful protest is one where there is clear evidence that the agency did not follow their own rules.

If you have won and your award is being protested, we recommend that you fight the protest vigorously, because if you lose, the next RFP may not be to your liking. The key to protecting your win is to thoroughly analyze the competitor's bid to uncover any competitor problems that the customer overlooked.

We rarely advocate protesting an award, because the odds of success are too slim. We recommend developing a superior strategy with the right price such that you have an uncontested victory.

Summary

After submitting the proposal, exhausted as you may be, it is not over. Your job is not finished when you submit the proposal. Just like a good book, the last chapter should bring all your efforts together. In fact, the post-proposal period is one of the most crucial periods in any pursuit. It can also be shrouded in mystery. This is the time when you are most likely to be tempted to do something drastic to ensure victory. But drastic action is exactly what you should avoid. If you have followed our strategy development process, pre-sold the customer, put together a good proposal and negotiated effectively, then you have done everything it takes to win. Any last minute divergence from this approach can undermine your position and cast doubts in the minds of the decision makers.

You usually don't know what's going on in the customer's offices, and this is one of the most worrisome times during the pursuit if you are unfamiliar with the customer's negotiating behavior. It is imperative to collect intelligence about how the customer conducts negotiations. Understanding their behavior allows you to effectively navigate these lasts steps of the competition. You must be wary; inept negotiating can erase an otherwise certain victory. It is equally important to monitor and counteract the competition. Many companies bungle these last steps by diving on price and squandering their good position just because they are nervous. In other cases, you must be ready to block a competitor's last-ditch effort to overturn the decision.

A Final Word

Chasing the big ones is a tough job. Winning is never easy, and big pursuits are complex. They are all different and there are no absolute rules. We have provided a process to help people bring organization to the complexity of a large pursuit, and have tried to give the reader the tools that will allow them to sort through a very complex endeavor and find simplicity in it. Winning is all about figuring out what's important to the customer and then showing them you can satisfy their needs better than the competition. If you can do that, you win. But, don't mistake something that's been made simple with something simplistic. If you can focus on executing a few things well, you can win, if you pick the right things. And it is all about execution. Thoughts, plans and ideas are interesting, but unimportant in winning without execution. The bottom line is this: you have to develop the right solution and sell it to the customer.

Our process is not foolproof. It relies on judgment, and sometimes there are simply forces beyond your control. However, when we look at our wins, many times we can clearly see how the process and tools we offer here transformed the campaign.

The big pursuits take a long time and they can make or break careers. As such, we invest part of our life in them. We hope that this book will help you with some ideas for winning, and make your life easier and more successful.

.

Acknowledgements

We want to thank Robert Hansen for coming up with the idea of writing a book to describe our lessons in winning. We also want to thank Harley Stein, Tom Bluesteen, Kelly Whalen, Don Brown, Jana O'Guin and Greg Kyprios, who invested their time to give us the excellent feedback that made this a more interesting and informative book. Also, we want to thank our excellent editor, Nancy Smay, who did a great job making this book readable. Thanks, also, to Eric VanGronigen for doing a superb job on the graphics and making the book easier on the eyes. Also, we want to thank Jana for her years of support and encouragement, which helped us to finish this book. Finally, we want to thank all of the clients who have helped us learn the lessons we discuss in this book.

How to Order Copies of this Book

Go to www.Lulu.com and search under "Winning the Big Ones"

If you would like to talk to the authors or have comments, thoughts, corrections or stories for the next edition, please email Michael O'Guin at Moguin@aol.com or call 949-858-2572, for Kim Kelly, email KimkellyCI@aol.com or call 703-378-6988.

Glossary of Select Terms

Acquisition Strategy Plan (ASP): A plan that defines how the customer intends to structure the acquisition, including: timing, schedule, work scope, how each piece of work scope will be contracted out, and who will be responsible for the procurement.

Best and Final Offer (BAFO): Term used in bids to indicate that no further negotiation on the amount or terms is possible.

Basis of Estimate (BOE): The rationale for discrete estimates that will be used in the cost build up of a proposal.

Bidding & Proposal (B&P): The costs incurred in preparing, submitting and supporting proposals.

Black Out: A time period defined by the customer where they do not allow any communications between potential bidders and the customer. This is usually right before RFP release and is initiated to ensure one contractor does not get any more information then the rest of the bidders.

Bill of Material (BOM): A listing of all of the components or parts comprising a system.

Bogies: Cost targets.

Business Review Board (BRB): An executive committee responsible for allocating new business resources, monitoring capture efforts and overseeing and refining the process. **Capture phase:** Starts with the initial opportunity identification and goes until award. This includes the investigation, positioning, proposal and negotiation phases.

Competitive intelligence: Organization of information to support management decisions. It consists of information about the competitors as well as the customer.

Commercial off the shelf (COTS): Item that is commercially available, leased, licensed, or sold to the general public and which requires no special modification or maintenance over its life.

Cost as an Independent Variable (CAIV): The evaluation of trade-offs and options to design a solution within a fixed cost or budget.

Design-to-Cost (DTC): An engineering discipline that meets the customer's cost requirements through an interactive process that balances cost and performance.

Draft Request for Proposal (DRFP): Initial request for proposal, which the customer publishes to obtain comments from the bidders.

Event driven schedule: A schedule with activities planned, which flexes as key milestones move.

Formal Opportunity Assessment Criteria (FOAC): The analysis of a potential pursuit against standard criteria to determine if the opportunity is one of the company's best few to pursue.

Freedom of Information Act (FOIA): A law that allows people to apply for access to government documents.

General & Administrative (G&A): General operating expenses and taxes that are directly related to the general operation of the company, such as executive salaries and support and all associated taxes related to the overall administration of the company.

Government Accountability Office (GAO): This is an independent, nonpartisan agency that works for Congress. Often called the "congressional watchdog," GAO investigates how the federal government spends taxpayer dollars.

Government Services Administration (GSA): is an independent U.S. agency that manages and supports the basic functioning of federal agencies.

Integrated Product Team (IPT): A multidisciplinary group of people who are collectively responsible for delivering a defined product or process.

Life Cycle Cost (LCC): The costs of a product beyond its initial production costs including maintenance, support and disposal.

Most Probable Cost (MPC): The result of an analysis performed by the customer of a bid, which determines the final evaluation price based on their judgment of the proposal and program risks.

Original Equipment Manufacturer (OEM): The original producer of equipment.

Operations and Support costs (O&S): Life cycle costs inclusive of disposal costs.

Pop Up: A potential opportunity that was not in sales forecast and is a surprise. Typically, the RFP is imminent.

Positioning phase: Starts after the pursue/no pursue and continues until the initiation of the proposal phase. Positioning is the critical time in the pursuit when a capture team should be cultivating the customer, influencing the customer and evolving their solution.

Program Objective Memorandum (POM): A document used in U.S. Department of Defense planning which identifies the program funding for next year's federal budget.

Price-to-Win (PTW): Externally focused analysis, which attempts to identify the highest price a company can bid and still win.

Pwin: Probability of Winning.

Red Team: A review conducted of the proposal that critiques the proposal, usually conducted so that it mimics the customer's process.

Request for Information (RFI): A customer's solicitation of information on a solution that generally does not include pricing

Request for Proposal (RFP): A solicitation for firm offers which become binding contracts upon acceptance.

Request for Quote (RFQ): A solicitation that usually includes pricing, but does not require a contractual commitment.

Request for Tender (RFT): When a customer formally asks a company for a price quote for products and services on an open or upcoming bid for proposal.

Rough Order of Magnitude (ROM): A cost estimate developed from data sources that may be incomplete, inaccurate or out-of-date, and serves until more reliable data and information is available.

Should Cost: An estimate of what the bid will cost if estimating inefficiencies, and over engineering are removed from bid.

Source Selection Advisory Council (SSAC): A committee of senior customers who oversee the source selection and usually make a recommendation on the award to the source selection authority.

Source Selection Authority (SSA): The customer responsible for making the award decision.

Source Selection Evaluation Board (SSEB): Customer team that conducts the technical evaluation and scoring of the proposals.

Source Selection Plan (SSP): A document that specifies how the source selection activities will be organized, initiated, and conducted.

Statement of Objectives (SOO): It is a document that provides basic, top-level objectives of an acquisition and is provided in the request for proposal (RFP) in lieu of a customer-written statement of work (SOW).

Statement of Work (SOW): A description of the products or services set forth in the specification and includes quantities, deliveries, performance data and requisite quality.

Storyboard: An outline used in proposal development that states key issues and covers strategy, layout, themes, discriminators and visuals for a specific section.

Teaming: Companies agree to work together on a pursuit, sharing work and investment commitments.

Terms and Conditions (T&Cs): Items that bound and caveat your proposal offer.

Total Ownership Cost (TOC): The sum of all costs from development, production and life cycle sustainment and disposal of a system.

Work Breakdown Structure (WBS): A detailed description of the work to be performed – decomposed into elements to provide visibility of all components of the product and who is responsible for each.

Selected Index

Symbols

A

B

C

K

KC-135 tanker Replacement Program. *See* tanker
KC-767. *See* tanker
KC-X. *See* tanker
key decision maker priorities 55, 83, 88–97, 135, 198, 228, 236, 279–280, 309, 312
key decision maker priority matrix 89–93
key decision makers 13, 15, 18, 49, 56–57, 66, 73–76, 78–97, 119–120, 130, 135, 153, 174, 177–178, 185, 198, 212, 220, 226, 228–229, 233, 237, 249, 254, 279, 283, 299

L

lessons learned 35–36, 40–42, 46, 105, 201, 258
Lockheed Martin 5–6, 11–13, 37–38, 60–61, 73–74, 107, 110–111, 152, 169, 187, 190, 243–245, 247, 262, 279–280, 288

M

magnify the competitor's weaknesses 106, 115–120
major subcontractors. *See* teaming
map decision making process 78–81
market forecasting 28–29
McDonnell Douglas 107, 152, 182, 274, 275
message sequencing 228
message timing 211, 229–232
messengers 237
metrics 23–25, 36, 41, 46, 206
Multi-Mission Maritime Aircraft (MMA) 11–12

N

negotiations 305–307, 313–316
neutralize your weaknesses 106, 120–123
Northrop Grumman 5, 73–74, 128, 133, 206, 225

O

opportunity assessment 45–72, 326
opportunity calendar 211, 219–222
opportunity champion 45, 47, 49, 52, 55, 58, 62, 65–67
orals 305, 307–310

P

personality analysis 53, 253–254, 269
persuasion process 109–110, 227
pink team 302–303
political insertion 318–320

T

U

V

W

Index

.

Made in the USA
Middletown, DE
02 July 2020

11809737R00201